Twelver Shiism

The New Edinburgh Islamic Surveys
Series Editor: Carole Hillenbrand

TITLES AVAILABLE OR FORTHCOMING

www.euppublishing.com/series/isur

Twelver Shiism

Unity and Diversity in the Life of Islam, 632 to 1722

Andrew J. Newman

EDINBURGH
University Press

For Gene Garthwaite,
who got me started

Andrew J. Newman, 2013

Edinburgh University Press Ltd
22 George Square, Edinburgh EH8 9LF
www.euppublishing.com

Typeset in 11/13pt Monotype Baskerville by
Servis Filmsetting Ltd, Stockport, Cheshire,
and printed and bound in Great Britain by
CPI Group (UK) Ltd, Croydon CR0 4YY

A CIP record for this book is available from the British Library

ISBN 978 0 7486 3330 2 (hardback)
ISBN 978 0 7486 3331 9 (paperback)
ISBN 978 0 7486 3190 2 (webready PDF)
ISBN 978 0 7486 7833 4 (epub)

Contents

Acknowledgements

I am very grateful to Carole Hillenbrand for having asked me to consider writing a volume devoted entirely to the Twelver Shia for her much respected *Islamic Surveys* series. I am grateful both to her and to my editor Nicola Ramsey also for their infinite patience, to my copy editor Lyn Flight for her 'good eye', as well as Rebecca Mackenzie and Eddie Clark.

I first became acquainted with the Twelver faith when I arrived in Iran in the Autumn of 1974. I spent two years in Iran and have been back to Iran on many occasions thereafter, most recently in 2008.

In the last decade or two I have also been fortunate enough to make the acquaintance of many non-Iranian Shia, both in my travels but also here in the United Kingdom. These personal contacts have only further reminded me of the faith's worldwide 'reach' and the consequent diverse backgrounds of the faithful.

In the years immediately following the Iranian Revolution, in the eyes of many Western commentators the Shia were vying with the Soviets for the role of 'world villain', with Shii-fomented revolution(s) perceived as being about to break out throughout the Middle East 'proper' if not elsewhere as well.

The vitriol poured out on the Twelvers as a group by some non-Shii Muslims was, and remains, particularly intense. As I have noted to students in my classes on Shiism, such elements consider the Twelvers to be more dangerous, and evil, than the Americans. Many do not even accept them as Muslims.

Both of these camps, trading on problematic images from the Iran–Iraq War, harped on the dangerous predisposition of the Shia for martyrdom and portrayed the faithful as sheep, immediately and directly under the absolute control of a single malevolent leader bent on the destruction of civilisation as we know it.

Such rhetoric speaks volumes about the agendas of those who promote it. It says precious little about the reality and, more importantly, the diversity of the Shii experience across the globe as I have come to know it since 1974.

The title of this volume bespeaks an interest in that diversity, across time and space, if not also in what the faithful might recognise that they have in common. The faith's, and the faithful's, diversity perhaps emerges more clearly herein than any unity, not the least because of the numerous, varied and repeatedly existential challenges, external but also internal, that the faithful have faced over the centuries in the different parts of the world they have inhabited.

I am grateful to all of those who have shared their experiences with me.

Thanks are due also to my wife and daughter, and also to colleagues in my department and elsewhere. In varying degrees all have tolerated my more than occasional disengagement in the service of this volume.

****

The present volume is directed primarily to the Western-language audience, particularly the non-specialist. Hence, instead of trying to transliterate Arabic and Persian words into English via a complicated system of diacritical markings, I have favoured a somewhat idiosyncratic system of transliteration based loosely on that used in the *International Journal of Middle Eastern Studies* (*IJMES*). Dates also are given only in their 'AD' version; where this makes for flagrant inaccuracy, two Christian years may be given as, for example, in 873–4 AD, corresponding to the Hijri year 260, the approximate year of the disappearance of the twelfth Shii Imam. While footnotes do refer to Persian and Arabic sources, care is also taken to refer to available translations of primary sources, secondary works by specialists available in English and other Western languages and 'introductory'/encyclopaedia entries that might be useful for the 'newcomer' to the field. The British bibliographical convention of omitting names of publishers is followed throughout.

Edinburgh
March 2013

Introduction

Shii[1] Muslims believe that after the death of the Prophet Muhammad in 632 AD his cousin and son-in-law Ali (d. 661) inherited Muhammad's spiritual and political authority over the *umma* (the Muslim community). Thus, the Shia reject the succession of the first three of Muhammad's successors (*khalifa*, caliph) until Ali himself became the fourth caliph (656–61). After Ali's assassination, the Shia believe that the succession lay with his male descendants, via his son al-Husayn. Each of these men is called 'Imam'.[2]

At present some 10–15 per cent of the world's 1 billion Muslims are estimated to be Shiites, that is between 154 million and 200 million.

Today there are three main Shii groups.

Of the three, the Ismailis are the second largest. They believe that Ismail, the eldest son of the sixth Imam, Jafar al-Sadiq (d. 765), did not die but went into hiding and had a son Muhammad, who also went into hiding or died. The Ismaili community then fragmented. The Nizari Ismailis, numbering some 5–15 million adherents, are the largest remaining of the Ismaili groups and follow a living Imam: as of 2013, the Agha Khan is the forty-ninth in the line. Today, Ismailis are found in the Indian subcontinent, central Asia, the Middle East and East Africa, as well as Europe and North America.[3]

The smallest of the three groups are the Zaydi Shia. They have their origins in those who gave allegiance to Zayd, son of the fourth Imam and half-brother of the fifth Imam. In 740, Zayd launched a revolt in Kufa against the Sunni Umayyad dynasty (661–750). This rising was crushed and Zayd was killed in the subsequent fighting. His followers then fragmented into different groups, with a number relocating to sites in modern-day Iran. The Zaydis believe that any meritorious member of the Prophet's household is eligible to be the Imam. Like the Nizari Ismailis, Zaydis follow a living Imam, although the last of these died in 1996. Zaydis comprise about 75 per cent of the Muslims in Yemen, but there are also Zaydis in Saudi Arabia.[4]

The largest of the Shii groups extant today are the Twelver Shia, the subject of the present volume.

The Twelvers believe that the spiritual–political leadership (the Imamate) of the community passed down through Ali's male descendants, via al-Husayn, until the twelfth Imam. The latter is understood to have been born in 870, but to have gone into *ghayba* (occultation) soon after his father's death in 874,[5] for safety's sake. He is still alive and will return when Allah determines it to be appropriate and safe. As the *Mahdi* (the Rightly Guided One), his return will inaugurate the processes associated with the last days; as part of that process Jesus also will return. Other titles ascribed to the twelfth Imam include *al-Muntazar* (the Awaited One), *Sahib* or *Imam al-Zaman* (The Lord, or Imam, of Time), *Sahib al-Amr* (The Lord of Authority), *al-Qaim* (the One Who Arises) and *al-Hujja* (the Proof [of Allah]).

In Iran, except for a brief hiatus in the mid-eighteenth century, Twelver Shiism has been the established faith since 1501 when Ismail I (d. 1524), the first Safawid shah, captured Tabriz and declared the faith to be his realm's official religion. The faith forms the basis of Iran's present-day Islamic Republic that came into being in 1979. Between 90 and 95 per cent of today's 75–77 million Iranians are professing Twelvers.

Just as not all Iranians are Shiites, however, so not all Shiites are Iranians. The Iranian Shia represent only 37–40 per cent of the world's Shii population.

Indeed, the majority of Iraqi (65–70 per cent) and Bahraini (65–75 per cent) Muslims – who are Arabs – also profess Shiism. The Shia also form sizeable minorities in other Arab countries such as Lebanon (45–55 per cent), Kuwait (20–25 per cent) and Saudi Arabia (10–15 per cent). Among non-Iranians and non-Arabs, as of 2009, between 10 and 15 per cent of Afghan Muslims were Shia. The Shia in Pakistan comprise between 15 and 25 per cent of the nation's population, some 17–26 million; as such, the Pakistani Shia may be the second largest Shii community in the world. Some 2 per cent of the population of India are Shii, that is, some 16–24 million. There are also Shia in eastern Africa, Nigeria, southeast Asia (Malaysia, Thailand, Indonesia and Singapore), Europe and North America. There are even Shia in Israel and the Caribbean.

Among all these non-Iranian Shia the Twelvers predominate.[6]

If there are three main Shii groups today, more than one thousand years ago, in the ninth and tenth centuries, the authors of different Shii sources and sources sympathetic to Shiism referred to the presence of between fourteen and forty-five Shii groups.[7]

The survival of the remaining three Shii groups, with the Twelvers emerging as the largest, and perhaps the most scattered of these, would seem to have been quite an accomplishment.

Twelver Shii Studies to 1979

As a distinct Western academic discipline Twelver Shii Studies has only recently appeared on the scene. The intellectual event that perhaps heralded the emergence of Twelver Shii studies as a distinct field – the Strasbourg colloquium 'Le Shi'isme imamite' – occurred only in 1968, but a decade before the onset of the Iranian Revolution.[8]

Up until that Revolution studies of the faith presupposed the division of its history into two periods.

The first of these was the period from the late ninth century up to 1501.

In these years the faith enjoyed a certain measure of tolerance during the Buyid period (946–1055) of the Abbasid dynasty (750–1258) and during the Mongol/Timurid periods (1258–1501). Nevertheless, the faith was a minority within a Sunni-dominated political structure and the Shii *ulama* (scholars) in the main composed their writings in Arabic.

In 1968, the 'Classicists', that is, scholars of the faith over these centuries, included W. Madelung, J. Eliash (d. 1981), E. Kohlberg and M. J. McDermott. The scholars mainly explored an eclectic series of issues in Twelver doctrine and practice based on reference to the Arabic-language texts. In this same tradition, H. Corbin (d. 1978) and S. H. Nasr, who, like Madelung and Eliash, also attended the Strasbourg colloquium, focused on aspects of medieval Islamic philosophy, highlighted the esoteric dimensions of the faith and explored the compatibility of certain aspects of Shiism with Sufism.

The second period of the faith's history was understood to have commenced with the capture of Tabriz in 1501, when Twelver Shiism became the official faith of Iran's Safawid dynasty (1501–1722).

Study of post-1501 Twelver Shiism overlapped with the study of the emergence of the modern Iranian nation-state. From this period the relevant sources included the religious texts, still mainly composed in Arabic, but also a plethora of Persian religious sources, non-religious sources, such as court chronicles, and numerous European-language sources.

Prior to 1979 research on the all-important Safawid period itself focused especially on the seventeenth century. This was understood to have begun with a burst of cultural and intellectual achievement, in an atmosphere of military, political and economic stability established by Shah Abbas I (*reg.* 1585–1629) only to end in the darkness of fanatical religious orthodoxy amid military, political and economic chaos. The last Safawid shah, Sultan Husayn (*reg.* 1694–1722), for example, was presented as being so attentive to the goodwill of courtiers and clerics – the latter including Muhammad Baqir al-Majlisi (d. 1699), 'an extremely bigoted *mujtahid*' and 'a rigid and fanatical formalist' – and so busy with ostentatious building projects that the state was unable to mount any credible response to Afghan raids. Following one such incursion, the Afghan capture of the Safawid capital Isfahan in 1722 was understood to have signalled the dynasty's end.[9]

The Safawid period formed the demarcation line between the two branches of the field. There was very little interaction between scholars in each, especially the closer one came to the modern day.

It was the religious texts, too, authored by a small number of identifiable scholarly elites whose examination revealed the un-linear process of the Twelver community's progression to the 'normative', if not 'orthodox', Twelver doctrine and practice of the present.

To be sure, the 1968 colloquium in Strasbourg was organised in the years after the appearance of such works as D. Lerner's *The Passing of Traditional Society* (1958) and M. Halpern's *The Politics of Social Change in the Middle East and North Africa* (1963). As applied to the Middle East, 'modernisation theory' – of which these two authors were among the early proponents – postulated that the Middle East was fast becoming secularised, assisted in this process by such modernising (and secular) leaders as Jamal Abd al-Nasr (d. 1970) in Egypt and the Shah of Iran, Muhammad Reza Pahlavi (*reg.* 1941–79; d. 1980).

In these years, envisioning Shiism as an exclusively Iranian phenomenon, Western scholars of Iran accepted the principle of modernisation theory. One struggles to find contemporary references to the faith in Iran as having any long-term 'traction' on the ground – let alone to what is now called 'political Islam' – in such surveys of modern Iran as former CIA agent R. Cottam's *Nationalism in Iran* (1964), P. Avery's *Modern Iran* (1965), J. Bill's *The Politics of Iran* (1972) and, even, F. Halliday's *Iran: Dictatorship and Development* (1979) (d. 2010). Although it was in Iraq in early 1970 that the Ayatollah Khomeini (d. 1989) delivered the lectures that would become his famous *Islamic Government*, such scholars accorded Khomeini, let alone Iraqi Shiism, little, if any, mention.[10]

With Shiism in Iran, and indeed Islam as a religion, consigned to eventual oblivion by nearly all Western political scientists and historians alike, what trajectory Shii Studies itself might have taken became a moot point when, in January 1978, anti-shah street demonstrations broke out in Iran. One year later to the month, Muhammad Reza Pahlavi fled Iran, and on 1 February 1979 the Ayatollah Khomeini returned to the country.

These events and, especially, the distinctly Twelver Shii character that the post-shah Iranian polity quickly assumed, as well as the subsequent Islamisation of opposition discourse throughout the region at large, caught Western analysts of Iran and Islam quite, if not completely, by surprise.

Years of expansion: Shii Studies in the aftermath of 1979

Notwithstanding the impact of the Iranian Revolution, and the distinctly Shii turn it quickly took, for and on Iran and its people, let alone the peoples of the Middle East, the Revolution's impact on the field of Shii studies was problematic.

Driven by the force of events – the Revolution itself, the Iraq–Iran War, the 1983 bombings of the US Embassy and the US and French military installations in Beirut, and the subsequent rise of Hizballah – both the population of Shii Studies and the disciplines in which this population was active underwent a rapid expansion. Prior to 1979, one row of a very small-sized bookshelf easily held all the Western-language works related to Shiism. Today, with respect to Twelver Shiism alone, an audience that ranges from the academic to the interested layperson faces a vast array of monographs – not to mention journal articles and chapters in edited volumes – across such varied disciplines as history, art, anthropology, politics, country-based studies, gender studies, international relations and Islamic studies.

That same bookshelf now not only holds such secondary sources – in a number of languages including Arabic and Persian – but a similar array of primary-source texts in Arabic and Persian, if not also other languages. Iran's Islamic government has itself sponsored, or at least encouraged, the first-time publication or re-publication of Arabic and Persian materials. In both Iran and elsewhere in the Shii world, semi-official or private organisations and, in the diaspora, faith-based groups have undertaken similar efforts in an effort not only to minister to the faith community, but also to reach out to non-Shiites.

Despite the post-1979 expansion in the resource base, in the years immediately following the Revolution the field was dominated by essentialist visions of the faith that reprised those extant prior to 1979.

Thus, for example, in his *The Shadow of God and the Hidden Imam* (1984), S. A. Arjomand, citing Corbin's and Nasr's equating of tendencies in Shiism and Sufism, argued that Shiism was characterised by 'pious antipathy toward political power', but that the Ayatollah Khomeini had utilised earlier 'mahdistic' tendencies within Shii Islam to promote a distinctly this-worldly political agenda. Echoing the pre-1979 picture of the Safawid period, he depicted the activities of al-Majlisi and like-minded co-religionists as 'an important cause' of the Afghan toppling of the Safawid dynasty.[11]

In the wake of *The Shadow* appeared contributions by other scholars who envisioned the faith in similarly essentialist way and, usually also, as diametrically opposed to all things Western. Chapters in M. Kramer's *Shiism, Resistance and Revolution* (1987), for example, pointed to the inherently expansionist tendencies of Iran's Shii revolution, the singular vision of the faith on offer in Iran and the imminent takeover of Gulf and other nearby states by Shii fifth-column elements, if not by Iran itself. S. H. Nasr, his son S. V. Nasr and H. Dabashi lent further credibility to the understanding, *pace* Arjomand, of 'real' Shiism as essentially apolitical and other-worldly in their collections of selected sections from earlier English-language contributions, *Shiism, Doctrines, Thought and Spirituality* (1988) and *Expectation of the Millennium: Shiism in History* (1989).[12]

In 1992, M. A. Amir-Moezzi, of the Classicists' tradition in the field, offered an understanding of the faith that echoed that of Arjomand. Amir-Moezzi characterised 'early Imamism' as 'an esoteric doctrine'. However, from the establishment of the faith in Safawid Iran could be dated the rise of 'the Doctors of the Law' – none of whom were identified – and the latter's promotion of themselves as the Imam's representatives to the community. Jurisprudence (*fiqh*) became the dominant discipline of study. 'Political ambition and power' took over and 'the 'jurist-theologian took the place of the Imam', with the intent 'to drag Imamism into the political arena, apply it on the collective level and crystallise it as an ideology'.[13]

It was in these same years that efforts to produce overviews of, or introductions to, the faith also appeared. The best known of these were M. Momen's *An Introduction to Shii Islam* (1985) and H. Halm's *Shiism* (1991).[14] Momen's detailed discussions on Shii communities outside Iran appeared at a time when little discussion of these was available in English.[15] Otherwise, however, the framework of their discussions was familiar. On al-Majlisi, for example, Momen cited only Browne and Lockhart. Also, despite his attention to the non-Iranian Shia, Momen's summation of the state of the faith – as those of Arjomand and Amir-Moezzi – primarily referenced Khomeini and Iran.[16]

More recent trends

In these very same years, however, the fruits of the research in the many diverse subfields that appeared in Shii Studies after 1979 also began to be published.

In the study of non-Iranian Shia, there appeared volumes on the faith in Lebanon by F. Ajami (1986) and A. R. Norton (1987); in the subcontinent by J. Cole (1988) and D. Pinault (1992); and in Iraq by J. Wiley (1992), C. Mallat (1993), Y. Nakash (1994) and M. Litvak (1998). G. Fuller (1999) looked at the Shia in Iraq in particular and L. Walbridge (1997) contributed a pioneering volume on the Shia in America.

Both the number and range of these such studies expanded only after the turn of the century. F. Jabar (2003) and N. Pelham (2008) wrote on the Shia in Iraq; R. Shanahan (2005), L. Deeb (2006), T. Chalabi (2006), M. Weiss (2010) and S. Winter (2010) contributed volumes on Lebanon.[17] F. Ibrahim (2006) authored a volume on the Shia of Saudi Arabia; Y. Nakash (2006) looked at the Shia in Bahrain, Saudi Arabia, Iraq and Lebanon; and S. A. Mousavi (2009) wrote on the Hazara Shia of Afghanistan. D. Pinault (2008) lamented the fate of the Pakistani Shia, J. Jones (2012) discussed the Shia in colonial India, while further east, C. Marcinkowski (2005, 2010) discussed the Shia in southeast Asia. L. Takim offered a work on the Shia in North America (2009).

A number of these authors might classify themselves as historians or political scientists. Pinault is an anthropologist, however, and a student of ritual, especially the commemoration of Ashura – the tenth day of the Muslim month of Muharram on which, in 680, the third Imam, al-Husayn, Ali's son and the grandson of the Prophet, was killed with many of his followers at Karbala during a rising against the Umayyads.

This commemoration – perhaps the most distinctive of all Shii 'rituals'

– had produced such earlier, but still useful, works as M. Ayoub's *Redemptive Suffering in Islam* (1978), as well as P. Chelkowski's *Taziyeh. Ritual and Drama in Iran* (1979).

The post-1979 period saw this interest expand greatly and encompass studies thereof outside Iran and across time. These included the special 1985 issue of *The Drama Review* on the Muharram commemorations as practiced across the Shii world, but also works by such observers as M. Heglend (1997, 1998), Pinault (1992, 1999), A. R. Saiyid (1981) and V. Schubel (1993) on the Indian subcontinent and on Turkey by E. Glassen (1993).

The commemorations continued to attract interest into the new millennium. Pinault (2001) was joined by T. Howarth (2005) and S. A. Hyder (2008) in discussing Ashura in the Indian subcontinent. N. Kazmi's film *10 Days* (2006) documented the commemorations as undertaken in rural Pakistan. A. R. Norton (2001) discussed Lebanon, and S. Mervin's film *The Procession of the Captives* (2006), addressed the re-creation of the forced march of the survivors of Karbala to the court of the Umayyad caliph Yazid (d. 683) by residents of a south Lebanon Shii village. K. Aghaie (2004) looked at evolving Muharram commemorations and discourse thereon over the past two centuries in Iran, and his 2006 work examined the role of women in these commemorations across the Shii world.

Several collections of articles also appeared after the onset of the millennium. These include such volumes as those by R. Brunner and W. Ende, L. Clarke, and L. Walbridge in 2001. A number of the chapters in these addressed non-Iranian Shii communities, as did the chapters in the 2007 collection of A. Monsutti *et al.*, and the 2010 collection edited by D. Hermann and S. Mervin. P. Khosronejad's 2011 collection even addressed aspects of Shii art and material culture.[18]

Efforts to promote Catholic–Shii inter-faith dialogue produced the edited volumes of J. Bill and J. Williams (2002), as well as those of 2004, 2006 and 2008 edited by A. O'Mahony *et al.*

Recent studies on the faith during the Safawid period in particular,[19] include C. Mitchell's 2009 study of religion and rhetoric in chancellery documents and B. Rahimi's 2011 study of Muharram commemorations in the period. The contributions of M. Kamal (2006), S. Rizvi (2007, 2009), I. Kalin (2010) and R. Pourjavady (2011) attest to rising interest in Safawid-period philosophy among a new generation of scholars.

The works produced on Shiism in post-1979 Iran are legion. To be sure, perhaps understandably, most deal with the faith and the state. Among those works that have privileged the faith rather more are A. Rahnema's 1998 work on Ali Shariati (d. 1977). Works of and about Abd al-Karim Soroush include the volume of his translated essays (2000), introduced by M. and A. Sadri; B. Ghamari-Tabrizi's 2008 volume on Soroush; and a 2009 volume of Soroush's essays edited by F. Jahanbaksh. Rahnema has produced a volume (2011) on religion and politics in Iran through the presidency of M. Ahmadinejad. N. Pak-Shiraz has examined Shiism as portrayed on contemporary Iranian cinema (2011).

Based on close-text analyses the 'Classicists' have also maintained a steady stream of research output in these years. Key volumes in this genre that have appeared in these years include E. Kohlberg's 1992 reconstruction of the library of Ibn Tawus (d. 1266), W. Madelung's 1988 study of the early caliphate and M. Bar-Asher's 1999 study of Shii *tafsir* (Quranic exegesis). F. Hamza's *Anthology of Quranic Commentaries, vol. I: On the Nature of the Divine* (2008) contains excerpts from a number of Twelver and non-Twelver Shii commentaries. R. Gleave contributed two important volumes (2000, 2007) on aspects of the Usuli/Akhbari debate within Twelver Shiism, and in 2009 Kohlberg and M. A. Amir-Moezzi revisited the debate on the authenticity of the Uthmanic Codex of the Quran within the early community and edited an early text key to this discourse. In 2011, N. Haider provided evidence for a process of self-differentiation among Shii groups in eighth-century Kufa.[20]

The faith community itself has made many contributions to the field in recent years. These may be divided into works of an academic nature and apologetic materials.

The former include the 1984 and 1993 monographs of H. Modarressi Tabatabai, and his 2003 bibliography of early Shii literature, as well as the 1981 and 1998 monographs of A. Sachedina. A. Lalani's 2000 study of Muhammad al-Baqir, the fifth Imam, also repays attention. A series of other works examined the lives and legacies of the Imams and key early scholarly figures.[21]

Works of an apologetic nature written specifically for Western audiences have been available since 1975. In the years since, these have since been supplemented by a series of works produced with both this audience but, arguably also, the growing Shia diaspora in mind.[22]

Despite the great growth in the field of Shii Studies and the appearance of a range of subdisciplines, features of the pre-1979 discourse still remain prominent.

The study of Twelver Shiism still ranges across the pre-1501 and post-1501 period, with scholars in each of the two groups still largely failing to interact with each other on any profound level. There is seldom any such interaction even between scholars in the many recently established subfields of the discipline, particularly those addressing post-1979 developments. The survival and trajectory of the faith through its formative years to some normative ideal today is assumed. The religious 'text' is still held to be the repository of the normative, and the tendency to see Shiism, if perhaps only in its post-1501 form, as mainly, if not solely, an Iranian phenomenon still permeates even the most recent discussions of the faith.[23]

A different agenda

Given the depth and breadth of the primary and secondary source materials on offer today, it is no longer feasible, or perhaps even advisable, to attempt to produce a single-volume summary view of all that is known about the faith across both time and space.

The better country and anthropological studies of recent years reveal the complexity of Shii life not only across the world's Shii communities today, but also within each of them. They demonstrate that what today, at first glance, might be taken as normative Twelver doctrine and practice is, in fact, not at all so. Rather, the normative is subject to debate and discussion and that there are many more 'voices' participating in these than just a handful of scholarly elites.

Studies of practices commemorating Muharram in particular reveal diverse and changing attitudes towards quietism and activism among Shia in all regions across the more recent centuries, as well as schisms between different lay elements across a variety of parameters, and between these and different elements of the clerical class. Revealed also is the extent to which, even today, some non-Shia participate in, and appreciate, the commemoration in some instances, while in other cases non-Iranian Shia participate in the commemoration as a means of publicly asserting the distinctiveness of their faith to non-believers.[24]

If Shii life today is so complex, why should the past have been any different?

This volume addresses the history and development of the faith from the time of the death of the Prophet Muhammad in 632 to 1722, the date of the 'political' end of Iran's Safawid dynasty when its capital Isfahan fell to an invading Afghan force.

In the process, the volume privileges the earlier observations that survival of the Twelvers as the largest, and perhaps the most scattered, of the myriad Shii groups attested in the ninth and tenth century would seem to have been quite an accomplishment, and that today most Shia are not Iranian. The volume also challenges the teleological approach favoured in discussions of pre-1722 Shiism in particular, especially those aspects of that approach that assume both the faith's survival from the first and that the sum total of the faith's 'spiritual scene' at any given point can be reconstructed based solely on reference to the 'normative' doctrines and practices enunciated by a handful of elites.

What emerges from the present study is that the views of the handful of those scholarly elites, with whose works Western scholars have long been familiar, were evolved in atmospheres of challenge and contention. The roots of the latter were external, of course. But, and to an extent not given sufficient attention to date, they were also internal. In fact, at any given moment in this period not only were the views of Twelver elites not uniform, they were most likely in the minority in their own times.

Such was the extent of the external and internal challenges over these centuries that at any given moment, also, the different ranks of the faithful, scattered as they were across the region, could not have taken for granted the future course or even the independent survival of the faith.

It was not until later in the seventeenth century that Twelver Shiism's very survival as anything more than a minor sect, if that, was assured.

The sources

A variety of sources have been utilised for the present discussion.

As for the very earliest centuries of Islamic history, the historical and 'religious' sources were not composed until some centuries later. Such sources include, for example, not only the biography of the Prophet completed by the late-eighth-century biographer Ibn Ishaq, but available only in the recension of Ibn Hisham (d. 883), but also the faith's various historical chronicles, from the earliest of these – by al-Yaqubi (d. 905),[25] al-Tabari (d. 923)[26] and al-Masudi (d. 956),[27] to later chronicles such as those of Ibn Miskawayh (d. 1030),[28] Ibn al-Jawzi (d. 1200), Ibn al-Athir (d. 1233)[29] and Ibn Kathir (d. 1373).[30] The authors of most of these are Sunnis,[31] but Shii sources, including the volume on the martyrdom of Imam al-Husayn by Abu Mikhnaf (d. 774) – used extensively by al-Tabari – and *Maqatil al Talibiyin* (*The Killing of the Talibids*, referring to descendants of the Prophet in the line of his uncle Abu Talib) of Abul-Faraj al-Isfahani (d. 967) (Cairo, 1368/1949), can also have their own biases.

Recently, G. Schoeler and A. Goerke, among others, have suggested that judicious use of such later works can, in fact, reveal more of the faith's early history than P. Crone and others have suggested.[32] For the first four chapters of the present work, covering the period from the death of the Prophet to the end of the Buyid period in 1055, such sources are used with care, and with a view to discerning the most important trends over these years as they pertain to the rise of Shiism.

From the time of the disappearance of the twelfth Imam in the early 870s, the sources used herein comprise, perhaps necessarily, the works of the scholarly elite themselves. The illiterate, the majority in any era of the pre-modern period, left no written records. But these works, when read carefully and 'against the grain',[33] often reveal evidence of non-elite 'voices' and their challenges to elites. We do not, and perhaps cannot, know as much about these other voices as we might like. But these voices are there nevertheless.

Appendix I comprises a listing of the numbers of scholars by their geographical points of association, based on the examination of the multi-volume *tabaqat* work by the well-known Shii scholar Agha Buzurg al-Tihrani (d. 1970) for the fifth to the twelfth Islamic centuries, that is, from approximately 1009 to 1785.[34] The term *tabaqat* refers to a genre of biographical literature in Islam that organises individuals or groups by the century in which they lived. The individuals whose biographical sketches al-Tihrani includes in these volumes can have names that contain a *nisba*. The term denotes the suffix of a word – often a place or vocation, for example – used to form an adjective and frequently used as part of an individual's name; in English the name 'Smith' referring, ultimately – in theory – to the occupation of some ancestor as that of a blacksmith, for example. The name of a person born on or otherwise associated with the island of Bahrain in the Persian Gulf often includes the term 'Bahrani' to refer to that association. Many of the figures listed in these volumes do not have *nisba*s. Many also kept or continued to be associated with a given *nisba* generations after the original geographical or vocational link denoted by the first holder of the *nisba* in question had ceased to have any real meaning. Al-Tihrani listed these figures alphabetically by first name and included a *nisba* where he could. He also cross-referenced all he could by *nisba*. The temptation would be to consult only the entry for the *nisba* itself (for example, Bahrani, Tabrizi, etc.) under which he listed all the individuals with that *nisba* and gave their proper name, and count them. One could, as has been the case for the present volume, also examine the entry on each and every individual in each volume from page 1 to make sure that there was some indication of a geographical link to an area beyond the *nisba* alone.

Even then care needs to exercised. The numbers cannot be absolute. The original exercise itself could only be carried out by al-Tihrani's examining written sources, including earlier works in the genre. These, as he notes, often contain poor/wrong or contradictory information, especially concerning scholars alive from 1055 to the later 1400s; this was an especially challenging period for the faith and the faithful as will be noted. Across any time period scholars who were born, trained, authored works and died far from or without otherwise having visited or been known by those at various of these centuries' larger Shii 'centres', might not have been noted in the works produced in those centres so as to have been recovered by al-Tihrani. Too, many named in these volumes were not scholars and, for others, it is not immediately clear from the entries that they were even Shiites.

Nevertheless, these numbers are 'indicative'. They suggest the continuous presence of pockets of believers scattered across the entire region; that is, as suggested, as in the present so in the past not all Shia were Iranian. The additional information al-Tihrani offers on scholars' movements and the making of manuscript copies suggests that these sites were also perceived as active centres of intellectual activity across the period. The data also suggests a marked decline in scholarly activity across the region over the thirteenth to the fifteenth centuries, precisely those years when the faith faced its greatest existential challenge. The data also suggests a marked upturn in Iran-based scholarly activity, particularly in the seventeenth century.

Appendix II comprises a database of the dateable manuscript copies of well-known texts of Twelver scholars who lived and wrote from the ninth to the sixteenth centuries. As for the data in Appendix I, the figures herein cannot be taken as absolute. Individual scholars may well have had access to personal or otherwise private copies of such works, for example. There is also no information available for the place of copying.

Nevertheless, the information can also be taken as 'indicative' of the extent to which copies of these key writings were generally available and accessible over the centuries. As such, they tell a story of the relative loss of heritage from 1055 and its 'recovery'. The date of the latter, the later seventeenth century, coincides with the upturn visible in numbers of scholars in Appendix I.

Appendix III lists selected *tabaqat* works produced in the Safawid period and their publication information, if any. Clearly, in the later Safawid period also there was much activity in this particular field of the religious sciences.

The same al-Tihrani also authored the famous twenty-five-volume bibliographical dictionary *al-Dharia*.[35] Appendix IV gathers information in this work on commentaries and marginalia produced by later scholars on the works of earlier generations, by the Islamic century in which the commentators, as best as can be assessed, died. As the data in the other appendices, so this data suggests that the Safawid period was a particularly active one for such texts, even if only a very few in the period were active in their production.

It might be assumed that such works, being what they are, contain little that was new or significant over and above the original.

The same might be assumed of the works produced by the scholarly elite across a range of the Shii religious sciences in these years, and that they contain little that might aid in the recovery of the complexity of community life over these centuries.

The proof, as is suggested, is in the reading.

Notes

1. Herein 'Shii', or sometimes 'Shiite', is used for the adjectival form and 'Shia' refers to the community of believers.
2. 'Imam' refers to these figures and 'imam' refers to the leadership role within the community, such as the imam of a mosque or the leader of a prayer service.
3. For an introduction to this community, see F. Daftary, *A Short History of the Ismailis* (Edinburgh, 1998).
4. There is as yet no introductory work on the Zaydis. The works of Momen and Halm, cited below, do give some useful background.
5. J. Hussain, *The Occultation of the Twelfth Imam. A Historical Background* (London, 1982), 69f, 57. H. Halm, *Shiism* (Edinburgh, 2004), 34, gives 869 as the year of the twelfth Imam's birth.
6. On the Shii populations, see The Pew Forum, 'Mapping the Global Muslim Population, A Report on the Size and Distribution of the World's Muslim Population', 7 October 2009, available at: http://www.pewforum.org/Muslim/Mapping-the-Global-Muslim-

Population%286%29.aspx, accessed 7 May 2012. On Israel, see K. Sindawi, 'Are there any Shi'ite Muslims in Israel?', *Holy Land Studies* 7(2) (2008), 183–99.

7. For the most thorough survey of the primary source discussion of the number and beliefs of the different Shii groups at the death of the eleventh Imam, see A. Iqbal's *Khwandan-i Nawbakhti* (Tehran, 1345), 140f, 246–67, citing Sad b. Abdallah al-Ashari al-Qummi (d. *c.* 911–914), *Kitab al-Maqalat wal-Firaq* (Tehran, 1963); Abu Muhammad al-Hasan b. Musa al-Nawbakhti (d. *c.* 912–922), *Firaq al-Shia* (Najaf, 1969); Ali b. al-Husayn al-Masudi (d. 956), *Muruj al-Dhahab*, 4 (Beirut, 1403/1982). See also Ali b. Ismail al-Ashari (d. 935–936), *Maqalat al-Islamiyyin*, ed. H. Ritter (Wiesbaden, 1980), 16f; H. Eisenstein, 'Sunnite Accounts of the Subdivisions of the Shia', in Frederick de Jong (ed.), *Shia Islam, Sects and Sufism. Historical Dimensions, Religious Practice and Methodological Considerations* (Utrecht, 1992), 1–9.

8. The papers were published as *Le Shi'isme imamite*, ed. T. Fahd (Paris 1970).

9. The quote is from L. Lockhart (d. 1975), *The Fall of the Safawi Dynasty and the Afghan Occupation of Persia* (Cambridge, 1958), 32–3, 70, 71 n. 1. The 'decline' narrative was on offer earlier in E. G. Browne (d. 1926), *A Literary History of Persia*, 4 (Cambridge, 1953, reprint of the 1924 edition), 4: 120, to which Lockhart's note refers, as well as 403–4, 194–5, 366. See also S. H. Nasr, 'The School of Ispahan', in M. M. Sharif (ed.), *A History of Muslim Philosophy*, 2 (Wiesbaden, 1966), 931. R. Savory's *Iran Under the Safavids* (Cambridge, 1980) remains the best pre-1979 exposition of the Safawid 'decline' narrative.

10. In the original, Cottam (see the 1979 edition, 308; Cottam's 1979 postscript begins on 320) mentions Khomeini as 'an unknown figure in Nationalist circles' leading the June 1963 riots. In his *The Political Elite of Iran* (Princeton, 1971) M. Zonis did mention Khomeini as well as Grand Ayatollah Burujirdi (d. 1961), but ranked 'principal religious leaders' as twentieth on a list of the thirty categories of the political elite (pp. 346–8). Avery's reference to Burujirdi (p. 505) is almost dismissive. Only Algar and Akhavi offered alternative agendas, seeing both believers and the faith as 'active' and meaningful in contemporary Iran. See N. Keddie, 'The Roots of the Ulama's Power in Modern Iran', in N. Keddie (ed.), *Scholars, Saints, and Sufis* (Berkeley, 1969), 211–29; H. Algar, 'The Oppositional Role of the Ulama in Twentieth Century Iran', in Keddie (ed.), *Scholars, Saints, and Sufis*, 231–55. See also Algar, *Religion and the State in Iran, 1785–1906* (Berkeley, 1969); S. Akhavi, *Religion and Politics in Contemporary Iran. Clergy–State Relations in the Pahlavi Period* (Albany, NY, 1980), the research for which pre-dated the Revolution (p. xiv).

11. S. A. Arjomand, *The Shadow of God and the Hidden Imam. Religion, Political Order, and Societal Change in Shiite Iran from the Beginning to 1890* (Chicago, 1984), 23, 261–3, 190f, 269–70, citing specifically Corbin's statement that 'Shiism is, in essence, the esotericism of Islam'.

12. In these years voices that questioned the narrative casting Iran and Shiism as anything less than a monolithic threat to the world order were decidedly in the minority. For an example of the latter, see J. Cole's and N. Keddie's collection of papers, *Shiism and Social Protest* (New Haven, CT, 1986).

13. M. A. Amir-Moezzi, *The Divine Guide in Early Shiism. The Sources of Esotericism in Islam*, trans. David Streight (Albany, NY, 1994), 125–6, 137–9. The original was published as *Le guide divin dans le shi'isme originel* (Lagrasse, 1992).

14. Halm's 1991 *Shiism* was a translation of a 1987 German volume; the 2004 version is a second edition of the 1991 edition. Halm's later 1997 *Shi'a Islam: from Religion to Revolution* was a translation of his 1994 *Schütische Islam*. See also Y. Richard's *Shiite Islam, Polity, Ideology, and Creed* (Oxford, 1995) originally appeared as *L'islam chiite, croyances et ideologies* (Paris, 1991). D. M. Donaldson's *The Shiite Religion. A History of Islam in Persia and Irak* (London, 1933), although still useful is usually overlooked.

15. The extent of the field's lack of awareness of non-Iranian Shii communities to this date can be seen in the paucity of secondary sources thereon available to Momen, *An Introduction to Shii Islam* (New Haven, 1985). See, for example, the 'sources' section for his chapter, 'Shiism in Modern Times, AD 1500–1900', 330–2, and that for his final chapter, 'Contemporary Shiism', 343–4.

16. Momen, *An Introduction to Shii Islam*, 115–16, 115 n.7, referring Browne, *A Literary History of Persia*, 4: 404, and Lockhart, *The Fall of the Safawi Dynasty*, 70, 297–9. On al-Majlisi, see also H. Halm, *Shiism*, 2nd edn (Edinburgh, 2004), 93. Notwithstanding the efforts of Momen and Halm (124f) to note the Shii presence outside Iran, a 1995 CIA map shows no Shia in the subcontinent: see http://www.zonu.com/detail-en/2009-09-18-7090/Sunni-and-Shiite-Muslims-in-the-World-1995.html, accessed 28 February 2013.

17. This is not to mention the many works on the Amal movement or Hizballah.

18. Listing the many journal articles published since 1979, or even since 2000 is beyond the scope of these remarks.

19. On pre- and post-1979 developments in Safawid studies to the early years of the century, see further my *Safavid Iran: Rebirth of a Persian Empire* (London, 2006), 1–9.

20. Just as this list includes only monographs, the careful reader will notice no works are listed in any of the European languages or Japanese. In French, for example, see M. A. Amir-Moezzi's *La religion discrete* (2006), now available in translation as *The Spirituality of Shii Islam* (London, 2011), a collection of some of the best of his essays. See also S. Mervin's several works on Lebanon, and works by D. Hermann and M. Terrier. In Italian, the work of M. Salati repays attention. In Japanese, see the work of K. Morimoto, who has also written in English.

21. These include S. H. M. Jafri, *The Origins and Early Development of Shia Islam* (New York, 1979); and, after 1979, Hussain, *The Occultation of the Twelfth Imam*; M. M. Shams al-Din, *The Rising of al-Husayn*, trans. I. Howard (London, 1985); S. W. Akhtar, *Early Shiite Imamiyyah Thinkers* (New Delhi, 1988).

22. One of the earliest of these was Allama Sayyid Muhammad Husayn Tabatabai's *Shiite Islam*, trans. S. H. Nasr (Albany, 1975), composed for a foreign audience. More recent examples of works in this genre include Ayatollah J. Sobhani, *Doctrines of Shii Islam*, trans. R. Shah-Kazemi (London, 2001), and M. A. Shomali, *Shii Islam* (London, 2003). Of Ayatollah Khomeini's works, see H. Algar's 1981 translation of Imam Khomeini, *Islam and Revolution*, and J. Burujirdi's 1984 translation of the Ayatollah's *Clarification of Questions*.

23. See, for example, V. Nasr, *The Shia Revival* (New York, 2006) and Dabashi's highly personalised *Shiism* (Cambridge, MA, 2011).

24. For Iran, see, for example, K. Aghaie, 'The Karbala Narrative: Shii Political Discourse in Modern Iran in the 1960s and 1970s', *Journal of Islamic Studies*, 12 (2001), 151–76; K. Aghaie, *The Martyrs of Karbala. Shii Symbols and Rituals in Modern Iran* (Seattle, WA, 2005); K. Aghaie, *The Women of Karbala. Ritual Performance and Symbolic Discourses in Modern Shii Islam* (Austin, TX, 2005). For the Indian subcontinent, see D. Pinault, *The Shiites. Ritual and Popular Piety in a Muslim Community* (New York, 1992); D. Pinault, *Horse of Karbala. Muslim Devotional Life in India* (New York, 2001); on Pakistan, see D. Pinault, *Notes from a Fortune-telling Parrot. Islam and the Struggle for Religious Pluralism in Pakistan* (London, 2008); M. Hegland, 'Mixed Blessing: The Majles – Shi'a Women's Rituals of Mourning in North-West Pakistan', in Judy Brink and Joan Mencher (eds.), *Mixed Blessings: Gender and Religious Fundamentalism Cross-Culturally* (New York, 1997), 179–96. In his 'The Flagellations of Muharram and the Shiite Ulama', *Islam*, 55 (1978), 19–36, Ende dissects the debate between Lebanon and Iraq in the early twentieth century. L. Deeb picks up Ende's story in her 'Living Ashura in Lebanon', *Comparative Studies of South Asia, Africa and the Middle East*,

25(1) (2005), 122–37. On contemporary disagreements among Shii scholars over the politi-
cal authority of the clerical class, see H. Mavani, *Religious Authority and Political Thought in Twelver Shiism*, forthcoming.

25. Thanks to Dr A. Marsham for suggesting 905 as the now-agreed death date for al-Yaqubi. See Ahmad b. Wadih al-Yaqubi, *Tarikh al-Yaqubi*, 3 vols (Najaf, 1384/1964).

26. Al-Tabari's *Tarikh al-Rusul wal-Muluk* (*The History of the Prophets and of the Kings*) has been translated into English by various scholars (Albany, 1989–2007).

27. A French translation of his *Muruj al-Dhahab* (*The Meadows of Gold*) was produced over 1861–77. A Sprenger's English translation of volume one appeared in London, 1841.

28. His *Tajarib al-Umam* is available as a partial edition. L. Caetani, 3 vols (Leiden 1909–17). The Arabic and an English translation were made available by H. F. Amedroz and D. S. Margoliouth as *The Experiences of Nations*, 7 vols (Oxford, 1920–1).

29. D. S. Richards has produced a multi-volume translation of the portion of *Al-Kamil fi'l-Tarikh* on the Saljuks and Crusades (Ashgate, 2008).

30. For an overview of these and other sources on Islamic history to 1050, see H. Kennedy, *The Prophet and the Age of the Caliphates* (London, 1986), 350f.

31. On al-Yaqubi, see Y. Marquet, 'Le shi'isme au XIe siècle à travers l'histoire de Ya'qubi', *Arabica* 19 (1972), 1–145, at 101–38; W. G. Millward, 'Al-Yaqubi's Sources and the Question of Shia Partiality', *Abr Nahrain*, 12 (1971/2), 47–74. My thanks, again, to Dr A. Marsham for directing me to these.

32. G. Schoeler's introduction to his *The Genesis of Literature in Islam* (Edinburgh, 2009), a trans-lation of the French original of 2002, rehearses the discussion on the sources. I have ben-efited much from conversations on these issues with Drs Goerke and Andrew Marsham of my own department in Edinburgh. For works by Dr Goerke, see Chapter 2, n. 1.

33. The phrase derives from the work of Walter Benjamin (d. 1940) as utilised especially within the field of Subaltern Studies.

34. Agha Buzurg al-Tihrani, *Tabaqat Alam al-Shia*, 6 vols, ed. A. N. Munzavi (Qum, n.d.).

35. Agha Buzurg al-Tihrani, *Al-Dharia ila Tasanif al-Shia*, 25 vols (Tehran and Najaf, 1353–1398).

CHAPTER 1

Shiism fragmented: the faith and the faithful from the seventh to the ninth century

The event that set in motion the trends and events that underlay the rise of Twelver Shiism as a distinctive body of doctrine and practice occurred in 632. In the summer of that year, in the city of Medina, after a few weeks of ill health, the Prophet Muhammad died.

This chapter offers a basic overview of the major events from 632 to the disappearance of the twelfth Husaynid Imam in 873–4.

The historical events that marked Islam's earliest years are recounted only in sources that began to appear only some centuries later and in such detail as to be, at the very least, quite problematic.

Nevertheless, certain events and trends across the period are discernible.

From the death of the Prophet to the fall of the Umayyads

The basic contours of early Islamic history are well enough known and accepted.

Muhammad – of the Banu Hashim clan of the Quraysh tribe – was, first and foremost, the messenger of Allah who revealed the Quran to the Arabs. This revelation commenced in the early 600s, when he was said to be 40 years of age. In the 620s, Muhammad fled the harassment of the Quraysh tribal elites in his hometown of Mecca for Medina. About a decade later, after an uneven series of military encounters, the Prophet appeared at Mecca with a large army and the Meccans surrendered the city. The Prophet later performed the pilgrimage to the city, but in 632 he became ill and died.

Elements of the *umma* (the Muslim community), composed of the *Muhajirun* (emigrants) – those who had left Mecca with him – and the *Ansar* (companions, helpers) – the converts at Medina – thereupon met in a nearby *saqifa* (hall). These chose Abu Bakr – a member of another tribe of the Quraysh – as the *khalifa* (caliph or successor) of the Prophet. During his two-year tenure, Abu Bakr defeated some rebellious Arab tribes and then oversaw politico-military expansion into modern-day Iraq, then under the Persian Sassanian dynasty, and Syria, then under the Byzantines.

Before he died in 634 Abu Bakr announced Umar, also a member of the Quraysh, as his successor. Under Umar, the Muslim victory over Sassanian forces at Qadisiyya in 636 allowed the Arab armies to advance east, through

Khurasan and, by 644, into modern-day Afghanistan. Muslim forces also moved through Egypt along the Libyan coast of the Mediterranean by 643 and north – taking Damascus and Jerusalem – into Byzantine territory by 638.

Umar died in 644, but he had convened a council to decide on his successor. This group chose Uthman, of the Umayyad clan of the Quraysh, and an early companion of the Prophet, to succeed Umar as caliph.

During the rule of Uthman (644–56), Sassanian rule over the Iranian plateau was finally ended and Muslim Arab armies moved into modern-day Pakistan. Other forces moved northward into the Caucasus and into the Byzantine territories of modern-day eastern Turkey. To the west, Sicily was captured and expeditions were sent through North Africa and into the Iberian Peninsula. To the south, Nubia was captured.

In 656, amid charges of nepotism and corruption, Uthman's house was besieged and attacked and he was killed. Delegations from the *Muhajirun*, the *Ansar* and the key provinces appealed to Ali, the cousin and son-in-law of the Prophet, to accept the post of caliph. He did, and Kufa became his capital.

Ali immediately faced opposition from Uthman's Umayyad clan, who sought revenge for his murder. Uthman's cousin Muawiya, the governor of Syria, refused to pledge his allegiance to Ali. In Mecca, Muhammad's wife Aisha also spoke against Ali. She and others travelled to Iraq to incite Basra and Kufa against him.

In 656, Ali, with some Kufan supporters, defeated these forces at the battle of the Camel and moved against the Syria-based opposition. At Siffin, in 657, Ali and Muawiya agreed to mediation. The result of a subsequent meeting, in 659, was a split in the caliphate: some, especially in greater Syria, declared for Muawiya and some, especially in Iraq, for Ali. In 661, at a mosque in Kufa, a renegade supporter attacked Ali.

Following Ali's death two days later, Muawiya (*reg.* 661–80) was recognised as caliph in the pro-Ali areas. Thus ended the period of the *Rashidun* (rightly-guided) caliphs and commenced the period of the Umayyad dynasty (661–750).

Internal divisions

If the basic events are clear, the later sources on which historians depend for their recounting reveal much less about the exact roots – the socioeconomic, political or cultural dimensions, for example, possibly underlying these and other events in early Islamic history – than historians today might deem desirable.[1]

The sources do, however, refer to manifestations of discontent over the years after the Prophet's death. These, as perhaps often in pre-modern societies, could be religious in nature.

Muhammad's spiritual leadership – in his role as the Messenger – was the basis of the political and military leadership that he exercised over the *umma*.

The sources agree that the Prophet made no formal reference to any plan of succession, nor did he explicitly name an immediate successor. The different sources offer many conflicting accounts of the discussions and the politicking between the various factions and personalities of those who gathered at the *saqifa* at the Prophet's death.[2] From a careful reading of these, it does seem that Umar, although he approved the choice of Abu Bakr by those present, was uneasy with the process. The meeting was held in the absence of many of the emigrants, many of the Prophet's family and clan and many Medinans. Ali, who had married the Prophet's daughter, is also agreed to have been absent, as he was attending to the Prophet's body. In addition, many of the *Ansar* who did attend did not pledge their loyalty to Abu Bakr as the designee. Some seem to have raised the name of Ali during the meeting, if only after the fact. Other prominent, named figures and some of the Quraysh also refused to pledge loyalty to Abu Bakr.[3]

The idea that Ali might be the Prophet's immediate successor was not entirely untoward.

The Prophet's cousin, Ali was the first male to accept the faith, at age 13. He was also Muhammad's son-in-law. He is said to have helped trick assassins sent against Muhammad on the eve of the flight to Medina. In Medina, when the Prophet commanded that all Muslims should have a brother, he designated Ali as such. Muhammad gave Ali a number of important tasks and the Prophet appointed Ali his deputy in Medina. In March 632, just a few months before his death, at the well of Ghadir Khumm on his return to Medina from his last pilgrimage to Mecca, the Prophet is said to have proclaimed Ali as his *mawla* (lord, leader) and asked Allah to 'support' those who supported Ali and to be the 'enemy' of those who opposed Ali.

The Quran itself would be collected and collated only during the reign of Uthman. Nevertheless, its verses were certainly in circulation beforehand and some refer to the special place of the families of the prophets previously sent by Allah. Terms such as *dhurriya* (offspring, progeny), *Al* (nearest relations by descent), *ahl* (referring to those from a common locality) and *bayt* (house, that is, household, the immediate descendants of the same house) occur repeatedly throughout the text. The term *Ahl al-Bayt* is used in reference to special status of the Prophet's family:

> Allah only wishes to remove from you [all kinds of]
> uncleanliness, O members of the family [of
> Muhammad], and thoroughly purify you. (33:33)[4]

Traditions ascribed to the Prophet collected in later Sunni collections also attest to special roles for Ali. The Sunni traditionist Ahmad b. Hanbal (d. 855) noted that the Prophet designated Ali to communicate Sura 9 of the Quran, not Abu Bakr, because the angel Gabriel had said that the Sura was to be communicated to the community only by the Prophet himself or 'someone from you', that is, his family. Muhammad is also said to have appeared with Ali, his wife Fatima and their two sons and all stood under a cloak. The five were thereafter referred to as *Ahl al-Kisa* (people of the cloak). In the collection of traditions entitled the *Sahih*, assembled by the Iranian Sunni traditionist Muslim b. Hajjaj (d. 864–5), there is mention of the five as gathered under the cloak, in reference to Quran 33:33, above. A number of Sunni collections contain traditions that report that Muhammad stated that he was leaving behind *thaqalayn* (two precious things) that, if followed, would produce no errors: the first was the Quran itself and the second was *Ahl al-Bayt*.[5]

Thus, although the exact details of certain events in these early years and the participants therein, as cited by later authors, are not so clear, two broad, and clearly different, visions of the succession question seem to have been abroad in the community. Some held that with the death of the Prophet the link with the Divine was now ended. The Muslim community could now depend only on its own resources, with just the mix of old and recently established sociopolitical hierarchies, and of old and recently established practices and *mores* as guides for the future. Others understood that the Divine intended that His link with the community and, therefore, the spiritual, political and military leadership that it bespoke, were to continue via the Prophet's family.[6]

In the event, the sources note that Ali did give his allegiance to Abu Bakr, but disagree as to when; some suggest he did so as many as six months later. Ali does not appear to have been consulted as to the appointment of Umar, however. At Umar's death in 644, Ali and Uthman were members of the council. There was no support for Ali among the others and Uthman was selected.[7]

The Shia and the Umayyads

The Arabic term Shia means 'follower', 'adherent' and, in this sense, 'party' or 'faction'. The term seems first to have appeared in reference to the supporters of Ali during the wars he fought as caliph against the partisans of the murdered Uthman.[8] Aside from the very few, and later-recorded names of, individuals – any might be taken to represent clan or other groupings – who supported Ali in the aftermath of the Prophet's death, the nature and strength of Ali's support from 632 to his own death in 661 is not at all clear. The often-mentioned Kufan support for Ali,[9] for example, cannot be shown to have been broad, deep or consistent, even after he became caliph in 656.

Ali and the Prophet's daughter Fatima had two sons: al-Hasan, aged about 37 when Ali died, and al-Husayn, aged about 35. At Ali's death, Muawiya advanced towards Kufa. What there was of support for al-Hasan in Kufa evaporated, with some supporters seemingly defecting to the Umayyads and others simply withdrawing. Undoubtedly aware of these realities, al-Hasan did not press his claim. He withdrew to Medina, refusing later requests from various delegations to undertake any 'political' activity. He died there in 669.

Two years later, in 671, ten years after Ali's death, one Hujr b. Adi and several others were said to have refused to curse Ali in public. They were executed and the caliph Muawiya adopted a series of political and economic measures that effectively disempowered the Kufans. Muawiya also designated his own son Yazid to succeed him.[10]

When Muawiya died in 680, al-Husayn was living in the Hijaz. He neither offered nor refused allegiance to Muawiya's son and successor Yazid. However, encouraged by Kufan opponents of the Umayyads, al-Husayn and less than one hundred family members and other followers set out for Kufa in September 680. The governor of Iraq blocked their entrance into the city and to the Euphrates as a source of water. Trapped in the desert on the plain of Karbala, on 10 Muharram 61/10 October 680, al-Husayn's party was attacked. He and most of the party, including his half-brother al-Abbas, were killed. Al-Husayn's head was carried off to Damascus. The women, including al-Husayn's sister Zaynab, and the children left living were marched through the dessert to Yazid's court in Damascus.[11]

Yazid himself ruled for only three years, until 683.

In 684–5, in the aftermath of Yazid's death, some of the Kufan tribal elements who had withdrawn their support for al-Husayn at the last minute – in total some thousand or more *tawwabun* (penitents) – are said to have left the city for Karbala weeping and making vows. A much larger Syrian force confronted them, and most of the *tawwabun* were killed.[12]

Most of the Arab tribes later cited as having taken part in all three of these risings were of south Arabian or Yemeni origin. These, it has been suggested, came from a culture used to dynasty-based kingly succession, and were accustomed also to the charismatic veneration of their rulers. Hence, they would have seen the issue of the succession to Muhammad as a family matter.[13]

At Yazid's death, a rival caliphate had been set up in Mecca. In 685, in the aftermath of the short-lived caliphate of his son Muawiya II and the nine-month rule of the latter's successor, one al-Mukhtar, the nephew of one of Ali's governors, proclaimed his leadership of the Kufan Shia in the name of Muhammad b. al-Hanafiyya. The latter was Ali's only surviving son by another woman.

Seizing the city, al-Mukhtar declared Ibn al-Hanafiyya the Imam and, crucially also, *Mahdi*. This was perhaps the first messianic use of this term in an Islamic context.[14]

Al-Mukhtar's supporters are said to have included *mawali*. Formally, the term refers to the non-Arab converts to Islam in the empire, especially Iranians, Turks and Egyptians, as well as Indians, Aramaeans and Christians. Although Islam preached a message of equality of all believers before Allah, the *mawali* (sing. *mawla*)[15] were required to have an Arab patron, often a tribe, and, although they had converted, to continue to pay the *jizya* (head, or 'poll') tax levied on all male non-believers. They also paid a higher rate of *kharaj* (land tax) on their land.[16]

During the reign of Muawiya, as efforts were made to expand agricultural production in Iraq, *mawali* elements were employed in great numbers to undertake this labour, along with many slaves; in fact, the Arabs often viewed the *mawali* as slaves.[17] *Mawali* numbers only grew as the empire expanded, and the resulting continued growth in *jizya* revenue was increasingly important to the treasury. At the same time, there were substantial numbers of *mawali* in Iraq, Kufa in particular.[18] The Arab tribal elite, especially those drawn from those who had first settled in these areas of Iraq, opposed any regularisation of the status of the *mawali*.

The numbers of *mawali* recorded as having allied with al-Mukhtar were not large. However, his apparently open appeal to them and their presence in the movement lent prominence to their grievances, if not to those of other aggrieved elements as well; indeed, the term was likely employed by the later chroniclers to refer to, and to denigrate, all opposition elements.[19] Some of al-Mukhtar's backers among the local tribal elite were alienated by the presence of such elements in the movement, however, and withdrew. Al-Mukhtar defeated both these and an Umayyad force in 686. In 687, tribal opponents who had left Kufa for Basra, and having allied with forces there, returned and crushed al-Mukhtar's rebellion.

At the death of Ibn al-Hanafiyya in 700–1, a group called the Kaysaniyya, their name derived from one of al-Mukhtar's *mawali* officers, were said to have advanced the idea that in fact he had not died but was *ghaib* (hidden, or in 'occultation').[20]

Coupled with the reference to the *Mahdi*, the belief that the latter was alive but in hiding and would return to bring justice to an unjust world was now on offer. Such a messianic tinge was to be detected in the discourse of many subsequent Shii movements. Together with the attention to al-Husayn, the focus on Ibn al-Hanafiyya also suggested that Shii discourse was now focusing on Ali's progeny. Finally, although the role of the *mawali* should not be exaggerated, the potential for the disaffected, whatever their backgrounds and the nature of their discontent, to sympathise and to identify with pro-Alid discourse was also now a reality. This was especially the case at times of political crises or at a caliph's death, when issues of succession came to the fore.

Shii risings in the later eighth century

If some maintained that Ibn al-Hanafiyya was in occultation, others seem to have acknowledged his death and gathered around his son Abu Hashim. At the latter's death in 718, rival claimants for the succession appeared. One was an Abbasid, that is, a descendant of the Prophet's uncle al-Abbas. Each of these had followers, and some of these were active in Khurasan among both Arab and Persian Muslims.[21]

In 737, one Bayan b. Saman, of one of the south Arabian tribes, joined with al-Mughira b. Said, who may have been a *mawla*, and a very small number of followers and rose in rebellion against the Umayyad governor in Iraq. The sources suggest that both some Arab tribes and some *mawali* were involved in the uprising and that the rising focused on the claims of the Imamate of Abu Hashim.[22]

Al-Mughira may initially have supported the Imamate of the fifth Imam, Ali's great grandson, Muhammad al-Baqir (d. 735). Later, however, he transferred his loyalty to a descendant of Ali's son al-Hasan, one Muhammad b. Abdallah, known as *al-Nafs al-Zakiyya* (the pure soul) (d. 762). [23]

Sometime between 738 and 744, soon after the crushing of this movement, another combined tribal/*mawali* outbreak occurred, launched by the Mansuriyya, named after its leader Abu Mansur. Abu Mansur was killed by the Umayyad governor of Iraq, and his followers then organised themselves around his son al-Husayn.[24]

In this period also Zayd, a half-brother of Muhammad al-Baqir, arrived from the Hijaz and in 740, encouraged by the Kufans, launched a rising. He may have been the first of the Banu Hashim – the sub-clan of the Quraysh of which the Prophet was a member - to lead an open rising himself. Clearly rejecting belief in a quietist or even a 'hidden' leader, he is identified with the view that the Imam can only lay claim to allegiance if he declares himself.

Kufan support, yet again, failed to materialise. Zayd fell in battle. His son Yahya escaped to Khurasan, where earlier Umayyads had exiled some Kufan Shia. There he was captured, released, launched a further anti-Umayyad rising in Herat and was killed in 743.[25]

In 743 also the caliph Hisham died. Walid II, Yazid III and Ibrahim succeeded him, in rapid succession. The period was marked by intense internal jockeying for the position of caliph that certainly further encouraged concerns about Umayyad longevity.[26]

In 744, about the time of Yazid III's death, Ibn Muawiya, a descendant of Ali's brother Jafar, rose in the name of the Banu Hashim generally. Although some of the defeated Zaydi forces in Kufa may have helped him, with broader Kufan support once again uneven, Ibn Muawiya fled to the east. Later sources suggest Qum, Shiraz and other areas acknowledged him. He also was said to have attracted *mawali* support. Once Marwan had secured his place as caliph in 747–8, he sent an army after Ibn Muawiya who was defeated and finally died in Khurasan. One account suggests that he was poisoned by Abu Muslim, an Iranian *mawla*, who saw in Ibn Muawiya a threat to his already well-developed pro-Abbasid network in Khurasan.[27]

Abu Muslim had been active in Khurasan, and Marv especially, since 745.

He may have had connections to al-Mughira, but the Abbasids themselves were also in possession of a broader Hashemite connection. The contemporary Abbasid leader, Ibrahim (d. 748), who had been Abu Muslim's patron, was then based in southern Jordan. Later sources note the claim that Abu Hashim, son of Ibn al-Hanafiyya, had formally transferred the Imamate to the house of al-Abbas.[28]

Marv was a garrison town in which many Arab tribal fighters and their *mawali* had long been settled. The former had long since come to identify with Khurasani affairs and concerns and to chafe under Umayyad efforts, from distant Damascus, to order their affairs.

In June 747, Abu Muslim rose in the name of an Imam, still unnamed but spoken of as *al-Rida* (the one who is acceptable [from the House of Muhammad]). His forces quickly took eastern Iran, and in September 749 reached Kufa. In January 750, the Umayyads were defeated in battle.

The Umayyads having murdered the Abbasid Ibrahim, the Khurasani army's leader al-Saffah became the first caliph. He oversaw the dispatching of the last Umayyads. At al-Saffah's death in 754 his brother became the second caliph and, taking the messianic title *al-Mansur* (the victorious), ruled until 775. To seal the loyalty of army to the Abbasid house more directly, in 755 al-Mansur had Abu Muslim murdered.

Any question that the Abbasids might be beholden, or subject, to pressure from Shii elements in Kufa was dispelled when, in 762, al-Mansur commenced building what would become the new Abbasid capital of Baghdad. Al-Mansur's son and successor, who reigned for ten years, formally abandoned the claim to have received the Imamate via Abu Hashim, and declared that Muhammad's uncle al-Abbas himself was the Imam. In so doing, he also dispensed with even paying lip service to the descendants of Ali as being entitled to lay claims to the Imamate. To further underline his credibility, he took the title *al-Mahdi*.[29]

This turn of events was not widely accepted among others of *Ahl al-Bayt* and their followers. To be sure, the evidence in the later, usually hostile, sources on the exact events and nature of the discourses associated with these later risings, as with earlier risings, is unclear and even contradictory. But, whatever their exact nature, Shii risings clearly did not abate with the fall of the Umayyads and the rise of the Abbasids. In fact, especially in later years, these attracted support from a growing range of sectors of society: tribal elements, *mawali* and, commensurate with the growth of such urban settings as Kufa over the period, even lower-ranking urban merchant elements. They also focused on personages associated with Ali and his family.

In Kufa, in 755, one Abul-Khattab, apparently an associate of the sixth Husaynid Imam, Jafar al-Sadiq, staged an unsuccessful rising. Abul-Khattab was soon executed in Kufa, but later sources suggest his followers split into perhaps as many as seven different groups, including one each purportedly led by a weaver, a corn merchant and a money-changer.[30]

In Medina, in 762, the Zaydi Hasanid al-Nafs al-Zakiyya finally rose up. He was said to have followers scattered as far afield as Egypt, Khurasan and even Sind. His brother Ibrahim also incited a rising in Basra. Both were crushed the same year.[31]

There were also those who believed that Abu Muslim had not in fact been killed, but was in hiding. In 775, elements of this group rose in Transoxiana. The movement spread across Marv, Bukhara and Samarqand before being put down.[32]

Medina witnessed a further Hasanid rising in 786 during the brief caliphate of the caliph al-Mahdi's son and successor al-Hadi (785–786).[33]

The Husaynid Imams in the later Umayyad period

Modern-day authors tend to utilise a composite of Twelver sources to discuss the events and details of the lives of the descendants of al-Husayn over the two centuries following Karbala. But these sources, as those for early Islamic history, only date to later centuries. There is often disagreement over even the birth and death dates of the Husaynid Imams and, as will seen in Chapters 3 and 4, even disagreement as to how they died.

Nevertheless, as for earlier Islamic history, for the two centuries after Karbala certain trends are discernible. First, neither Sunni nor Shii sources offer any evidence that from 680 to the early Abbasid period, any of Imam al-Husayn's direct descendants was himself immediately and directly involved in any of the various Shii risings. Secondly, the number of followers of those understood to be the Husaynid Imams was small and, at the death of each, almost always became smaller.

In the aftermath of Karbala, al-Husayn's son Ali, later given the title *Zayn al-Abidin* (the Ornament of the Worshippers),[34] was taken prisoner and then released. He is said to have spent the rest of his life in Medina, with no direct connection to the many risings – from those of the 'penitents' to that of al-Mukhtar and the rise of the Kaysaniyya – that took place over the years to his death (*c.* 713). At his death, it has been suggested that the majority of Shia followed Ibn al-Hanafiyya and then his son Abu Hashim, not al-Baqir.[35]

His son Muhammad, the fifth Imam, was born in 676 and was given the title *al-Baqir* (shortened form of *Baqir al-Ilm*, meaning one who splits knowledge open, based on the great knowledge attributed to him). He also avoided the various risings during his lifetime, including those of the Kaysaniyya, Ibn al-Hanafiyya's son Abu Hashim, Bayan b. Saman, al-Mughira, Abu Mansur and that of his own half-brother Zayd.[36]

Not all of his followers appear to have accepted the succession of the Imamate to his son Jafar, however. A Kufan was later said to have considered al-Baqir to be the hidden *Mahdi*, that is, that the line of Imams ceased with him.[37]

Jafar, later called *al-Sadiq* (he who speaks the truth), was in his late thirties when his father died.[38] Even more so than his father, the sixth Imam lived through times that were turbulent for both the Shia and the *umma* as a whole. These years witnessed the Kufa-based Shii risings already cited above, that of his own uncle Zayd in 740, of Ibn Muawiya in 744 and the Abbasid rising itself. These risings were followed by the 755 revolt of Abul-Khattab and that in 762 in Medina – where Jafar was based – of the Hasanid al-Nafs al-Zakiyya.

These years also witnessed the death, in 767, of the Kufa-based Abu Hanifa – the eponymous founder of the Sunni Hanafi school of law – a wealthy silk merchant whose forebears were eastern Iranian, and perhaps even Kabuli, in origin. Abu Hanifa had supported the rising of Zayd, initially welcomed the Abbasids, but then opposed them and was jailed by them until his death.[39] In these years also, in the Imam's hometown of Medina, the Sunni Malik b. Anas (d. 795), the 'founder' of the Sunni Maliki school, produced his *Al-Muwatta*, the first written collection of nearly 2,000 traditions of the Prophet and his companions at the request of the Abbasid caliph al-Mansur.[40]

Like his own father, Imam Jafar avoided the religiopolitical nightmare of Kufa and any entanglements with the Abbasid court.[41] At his death in 765 he was buried in Medina – the last of the Imams to be buried there.

At this date, later sources note the appearance of a number of splinter groups. One group, later called the Fatahiyya, or Aftahiyya, believed that the successor was always to be the oldest son, in this case Abdallah *al-Aftah* (the Broad Headed). At the latter's death some understood Imam Jafar's son Musa, born in either 737 or 745, to be the next in line. Others seem to have expected the Imam's son Ismail, who had predeceased his father, to return as the *qaim* (the one who arises), or *Mahdi*, or they followed his progeny. Those believing in the Imamate of Ismail's son Muhammad and his descendants would become the Ismailis. Still others were later said to have believed that Imam Jafar himself was in occultation and was the *qaim*.[42]

Those who understood Musa, also known as *al-Kazim* (the reserved), to be his father's successor were, in any case, clearly fewer in number than those who had gathered around his father.

The Husaynid Imams over the later Abbasid period

There is general agreement that the personal situations of the Imams under the early Abbasids worsened, at least partly because of Abbasid suspicions as to their involvement in the continued uprisings by more militant Shii movements.

Later sources suggest that Imam Musa was generally ignored by al-Mansur during the remaining years of his caliphate. After his accession in 774, the

Caliph al-Mahdi is said to have reached out to other Shii groups, including the Zaydis, to enlist them in the legitimisation of the Abbasid line.[43]

In 785, during the very brief caliphate of al-Mahdi's successor al-Hadi (785–6), a Hasanid rising failed and many Alids were killed by Abbasid forces at the battle of Fakhkh, near Mecca. Abbasid suspicions of all Alids increased markedly.[44]

At al-Hadi's death an internal coup resulted in the accession to the caliphate of the fifth Abbasid caliph, Harun al-Rashid (786–809).

In the meantime, two brothers of the Hasanid al-Nafs al-Zakiyya had fled from Fakhkh. Within three years, Idris had founded the Idrisid Shii state in Morocco. In 793, Idris was poisoned, apparently by a Zaydi agent of the caliph, but the Berber tribes who had flocked to his banner thereupon installed his young son in his place. The other brother fled to Daylam, along the Caspian Sea in Iran, and launched a rising there in 791. The caliph eventually succeeded in luring him to Baghdad and had him killed.[45]

These risings can only have encouraged Harun's very anti-Shii tendencies. Al-Tabari records that in 787 he exiled all the Alids in Baghdad to Medina. In 795, Harun brought Imam Musa back to Iraq with him after his pilgrimage and had him put under house arrest. The Imam died in 799, and was buried in Baghdad.[46]

At Musa's death, as with the deaths of previous Imams, later sources suggest that the already small community of followers experienced further splits. Some maintained that Musa himself was the promised *qaim*. Within this group were those who maintained that the Imam had died and others who held that he was in occultation. The latter were called the *Waqifa* (those who stopped), signalling their belief that the line of imams went no further. Others believed that the Imamate had passed to Musa son's Ahmad. Finally, some maintained that the Imamate had passed to Musa's son, and Ahmad's brother, Ali al-Rida, born in 765, based in Medina.[47]

The nearly twenty years of al-Rida's Imamate were similarly marked by both intellectual and 'practical' developments and challenges.

In these years Mutazilism also appeared, privileging *aql* (reason) above the revelation, and identified with the development of *kalam* (systematic theology) in Islam and for its Basran and Baghdadi 'schools'. Participants in this discourse were drawn from across sectarian lines, including members of various Shii groups.[48]

Perhaps more importantly, at Harun's death in 809 the empire descended into a brutal civil war over the succession between Harun's two sons, al-Amin based in Baghdad and al-Mamun in Khurasan. The war came to an end only *c.* 817, with the latter victorious.

In the midst of this turmoil over the succession, Alid affections again came to the fore. In 815, in Kufa, one Abul-Saraya rose up in the name of a Zaydi

Hasanid Muhammad b. Ibrahim, known as Ibn Tabataba. The rebellion gripped southern Iraq and nearly reached Baghdad. Several attempts to crush the rising failed. In Basra, the rebels burned large numbers of houses belonging to the Abbasid family. Elsewhere, a *hajj* caravan was plundered. In Mecca, the Husaynid governor seized the treasure in the Kaba and plundered the wealth of local Abbasids.

Abbasid forces did finally crush the rising. Two years later, in 817–18, the brother of Abul-Saraya launched a further rising in Kufa that also was quickly suppressed. The same year, Imam Ali al-Rida's brother was made governor of Kufa. The insertion of the caliph's name first in the Friday prayer – not that of the Imam himself – is said to have caused riots in the city and an attack on Baghdad.[49]

At this point, some who had maintained the Imamate of Imam Musa's son Ahmad now accepted that Imam Musa was the *qaim*. Others in the Hijaz now swore allegiance to Imam Jafar's fourth son Muhammad.[50]

In March 817, al-Mamun, still in Marv, proclaimed the eighth Husaynid Imam, al-Rida, his heir. From a theological viewpoint, this was astute. The appointment addressed aspects of Mutazili discourse, which allowed for the legitimacy of the first four caliphs but permitted some recognition of Alid claims, representing an 'intermediate position', a Mutazili precept.[51] From a political point of view, also, Abul-Saraya's very activist Shiism was thereby contrasted with that of the Husaynid Imam, whose attitude towards the political establishment was more 'realistic'. Indeed, the Imam accepted the designation, albeit on his own terms. He also acquiesced to al-Mamun's demand that he join the caliph in Marv, apparently via a route that avoided the most notorious of the Iraqi Shii centres.[52]

The Imam did reach the court of the caliph. His acceptance of the appointment as heir caused some discontent back in Iraq and the caliph set out for Baghdad in 818. On the way, near Tus, the Imam took ill and died. The caliph ordered him buried near the tomb of Harun al-Rashid.[53]

During the Imam's stay in Marv his sister Fatima set out from Medina to visit him. She died at and was buried in Qum, a city strongly Shii since its founding in *c.* 712 by a member of the Ashari tribe, of south Arabia, fleeing the persecutions of Kufan Shia by the city's governor al-Hajjaj (d. 714).[54]

At the Imam's death, later Shii sources record a meeting in Baghdad. Al-Rida's son al-Jawad was but seven years old at his father's death, and two groups are said not to have countenanced his succession to the Imamate on account of his age. One supported the Imamate of his uncle, al-Rida's brother Ahmad. The other declared that Imam Musa was the *qaim*. The remainder are said to have supported the succession of al-Jawad.[55]

During these years, al-Mamun, now successfully ensconced in Baghdad, maintained some of his pro-Ali and pro-Mutazili policies. Thus his meetings, from 820, with both Zaydi and other Imami elements, his short-lived decision in 826–7 to persecute anyone mentioning the name of Muawiya and the giving of his daughters in marriage to Imam Al-Rida and the Imam's son, and successor, al-Jawad.[56] In 827–8, the caliph also promulgated the doctrines of the createdness of the Quran and the *tafdil* (pre-eminence) of Ali after the Prophet himself. In 833, he instituted a *mihna* (inquisition) against all who did not hold with the createdness of the Quran. But, with regard to the Alids in particular, he retreated from his close affiliations: in 821 he ordered all Alids to wear black and forbade them from entering his palace. To reduce popular support for Shii militancy, he reduced land tax on the peasants of the Sawad area in southern Iraq.[57]

Nevertheless, Alid risings continued apace. In 822–3, there was a rebellion against tax-collecting in the Yemen led by an Alid. On the Iranian plateau, in 825, the Shii Qummis demanded a reduction in tax from the caliph and when they refused to pay, the caliph sent the army and pulled down the city wall. Another Qummi revolt in 829 was also crushed.[58] In 834–5, the first year of the reign of the new caliph, al-Mamun's brother al-Mutasim, a Husaynid, rebelled in Taliqan. Captured and sent to Baghdad, he escaped and disappeared.[59]

Al-Jawad, however, maintained his distance from all of this. Nevertheless, the new caliph summoned the Imam and his wife, the daughter of al-Mamun, and put him under house arrest. There he remained until his death in 835, aged 25. He was buried in Baghdad near Imam Musa.[60]

Like his father, Imam Ali b. Muhammad, called *al-Hadi* (the Guide) (d. 868), the tenth Imam, was young – perhaps no more than seven when he assumed the Imamate.[61] That Imamate, however, lasted more than three decades, through the reigns of six caliphs. During the reigns of the first two, al-Mutasim (*reg.* 833–42) and al-Wathiq (*reg.* 842–7), the pro-Mutazili policies of earlier years were continued. Indeed, a rising against the Inquisition was suppressed in 846.[62]

Al-Mutawakkil (*reg.* 847–61), however, pointedly reversed his predecessors' pro-Alid, pro-Mutazili policies and instituted a series of anti-minority measures. Ali was cursed, for example, and Shiites, Jews and Christians were excluded from government appointments and their houses were taxed. In 850–1, the caliph ordered Imam al-Husayn's grave at Karbala to be destroyed[63] and, in 855–6, he ordered a wealthy perfume merchant who had openly cursed Abu Bakr, Umar and Aisha to be flogged.[64]

Al-Mutawakkil had the Imam, and his son, put under house arrest in Samarra – whence the capital had been moved by al-Mutasim. He remained a prisoner there through the reign of al-Mutazz (*reg.* 866–9), and died in 868.

The nine years of anarchy in Samarra following al-Mutawakkil's assassination in 861 saw four caliphs succeed each other. Of these, three were murdered.

During the year he was caliph, following his participation in his father's murder, al-Muntasir briefly restored the Alids to favour. He also allowed visits to tomb of al-Husayn.[65]

These last few years of the Imam's life witnessed a series of Shii risings, concomitant with, if not encouraged by, the political turmoil of the period. In 864–5, there were two Zaydi Shii rebellions. One was in Kufa, and apparently enjoyed widespread support there and in Baghdad. When its leader was killed, the attempt to display his head in Samarra caused riots in Baghdad.[66] The same year another Zaydi rose in Tabaristan and took Rayy, Zanjan and Qazwin. In Rayy, in the same year, there was Zaydi rising, and in Qazwin there was a Husaynid rising. In the mid-860s a Hasanid rose in Kufa.[67] In 865–6, as the army of al-Mutazz entered and looted Baghdad and a civil war as vicious as that witnessed earlier in the century broke out in the city, Alid risings in Rayy and in Mecca are also reported.[68]

At the tenth Imam's death in 868, the caliph al-Mutazz sent his brother to pray at the Imam's funeral in Samarra, perhaps in an effort to placate, or at least indicate sympathy for, local Shii concerns, if not also to gauge their extent. Al-Yaqubi (d. 905), now – as al-Tabari (d. 923) – a contemporary source, reported that large crowds attended the proceedings, suggesting continued widespread sympathy with Shii discourse. [69]

The tenth Imam's death seems to have occasioned further splits within the community. One Muhammad b. al-Nusayr was later said to have claimed that the Imam was Allah, and that he, Muhammad, was his prophet.[70]

As to the Imam's son, al-Hasan *al-Askari* (of the military, so-called because he and his father were under house arrest in Samarra, a military camp) was born in 846. He was in his twenties at the death of his father.

In the few years that he was the Imam, before his death in 873–4, there was no let up to the turmoil engulfing the caliphate.

The second civil war of the 860s exacerbated the political fragmentation of the Abbasid polity. In the east, the Saffarids had been a force with which to be reckoned since 861, the year of al-Mutawakkil's assassination. In these years they moved through Khurasan, and in 876 they were defeated barely 50 miles from Baghdad. An arrangement reached with the caliph allowed them to retain control of Fars, in Iran, but the loss of this area was a severe blow to the Abbasids.[71]

The drop in the centre's revenues from the loss of Egypt and the Iranian provinces was exacerbated by the deteriorating conditions in Iraqi agricultural centres, particularly the Sawad. These areas were badly damaged in the second civil war.

Again, the turmoil engendered spiritual unrest. In 868–9, two Hasanids rebelled in Kufa, killing a local official. In the same year there was a Shii revolt in Upper Egypt.[72]

But it was in the Iraqi marshes that the most serious unrest manifested itself. The first, that of the Zanj (868/9–883), was Zaydi in tone. The Zanj leader, Ali b. Muhammad, was born in Rayy. Initially, he identified himself with claims that he was the returned, popular Yahya b. Umar – the Zaydi whose rising in Kufa was crushed in 864–5. When he connected with the Zanj slaves who cleared the salt marshes near the Shatt al-Arab waterway in the Sawad to prepare the land for cultivation, the Zanj assumed the characteristics of a mass movement. Zanj forces sacked Basra in 871, the same year the Saffarids entered Fars; Ahwaz in 874–5, about the time of the disappearance of the twelfth Imam; and Wasit in 877–8. [73]

At the death of the eleventh Husaynid imam in 874, it is clear that there was little agreement as to the way forward.

As already noted, the contemporary Abu Muhammad al-Hasan b. Musa al-Nawbakhti (d. *c.* 912–22), the nephew of the then Shii state secretary Abu Sahl Ismail al-Nawbakhti, stated that after the death of al-Hasan al-Askari the Shia broke up into fourteen sects. His contemporary Sad b. Abdallah al-Qummi al-Ashari (d. *c.* 911–14) noted fifteen. Others noted more.[74]

Among these, some were said to have maintained that the eleventh Imam had no son and that the Imamate had ended with his death. There were also those who felt that he was in occultation, and those who felt that the line had ended with the tenth Imam who would return. Some held that the eleventh Imam's brother Jafar was now the Imam, and others believed that the eleventh Imam's other brother Muhammad was the Imam, though he had died.[75]

Those who believed that the eleventh Imam had a son who had became the Imam at his father's death, but had then gone into hiding – the Twelver Shia – were but one of many contemporary Shii groups and were very few in number at that.

Summary and conclusion

Though we are dependent for the study of early Islamic and early Shii history on sources composed centuries later, careful attention to these does suggest certain trends at work over the two-and-a-half centuries following the death of the Prophet. In the absence of a mandated line of succession to the Prophet, the feeling that the Prophet's family ought to be invested with such a role was clearly extant. Such pro-Alid and increasingly messianic sentiments were particularly associated with not-infrequent anti-establishment risings. The repeated failure of such risings over the period, and even the anti-Alid turn later taken by the only successful Shii rising of the period, that of the Abbasids, did not check such sentiments. Indeed, in these years the potential for such discourse to attract a mass following was clear.

The Imams of the Husaynid line refrained from associating with these repeated risings and from involvement with both the Umayyad and the Abbasid political establishment.

Over these years, however, their lineage and aversion to politics did not guarantee popularity. Indeed, at the successive death of the imams, splits occurred and numbers dwindled. At the death of the eleventh Imam, the followers of his brother Jafar may have been the largest of the extant Imami groups.[76]

Notes

1. These are discussed in the Introduction. The most useful of the recent scholarship that makes critical use of such early sources includes the works of G. Schoeler, such as *The Biography of Muhammad. Nature and Authenticity* (Abingdon, 2010). See also n. 1 of Chapter 2.

2. See, for example, in chronological order by author's death date, Ibn Ishaq (d. 761), *The Life of Muhammad*, trans. A. Guillaume (London, 1955), 683–7; Ahmad b. Wadih al-Yaqubi, *Tarikh al-Yaqubi* (d. 895) (Najaf, 1384/1964), 2:113–16; Muhammad b. Jarir al-Tabari (d. 923), *The History of al-Tabari*, 9, trans. I. K. Poonawala (Albany, 1990), 189–206. For an early, easily available Twelver Shii account, see al-Shaykh al-Mufid [Muhammad b. Muhammad b. al-Numan] (d. 1022), *Kitab al-Irshad* (in English), trans. I. K. A. Howard (London, 1981), 2f.

3. W. Madelung discusses, and has made the most sense of, the relevant sources on the events through Ali's caliphate. See his *The Succession to Muhammad. A Study of the Early Caliphate* (Cambridge, 1998), *passim*, esp. 33–41.

4. These texts and other arguments for Ali as successor are reviewed in Jafri, *Origins and Early Development of Shia Islam*, 18–21; Momen, *An Introduction to Shii Islam*, 11f.

5. Madelung, *The Succession to Muhammad*, 15–16; Momen, *Introduction to Shii Islam*, 13–14.

6. Indeed, al-Yaqubi (*Tarikh al-Yaqubi*, 2:116) credits the Prophet's uncle, al-Abbas – from whom the later Abbasid dynasty, during whose reign al-Yaqubi lived, claimed lineage – as stating to those at the *saqifa*, after a very long speech, that 'Allah's Messenger is like a *shajara* (tree): we [i.e., the family] are its branches'. On al-Yaqubi's Shii tendencies, see n. 31 of the Introduction.

7. See those sources cited in n. 2; Madelung, *The Succession to Muhammad*, 70f.

8. Madelung, 'Shia', *EI2*.

9. See, for example, Halm, *Shiism*, 8.

10. Madelung, 'Shia'; W. M. Watt, 'Shiism under the Umayyads', *Journal of the Royal Asiatic Society*, 3(4) (1960), 158f, citing the tenth-century chronicler al-Tabari. See also G. R. Hawting, *The First Dynasty of Islam. The Umayyad Caliphate ad 661–750* (London, 2000), 41.

11. For al-Tabari's account of these events, as translated into English, see al-Tabari, *The History of al-Tabari*, 19, trans. I. K. A. Howard (Albany, 1990), 16–183.

12. Madelung, 'Shia', suggests a figure of 4,000. R. Buckley, 'The Early Shiite *Ghulah*', *Journal of Semitic Studies*, 42(2) (1997), 315, n. 65, cites Ibn al-Athir that of some 6,000 followers only 700 were Arabs. Jafri's very detailed accounts (*Origins and Early Development of Shia Islam*, 174f, 22–32) are based on a composite of later sources.

13. Watt, 'Shiism under the Umayyads', 160–1; Madelung, *The Succession to Muhammad*, 5. On the Ashari tribe of South Arabia, see below at n. 54.

14. Watt, 'Shiism under the Umayyads', 162f; Madelung, 'Shia'; Jafri, *Origins and Early Development of Shia Islam*, 262f.
15. The term was that applied to Ali by Muhammad at Ghadir Khumm, but in this case it is often translated as 'client'.
16. Watt, 'Shiism under the Umayyads', 163–4.
17. Kennedy, *The Prophet and the Age of the Caliphates*, 88, 94–5, 106–7. See also P. Crone, 'Mawla', *EI2*.
18. On the settlement of Iranian *mawali* in Kufa, see Watt, 'Shiism under the Umayyads', 165.
19. Kennedy, *The Prophet and the Age of the Caliphates*, 96.
20. It has been suggested that this group was influenced in its notion of the *ghayba* by an earlier group known as the Sabaiyya who believed that Ali himself had not died. See Buckley, 'The Early Shiite *Ghulah*', 316; W. al-Qadi, 'The Development of the Term "Ghulat" in Muslim Literature with Special Reference to the Kaysaniyya', in E. Kohlberg (ed.), *Shiism* (Aldershot, 2003), 169f; S. Anthony, 'The Legend of Abdallah ibn Saba and the Date of Umm al-Kitab', *Journal of the Royal Asiatic Society* 21 (2011), 1, notes Sunni tendencies to exaggerate Ibn Saba's role – as a Yemeni convert from Judaism – as progenitor of Shiism. See also W. F. Tucker, *Mahdis and Millenarians* (Cambridge, 2008), 9f; S. Anthony, *The Caliph and the Heretic. Ibn Saba and the Origins of Shiism* (Leiden, 2011).
21. A. Lalani, *Early Shii Thought. The Teachings of Imam Muhammad al-Baqir* (London, 2004), 42f.
22. Hawting, *The First Dynasty of Islam*, 110. Tucker consistently notes the problems of using later sources to discuss the various risings and the often *ghali* (extreme, exaggerated) beliefs attributed to some of these figures. Tucker notes the 'contradictory accounts' of Bayan's discourse (*Mahdis and Millenarians*, 42), for example. He also notes (40f) that the idea of a prophetic succession was also extant among such contemporary groups as the Manicheans, gnostic elements and the Persian Jewish Isawites. On the *ghulat* (sing. *ghali*, exaggerator), so-called because they held 'extreme' views about the persons and natures of the Imams, including that they were divine, see H. Halm, 'Golat', *EIr*; M. Moosa, *Extremist Shiites* (Syracuse, NY, 1988).
23. Al-Mughira may himself have claimed the Imamate in preparation for the rising of the *Mahdi*, i.e., al-Nafs al-Zakiyya. On later, 'hostile' accounts, see Tucker, *Mahdis and Millenarians*, 71–87.
24. For later accounts, see Tucker, *Mahdis and Millenarians*, 71–87. Watt ('Shiism under the Umayyads', 164f) notes Abu Mansur as possibly representative of a Christian presence among the early *mawali*.
25. Watt, 'Shiism under the Umayyads', 169. The term 'Rafidi' (rejectionist, i.e., of Abu Bakr and Uthman, or all the Companions of the Prophet), as a pejorative reference to the Shia, may date to these years. See E. Kohlberg, 'al-Rafida', *EI2*; W. M. Watt, 'The Rafidites: a Preliminary Study, *Oriens*, 16 (1963), 116f.
26. On this period in Umayyad history, and the conflicts over the caliphate which marked the 'third civil war', see Hawting, *The First Dynasty of Islam*, 90f.
27. Ibn Muawiya is often associated in the later sources with such heretical ideas as *al-hulul* (incarnation) and *al-tanasukh* (the transmigration of souls), and with permitting certain forbidden practices on the theory that whoever knew his Imam could do as he wished. See Tucker, *Mahdis and Millenarians*, 88–108.
28. Watt, 'Shiism under the Umayyads', 171.
29. Watt, 'Shiism under the Umayyads', 171.

30. M. A. Amir-Moezzi, 'Khattabiyya', *EIr*; Madelung, 'Khattabiyya', *EI2*. On the number of Kufan money changers among the followers of Imam Jafar and the later Imams, see M. Asatryan, 'Bankers and Politics: The Network of Shii Moneychangers in 2nd/8th-century Kufa and their Role in the Shii Community', forthcoming.

31. F. Buhl, 'Muhammad b. Abd Allah ... al-Nafs al-Zakiyya', *EI2*; H. Kennedy, *The Early Abbasid Caliphate* (London, 1981), 200f.

32. These were later said to believe that all the prophets to Muhammad, including Abu Muslim, were incarnations of the Divine. See Ed. 'al-Mukanna', *EI2*. See the discussion on the veneration of Abu Muslim in the Safawid period in Chapters 7 and 8.

33. Kennedy, *The Early Abbasid Caliphate*, 205–7; Kennedy, *The Prophet and the Age of the Caliphates*, 132–4, 140; Halm, *Shiism*, 17–20, 33, 206f, 210–1; M. A. Shaban, *Islamic History. A New Interpretation*, 2 (Cambridge, 1978), 14–15.

34. Amir-Moezzi, *The Divine Guide*, 174, cites the names, titles and patronymics of all the Imams.

35. Jafri, *Origins and Early Development of Shia Islam*, 238–45.

36. The dates of the Imam's death range from 732 to 743, and possibly between 737 and 739, the year of Zayd's revolt. See Jafri, *Origins and Early Development of Shia Islam*, 255, citing later sources but, agreeing with al-Yaqubi, that he had died before Zayd's revolt. See also Lalani, *Early Shii Thought*, 55–6.

37. Amir-Moezzi, *The Divine Guide*, 101, n. 538, citing later Twelver biographies; Jafri, *Origins and Early Development of Shia Islam*, 255, citing Nawbakhti and the Iranian Sunni al-Shahristani (d. 1153), author of a well-known book on sects *Kitab al-Milal wa al-Nihal* (*The Book on Sects and Beliefs*).

38. Momen, *Introduction to Shii Islam*, 38, gives his various birth dates as 699, 702 and 705.

39. He is said to have met the fifth and sixth Imams. See U. F. Abd-Allah, 'Abu Hanifa', *EIr*.

40. See Y. Dutton, *The Origins of Islamic Law. The Qur'an, the Muwatta' and Madinan Amal* (Richmond, 1999).

41. Jafri, *Origins and Early Development of Shia Islam*, 273, citing such later sources as al-Tabari, al-Jahshiyari (d. 942) and al-Masudi, says the victorious Abbasids invited Imam Jafar and other potential claimants to come to Kufa.

42. Hussain, *The Occultation of the Twelfth Imam*, 34, citing Nawbakhti. Like Jafri, Hussain generally uses a composite of later accounts. See also Momen, *Introduction to Shii Islam*, 54. On the Ismailis, see also Daftary, *A Short History*.

43. Amir-Moezzi, *The Divine Guide*, 65 citing al-Mufid (d. 1022), *Maqatil al-Talibiyyin* of al-Isfahani, and the notorious anti-Shii Ibn Taymiyya (d. 1328). See also Hussain, *The Occultation of the Twelfth Imam*, 34–5, citing al-Tabari.

44. Hussain, *The Occultation of the Twelfth Imam*, 36, citing al-Tabari and al-Masudi.

45. Hussain, *The Occultation of the Twelfth Imam*, 37. Kennedy, *The Prophet and the Age of the Caliphates*, 143; Kennedy, *The Early Abbasid Caliphate*, 109–10.

46. See the various dates for his death in Momen, *Introduction to Shii Islam*, 40; Halm, *Shiism*, 31; Hussain, *The Occultation of the Twelfth Imam*, 38–9.

47. Hussain, *The Occultation of the Twelfth Imam*, 39, citing Nawbakhti and al-Ashari. See also A. Buyukkara, 'The Schism in the Party of Musa al-Kazim and the Emergence of the Waqifa', *Arabica* 47(1) (2000), 78–99.

48. W. M. Watt, *The Formative Period of Islamic Thought* (Edinburgh, 1973), 151f.

49. On these and the risings below, see al-Tabari, *The History of al-Tabari*, trans. C. E. Bosworth *et al.* (Albany, NY, 1985f), 32–8; 32: 69, 71, 130, 182; 33: 5; 34: 89f, 95, 110, 106; 35: 15–26.

50. Hussain, *The Occultation of the Twelfth Imam*, 41–2, citing later Twelver sources as well as al-Tabari.

51. Watt, *The Formative Period of Islamic Thought*, 175–9.

52. See J. Irfanmunsh, *Jughrafiye-yi Tarikihi-yi Hijrat Imam Rida Az Madina ta Marv* (Tehran, 1382). My thanks to Mr R. Jafarriyan for directing my attention to this work.

53. Hussain, *The Occultation of the Twelfth Imam*, 42–4, citing such later sources as al-Yaqubi, al-Tabari, al-Masudi and Shii sources.

54. On Qum, see our *The Formative Period of Twelver Shiism* (Abingdon, 2000), 38f. On the Ashari as a south Arabian tribe, see Watt, *Shiism*, 160.

55. Hussain, *The Occultation of the Twelfth Imam*, 45, citing Nawbakhti and al-Ashari.

56. Al-Yaqubi, *Tarikh al-Yaqubi*, 3:189; al-Tabari, *The History of al-Tabari*, 32: 175, 177, 71, 83. See also Watt, *The Formative Period of Islamic Thought*, 179f; Shaban, *Islamic History*, 2: 54–5.

57. Hussain, *The Occultation of the Twelfth Imam*, 44–5, citing al-Tabari and Ibn al-Athir.

58. Al-Tabari, *The History of al-Tabari*, 32: 166–7, 182, 190, 197; Hasan b. Muhammad b. al-Hasan al-Ashari al-Qummi, *Tarikh-i Qum*, trans. Hasan b. Ali al-Qummi, ed. Jalal al-Din al-Tihrani (Tehran, 1313/1934–5), 35, 163, 189–90.

59. W. Madelung, *Religious Trends in Early Islamic Iran* (Albany, NY, 1988), 87; R. Jafariyan, *Tarikh-i Tashayyu dar Iran* (Qum, 1375), 1: 170–1, 176–7, 287f. See also Kennedy, *The Prophet and the Age of the Caliphates*, 132–4, 140; Kennedy, *The Early Abbasid Caliphate*, 200f.

60. Hussain, *The Occultation of the Twelfth Imam*, 47, citing al-Tabari and al-Masudi.

61. Hussain, *The Occultation of the Twelfth Imam*, 48, citing al-Ashari.

62. Al-Tabari, *The History of al-Tabari*, 34: 34, 135, 110–11.

63. Al-Yaqubi, *Tarikh al-Yaqubi*, 3: 219; al-Tabari, *The History of al-Tabari*, 34: 89f, 110–11.

64. Al-Yaqubi, *Tarikh al-Yaqubi*, 3: 234; al-Tabari, *The History of al-Tabari*, 34: 135, 155.

65. Al-Yaqubi, *Tarikh al-Yaqubi*, 3: 189; al-Tabari, *The History of al-Tabari*, 32: 71, 83, 82, n. 262; al-Masudi, *Muruj al-Dhahab*, 4: 135; Kennedy, *The Prophet and the Age of the Caliphates*, 173.

66. Al-Tabari, *The History of al-Tabari*, 35: 15f, 108–9, 150–1; al-Masudi, *Muruj al-Dhahab*, 4: 153–4.

67. Al-Yaqubi, *Tarikh al-Yaqubi*, 3: 236; al-Tabari, *The History of al-Tabari*, 35: 88–90, 141–2, 65, 108–9, 144, 163, 115; 36: xv; al-Masudi, *Muruj al-Dhahab*, 4: 180, 307.

68. Al-Masudi, *Muruj al-Dhahab*, 4: 135; D. Waines, 'The Third Century Internal Crisis of the Abbasids', *Journal of the Economic and Social History of the Orient*, 20 (1977), 299–301.

69. Al-Yaqubi, *Tarikh al-Yaqubi*, 3: 234; al-Tabari, *The History of al-Tabari*, 34: 135, 155.

70. He was the eponymous 'founder' of the Nusayri sect of Shia. Momen, *Introduction to Shii Islam*, 58, notes that the sources disagree on the claims associated with him. See Moosa, *Extremist Shiites*, 261. Others looked to al-Hadi's younger son Jafar.

71. C. E. Bosworth, 'Saffarids', *EI2*; Kennedy, *The Prophet and the Age of the Caliphates*, 178–9.

72. Al-Yaqubi, *Tarikh al-Yaqubi*, 3: 236; al-Tabari, *The History of al-Tabari*, 35: 65, 88–90, 141–2, 108–9, 144, 163, 115; 36: xv; al-Masudi, *Muruj al-Dhahab*, 4: 180, 307.

73. Al-Yaqubi, *Tarikh al-Yaqubi*, 3: 236; al-Tabari, *The History of al-Tabari*, 36: 29, n. 114, n, 115; 35: 125f, 119–20, 165, 35: 115, n. 333, 190f; al-Masudi, *Muruj al-Dhahab*, 4: 194–5. On the Zanj, see A. Popovic, *The Revolt of the African Slaves in the Third/Ninth Century* (Princeton, 1999).

74. See n. 7 in the Introduction.

75. Amir-Moezzi, *The Divine Guide*, 214–15, nn. 556, 557, and Hussain, *The Occultation of the*

Twelfth Imam, 57–66, respectively, offer brief and longer summaries of the views on offer in the sources cited in n. 7 of the Introduction.

76. H. Modarressi, *Crisis and Consolidation in the Formative Period of Shiite Islam. Abu Jafar Ibn Qiba Al-Razi and His Contribution to Imamite Shiite Thought* (Princeton, 1993), 81, 84.

CHAPTER 2

Bereft of a leader: The early traditionists and the beginnings of doctrine and practice

In the later 870s those who believed in the Imamate of the twelfth Husaynid Imam, and who now understood him to be in occultation, were few in number and but one of a plethora of different Shii groups.

Nevertheless, the Imams had left behind two concrete legacies. The first was a body of statements or 'traditions' (variously called *ahadith*, *hadith* singular, statement; or *akhbar*, sing *khabar*, news, report) ascribed to them or recounting their actions. The second comprised the pockets of the faithful scattered across the region.

From the 870s to the arrival of the Zaydi Buyids at Baghdad in the 940s, the manner in which the faithful tried to come to grips with the Imam's disappearance is perhaps best explained with reference to their own particular situations. In these years it was those in Qum, on the Iranian plateau, and to the west, in the Abbasid capital of Baghdad, who left the written works that are among the first visible evidence of such efforts. The former set about compiling the Imams' traditions for both reassurance and guidance. The latter engaged with non-textual methods of discourse on offer in Iraq-based Sunni Mutazili circles for some years. Taken together the efforts of both groups marked the creation of a legacy for future generations unmatched by those associated with the myriad of other Shii groups of the day.

Elements of both of these groups, however, if not also believers elsewhere, seem to have assumed the Imam's imminent return.

Pockets of believers: the traditionists of Qum

A *hadith*, or *khabar*, consists of two parts: the *matn* (the text of the tradition itself) and the *isnad* (sing. *sanad*, the list of the chain of transmitters/narrators of the tradition back to the figure who made the statement).[1]

These traditions, even as gathered together in such an early collection of the Imams' traditions as the *al-Kafi* of al-Kulayni (d. 941), refer to the Imams' agents and believing communities over the Imamates of the fifth Imam, al-Baqir, through to at least that of the tenth Imam, al-Hadi. These included such locales as the Maghreb, Egypt, the Hijaz, Kufa, Basra, Baghdad, Qum, Daylam and Khurasan.[2]

Nevertheless, it was on the Iranian plateau that some of the earliest efforts to come to grips with the absence of the twelfth Imam took written form.

In Iran, among those Arabs who had settled on the Iranian plateau, traditionism, that is a concern with *ahadith*, prevailed. Indeed, many of the Sunni traditionists of this century, though Arab, were in fact born in Iran and commenced their collection of the Prophetic traditions in such rapidly expanding conurbations as Marv, Bukhara, Samarqand and Nishabur. Together with their residencies in Baghdad, Kufa and the Hijaz, these compilers' perception that events and trends across the ninth century portended the disintegration of the caliphate and the rise of Shiism encouraged a rising interest in compiling traditions from, and thereby, not coincidentally, the idealisation of, the very earliest years of the *umma*.[3]

Shii influences in Iran are discernible from the late seventh and eighth centuries in the aftermath of the failed risings of al-Mukhtar and Ibn Muawiya. By the late ninth century, Zaydism had laid down roots in the Tabaristan region, having first appeared in the region after the flight of Zayd's own son to Khurasan.[4] Zaydi activity in Rayy – south of modern-day Tehran – is attested in the 860s and the late 880s. In the early tenth century, an Ismaili presence was also extant along the Caspian, in Khurasan and also near Rayy, especially, the village of Kulayn.[5]

The plateau's direct association with the Husaynid Imams in particular began with the route that the eighth Imam, Ali al-Rida, took to join the caliph al-Mamun in Marv at the latter's command, following the caliph's 817 designation of the Imam as his heir. Ordered to avoid contacting sympathisers in Kufa, the trip through Basra, Ahwaz and Fars to Khurasan, coupled with a nearly two-year sojourn in Marv, allowed for direct and indirect contacts with adherents in these areas. It certainly also stimulated a growth in the numbers of followers. Later sources identify many of the Imam's companions as Arabs who had taken Iranian *nisbas* that associated them with such areas in Iran as Hamadan, Rayy, Qazwin, Nishabur, Taliqan, areas in Gurgan, as well as Marv and Balkh. But a number of Razis – the *nisba* denoting someone associated with Rayy – were counted among the companions of the seventh and, especially, the eighth to the eleventh Imams.[6]

Qum itself is said to have been founded by a member of the south Arabian Ashari tribe following the various anti-Umayyad Shii risings in the seventh century. Members of the tribe were later said to have been companions of the fifth to the eleventh Imams.[7] Some of the tribe's *mawali* were also said to be Shia. During the Umayyad period it was to Qum, and to Shiraz, Isfahan and Kashan, that various Alids and their associates fled, as judged by grave sites dating from this period. In Qum they were given land.

In 816, the sister of Imam Al-Rida, Fatima, travelled through the area to visit her brother at the court of al-Mamun in Marv. She fell ill and was taken to Qum. She lodged in the *saray* of a member of the Ashari clan, but afterwards died. Other relatives of the Imam also appeared in the city and were welcomed.

Following the onset of the Zanj rebellion in the late 860s, a number of sayyids also came from Iraq to Qum, where they intermarried with members of the clan.[8]

Over the Abbasid period, through to the disappearance of the twelfth Imam and into the tenth century, the Qummi attitude towards the established political authority in Baghdad was distinctly confrontational.

In the ninth century, in particular, the Qummis were said to have sent *al-khums* (the Islamic 'one-fifth' tax/tithe on one's income) revenues to the Imams, but to have been openly dilatory in sending other taxes to Baghdad.

This recalcitrance also manifested itself in risings against Baghdad in 825–6, 831–2 and 865. In response, Baghdad repeatedly sent punitive expeditions against the city: for example, in 800–1, in 825–6, when al-Mamun's armies levelled the city's walls, in 832–3, 868, the 870s and 903–4. The centre also made repeated, not always successful, efforts to survey the taxable land.[9]

The earliest compilations of the Imams' traditions: the Qummi responses of al-Barqi and al-Saffar

In such an atmosphere Qum-based scholars assembled the two earliest major compilations of the Imams' traditions. The *isnad* of these compilations' traditions reflect the growing role of the Ashari and non-Ashari elite of the city in the transmission of traditions about faith's distinctive doctrines and practices. Unsurprisingly, these traditions reflect a robust sense of politico-spiritual independence.[10]

The first of these was *al-Mahasin* (*The Beauties*) of Ahmad b. Muhammad Barqi (d. *c.* 894). Al-Barqi was a descendant of Kufan *mawali* of the Ashari clan. An ancestor was jailed in the aftermath of the failed 740 rising of Zayd against the Umayyads. The latter's son and grandson fled to Qum. Al-Barqi's father was said to have been a companion of the seventh, eighth and ninth Imams. Al-Barqi himself was a companion of the ninth and the tenth Imams.[11]

Of the original text only between one-sixth and one-seventh remains.[12] The chapter titles of the complete text are recorded, however. These suggest that the original was intended to be an encyclopaedic work and, as such, the forerunner of later comprehensive Twelver collections such as *al-Kafi* and *Bihar al-Anwar* of the late Safawid period scholar, Baqir al-Majlisi, comprising traditions on a broad range of issues of both doctrine and practice.

The extant 2,606 of *al-Mahasin*'s traditions reveal something of the manner in which the embattled Shia of Qum were already engaged in delineating a body of doctrine and practice distinctive from that of contemporary Sunni and non-Twelver Shia around them. Such traditions can have served only to encourage them in their faith.

Unsurprisingly, many of these traditions stress the special position of the

Imams and their adherents, and the special importance of their traditions as a source of reference for matters of doctrine and practice.

Thus, for example, in four traditions Imams al-Baqir, Jafar (twice) and al-Rida[13] stated that Allah had created the believer from His *nur* (light). Elsewhere, al-Baqir said that believers had been created from the same *tin* (clay) as the Imams. Imams al-Baqir and Jafar refer to a time before the creation of the world when Allah agreed with the Shia, when they existed in the form of *dharr* (particles), a pact in which they pledged *walaya* (affection) for the Imams. Imam Jafar said that believers were guaranteed entrance into paradise. Imams Jafar and Baqir explained such Quranic references as 'those who know' and 'men of understanding' (Quran 39:9) as referring to the Imams and their Shia. The same two Imams also attested to the Shia as the closest of Allah's creatures to Him.[14]

Legal rulings were to be based on *ilm* (knowledge), and Imams al-Baqir, Jafar and Musa all condemned recourse to *bida* (innovation), *qiyas* (analogy) and *al-ray* (opinion), all well-known Sunni jurisprudential devices. The Imams also extolled the importance of exercising caution in the faith and of recourse to the *Sunna*: Imam Jafar, for example, cited his father as having said that the *faqih* (the legist, pl. *fuqaha*) was an ascetic in this world and always 'seeking after' the next world, holding firmly to the *Sunna* of the Prophet. Some twenty traditions underscored the importance of seeking *ilm* and that it was to be found in the revelation.[15]

The importance of basic Muslim practices was also stressed, even as these were given a distinctly Shii dimension. Thus, the 143 traditions in the seventy chapters of book three detail punishments for failure to pay *al-zakat* (alms), failure to attend Friday prayer, and others for murder, adultery and the drinking of intoxicants. In one of two traditions on the Friday prayer, for example, al-Baqir called the prayer a *fard* (religious obligation) when the Imam was present to lead it. In traditions on *al-zakat*, for example, Imam Jafar stated that when *al-qaim* returns he would cut off the head of whoever fails to pay alms. Three traditions – including one each from al-Baqir and Jafar – enjoin the importance of knowing one's Imam. One referred to *Aimma al-Haqq* (the Imams of Truth) and four immediately following traditions – three from al-Baqir – condemned reference to *Aimma al-Jawr* (the Imams of Tyranny), although without defining either.[16]

In a chapter of twelve traditions, the Imams addressed the essential, but distinct, practices of both Islam and Shii Islam. In one, Imam Jafar stated that the bases of Islam were five: prayer, alms, the pilgrimage, fasting and *al-walaya* (affection, that is, for the family of the Prophet).[17]

There are references herein to other beliefs and practices that distinguished the faithful. Twelve traditions – eight from Imam Jafar and three from al-Baqir – attested that Allah would never leave the world without an *alim* (i.e., an Imam). Twenty-seven traditions – twenty-two narrated from Imam Jafar and four from al-Baqir – addressed the doctrine of *taqiyya* (dissimulation of one's true faith). In one the Imam stated that whoever did not practice *taqiyya* was in fact without faith.[18]

Also in Qum, and less than a generation later, Muhammad b. al-Hasan, al-Saffar al-Qummi (d. 902–3) compiled his *Basair al-Darajat*, a collection of 1,881 traditions dealing with issues of Twelver theology.

Al-Saffar was a companion of the eleventh Imam. That he, like al-Barqi, was also an Ashari *mawla* suggests the continued interest of the city's elites in, and their approval of, such projects.[19] Al-Barqi collected the largest number of the traditions in the extant version of his collection from his own father, then immigrant Kufans, then Basrans, and then those based in the Iranian cities of Isfahan, Kashan and Nishabur. Al-Saffar, however, collected a larger number of traditions from Qummis. Qummis narrated 793 of the 1,881, 42 per cent. Asharis narrated 422, 22 per cent.

The title of the collection[20] suggests that the aim of the work was to demonstrate that the Imams had been endowed with special knowledge and unique abilities, and that, as such, believers were enjoined to obedience to, and affection for, them. Such stress on the Imams' authority and power in traditions narrated via the city's elites could only encourage fellow believers in this beleaguered Shii city-state as they confronted both the spiritual challenge of the Imam's disappearance and the military/political challenge from Baghdad.[21]

The earliest of the volume's ten sections portray the Imams as enjoining the seeking of *ilm* – as had traditions cited by al-Barqi – and also the Imams as sole possessors of that *ilm*. In this collection traditions from Imams al-Baqir and Jafar also feature widely: in thirty-six traditions on *ilm*, for example, twenty-six were narrated from Imam Jafar and eight from al-Baqir.

But *Basair*'s traditions also showed the Imams' *ilm* to have been miraculous in nature. Thus, for example, in some sixty-one traditions – thirty-nine ascribed to Imam Jafar and nine from al-Baqir – over six chapters, the Imams are said to have knowledge of aspects of their own deaths and to know who will receive their authority after them.[22] In some 100 traditions the Imams claimed knowledge of and/or access to such 'secret' books as those variously entitled *al-Sahifa* (*The Page*), *al-Mashaf* (*The Book*) or *al-Jamia* (*The Comprehensive*), *al-Jafr*. The latter comprised the white and the red *Jafr*, the former contained the books of Abraham, Moses (the Torah and the *alwah* (tablets)), David (*al-Zabur*, i.e., the Psalms), as well as Jesus (*al-Injil*, i.e., the Gospels). There are references also to *The Book of Fatima*: a text on the Prophet's last condition and about her own descendants, that is, including the Imams, that the angel Gabriel revealed to Fatima after the Prophet's death and which she then dictated to Ali – and *al-Furqan*.[23]

In some seventeen traditions – thirteen from Imam Jafar and nine from al-Baqir – the Imams also laid claim to possessing the authentic version of the Quran and the authoritative *tafsir* on it.[24]

In forty-one traditions, the Imams were spoken of as *muhaddath* (those who were spoken to, that is, by the angel), meaning that they were participants with the Prophet himself in the original revelation. In several the Imams are spoken of as 'the twelve who were spoken to', a clear indication that in these years the final number of the Imams as twelve was already in circulation in Qum if not also elsewhere.[25]

In fifty-eight traditions, the Imams stated that they had in their possession items from the Ark of the Covenant, as well as the tablets of Moses, the cloak of Adam, that of Joseph, the *khatim* (the seal) of Solomon, the staff of Moses, the *sayf* (sword), *dur'* (armour) and *silah* (weapon) of the Prophet Muhammad and his famous double-edged sword *Dhul-Faqar*.[26]

Al-Mahasin had contained four traditions on the pre-existential pact concluded between Allah and the Shia. Al-Saffar collected fifty-eight.[27]

Al-Saffar also included traditions on the miraculous gestation and birth of each Imam.[28] Forty-three traditions referred to the Imams' ability in 'the language of the birds (Quran 27:16)', as the Prophet himself.[29] In thirty-eight, the Imams were seen communicating with now-dead prophets and Imams, arranging that others might also have such visions, and addressing the teaching that Ali received from Muhammad after the latter's death.[30]

The Quran contains references to the raising of the dead and the curing of the sick. Quran 3:49 refers to Jesus as having the ability to 'heal . . . [the] blind, and the leper and . . . raise the dead, by Allah's leave'.[31] Al-Saffar collected thirteen traditions in which the Imams also were seen to be exercising these powers.[32]

Pockets of believers: . . . and Baghdad

Where Qum was clearly a Twelver city-state, if a small one, in Baghdad, to the west, the resident Shia were in the minority, organised in a limited number of quarters. On the western bank of the Tigris River, al-Karkh was home to a strong mercantile/commercial community and a largely Shii population, along with some seven other quarters, of a total of seventeen. Of the seven quarters on the eastern side, Bab al-Taq was perhaps the most important of the three Shii quarters, with many Shii inhabitants and a large merchant sector.[33]

To the west of Qum, in the later ninth century there was no let up in the Shii-associated violent, and successful, uprisings. Less than two decades after defeating the Zanj, the caliph al-Mutamid (*reg.* 870–92) had to confront the second great Shii menace of the century: the Qaramatians. In spite of early apparent links with the Zaydi Zanj, the Qaramatian rising heralded the rise of the Ismaili Shia. In 898–9 and 900, two decades after the Imam's disappearance, the Qaramatians plundered a merchant caravan and threatened Basra. Kufa was threatened, the Kufa–Hijaz road was cut and other *hajj* caravans were also seized. The Qaramatians entered Basra in 923, and in 927–8 Baghdadis feared an imminent Qaramatian attack. In 930, Qaramatian forces seized Mecca and took away the Black Stone, which they returned only in 951.[34]

In these same years several prominent Shii families jockeyed for prominent positions at court. Their fortunes rose and fell based on shifting local political as well as external factors.

In the early 880s, as the caliph al-Mutamid seized the Zanj capital, the Shiite Ismail b. Bulbul[35] began to exercise the functions of the vizier. Ismail, in turn, appointed members of the Shii merchant family Banul-Furat to key posts and surrounded himself with other Shiites such as the Banul-Nawbakht.

Ismail's appointment suggested a positive signal to Shii elements of the desire for an alliance to counterbalance the influence of the military/merchants/Sunni traditionist alliance that had dominated caliphal politics since al-Mutawakkil's accession in 847. Indeed, al-Mutamid permitted the distribution of funds sent by the Tabaristani Zaydis to the Iraqi and Hijazi communities, and actively promoted the public cursing of Muawiya. He also restricted theological discussions at the city's two main mosques and forbad public storytellers, vendors in their stalls and water boys from invoking blessings on Muawiya.[36]

However, during the reign of al-Mutadid (reg. 892–902), and following the Qaramatians' 898–9 plundering of a merchant caravan, their appearance in Bahrain the next year and their routing of an Abbasid force, the Banul-Furat were replaced by the Banul-Jarrah. The Banul-Jarrah, originally Nestorian Christians, had developed close connections to Baghdad's great Sunni merchants and favoured closer cooperation with the military.[37]

The long reign of al-Muqtadir (reg. 908–32) witnessed some fifteen changes of viziers and five coups owing to, or at least accentuated by, the rivalry of these two families, and the Banul-Nawbakht as allies of the Banul-Furat, as well as external events. Thus, the Qaramatians sacked Basra in 919–20 and attacked *hajj* caravans in 924 and 925. Following these events, the Shii vizier was arrested on the caliph's orders, and he and his son were executed. In 925, the caliph, bowing to Sunni pressure in Baghdad, especially from traditionist elements – whose ranks were swelled in these years by the defection from Mutazilism of the Baghdad-based Ali b. Ismail al-Ashari (d. *c*. 935), with whom the Ashari, text-oriented 'school' is identified – ordered the levelling of the Baratha mosque in the al-Karkh quarter of Baghdad.[38] In 929, the year after the Qaramatians had seized the Black Stone, a palace coup forced al-Muqtadir's abdication. His brother al-Qahir was briefly caliph. During his short reign (932–4), a member of the Al Furat was made vizier. Subsequent official discussion about introducing the public slandering of Muawiya sparked widespread rioting in the city, including attacks on both the Shia and the Imams' tombs. Al-Qahir was deposed and al-Radi (reg. 934–40), son of al-Muqtadir, became caliph.

In 934 also, the Daylam-based Zaydi Buyids defeated a larger Abbasid force, signalling the rise and expansion of the Buyids as a force in the region. The Sawad, Iraq's 'breadbasket', had fallen under the effective control of the Shii Banul-Barid, who frequently withheld revenue from the centre. As the Buyids extended their control over nearby Fars the Baridis reached an agreement with them against the centre. As a result, by 936 the writ of the caliph covered only Baghdad. Nevertheless, al-Radi, who had permitted the rebuilding of the Baratha mosque, died peacefully in his sleep.[39]

The mosque's rebuilding generated much opposition among Hanbali tra-ditionist elements – intellectuals and popular elements alike. The latter sacked the city's financial quarter, mainly inhabited by Jews, and attempted to destroy the mosque. Probably in response thereto, pilgrimages to the Imams' tombs were banned. Al-Muttaqi (reg. 940–4) had the mosque guarded, but also, in 943, arrested the head of the Shia community in Bab al-Taq.[40]

In the context of the disappearance of the Imam, the rise of other militant Shii and proto-Shii movements, such as the Zanj and the Qaramatians, and the reaction of Sunni traditionism, supported by military and merchant circles, the written legacy of the Nawbakhtis attests to an effort to rekindle the Mutazili–Shii confluence of interests that al-Mamun had encouraged in early ninth-century Baghdad. The Nawbakhtis, and their like-minded co-religionists, aimed to integrate key aspects of Mutazili doctrine on the attributes and justice of Allah, as well as man's free will, into a doctrinal statement. Such discourse also argued for the doctrine of the Imamate in the absence of the Imam, and laid the groundwork for the assumption of authority over community doctrine and prac-tice by scholars who adhered to and were versed in such rationalist theology. This Mutazili–Shii alliance presupposed, as it had a century earlier, a working accommodation between such Shii elites and the established political institution. The goal was the safeguarding, if not also the advancing, of the interests of the community and of defending the faith against Sunnis and non-Twelver Shia.[41]

The sometime vizier the Shiite Abu Sahl Ismail al-Nawbakhti (d. 923), was well known for his philosophical and the distinctly Shii dimension to his Mutazili inclinations. He is credited with a number of works arguing for the Imamate of the son of the eleventh Imam and refuting ghulat elements, the Waqifi Shia, the legality of qiyas and Mutazili ideas about the attributes of Allah.[42]

Abu Sahl's nephew al-Hasan b. Musa al-Nawbakhti (d. 912) authored the heresiographical work Firaq al-Shia, as well as refutations of the Waqifi Shia, of the Mutazila on the Imamate and other issues, of the ghulat – in which he listed various such groups, including those who believed in the transmigration of souls – and of non-Twelver Shia. On legal issues, he also composed a work on the legal validity of rulings based on akhbar al-ahad (traditions related via only one or very few individuals) and another heresiography, now lost.[43]

The al-Nawbakhti family continued to associate with the caliphate, par-ticularly during and after al-Muqtadir's reign. Indeed, one family member was in charge of the caliph's personal domains, and his home became a popular meeting place for notables and other administrators. Others served in various court-appointed positions.[44]

The involvement of the Banul-Nawbakht in the affairs of the extremist Iranian Sufi al-Husayn b. Mansur al-Hallaj (d. 922)[45] and Muhammad b. Ali al-Shalmaghani (d. 934) further affirms both their efforts to safeguard the interests of the community and also the influence of political manoeuvrings at court and in Baghdad itself.[46]

The Qummi response to Baghdadi discourse: al-Kulayni's *al-Kafi*

The compiler of the third of the great compilations of this early period of Twelver history, *al-Kafi fi Ilm al-Din* (*The Sufficient, on the Knowledge of the Faith*), was Muhammad b. Yaqub al-Kulayni (d. 941). Al-Kulayni completed *al-Kafi* in Baghdad, where he resided during the last years of his life. Before that he had divided his time between Rayy, which he left *c.* 893, and Qum.[47]

His residence in the Shii quarter of al-Karkh would have given him first-hand experience of Baghdad's Twelver and non-Twelver Shii discourse, as well as the precarious situation of the faithful in the face of contemporary resurgent Sunni traditionism as allied with the political establishment. In this context, where neither al-Barqi nor al-Saffar seems to have prefaced his work, al-Kulayni's short preface repays attention.

According to al-Kulayni, he received a query from a believer who wanted to 'act on the basis of the correct statements' of the Imams, but saw that there was disagreement between the traditions. Al-Kulayni admonished his 'brother' that no one was permitted to make choices between the *ikhtilaf* (disagreement) in the Imams' narrations on the basis of *ray* (personal opinion). Nothing, he said, was 'more careful' or 'more sufficient' than tracing knowledge on all matters back to the Imam and accepting what he had said.[48]

The question suggests that in the early years of the tenth century, under the pressure of events, the seeming pre-eminence of rationalist discourse in the city and the Twelver community, especially among its elites, was now in question. A rising interest in the traditions, but awareness of their apparent contradictions, had, however, produced frustration. *Al-Kafi* was thus a response to a need for a traditionist exposition of the faith by those seeking meaning in, but lacking experience with, this material. It was also a distinctly Qummi traditionist response. Compared with *al-Mahasin* and even *Basair*, the bulk of al-Kafi's traditions were narrated from just a handful of Qummi and, especially, Ashari traditionists. Finally, it also 'spoke' both to contemporary Twelver rationalists and to Sunnis as well.[49]

Indeed, the compilation was clearly assembled with a dual purpose. Slightly more than one-quarter of the collection's traditions – those found in the first two volumes, *al-Usul* (*The Origins*, or *Principles*) and, to a lesser extent, *al-Rawda* (*The Garden*) – the eighth and last volume – laid the theological bases for seeing the Husaynid Imams as the authoritative and definitive source of *ilm*, that is, not *aql* (reason), as promoted by Twelver rationalists. This al-Saffar had done, albeit with many fewer traditions, in the opening sections of *Basair*.

In *al-Usul*, Qummi disavowal of recourse to *aql* alone was clear from the start: the first thirty-four of the compilation's traditions made it clear that *aql* was insufficient to attain *ilm*. The Imams alone were the repositories of that *ilm*: a tradition transmitted in both *Basair* and *al-Kafi*, via two slightly different *isnad*, who quoted Imam Jafar[50] as stating:

> We are the possessors of *ilm*
> and our *Shia* are those seeking *ilm* and
> the rest of the people are *ghutha* (scum).[51]

The *fuqaha* (sing. *faqih*, legal scholar) were depicted as the inheritors of that legacy. They were enjoined not to become subservient to the established political institution: Imam Jafar cited the Prophet as stating:

> The *fuqaha* are the *umana* (trustees) of the prophets as
> long as they do not become involved in the world.

The Prophet was asked:

> What do you mean by their 'becoming involved in the world'?
> He said: Complying with *al-Sultan*.

The community was enjoined to compile the Imams' traditions, but not to subject them to such tools of subjective interpretation as *ray*, *qiyas* and *bida* – all of which had also been condemned in *al-Mahasin*. Where the believer was uncertain how to proceed, he should consult the Imam.

If the Imam were not present? The well-known tradition of Imam Jafar transmitted via Umar b. Hanzala embodied the Qummi rejoinder to Baghdadi rationalism *par excellence*. Here, too, the Imam condemned the seeking of judgement from *al-sultan* (the political authority) or *al-qudat* (judges) in favour of seeking out someone who transmits

> our *hadith* and who has examined what we have permitted
> and what we have forbidden and knows our *ahkam*
> (judgements). Accept his judgement. I have made him
> a *hakim* (judge) among you.

The traditions were the ultimate source of knowledge. The believer should accept 'what is agreed upon by your fellow believers as our judgement' and ignore 'the irregular which is not well-known among your fellow believers'. In difficult issues, 'one is to trace his *'ilm* back to Allah and the Prophet'. In the end, however, the Imam cautioned that if one was still unsure as to what course of action to pursue, 'wait until you meet your Imam. Indeed, *al-wuquf* (hesitation) at points of doubt is better than leaping into destruction.'[52]

Thus, while the traditions were the source of the normative, the individual, if not the community as a whole, had a role in determining whom to seek out for their interpretation. If there was still uncertainty, however, action should be delayed until the Imam could be consulted.

As to the Imams, as in a texts cited in *Basair*, in *al-Kafi* traditions described the Imams as *hujja* (the proof), *bab* (the gate), *lisan* (the tongue), *wajh* (the face) and *ayn* (the eye) of Allah *fi khalqihi* (to His creation). They were His *nur* (light) on earth and the *arkan* (pillars) of the earth. They were *mutahhar an al-dhunub* (free from sin) and *masum* (infallible), inheritors of both the knowledge of the Prophet and that of all the preceding *anbiya* (messengers) and *awsiya* (legatees), and – as in earlier collections – with access to the books of earlier prophets and a number of other texts.[53]

As in *Basair* also, the Imams were said to have the complete much longer version of the Quran itself,[54] and *al-Kafi* listed sections missing from the Uthmanic Codex.[55] They also possessed various effects of the earlier prophets, claimed to know the future and distinguished themselves also as *muhaddathun*.[56]

Nevertheless, in a clear nod to earlier events that would only also have resonated among the early tenth-century community, al-Kulayni included traditions in which the Imams also warned of the danger of rising up or permitting their names to be mentioned in connection with such moves; 'the one whose birth is concealed from the people' (that is, the twelfth Imam) would organise that final, implicitly successful – and violent – uprising.[57] With meaning for both past but especially also contemporary audiences, believers were enjoined also against becoming too hasty in their expectation of the Imam's return to the community. They were also cautioned that during the occultation false claimants to the Imamate would arise.[58]

A large body of traditions followed in which each Imam was seen to designate his successor, and on the births, sometimes clearly miraculous in nature,[59] of the Imams, including that of the twelfth Imam, in which he was seen before going into occultation. The Imams are also seen to address the fact of the occultation. But, to be sure, of the thirty-one traditions in a chapter on the occultation, in some the Imams spoke of *al-qaim* as having but one occultation where other traditions pointed to two, one shorter and one longer.[60]

These same texts contained references by the Imams to networks of *wukala* (sing. *wakil*, 'agent', usually a financial agent) scattered throughout the region – including Yemen, Nishabur, Egypt and Qum – but also refer to local believers' wariness of those who spoke on behalf of the Imams and to the political establishment's hostility to those known to be agents of the Imams. There are also accounts of believers themselves being confused over the fate of the eleventh

Imam. However, although the Imams' temporary absences were referred to, there is no reference to any formal delegation of authority, let alone named duties to any individual during any such absences or during the forthcoming periods of occultation.[61]

The subsequent five volumes that made up *al-Furu min al-Kafi* (the branches of *al-Kafi*) contain nearly 12,000 traditions – nearly three-quarters of the entire collection – on *ahkam* (precepts). They spoke to the second purpose of the collection, the delineation of a body of individual and community, or private and public, daily practice and behaviour, based on the Imams' *ilm*, as distinctively Twelver as the doctrinal beliefs outlined in the preceding theological sections. These traditions addressed issues such as ritual cleanliness, funerals, prayer, *al-zakat*, fasting, the pilgrimage, holy war, *al-maisha* (livelihood) – including commercial transactions – marriage, divorce, the manumission of slaves, hunting, slaughtering, food, drinks, adornment, domesticated animals, legacies, inheritances, *al-hudud* (punishments), blood money, witnesses, arbitration and legal judgements and oaths, vows and penances.

The offering up of such traditions implicitly pointed up the inability of the rationalist jurisprudence offered by such figures as the al-Nawbakhtis to produce a body of material on such a detailed scale. *Al-Furu* could only have encouraged believers in their demonstration to contemporary Sunni traditionists that the Twelvers too had access to a body of revelation that addressed such a broad range of issues in detail. Indeed, in many of these traditions the distinctly Shii interpretations were quite explicit.

Thus, in *al-Kafi*'s traditions on *al-khums* the Imams asserted their claim to the revenue as equal to that of Allah and the Prophet, and affirmed their own role in its collection and distribution. In one, Imam al-Rida stated that balancing the needs of the different groups of recipients was the Imam's responsibility. In another tradition, the Imam referred to a *wali* as an intermediary in the collection and distribution process. But, although other traditions in the volume both addressed the occultations and mentioned agents for collection of *al-khums* being in place, nowhere were the Imams cited as formally making provisions regarding *al-khums* during their absence from the community.[62]

The role of the Imams and their agents in the collection and distribution of *al-zakat*, based on Quran, 9:60,[63] was also seen to be paramount in the 528 traditions on the subject. Nevertheless, there were also references to believers' distributing the revenues directly to the recipients.[64]

This was the case also with regard to *al-hudud* (judicial punishments), on which al-Kulayni collected some 448 narrations.[65] In a number of these the Imam refers to the implementation of the relevant laws by both the Imams and individuals acting on the Imam's behalf.[66] There was no formal delegation of any authority to undertake these on behalf of an Imam, as in the case of *al-qada* (judicial authority) and the tradition of Umar b. Hanzala. In one text, however, the fifth Imam stated that the questioner might deal with a situation himself rather than refer it to the Imam, since the outcome would be the same.[67]

The Imams also stressed the importance of attendance at congregational prayer services in place of the *zuhr* (noon) prayer on Friday. In one text, for example, an unnamed Imam stated that whoever did not attend a prayer gathering without a reason would be considered not to have performed the prayer at all. But there were also provisions for performance of the prayer by oneself, in a group or prayers in lieu of this prayer. The Imams also made clear their preference for the presence of a prayer leader to conduct the service, but a wide range of individuals was permitted to be designated as such, even a young boy who had not attained the age of puberty. The Imams also stated that the presence of the prayer leader was not always an absolute guarantee of the prayer's validity.[68]

As to prayer venues, there were traditions in this book on the virtues of certain mosques in Kufa, including the city's grand mosque, but also the effective censuring of other sites.[69]

In the realm of distinctively Shii practices also, *al-Kafi*'s book on the *hajj*, with some 458 traditions, contains a subsection of fifty texts on the *ziyarat* (visitation) to the grave sites of the Imams, ranging from those of Imam Ali and Imam al-Husayn in Iraq to Imam al-Rida in Tus. These included the texts of prayers to be said at each, and traditions in which the Imam extolled the virtues of such *ziyara*. In one of eleven traditions on visiting the grave of Imam al-Husayn, Imam Jafar stated that the visit would erase one's sins. In another, the same Imam said a visit to any one of the Imams' graves was equivalent to *ziyara* to the Prophet himself. These traditions also extolled the properties and curative powers of the *tin/turba* (soil) of the Imams' graves beyond such texts as were on offer in *al-Mahasin*.[70]

Nevertheless, the Imams also advised believers to be cautious in relation to actions that might cause them to be unnecessarily visible. Indeed, traditions in volume 2 of *al-Usul* stressed the importance of the practice of *taqiyya*. In one, Imam Jafar extolled *taqiyya* as a condition of the faith.[71]

There are some seventy-six texts on *muta* (temporary marriage). The practice is derived from Quran 4:24, a fuller version of which seems to attest to its practice in the early *umma*. To be sure, as elsewhere herein, many of the exact details associated with the practice – how many such marriages might be allowed and their durations, for example – were not easily discernible in these traditions. Indeed, Imam Jafar cautioned against its practice whilst in Medina lest practitioners be identified as 'companions of Jafar'.[72]

In the 146 traditions of the collection's *Kitab al-Jihad* (*The Book of Struggle*), believers were reminded that the necessity to fulfil this obligation had limits. In one text, Imam Jafar explained that the obligation fell only on those able to undertake it. In another, the same Imam stated that a believer was accorded merit if, when he saw something indecent, Allah knew he had disapproved of it in his heart.[73]

The Imams' wariness as to entanglements with the political establishment has been noted. Further traditions on the subject are scattered throughout *al-Furu*. In a chapter of fifteen traditions, the Imams counselled the believer against undertaking any activity on behalf of the secular powers. In one, Imam Jafar prohibited a man from taking up government service, saying 'the hurt they have done to this *umma* is greater than that done by the Turks and the people of Daylam'. Nevertheless, as in the other instances above, and bespeaking concern for those Twelver elites in Baghdad who had served the court, al-Kulayni also included traditions in which the Imams were sympathetic to individual circumstances. Imam Musa stated that 'if you are compelled to do so [i.e., to undertake such service], then protect the property (*al-amwal*) of the Shia'.[74]

Summary and Conclusion

In the last years of the ninth and the early tenth centuries, Qum and Baghdad were the most active of the many pockets of believers scattered throughout the region, as judged on the basis of their extant legacy.

The alternative understandings of the faith on offer in each in turn reflected the larger dynamic in which the faithful of each was a part. Their respective discourses, in the absence of other sources, thus offer glimpses, even if imperfect and incomplete, into this clash of visions as the faithful struggled also to distinguish themselves from other Shii discourses, as well as rampant Sunni traditionist discourse in the midst of on-going, broader political and religious discord that marked these years. The Qum-based traditionist vision encouraged a stronger sense of separatism, while the Baghdad-based rationalist vision was both more accommodationist in nature and entailed a distinctly hierarchical vision of the structure of the community during the Imams' absence. *Al-Kafi* reminded the faithful in Baghdad of the ultimate source of their differences with these other discourses: the Imams' statements and actions.

Believers' actual practice in these years is more difficult to ascertain. There is some suggestion that certain distinctive practices had been extant in Kufa – a hotbed of diverse religious discourses – as early as the eighth century, that is at least a century before the disappearance of the twelfth Imam.[75]

At the same time, the fact that over the ninth and up to the early tenth century both Qummi and Baghdadi elites involved themselves in addressing aspects of Twelver doctrine and practice suggests they perceived a need to do so. That is, their contributions[76] attest to their understanding of 'fluidity' of boundaries on issues of both doctrine and practice 'on the ground' among and between the many Shii groups extant in this period, let alone between these elements and Sunni groups. Sunni elements' simultaneous work in evolving distinctive bodies of doctrine and practice – *viz* the appearance of Sunni *hadith* collections – suggests that they also perceived that 'on the ground' these distinctions were fluid.

In fact, in the last years of the ninth and early tenth centuries the situation of even those in these locations who accepted that the eleventh Husaynid Imam, al-Hasan al-Askari, had a son who became the Imam at his father's death, but had then gone into hiding could not have appeared to have been secure. The Shii city-state of Qum was under continued attack from the Baghdad-based caliphate. In Baghdad, the fortunes even of the elites among the faithful were at the mercy of factors beyond their own control. And the views as to the way forward for the faith held by elites in each of these two pockets could not have been more different.

Al-Kulayni's petitioner gave voice to the contemporary, resulting uncertainty.

Traditions on both the number and length of the occultation(s) were contradictory. Also, although the Imams made numerous references to networks of agents, those named and the activities they undertook related only to the period of the Imams' presence. If the Imams' traditions in *al-Kafi* in particular did lay down the bases for distinctively Twelver theological doctrine and daily personal and communal practice, they offered no provisions for the further interpretation of that doctrine and practice or even the continuation of that practice during the occultation.

To the extent that the tradition of Ibn Hanzala offered any guidance, however, it was to be cautious, to wait until the Imam himself was available to be questioned directly. That day was perceived by some as not so far off.

Al-Kafi also contained traditions that identified the *alamat* (signs) whose appearance would precede, and thus herald, the return of the Hidden Imam. In one, Imam Jafar called attention to the splits and weakness among the 'sons of al-Abbas', for example.[77]

Momentous events were certainly in evidence in the years preceding al-Kulayni's death in Baghdad. The rise of the Zaydi Buyids on the Iranian plateau and their defeat of a larger Abbasid force in 934, the many traditions suggesting that most of the Imam's supporters at his return would be Iranians[78] and the feeling among some in the community that the Imam would return whilst still a young man,[79] could only have encouraged expectations that the last days were imminent.

Notes

1. It is the Sunni traditions and, especially, their authenticity, that have preoccupied most Western scholars to date. See Newman, *The Formative Period of Twelver Shiism*, xiv. Signs of moving past such a circular debate are on offer in the works of G. Schoeler and A. Goerke, among others. See, for example, A. Goerke *et al.*, 'First-century Sources for the Life of Muhammad? A Debate', *Der Islam* 89 (2012), 2–59.
2. See the discussion on *al-Kafi*, below.

3. Newman, *ibid.*, 13–14. These included such scholars as al-Bukhari (d. 870), Muslim b. Hajjaj (d. 874) and al-Sijistani (d. 888). On the Sunni traditionists and their backgrounds, see M. Z. Siddiqi, *Hadith Literature, its Origin, Development and Special Features* (Cambridge, 1993). On the first two, see also J. Brown, *The Canonization of al-Bukhari and Muslim: the Formation and Function of the Sunni Hadith Canon* (Leiden, 2007).

4. Madelung, *Religious Trends*, 86–90.

5. Jafariyan, *Tarikh-i Tashayyu*, 1: 220, 226–30; F. Daftary, *The Ismailis. Their History and Doctrines* (London, 1992), 120–3, 125, 131; Madelung, *Religious Trends*, 96.

6. See Chapter 1, n. 52. See also Ahmad b. Muhammad b. Khalid al-Qummi al-Barqi, *al-Rijal*, ed. J. M. Urmawi (Tehran, 1342, together with Ibn Daud's *Kitab al-Rijal*), 47–53, 53–5, 57, 58. See also Ahmad b. Ali al-Asadi al-Najashi, *Rijal al-Najashi*, ed. M. al-Zanjani (Qum, 1407), 109, 185; Muhammad b. al-Hasan al-Tusi, *Rijal al-Tusi*, ed. Bahr al-Ulum (Najaf, 1380/1961), 373, 393, 400, 401, 403, 407, 410, 416, 429, 431, 426. See also Jafariyan, *Tarikh-i Tashayyu*, 1: 249, 250–2, 250, n. 8; Madelung, *Religious Trends*, 84.

7. On the fifth Imam, see al-Tusi, *Rijal al-Tusi*, 107, 116, 133, 136, 138. On the sixth Imam, see al-Barqi, *al-Rijal*, 27–8; al-Najashi, *Rijal al-Najashi*, 104; al-Tusi, *ibid.*, 149, 150, 172, 178, 256, 266, 145, 154. On the seventh Imam, see al-Barqi, *ibid.*, 48, 51; al-Tusi, *ibid.*, 347. On Imam al-Rida, see al-Barqi, *ibid.*, 51, 55; al-Tusi, *ibid.*, 367, 377, 378, 381, 382, 386, 388, 389, 391, 395; Muhammad b. al-Hasan al-Tusi, *al-Fihrist*, ed. M. Bahr al-Ulum (Najaf, 1937), 99, 145. On al-Jawad, see al-Barqi, *ibid.*, 56, 54, 57, 59; al-Tusi, *Rijal al-Tusi*, 397, 398, 404, 409, 410, 422, 423, 426; al-Tusi, *al-Fihrist*, 26. On the eleventh Imam, see al-Barqi, *ibid.*, 60, 61; al-Tusi, *Rijal al-Tusi*, 427, 431; al-Tusi, *al-Fihrist*, 101. See also Chapter 1, n. 54.

8. Qummi, *Tarikh-i Qum*, 279, 213, 226–7, 215–16, 226–7, 229; Jafariyan, *Tarikh-i Tashayyu*, 1: 193, 180–1, 198–202, 201.

9. Qummi, *Tarikh-i Qum*, 28–31, 37, 279; 163–4, 156–7, 104–5, 35; 39, 102–6, 142. See also al-Tabari, *The History of al-Tabari*, 32: 166–7, 182, 190, 197; Qummi, *ibid.*, 35, 163, 189–90; and Jafariyan, *Tarikh-i Tashayyu*, 1: 180, 297, 203–66.

10. Earlier, scattered efforts to compile collections of the traditions of the Imams include the 'Four Hundred *Usul* (sing. *asl*)', most of which were assembled by followers of Imam Jafar. Less than a score have survived and these comprise traditions on a variety of subjects. See E. Kohlberg, 'al-Usul al-Arbaumia', *Jerusalem Studies in Arabic and Islam* 10 (1987), 128–66.

11. Al-Najashi, *Rijal al-Najashi*, 335, 76–7, 61; al-Tusi, *al-Fihrist*, 20–2; al-Tusi, *Rijal al-Tusi*, 386, 398, 398, n. 1, 404, 410. On Qum generally, and for a more thorough biography and discussion of this work, see Newman, *The Formative Period of Twelver Shiism*, 32f, 50f. More recently, see also R. Vilozny, 'A Shii Life Cycle according to al-Barqi's *Kitab al-Mahasin*', *Arabica*, 54(3) (2007), 362–96.

12. Complete copies of *al-Mahasin* seem to have been lost by the thirteenth century, if not earlier. See E. Kohlberg, *A Medieval Muslim Scholar at Work. Ibn Tawus and his Library* (Leiden, 1992), 241.

13. The ninth-century Twelver scholar al-Kashshi, on whom see Chapter 4, n. 54, as cited in Jafri, *Origins and Early Development of Shia Islam*, 253–4, stated that the fifth Imam, al-Baqir, 'taught them and explained to them the knowledge [of law], and they began to teach other people from whom they were previously learning'. Indeed, Amir-Moezzi (*The Divine Guide*, 26, n. 143, 133) noted the preponderance of texts attributed to al-Baqir and his son Jafar, the sixth Imam, in the early collections of the Imams' traditions. This is attested in the collections discussed in this chapter.

14. Al-Barqi, *al-Mahasin*, ed. Jalal al-Din Muhaddith Urmawi (Tehran, 1370/1950–1), 131–3, 135–6, 146, 158, 169–71, 181–2.

15. Al-Barqi, *ibid.*, 207–15, 220–9.
16. Al-Barqi, *ibid.*, 85–8, 92–3.
17. Al-Barqi, *ibid.*, 286–90. Sunni Islam does not include the last and holds the first as the *sha-hada* ('bearing witness' that there is only one god and Muhammad is His messenger).
18. Al-Barqi, *ibid.*, 234–6, 259.
19. On al-Saffar, see also Newman, *The Formative Period of Twelver Shiism*, 67f.
20. The original full title *Insights into the Degrees, on the Knowledge of the Family of Muhammad and That with which Allah Endowed Them* differs slightly from that given the work, *The Insights of the Degrees on the Virtues of the Family of Muhammad*, by the publishers of the Qum 1404 edition: *Basair al-Darajat fi Fadail Al Muhammad*, ed. M. Kuchabaghi (Qum, 1404). Cf. al-Tihrani, *Al-Dharia*, 3: 124–5.
21. Thus, unlike *al-Mahasin* and *al-Kafi*, *Basair* includes no traditions on *ahkam* (precepts); biographies of al-Saffar note that he did compile collections of traditions on precepts, on prayer and ablutions, for example, but these are no longer extant. See al-Najashi, *Rijal al-Najashi*, 354; al-Tusi, *al-Fihrist*, 143–4; al-Tusi, *Rijal al-Tusi*, 436.
22. Al-Saffar, *Basair al-Darajat*, 464–6, 480–4, 470–5.
23. Al-Saffar, *ibid.*, 142–6, 150–61, 324–6, 132–5, 135–42, 340–1, 162–8. Seventy-one of the 100 were narrated from Imam Jafar, and eighteen from al-Baqir.
24. Al-Saffar, *ibid.*, 193–6. The reference was to a Shii variant on Quran 22:52: 'Never did we send a messenger or a prophet [or someone spoken to] before you.' See M. M. Bar-Asher, 'Variant Readings and Additions of the Imami Shia to the Quran', *Israel Oriental Studies*, 13 (1993), 64–5; E. Kohlberg, 'The Term *Muhaddath* in Twelver Shiism', *Studia Orientalia Memoriae D. H. Baneth Dedicata* (Jerusalem, 1979), 39–47.
25. Al-Saffar, *ibid.*, 319–20; thirteen were narrated from Imam Jafar and nine from al-Baqir. See also Kohlberg, 'The Term *Muhaddath* in Twelver Shiism'. To be sure, as noted by Amir-Moezzi (*Divine Guide*, 101, 101, n. 537), what remains of *al-Mahasin* had contained no references to the occultation *per se* or the final number of the Imams as twelve. But by this time in Qum, the twelfth Imam and his occultation were acknowledged facts: Abdallah b. Jafar al-Himyari (d. after 910), from whom al-Saffar narrated texts, authored a book on the occultation, and the first recorded reference to the number of Imam as twelve, along with their names, was in the *tafsir* (Quran commentary) of Ali b. Ibrahim b. Hashim al-Qummi (d. after 919). As will be noted in the following chapter, writing in Qum at the same time, Ali b. Babawayh (d. 941) also referred to twelve as the number of Imams. See Amir-Moezzi, *ibid.*, 216, n. 566; Modarressi, *Crisis and Consolidation*, 100, n. 251; E. Kohlberg, 'From Imamiyya to Ithna' Ashariyya', *Bulletin of the School of Oriental and African Studies*, 39 (1976), 521–34.
26. Al-Saffar, *ibid.*, 174–90. Of these, twenty-four were narrated from Imam Jafar and seventeen from al-Baqir.
27. Al-Barqi, *al-Mahasin*, 135–6; al-Saffar, *ibid.*, 67–90. Of the latter, thirty-four were narrated from Jafar and twenty-nine from al-Baqir.
28. Al-Saffar, *ibid.*, 431–3. In these it was said that the Imam could hear whilst still in the womb, was born with the words of Quran 6:116 inscribed on his arm and that columns of light transmitted Allah's knowledge to the Imam.
29. Al-Saffar, *ibid.*, 341–54. Eighteen of these were narrated from Imam Jafar and twelve from al-Baqir.
30. Al-Saffar, *Basair al-Darajat*, 274–87. Nineteen of these came from Jafar and six from al-Baqir.
31. See also Quran 5:110; 2:73, 2:260, 22:6; 42:9, 46:3.
32. Al-Saffar, *Basair al-Darajat*, 269–74. Of these texts, nine came from Jafar and one from al-Baqir.

33. S. Sabari, *Mouvements populaires à Bagdad à l'époque 'Abbasside, IXe–XIe siècles* (Paris, 1981), 12, 14, 37, 38.

34. Al-Tabari, *The History of al-Tabari*, 38: 77, 82–3, 96, 99, 11–15, 119, 147, 163, 166, 173–4, 176–7, 197; al-Masudi, *Muruj al-Dhahab*, 4: 270, 280, 304–5; Abd al-Rahman b. Ali, Ibn al-Jawzi, *al-Muntazam*, 5–6 (Hyderabad, 1357), 6: 33, 46, 109, 153, 208, 223–4, 295–6, 300–1; Daftary, *The Ismailis*, 117–19, 125–8, 130f; Madelung, *Religious Trends*, 95–6; Kennedy, *The Prophet and the Age of the Caliphates*, 185–6, 193–4, 287–92, 315–16, 320–1, 323.

35. Massignon identified Ismail as a member of the extremist Mukhammisa (fiver) Shii sect, whose members venerated Muhammad, Ali, Fatima and their two sons as the five incarnations of Allah. See L. Massignon, 'Recherches sur les shîites extrémistes à Bagdad à la fin du troisième siècle de l'Hégire', *Opera Minora*, ed. Y. Moubarac (Paris, 1969), 1: 524–5 (originally published in 1938). See also Moosa, *Extremist Shiites*, 255–66, 85, 356, 392; al-Tabari, *The History of al-Tabari*, 35: 204, n. 611.

36. Al-Tabari, *The History of al-Tabari*, 38: 24–25, 46–64; al-Masudi, *Muruj al-Dhahab*, 4: 270–1; Ibn al-Jawzi, *al-Muntazam*, 5: 150–1, 171.

37. Al-Tabari, *ibid.*, 38: 77, n. 393, 81–8; Ibn al-Jawzi, *al-Muntazam*, 6: 18; Shaban, *Islamic History*, 2: 121, 130–1, 140–1; Waines, 'The Third Century Internal Crisis of the Abbasids', 305; Kennedy, *The Prophet and the Age of the Caliphates*, 182.

38. The historian Ibn al-Jawzi (d. 1200) (*al-Muntazam*, 6: 195–6), himself a Hanbali, records that Sunni clerics claimed the mosque was full of *kuffar* (unbelievers) who were slandering the companions of the Prophet.

39. Miskawayh, *The Eclipse of the Abbasid Caliphate*, 1: 364–5 (ad. 323); Ibn al-Jawzi, *al-Muntazam*, 6: 281, 288–9; D. Sourdel, 'Ibn al-Furat', *EI2*; Waines, 'The Third Century Internal Crisis of the Abbasids', 283, n. 3; Kennedy, *The Prophet and the Age of the Caliphates*, 196–9, 229; K. Zetterstéen, 'al-Radi', *EI2*.

40. J. Kramer, *Humanism in the Renaissance of Islam. The Cultural Revival of the Buyid Age* (Leiden, 1986), 61–2, citing Miskawayh, Ibn al-Athir and Ibn Kathir.

41. On the earlier generations of Twelver rationalists, see Iqbal, *Khwandan-i Nawbakhti*, 77–94; Modarressi, *Crisis and Consolidation*, 111, 59, n. 25, 9, 11–14, 113, 33, 61, 113–14, 127, 39, 45, 66, 92, 127; al-Najashi, *Rijal al-Najashi*, 175, 434, 212; al-Tusi, *al-Fihrist*, 74–5, 131–2, 174, 293, 181–2. See also W. Madelung, 'The Shiite and Kharijite Contribution to Pre-Asharite *Kalam*', in P. Morewedge (ed.), *Islamic Philosophical Theology* (Albany, NY, 1979), 121–2, 125. These elements included the two Nawbakhtis themselves (see below) and Ibn Qiba al-Razi of the early tenth century. The latter was a Mutazilite who became a Shii. See al-Najashi, *ibid.*, 75–6, 380, 63; al-Tusi, *al-Fihrist*, 132, 190, 193; Iqbal, *ibid.*, 83–4, 94–5; Modarressi, *ibid.*, 117–31. See also W. Madelung, 'Imamism and Mutazilite Theology', in T. Fahd (ed.), *Le shi'isme imamite* (Paris, 1970), 15–16. Ibn Qiba authored refutations of the Mutazila, of those claiming the Imamate for the younger son of the tenth Imam and of the Zaydis. These are included in Modarressi, *ibid.*, 133f.

42. Modarressi, *ibid.*, 88–89, 95, n. 223, 99–100, 247. Only fragments remain of his *Kitab al-Tanbih*, in which he argued that the son of the eleventh Imam, now in hiding, would reemerge as the *qaim* to establish a new order. See also Amir-Moezzi, *The Divine Guide*, 222, n. 621. For a list of his works see Iqbal, *ibid.*, 116–23; Modarressi, *ibid.*, 99–100, 60, 87.

43. Modarressi, *ibid.*, 99–100, 116–18. On his works, see Iqbal, *ibid.*, 128–40. See also Madelung, 'Imamism and Mutazilite Theology', 14–16.

44. Modarressi, *ibid.*, 42, 67, 93–4; Hussain, *The Occultation of the Twelfth Imam*, 120–1, 122–5.

45. L. Massignon [L. Gardet], 'al-Hallaj', *EI2*, Iqbal, *Khwandan-i Nawbakhti*, 97–8, 110, 111–16.

46. Ch. Pellat, 'Muhammad b. Ali al-Shalmaghani', *EI2*; Iqbal, *Khwandan-i Nawbakhti*, 222–38. Iqbal (pp. 225–6) notes that the sources on al-Shalmaghani's unorthodox beliefs were all later sources. See also Hussain, *The Occultation of the Twelfth Imam*, 127–30.

47. Newman, *The Formative Period of Twelver Shiism*, 94f; Akhtar, *Early Shiite Imamiyyah Thinkers*, 1–23.

48. Muhammad b. Yaqub al-Kulayni, *al-Kafi*, ed. A. A. al-Ghaffari, 8 vols (Tehran, 1377–9/1957–60), 1: 2–9.

49. Newman, *The Formative Period of Twelver Shiism*, studied 7,599 of *al-Kafi*'s 16,199 traditions, and confirmed that al-Kulayni narrated 72 per cent of these from Qummis, of which 35 per cent were narrated from three Asharis alone. One of these and another non-Ashari Qummi narrated more than half of all those studied.

50. Traditions from the fifth and sixth Imams dominate this collection as they had the earlier compilations.

51. Al-Kulayni, *al-Kafi*, 1: 34; al-Saffar, *Basair al-Darajat*, 8. See also 1: 34, and compare with *Basair* (9). A single tradition in another chapter (1: 37) had been cited in *al-Mahasin* (233).

52. Al-Kulayni, *ibid.*, 1: 46, 67–8. A shorter version of the Ibn Hanzala tradition appeared in the later chapter on *al-qada* (judicial arbitration), 7: 412. The tradition was cited by Ayatollah Ruholllah Khomeini (d. 1989) in his famous early 1970s' *al-Hukuma al-Islami-yya* (Islamic Government). See Khomeini, *Islam and Revolution*, trans. H. Algar, 93. For a tradition narrated via one Abu Khadija, in which the Imam stated 'look to one among you who knows something of our judgements and make him a *qadi* among you', see al-Kulayni, *ibid.*

53. Al-Kulayni, *ibid.*, 1: 145; al-Saffar, *Basair al-Darajat*, 61; al-Kulayni, 1: 194–8; al-Saffar, 199–200; al-Kulayni, 1: 198–205, 223–8.

54. Al-Kulayni, *ibid.*, 1: 228–9. See also 2: 633, 8: 386–7.

55. Al-Kulayni, *ibid.*, 1: 414, 416, 418; 2: 617–18, 628, 631, 633–4; 8: 208, 210, 211, 435, 437, 440, 502, 570, 571, 586, 596.

56. Al-Kulayni, *ibid.*, 1: 232–8, 258–60, 270–1. See also 1: 196–8, 258–62, 341. On 341, al-Baqir cited Quran 81: 15–16, as indicating the year in which an Imam would go into occultation.

57. Al-Kulayni, *ibid.*, 1: 342. On failed uprisings see also 1: 366, 369. See also 1: 330–1, 8: 264, on the secrecy surrounding the birth and early life of the twelfth Imam. The faithful were even cautioned against pronouncing the name of the Hidden Imam (1: 333).

58. Al-Kulayni, *ibid.*, 1: 368–9, 372–4. See also 1: 374–6, where the traditions refer to *Aimma al-Jawr* (the Imams of Tyranny) or *Aimma al-Zulm* (the Imams of Oppression), as opposed to *Aimma al-Haqq* (the Imams of Truth) or *Imam Adil min Allah* (the Just Imam from Allah).

59. See, for example, al-Kulayni, *ibid.*, 1: 385.

60. Al-Kulayni, *ibid.*, 1: 276, 329–32. On the occultation itself, see 1: 335–43.

61. Al-Kulayni, *ibid.*, 1: 286–332, 439–535. In one (1: 518–19) an agent who denied that the eleventh Imam had a son was dismissed. See also Asatryan, 'Bankers and Politics'.

62. Al-Kulayni, *ibid.*, 1: 539–43, 544, 335–43, 517–18. *Al-Khums* is based on Quran 8:41:

> Know that whatever you have captured
> of booty, a fifth of that is for Allah, and
> for the Prophet, and for *al-qurba* (the
> kinsmen of the Prophet) and *al-yatima*
> (the orphans) and *al-maskin* (the needy)
> and *ibn al-sabil* (the wayfarers).

63.   *Al-sadaqat* (the alms) are for *al-fuqara* (the poor)
        and *al-miskin* (the needy) and *al-amilun* (those who
        collect them, and *al-muallafa qulubihum* (those
        whose hearts are to be reconciled [to free] the captives and
        the debtors, and *fi sabil Allah* (for the cause of
        Allah) and *ibn al-sabil* (the wayfarers).

64.   Al-Kulayni, *al-Kafi*, 3: 496f, especially 3: 496–7, 497, 536–9, 549–50. Seventy per cent of these were collected from Qummis, and one individual narrated 33 per cent. See also the traditions on *al-sadaqa* (alms), in al-Kulayni, 4: 2–61

65.   Al-Kulayni, *ibid.*, 7: 174–270. 310, 70 per cent were narrated from two Qummis.

66.   For this use of the term see, for example, al-Kulayni, *ibid.*, 7: 197, 206, 251, 254, 258, 259, 262.

67.   Al-Kulayni, *ibid.*, 7: 252.

68.   Al-Kulayni, *ibid.*, 3: 372, 421, 371, 376, 377–9, 377–8, 358–62.

69.   Al-Kulayni, *ibid.*, 3: 489–90, 490–5.

70.   Al-Kulayni, *ibid.*, 4: 569f, 580–3, 585–6, 588f; 6: 265f, 6: 378; al-Barqi, *al-Mahasin*, 2: 500. (Interestingly, Ashura by name, as a particularly significant day in the Shii calendar, was referred to herein only in the context of fasting in *al-Kafi* (4: 86, 145–7).) A contemporary of al-Kulayni living in Aleppo and Damascus mentions, and indeed encourages, visits to Imam al-Husayn's grave in a number of his poems. See K. Sindawi, 'Visit to the Tomb of al-Husayn b. Ali in Shiite Poetry: First to Fifth Centuries AH (8th–11th Centuries CE)', *Journal of Arabic Literature*, 37(2) (2006), 248–9, 253. Earlier references herein to al-Mutawakkil's destruction of the Imam's grave in 850–1, visits to the site during the reign of al-Muntasir and the banning of such visitations in the 940s would seem to confirm the site as a place of importance for the faithful by this period, if not also before. Cf. Y. Nakash, 'An Attempt to Trace the Origin of the Rituals of Ashura', *Die Welt des Islams*, 33(2) (1993), 164, mainly citing traditions from later collections. In these texts Imam Ali is referred to as *Wali Allah* and *Khalifa Allah* (al-Kulayni, 4: 569–70). Imam Musa is also referred to as *Wali Allah*, while he and Imam Husayn are also referred to as *Hujjat Allah* (the proof of Allah) (4: 578).

71.   Of the twenty-three texts in the chapter on *taqiyya* (al-Kulayni, *ibid.*, 2: 217–21), none of *Basair*'s traditions were cited, although seven of *al-Mahasin*'s twenty-seven were. See also al-Kulayni, *ibid.*, 2: 221–6.

72.   Al-Kulayni, *ibid.*, 5: 448–67, esp. 451–2, 459–60, 449, 467. See also I. Howard, '*Muta* Marriage Reconsidered in the Context of the Formal Procedures for Islamic Marriage', *Journal of Semitic Studies*, 20 (1975), 82–92. The verse reads:

        Also (prohibited are) women already married, except those whom your right hands possess: Thus hath Allah ordained against you: Except for these, all others are lawful, provided ye seek them with gifts from your property, desiring chastity, not lust, seeing that ye derive benefit from them, give them their dowers as prescribed; but if, after a dower is prescribed, agree mutually, there is no blame on you, and Allah is All-knowing, All-wise.

73.   Al-Kulayni, *ibid.*, 5: 2f, esp. 59–60. Forty-seven per cent of these were collected from one Qummi.

74.   Al-Kulayni, *ibid.*, 5: 106, 110. Given other references by Imam Jafar to the Umayyads; 'they' likely refers to them here as well, even though his Imamate spanned the rule of both the Umayyads and the Abbasids. See also 3: 543. The faithful were also enjoined not to

seek power in eight traditions, of which six were narrated via Imam Jafar. See al-Kulayni, 2: 297f.

75. See N. Haidar, *The Origins of the Shi'a. Identity, Ritual, and Sacred Space in Eighth-century Kufa* (Cambridge, 2011). Haidar, using a variety of collections of the Imams' traditions, points to evidence for the presence of a distinct, independent Twelver identity by this period.
76. Biographies of al-Kulayni note his refutation of the Qaramatians. Al-Najashi, *Rijal al-Najashi*, 377–8; al-Tusi, *al-Fihrist*, 135–6.
77. Al-Kulayni, *al-Kafi*, 8: 224–5.
78. Al-Kulayni, *ibid.*, 1: 369f.
79. Al-Kulayni *ibid.*, 1: 536.

CHAPTER 3

The challenge of 'the Uncertainty'

Such traditions as that of Umar b. Hanzala, in which Imam Jafar cautioned the faithful to wait to bring particularly problematic matters to the Imam himself, and traditions referring to the signs that would precede the Imam's return must have given further hope to some that the return was imminent. That the Imam did not reappear caused many across the region to fall into doubt and some to abandon the faith. Others overcame these doubts, some at least by, again, referring to the traditions themselves for guidance.

At the time, the period was referred to as *al-Hayra* (the Uncertainty).[1] The reality of, and the responses to, this challenge across the region's scattered pockets of the faithful can be traced via compilations of the Imams' traditions completed over the tenth century. From mid-century the rise of the Buyids – who entered Baghdad in 946 and who, as Zaydis, were tolerant of Twelver discourse – facilitated the resolution of the challenge, but also presented challenges to the nascent Twelver community.

The reality of *al-Hayra*: 'the Imamate and the Enlightenment'

The Qummi origins of the majority of *al-Kafi*'s contradictory traditions on the occultation reflected broader uncertainties over the nature and length of the Imam's absence from the community. In Qum itself, however, efforts to address these questions were underway even as al-Kulayni himself was finishing his compilation in Baghdad.

One of the earliest of these efforts was a volume of traditions completed by one Ali b. al-Husayn b. Babawayh, who died in 941 in Qum, the same year that al-Kulayni died in Baghdad.

Born some ten years before the occultation, Ali b. Babawayh, as he is often called,[2] completed his short compilation *Kitab al-Imama wal-Tabsira min al-Hayra* (*The Book of the Imamate and Enlightenment from the Uncertainty*) in c. 937.[3] The volume represented an acknowledgement of the reality facing the community and proffered some measure of reassurance.

Although he visited Baghdad and met al-Husayn b. Ruh al-Nawbakhti (d. 937), Ali b. Babawayh's strongest ties were with Qum's Twelver community, especially its religiopolitical elite.[4] In fact, he collected some two-thirds of the ninety-nine traditions in this collection from two of those from whom al-Kulayni had collected traditions in *al-Kafi*.[5] But those traditions appeared in *al-Kafi* along-side traditions on a wide variety of topics. *Al-Kafi*, even if completed well before al-Kulayni's death in 941, would not yet have been in widespread circulation.

Ali b. Babawayh's opening remarks – in which he cited a tradition, that also appeared in *al-Kafi*, in which Imam Ali stated that *al-hayra wal-ghayba* (the uncertainty and the occultation) would last 'six days, six months, or six years' – bespeak his understanding that the lack of clarity therein called for a 'dedicated' response.[6]

The collection's twenty-three chapters deal with three issues: the Imamate itself (1–3); the Imamate as being invested in a particular line of the Prophet's family (4–17); and, finally, the importance of knowing one's Imam (18–22).[7]

The twenty-seven traditions in chapter two, as such the volume's largest chapter, suggests the compiler's sense that the issue herein – the Imams' promise that the Earth would never be devoid of a *hujja* – was in special need of renewed emphasis. These traditions included Imam Jafar's famous statement – cited by al-Saffar and al-Kulayni – that even if there were but two individuals on earth, one would be the Imam. In another, previously cited by al-Saffar, Imam al-Baqir stated that the Earth would never be without an Imam, whether he was *zahir* (open, visible) or *batin* (hidden).[8]

The forty-eight traditions in chapters 4–17 stressed that the Imamate was invested in the Husaynid line. Chapters 8 and 15 contain statements that the Imamate would never again be invested in two brothers, and declared as false the claim that the Imamate had passed to another son of Imam Jafar. Chapter 14's single text upheld the falsity of the claim thereto for Ismail b. Jafar.

In one of the seven miscellaneous traditions in the collection's last chapter, a tradition not cited in earlier collections, Imam al-Baqir stated that the Imam possessed four features of earlier prophets, including that of Jesus, 'that he died but did not die'.[9]

The inclusion of such traditions suggests the need of believers for reassur-ance, both as to the promise that an Imam would always be with them and as to the Imams' lineage. As to the latter, Ali b. Babawayh clearly considered the claims of nascent Ismaili elements – a force in the area of Rayy in these years – as a discourse with which to reckon.

But the collection did not address the thornier question of the nature, and length, of the Imam's absence.

Al-Numani's *Kitab al-Ghayba*

Ali b. Babawayh was one of those from whom al-Kulayni's student Muhammad b. Ibrahim, Ibn Abi Zaynab al-Numani (d. *c.* 961), narrated traditions. Known as *al-Katib* (the Scribe), based on his study with al-Kulayni, al-Numani was of that generation who knew only the reality of the Imam's absence. He also studied in

Shiraz and Baghdad, and in 944–5 was visiting Damascus and Aleppo. He died in Syria. In *c.* 954, after the Buyids had taken Baghdad, he compiled a volume of traditions entitled *Kitab al-Ghayba* (*The Book of the Occultation*).[10]

References in the volume, the introduction especially, make it quite clear that among the faithful in the west, where al-Numani was travelling, there was considerable uncertainty about, if not actual denial of, the existence of the Hidden Imam. Al-Numani notes that some were saying that the Imam had died, or asking how long he could possibly be alive, as he would now be more than 80 years old. Others maintained the Imamate had passed to others or that he had never existed at all. They did not believe, al-Numani wrote, in Allah's power to extend life beyond human comprehension and experience, as Musa (Moses), for example.[11] But believers in these same pockets also had access to traditions with which to respond to this uncertainty.

Al-Numani's more than 470 traditions,[12] in twenty-six chapters, address many issues covered in the earlier collections of al-Kulayni and Ali b. Babawayh, suggesting continued doubt on them all. These include, for example, traditions on the designation of the Imam being a matter for Allah alone; the fate of those who die without knowing the Imam; the number of the Imam as twelve; that if even only two people were left alive on earth, one would be the Imam; the inability of humans to set the time of the Imam's return; the situation of the faithful at the time of his rising; and how long the Imam would rule.

Chapter 10, with 105 traditions, was by far the largest of the volume's chapters.[13] Entitled 'That which is related concerning the occultation of *al-Imam al-Muntazar al-Thani Ashar*' (the Twelfth, awaited Imam), twenty-seven of the 105 were among the thirty-four traditions in *al-Kafi*'s corresponding chapter on the occultation.[14] However, the majority of the chapter's traditions were 'new' to this volume. Of these fifty-five, 52 per cent, were gathered from non-Qummis, including narrators associated with such communities to the west of Qum as Kufa and Mosul.

In the eleven numbered and five unnumbered traditions of section four, the latter all also cited in *al-Kafi*, the Imams stated that the most difficult time for the community was when they could not see the *hujja*. They compared the absence of the *hujja*, or *Sahib al-Amr*, to the absences of Musa (Moses), Isa (Jesus), Yusuf (Joseph) and Muhammad himself. In the sixth tradition, for example, not cited in earlier compilations, Imam Jafar stated that *al-qaim* would be in occultation before he arose, that some would say his father died without children, others that a child was still in his mother's womb, that he was hiding or that he had predeceased his father. This was a test, the Imam explained.

In five traditions, of which four were 'new', the Imams stated that the birth of one who would undertake the *khuruj* (the coming out) would be secret, that Allah would chose the child of whose birth and whose life nothing would be known, and that the Imam would be in occultation.[15]

In the forty-six numbered traditions of section five, a shorter and longer occultation were noted, and the signs that would precede the Imam's return were listed. In asides, al-Numani explained that during the first occultation *sufara* (intermediaries) between the Imam and the people would deal with issues and problems posed to the Imam. 'The second occultation', al-Numani explained, was that in which 'the intermediaries and *al-wasait* (mediators)' who assumed certain tasks for which Allah had prepared them – citing Quran 3:179 – were no longer present. 'This age is upon us now', al-Numani said.[16]

In several of the last seven traditions of this section, the Imams stated that *al-qaim* would live more than 120 years and would reappear as a 32-year-old to fill the earth with justice.[17]

The sixth and last section in this chapter contained five numbered traditions – all 'new' – which, al-Numani commented,

> confirm the matter of the occultation and attest to its
> reality and its existence and to the situation of *al-hayra*
> in which people are now and that there will be discord *fitna*
> (discord) and that no one will be saved unless he is steadfast.

Allah, he concluded, would decide when to return the Imam and those who had held fast would be delivered.[18]

The coming of the Buyids

The Buyids, or Buwayhids, appeared in Daylam in the early tenth century, as one of the polities that had emerged in the eastern reaches of the Abbasid realm. The Buyids were originally Zaydi Shia, no doubt owing to the arrival of Zaydi elements in Daylam in the aftermath of the many failed Zaydi risings since the eighth century.

In January 946, at the end of a campaign beginning in the 930s with a move on the area of Fars, the Buyids entered Baghdad. Eventually, they also came to control southern Iraq and Khuzistan, and faced opposition from the Hamdanids, based on Mosul and northern Iraq.

The Buyids were less a single empire than a federation of amirates ruled by different members of the family from centres in Shiraz, Rayy and Baghdad. Each ruler was an *amir* (prince), not caliph, as the Buyids portrayed themselves as ruling in the name of the Abbasid caliph. These lands were predominantly Sunni in faith.[19]

Beyond *al-Hayra*: *al-Ziyarat* in theory and practice

Kamil al-Ziyarat (*The Complete of the Visitations*), a compilation produced by another student of al-Kulayni, Jafar b. Muhammad al-Qummi, known as Ibn Qulawayh

(d. 979–80), offers further evidence that by mid-century elements in Qum and elsewhere were moving beyond *al-Hayra*.

Ibn Qulawayh's father was an associate of Sad b. Abdallah al-Qummi al-Ashari (d. 911–13), a noted Qummi traditionist, clan and political leader. Sad was a key source of narrations for both al-Kulayni and Ali b. Babawayh, and for a relative from whom al-Numani collected traditions.[20] Ibn Qulawayh himself, like al-Numani, had no experience of his faith other than without the Imam. But he had studied with al-Kulayni, as had Ali b. Babawayh and al-Numani.[21]

Kamil demonstrates the continued interest in the traditions in both Qum and the west. Of the 801 traditions in the text, some 488 texts, 61 per cent, were collected from Qummis, including Ibn Qulawayh's own father. However, a prominent Kufan, Muhammad b. Jafar, al-Bazzaz (d. 925), who appears to have stayed in the west, narrated 105, 13 per cent. Ibn Qulawayh also seems to have had connections to co-religionists with links to Baghdad and Egypt[22] in the years before the Fatimid establishment of Cairo in 969.

Kamil's traditions suggest that some had begun to evolve rituals whose open, very public display marked them off from Sunni and some Shii elements and, as such, reflect an increasingly stronger sense of self-identity and self-assurance. In this case, the ritual involved *ziyara* (visitation) to the gravesite of the third Imam, al-Husayn, killed at Karbala in 680, a practice either in its infancy at the time or well underway.[23]

To be sure, visiting the grave of the Prophet himself, and his mosque in Medina, was also considered important, as attested in some fifty-three traditions. But these are all grouped in the first seven of the collection's 108 chapters.

The distinctly Shii nature of the compilation becomes apparent immediately thereafter. First, in chapters 8–15, fifty-two traditions address *ziyarat* to the grave of Imam Ali and nearby sites. In the remaining chapters the grave of the third Imam receives the bulk of the attention; indeed, some 552 of the 800 traditions, 69 per cent, refer to visitations to his gravesite.

Thus, for example, in chapter 59, in fourteen traditions – seven narrated from Ibn Qulawayh's father – the Imams equate visiting al-Husayn's grave with visiting that of the Prophet himself or Allah on his throne, and that such a visitor would be recorded as being at the highest level of the Paradise.[24] In the nine texts of chapter 62 – four narrated from Ibn Qulawayh's father – the Imams state that visiting the site mitigates *dhunub* (sins). In chapter 71's nine texts – one from Ibn Qulawayh's father – the Imams extol the *thawab* (virtue) of visiting the grave on the very anniversary of his death, the tenth day of Muharram. Chapter 78 contains a tradition – also narrated from his father – in which Imam Jafar stated that someone who did not make the visit was among those consigned to Hell.[25]

Chapters 91–95 contain thirty-five traditions on the earth (*tin*) of the grave site itself. In a number of these, the Imams stress its curative powers. Ibn

Qulawayh's father narrates a tradition from Sad b. Abdallah in which Imam Jafar says the earth of the site 'is a cure for every affliction'.[26] *Kamil* is also one of the earliest collections in which al-Husayn is explicitly referred to as both *Sayyid al-Shuhada* (chief of the martyrs) and *wasi* (legatee).[27]

Ibn Babawayh and the Imams' traditions

The career and several of the contributions of Muhammad b. Ali al-Qummi (d. 991–2), known as al-Shaykh al-Saduq, Ibn Babuya or Ibn Babawayh, shed further light on the manner in which various pockets of the faithful in the later years of the century were both affected by, but also transcending, 'the Uncertainty'.

Ibn Babawayh was born in Qum *c.* 918. His birth was said to have been blessed by the Hidden Imam himself, after his father Ali b. Babawayh had journeyed to Iraq to ask for a son. Ibn Babawayh studied with his father, who died just before the Buyids entered Baghdad, and with several of al-Kulayni's students, including Ibn Qulawayh. Like both al-Numani and Ibn Qulawayh, Ibn Babawayh was of that generation who knew nothing other the Imam's absence.

Ibn Babawayh was also especially well travelled, perhaps more than some of his predecessors. Sometime between 949 and 957 he moved to Rayy. He made at least three trips to Khurasan, journeying as far as Transoxiana, southern Uzbekistan and Samarqand. He is said also to have visited Gurgan and Astarabad. To the west, in the 960s he was in Hamadan and Kufa, as well as Baghdad and the Hijaz. He was in Kufa in 978. Rayy, a Buyid capital, appears to have been his chief residence, however. Ibn Babawayh seems to have returned to Rayy between most journeys, and it is there that he died.[28]

His move from Qum to Rayy owed itself to an invitation from Rukn al-Dawla (d. 976), the first Buyid amir of northern and central Iran – whose vizier from 939 to his death in 970 was Abul-Fadl b. al-Amid, a Qummi Shii – from whom Ibn Babawayh asked permission to visit Tus in 962. At court Ibn Babawayh participated in debates with scholars of other faiths. His *Uyun Akhbar al-Rida*, discussed below, was completed at the request of al-Sahib b. Abbad (d. 995), the vizier to the Buyid amir Muayyid al-Dawla (*reg.* 976–83). The latter was the son of Rukn al-Dawla.[29]

Western scholars usually identify Ibn Babawayh with reference to his compilation of the Imams' traditions entitled *Man la Yahdaruhu al-Faqih* (*He Who has no Jurisprudent with Him*, hereafter *al-Faqih*), which, with *al-Kafi* and two works of Muhammad b. al-Hasan al-Tusi (d. 1067), were later dubbed 'the four books'.[30]

In fact, however, Ibn Babawayh also assembled a number of other compilations. Taken together, these contain slightly more traditions than the approximately 6,000 in *al-Faqih*.[31] Read carefully, these shed light on the state of various pockets of the faithful over the mid- to late tenth century.

Confronting the confusion: *Kamal al-Din*

Ibn Babawayh's *Kamal al-Din wa Tamam al-Nima fi Ithbat al-Ghayba wa Kashf al-Hayra* (*The Perfection of the Faith and the Completeness of the Blessings on the Certainty of the Occultation and the Examination of 'the Uncertainty'*) is arranged in fifty-eight chapters, in two sections, and contains over 580 traditions.[32]

While Ibn Babawayh did collect many of *Kamal*'s traditions from his father,[33] others from whom he narrated these had *nisba*s suggesting connections with Egypt, Baghdad, Hamadan, Rayy, Isfahan, Ahwaz and Nishabur, as well as Taliqan, Samarqand and Aylaq, near Balkh.

Kamal, dated to *c.* 970–1, and perhaps as early as 964–5, with its title taken from Quran 5:3,[34] attests to the still widespread confusion about the Imam's absence among pockets of the faithful scattered across the region in these years.

In his lengthy introduction, Ibn Babawayh notes that in Nishabur, perhaps during his first visit to the area in the early 960s, he met some believers thrown into confusion by the occultation. He also met a prominent Qummi scholar, who had lived in Bukhara and was in a similar state. He refers also to a Baghdadi who spoke of doubts abroad about the Imam's continued absence, and to another who queried Ibn Babawayh's reference to 'the Unseen' in Quran 12:102 in their discussions about the Imam and his absence.[35]

Other comments refer to non-Twelver Shii discourses. Thus, Ibn Babawayh pointedly referred to the reality of the death of Muhammad b. al-Hanafiyya, as well as that of Musa b. Jafar and the eleventh Imam himself. He mentioned also the short rebuttal by Ibn Qiba to a supporter of the Imamate of Jafar, the younger son of the tenth Imam, and noted rebuttals to numerous Zaydi objections. He closed the introduction by referring to Abu Sahl al-Nawbakhti's various refutations and to Ibn Qiba's refutation of the Zaydis, in which the latter critiqued the Fatahiyya and the Qaramatians.[36]

Kamal's chapters across both sections in order of those with the most traditions reflect the compiler's perceptions of those questions that most needed attention.

Of the first section's 254 texts, 176 – 69 per cent – appear in five chapters. The largest chapter, chapter 22, contains sixty-six texts.[37] These address a point that also received the most attention in his father's *al-Imama*, the promise that the Earth would never be devoid of a *hujja*. Ibn Babawayh's chapter 24, with thirty-six texts, noted that the Prophet himself had said the *qaim* would be the twelfth of the Imams. The thirty-three traditions in chapter 26 also included references to the *qaim* as the twelfth Imam – suggesting lingering doubt on the matter. Chapter 21, on the reason why an Imam was needed, contained the next largest number of texts, with twenty-three. The eighteen texts in Chapter 32, the next largest number, also included a reference, by al-Baqir, to the twelfth Imam as *al-qaim*.[38]

Section two, from chapters 33 to 58, contains some 332 texts, 226, 68 per cent, of which are found in seven chapters. Sixty texts are cited in chapter 33 – the second largest chapter in the volume, after chapter 22 – on statements by Imam Jafar on *al-qaim*, his absence and, yet again, his being the twelfth Imam. Chapter 45's fifty-two texts referred to written communications from the Hidden Imam himself.[39]

Ibn Babawayh used the last chapter's thirty-two miscellaneous traditions – of which nine each were cited from his father and Ibn Babawayh's fellow Qummi traditionist Muhammad b. al-Hasan, Ibn al-Walid (d. 954–5), and four had been cited by al-Kulayni and three by al-Numani – to reiterate his main concern.

Following the first text, Ibn Babawayh pointedly rejected the allegation by some that the Imamate had ended. This

> is contrary to the Truth, based on the many extant traditions that
> the Earth would not be devoid of a *hujja* until the Day of
> Judgement . . . and we have cited these in this book . . . the Imamate
> has not come to an end and it is not possible for it to end.

Ibn Babawayh noted that some even cited Quranic verses[40] to argue that there would be no messenger, prophet or *hujja* between Jesus and Muhammad. He countered with traditions that promised that each age would have a 'guide' and that cited verses which referred to the *qaim*[41] and that he would be of the Prophet's family. Other traditions cited the earlier Imams as having seen *al-qaim*.

How, he asked – clearly reflecting another strand of thought abroad in the community – could there be a discussion about choosing the Imam? Allah had granted the prophets and the Imams His knowledge and wisdom that was far over and above that available to the people of any age. How could there be choice with respect to the Imams, as members of the Prophet's family.[42]

The twenty-nine traditions in Chapter 57 cited signs whose appearance would portend the appearance of the Imam. Some themes therein are familiar from *al-Kafi* and al-Numani's book on the occultation, although twenty-seven of the twenty-nine were 'new' to this collection.[43] Chapter 43, with twenty-six numbered and many unnumbered traditions, included reports in which individuals, oftentimes named and some designated as *wakils*, had seen the Imam since he had gone into occultation. In one, Muhammad b. Uthman al-Umari (d. 916 or 917), a *wakil*, stated that he had seen the Imam performing the pilgrimage.[44]

Chapter 42's sixteen texts contain details of the birth of the Hidden Imam. In one, the eleventh Imam shows his son to his companions and says:

> This is your *sahib* (leader) after me, and I leave
> him as my *khalifa* to you. He is the *al-qaim* . . . Lo,
> the world is filled with tyranny and oppression.
> When he comes forth he will fill it with fairness
> and justice.

In a text new to this compilation, in which the twelfth Imam's birth was cited as a Friday in the month of Shaban of 256 (870), the *wikala* (agency) was said to have passed from Uthman b. Said al-Umari to his son Muhammad b. Uthman, to Abul-Qasim al-Husayn b. Ruh al-Nawbakhti and then to Abul-Hasan Ali b. Muhammad al-Sammari. At the latter's death – in 941, the same year that al-Kulayni and Ibn Babawayh's father died – the question of to whom the *wikala* should be entrusted was then posed. The answer was: '*al-Ghayba al-Tamma* (the full occultation) is what set in after the passing of al-Sammari'.[45]

'Speaking truth to power': *Uyun Akhbar al-Rida*

Although the 941 traditions in *Uyun Akhbar al-Rida* (*The Sources of The Statements on al-Rida,* that is, the eighth Imam) were collected during earlier visits to the Khurasan,[46] these were finally assembled into the volume at the request of the vizier al-Sahib b. Abbad.

The latter is noted for his Zaydi Shii leanings and his poetry, in some of which he addressed pilgrims visiting the tomb of Imam al-Husayn, and even asked them to give the Imam and the other Karbala martyrs his greetings.[47]

But the vizier is also known for his Mutazili sympathies. In 977, shortly after becoming vizier, he invited Abd al-Jabbar b. Ahmad (d. 1024–5), the noted Sunni Mutazili scholar, to become chief judge in Rayy and its environs. Abd al-Jabbar, whose hostility to reliance on traditions by Sunnis and the Shia is well attested, remained in post until his patron's death in 995, four years after Ibn Babawayh's own death. The vizier is said to have clamped down on Sunni and Shii traditionists, including Ibn Babawayh; if true, this crackdown likely coincided with Abd al-Jabbar's appointment.[48]

Assembled amidst, and thus in spite of, mounting court-approved criticism of the recourse to traditions, *Uyun* clearly reflects Ibn Babawayh's sense of self-confidence that followed on his efforts to move past *al-Hayra*. Indeed, the account of the Imam's life herein attests both to the fate that ultimately befell the Imam – that he was killed by caliph al-Mamun – but in the process also affirmed the ultimate religious superiority of the faith, even if by means of the traditions. Ibn Babawayh was thus as much 'speaking truth to power' as these traditions show the eighth Imam had done more than a century earlier.

Ibn Babawayh begins the collection citing the versified greetings of al-Sahib b. Abbad that the vizier had asked him to recite at the Imam's grave site in Tus, this after Ibn Babawayh had asked permission to undertake a visit to the site. Implicitly, the citations sought to establish common ground with the vizier in the mutual veneration of patron and author for the Imam.

Given the atmosphere in which Ibn Babawayh was then living and working, it is precisely the encounters between the Imam and the caliph that repay attention, although they comprise only sixty-two of the 634 traditions, that is, nearly 10 per cent, in some eleven of the two-volume compilation's sixty-nine chapters.

Indeed, in the first volume, chapter 12, the first of those chapters involving the Imam and the caliph, the sole, very long tradition therein, collected from a Qummi traditionist in Aylaq, shows the Imam debating with representatives of the Catholic, Jewish, Hindu, Zoroastrian, Roman (Rumi)/Latin-speaking and other, unnamed, religious communities in the presence of the caliph. The Imam ignores warnings from a follower, who claimed that the debate was a trick by the caliph to confuse and to intimidate the Imam. The Imam uses evidence from the books of his opponents to prove the truth of the message of Islam and the prophethood of Muhammad. Although he is not seen to have taken an especially overt Twelver line in these discussions, the Imam's associates worry that his discourse was so masterful that the caliph might order the Imam hurt or killed.[49]

Chapter 13's sole, also long, tradition, via the same narrator, recounts a debate on the unity of Allah held in the caliph's presence between the Imam and a local Sunni theologian. The intention of the caliph, it is noted herein, was for the Sunni to best the Imam. In the end the caliph himself proclaimed the Imam to be the most learned of the Banu Hashim. Citing Quran 40:51, Ibn Babawayh said Allah would not let the Imam be defeated.[50]

Chapter 23's single, very long, tradition discusses a debate in Marv between the Imam and some scholars from Iraq and Khurasan. The Imam explained that Quran 35:32 referred to al-Itra al-Tahira (the pure descendants, that is, Ahl al-Bayt). Those attending agreed. When the caliph asked for further Quranic citations attesting to the Family and the Imam offered a further twelve, all were convinced.[51]

Volume 2 contained a further seven chapters of sixty-four texts. Chapter 40 comprises some thirty traditions on the Imam's acceptance of al-Mamun's designation of himself as the heir of the caliph. Of these, a Bayhaqi scholar narrated thirteen, nearly half, and a Hamadani scholar four. In these the Imam said he would have been killed had he not accepted the caliph's call, as Yusuf (Joseph) had said service to the king of Egypt was necessary. The Imam is also seen to have accepted the designation with certain conditions, notably that he would not issue orders or render judgements.[52]

Chapter 41's single tradition, narrated via the eleventh Imam, notes that after al-Rida's appointment it did not rain for a long time, and that many blamed the appointment for this situation. The caliph asked the Imam to pray for rain. The Imam did so and it rained. The caliph now realised he had made a mistake in appointing the Imam as his successor and set about denigrating him. Another debate was organised with all the realm's elites in attendance. An opponent challenged the Imam that the rainfall could have occurred by chance and that as the caliph appointed the Imam to his post, he was not superior to the figure who made the appointment. The Imam countered that Allah made the appointment.[53]

Other chapters in the collection also repay attention. The thirty-seven traditions in chapter 66, and the single, long text in chapter 68, address the importance of pilgrimage to the tomb of the Imam near Tus. Of these, thirty had not been cited in earlier collections. In one, the Imam predicted his death by poison, though not the culprit, that he would be buried in a 'strange' land and that whoever visited his tomb would be accorded a merit equivalent to 100,000 performances of the *hajj*. In another, the Prophet stated that a family member would be buried in Khurasan and that the sins of a visitor to the tomb would be forgiven.[54]

The thirteen traditions in chapter 69 offered first-hand experiences of the miraculous nature of the tomb. None of these had been cited in earlier collections, eight were cited from those with Nishabur associations and one from someone connected to Herat. In one, the ruler of Tus prayed at the site for children and was granted a son. Ibn Babawayh noted that Rukn al-Dawla himself had said he had visited the site and that all his prayers had been granted. Even Sunnis are recorded as having been won over to the faith based on their experiences at the site.[55]

Al-Itiqadat: a challenging précis

In 978, Ibn Babawayh was again in Nishabur. Sometime thereafter he completed his *al-Itiqadat* (*The Beliefs*), in effect a précis of the faith's basic doctrines. Although this is mainly a work of theology, Ibn Babawayh does cite many traditions in the course of addressing some forty-five different topics involving the beliefs of the Imamis – his term for the Twelvers.[56] But the volume also offers further evidence that, as represented by Ibn Babawayh himself, certain sections of the community were overcoming the self-doubt and uncertainty that marked *al-Hayra* and gaining a new sense of self.

The volume itself may be divided into two sections. Through to chapter 34, Ibn Babawayh seems at pains to demonstrate that Imami theology had much in common with 'mainstream', that is, Sunni, Muslim theology, even if the former did not conform to any exactly/exclusively idealised Mutazili or Ashari argument; the latter, of course, was, in this period, only extant in its nascent form.

Thus, Ibn Babawayh argues that where both the Imams and the Quran refer to His apparently human characteristics, these were, in fact, clearly metaphysical in nature – an argument more akin to Mutazili formulations than not. In these early chapters, too, most references are to the Quran, suggesting an effort to win over a potential Sunni audience, and some doubtful Shia. On the issue of free will, citing a statement of Imam Jafar, Ibn Babawayh notes that Allah knows human actions before they are undertaken, but He does compel people to act in a given manner – a middle position between Mutazili and Sunni traditionism.[57]

Citing both the Quran and, as the volume progresses, increasingly the Imams' traditions, Ibn Babawayh also upheld Twelver commitment to many of the conventional doctrines associated with Islam in general. These included, for example, the realities of death, the day of Judgements and the Resurrection. He rejects, too, the transmigration of souls, as this doctrine denies the reality of Paradise and Hell and the promise of reward for good actions. Ibn Babawayh also affirms the authenticity of the Uthmanic Codex of the Quran.[58]

But at the core of Twelver belief was the acceptance of the unique place and role of the Imams. Having used more than half of the chapters to demonstrate the faith's acceptance of Islam's 'core' belief system, in the thirty-fifth of the essay's forty-five chapters Ibn Babawayh draws his line in the sand, as it were, both for the faithful and for those outwith that community.

Herein he identifies 'the *hujaj* (proofs; sing. *hujja*) of Allah for the people' as 'the Twelve Imams'. The last Imam, 'Muhammad b. al-Hasan' is 'the *hujja* . . . the Lord of the Age, *Khalifat al-Rahman* [the Vice-regent of the Beneficent, the latter referring to Allah] on His earth, the one who is present in the earth but *ghaib* (absent) to the eyes.' The Imams are 'the repositories of His knowledge . . . immune from sins and errors'. They also can perform miracles.

> Obedience to them is obedience to Allah, and disobedience
> to them is disobedience to Allah . . . their enemy is the enemy of
> Allah. We believe that the earth cannot be without the *hujja* of
> Allah to His creatures . . . either *zahir* (present) . . . or *khafi* (hidden).
> When he appears Jesus, son of Mary, will descend upon the
> earth and pray behind him.[59]

In chapter 37, he also maintains that the fourth to the eleventh Imams had been poisoned, and names the caliphs who had so ordered. Here also he defined and condemned *zalimun* (oppressors) as false claimants to the Imamate and those who advanced such claims for others. Ibn Babawayh offered also a lengthy discussion of the obligatory nature of *taqiyya* until the return of the Imam, in the process citing a series of statements ascribed to the Prophet and the Imams. He also cited a preference for the principle of *ibaha*, that something is assumed to be permitted unless there was a specific prohibition against it.[60]

In his last, rather long, chapter he addressed how to deal with contradictory traditions. 'Authentic' traditions did not contradict the Quran, he began. Too, sometimes there are obvious, specific reasons that traditions might appear to differ, while in other cases one might override another. Some might be handed down based on *taqiyya*. Imam Ali had stated that all traditions come from one of four sources: a hypocrite; someone who hears the statement imprecisely, perhaps deliberately so; someone who hears the statement but not a later statement abrogating the first; someone who hears it correctly and knows if it has/has not been abrogated later.

Imam Ali is then cited as referring to such exegetical pairs of analysis as *nasikh* (abrogating) and *mansukh* (abrogated), *khass* (particular) and *amm* (general), as well as *muhkam* (definite) and *mutashabih* (ambiguous), as were being adopted by Sunni and Shii 'rationalists'.[61] The Imam said that often the Prophet spoke to him in private, explaining the *tawil* (the true meaning) of something in the Quran or taught him both its apparent and hidden significance. Ibn Babawayh also explained that the Prophet's reference to 'those in authority' in Quran 4:59[62] meant the Imams, who were 'with the Quran and the Quran is with them'. They will guide the community 'and by them will calamity be averted'.[63]

Al-Faqih: Ibn Babawayh and the *Ahkam*

Al-Faqih, completed in 983, was another work inspired by Ibn Babawayh's travels into Khurasan. He completed the work at the request of a descendant of Imam Musa whom he met in Aylaq.

Like *al-Kafi's furu*, which contained some 12,000 of *al-Kafi's* 16,000 texts, and, as with Sunni compilations of the Prophetic *hadith*, Ibn Babawayh's *al-Faqih* was a collection of traditions organised into chapters on *furu* issues. But, *al-Faqih* contained only some 6,000 traditions, about half of the number cited by al-Kulayni.

Ibn Babawayh dropped traditions that were similar to those in *al-Kafi* or to traditions 'new' to *al-Faqih*, as well as those presenting problems of reconciliation with texts he did cite. He also occasionally offered a formulation or otherwise explained the meanings of some texts. Ibn Babawayh did include many texts not previously cited by al-Kulayni, which is not so surprising given his more extensive travels. In general, however, he cited far fewer texts on a given subject covered in *al-Kafi*.[64] Finally, unlike al-Kulayni and even unlike his other collections of the Imams' traditions, in *al-Faqih* Ibn Babawayh did not include the full *isnad* for every tradition, but only the last few names in the link to the Imam, reflecting his stated intention to assemble for his petitioner what Ibn Babawayh himself called a *marja* (authoritative source of reference). Such a work, though intended to fulfil the request of his petitioner, was also useful for the 'ordinary', if literate, members of the community. These, as he wrote in the introduction, were more interested in the 'ruling' itself.[65]

For these several reasons *al-Faqih* was shorter and therefore, as apparently intended, 'handier' than *al-Kafi*, even if the range of legal matters covered in *al-Faqih* was not quite as comprehensive.

While at first glance it might seem that *al-Faqih's* traditions broke little or no 'new ground' with those in *al-Kafi*, this was not always the case. Thus, with regard to *al-qada* (judicial authority), in both *al-Kafi* and the corresponding sections of *al-Faqih*, the Imams are seen as delegating authority in matters of judicial arbitration and interpretation. They also emphasised the importance of recourse to the revelation and that the qualification that distinguished judges was knowledge of the Imams' judgements. In one of three traditions, for example, Imam Jafar was questioned as to how to proceed if two 'just' individuals disagreed on a ruling. The Imam stated:

> Look to the one who is more
> knowledgeable and more knowledgeable
> in our traditions and more pious.

Ibn Babawayh even included a truncated version of the famous tradition from Imam Jafar cited via Umar b. Hanzala.[66]

As had al-Kulayni, Ibn Babawayh included traditions, some cited previously, in which both the Imams and individuals were described as implementing *al-hudud* – the latter especially with regard to personal matters. Ibn Babawayh also cited a tradition that had not appeared in the earlier collections in which provision for the Imam's absence, if not the occultation itself, appears to have been made. Here, Imam Jafar was asked:

> Who implements *al-hudud*, al-Sultan or
> *al-qadi*? He [the Imam] replied,
> The implementation of *al-hudud* is
> to him to whom is *al-hukm*.[67]

Thus, the *qadi* was equally, at least implicitly, authorised to undertake the implementation of *al-hudud*, where in *al-Kafi*, the Imams had portrayed the Imams as having delegated only the authority to undertake judicial arbitration.

Al-Faqih's traditions on the Friday congregational prayer also broke new ground. To be sure, Ibn Babawayh, as al-Kulayni, cited no statements by the Imams delegating authority to lead these services, nor did the Imams make provisions for the conduct of the services during the occultation *per se*. But, more so than had *al-Kafi*, *al-Faqih*'s traditions stressed the obligatory nature of attendance.[68] Herein also the Imams gave a central role to the prayer leader and added new grounds on which some might be excluded from undertaking this role. In one such newly cited tradition, the Imam forbad *al-ghali*, even if he were of one's own faith, the openly corrupt and someone unknown by the community from leading prayer. In another new text, the Imam was quoted as saying *man yaquluh bil-jism* (the anthropomorphist) should not receive *al-zakat* nor be a prayer leader. The Imams also prohibited believers from being led in prayer by those not professing belief in all twelve Imams, an unbeliever, someone who had yielded to sin, someone who had denied Allah's power, or other enemies of the faith.

Ibn Babawayh closed the section with a statement of his father's, making a point also not included in *al-Kafi*. His father had stated that one should be lead in prayer by only two persons. The first, was the person whose faith and piety could be trusted. The second, was one whose sword, influence and condemnation of the faith the believer feared. The believer should pray with the latter based on *taqiyya* and *mudara* (social intercourse).[69]

Al-Kulayni had cited a variety of texts on the status of the prayer leader as guarantor of the prayer's validity, but these included provisions for prayer by oneself or in a group without a leader. Citing both 'new' traditions and those available in *al-Kafi*, Ibn Babawayh in effect ruled that the imam guaranteed the prayers of whoever was in attendance unless the person being led in prayer intentionally neglected something.[70] Too, in a comment offered in a chapter of thirty-four four traditions on the prayers of the two festival days of *al-Iftar* (at the end of Ramadan) and *al-Adha* (marking Ibrahim's willingness to sacrifice his son), only four of which had been cited in *al-Kafi*, Ibn Babawayh concluded that unless a believer attended prayer supervised by a prayer leader on these days he would not be judged to have performed prayer.[71]

Al-Faqih's traditions on *al-zakat* provided more details as to the categories of *al-zakat* recipients than had the traditions in *al-Kafi*. To be sure, as in *al-Kafi*, the Imams stated no preference as to a single method by which *al-zakat* was to be collected and distributed during the occultation, let alone the period of the Imams' presence within the community.[72]

Although Ibn Babawayh cited relatively few of *al-Kafi's* traditions on *al-khums*, in both collections the Imams were cited as claiming their right to *al-khums* after the Prophet. But, as in the case of *al-zakat*, Ibn Babawayh's traditions contained additions to *al-Kafi's* list of items subject to *al-khums*. The Imams in *al-Faqih* also made no mention of the involvement of agents or other intermediaries collecting and distributing the tax, and no mention of its collection and distribution during the Imam's absence. Thus, Ibn Babawayh did not cite from *al-Kafi* the tradition in which the Imam spoke of a *wali* who might be entrusted with its collection and distribution, or other traditions in which the Imams referred to intermediaries between the donor and the recipients of *al-khums*.[73]

In *al-Faqih*, the Imams also took a more lenient attitude towards associating with the secular political establishment – *al-sultan* – than had been the case in *al-Kafi*. If, as in *al-Kafi*, the Imams were not seen to provide an objective, working definition of what constituted *jawr*, in *al-Itiqadat*, the latter was defined as a false claimant to the Imamate.

Thus, in a previously uncited tradition, the Imam permitted an Imami *qadi*, when among non-Imamis, to render judgements in accordance with non-Imami principles in order to avoid persecution or death.[74] In another 'new' tradition, Imam Jafar was quoted as saying:

> The *kaffara* (atonement) of working
> for *al-sultan* is the satisfaction of
> the needs of the brethren.[75]

Moreover, while in *al-Kafi* the Imams had permitted such service if the believer feared for his life if he refused such service, texts in *al-Faqih*'s traditions did not mention such fear as a reason for accepting a position with the government. Such texts could only have reassured Abul-Fadl b. al-Amid, Rukn al-Dawla's Shii vizier.

Ibn Babawayh also included traditions on *ziyara* to the tombs of *Ahl al-Bayt* but not, as his teacher Ibn Qulawayh, to the point where visitation to Karbala predominated. These fifteen traditions were included within the section on the *hajj*. They included traditions on *ziyara* to Fatima and others of the family buried in Medina, including Imam Jafar, Imam Ali in Najaf, and one on the grave of Imam Husayn, as well as one on visiting the site under the guise of *taqiyya*; the latter was new to this collection. There were two traditions on the curative powers of the *turba* of al-Husayn's tomb, both cited from Ibn Qulawayh, and traditions on visiting the tombs of the other Imams including that of Imam al-Rida.[76]

Al-Faqih also included a number of scattered traditions on *taqiyya* itself, though many of these related to prayer.[77]

Alternative approaches

If the extant written record suggests traditionism waxed strong in this period, especially to the east, other approaches were on offer.

There were, for example, some 'rationalist' elements within the community. Two figures in particular were associated with such discourse in this period: al-Hasan b. Abi Aqil al-Umani, of the early tenth century; and Muhammad b. Ahmad al-Katib al-Iskafi, known as Ibn Abil-Junayd (d. 991–2). The former authored a work on *fiqh* and another on the Imamate. He also devoted great attention to rationalist theology.[78]

The al-Iskafi family were based in Baghdad. Ibn Abil-Junayd himself recognised the revealed texts, accepting some traditions to prove those of his points that others denounced as lacking multiple attestation and therefore as not being a source of law. But he was an active proponent of the use of rationalism in the formulation of Twelver theology and law, approved the use of *qiyas* – accepted by the Sunnis as a source of law – and was said to be especially proficient in *dhann* (speculative opinion), also accorded importance as a legal source by the Sunnis.

Ibn Abi Aqil and Ibn Abil-Junayd, subsequently referred to as *al-qadimayn* (the two ancients), together attempted to legitimise both the recourse to 'speculative analysis and rational argument' and the process of reconciling apparently contradictory sources into uniform legal opinions. They often reached similar conclusions on certain legal issues.[79]

In that sense, then, both carried on the work begun prior to the Buyids' arrival in Baghdad both by the Nawbakhti family and Ibn Qiba al-Razi who, it would seem, had died before the arrival of the Buyids. In fact, Ibn Abil-Junayd was the intellectual link between this tradition and the later Buyid period rationalist al-Shaykh al-Mufid (d. 1022), being his teacher, just as Ibn Qulawayh and Ibn Babawayh were al-Mufid's links to the Qum traditionist school, being his teachers.

Summary and conclusion

In the face of the Imam's continued absence, compilations of traditions over the century, beginning with that of Ali b. Babawayh, attest to the presence of doubt on a range of issues fundamental to the Imamate among the faithful across the region in the early tenth century. But the same compilations point also to the growing availability of responses to the quandary.

Al-Numani, in particular, utilised available and 'new' traditions, coupled with explanations on the basis of which he offered the understanding that there would be a shorter and longer occultation, that during the first, shorter occultation the community was in contact with the Imam via intermediaries, and that the second, in which the community was now living, would be prolonged and that its end was a matter for Divine, not human, determination.

In evidence also is the evolution of distinct bodies of both what today is called ritual as well as personal and communal practices. Decades after *al-Kafi* was assembled, Ibn Qulawayh's *Kamil* represents a decisive, definitive favouring of *ziyara* to al-Husayn over not only the Prophet, but also the graves of the other Imams and even such other notables as Fatima in Qum. In the face of *al-Hayra*, this collection reveals some Twelvers as already engaged in delineating aspects of what publicly defined themselves as such both to others in the broader Shii community and to non-Shia as well.

Ibn Babawayh's *Kamal* completed the reconciliation of the contradictions as to the nature, number and length(s) of the occultation(s) on offer in *al-Kafi* and first offered in written form by al-Numani. His other works also exhibit the emergence of a new self-confidence, reminiscent of that present in Qum a century before. Clearly, some of the region's faithful were in the process of overcoming the existential doubts that arose in the aftermath of the Imam's failure to return to his followers in the early years of the century.

Al-Numani's and, especially, Ibn Babawayh's contributions also highlight something of a transition in the nature of scholarly activity in the community. Both assembled traditions. But both also sought, and offered, solutions to key problems; Ibn Babawayh addressing issues both of theology and daily personal and community practice. In the process, as attested in *al-Itiqadat* and *al-Faqih*, Ibn Babawayh also stood for the evolution of methodologies which incorporated recourse both to the traditions and to certain human-derived, if not Divinely inspired, tools of analysis in their interpretation and application. These were tools with whose use not all among the faithful might be equally skilled.

Notes

1. Modarressi, *Crisis and Consolidation*, 98, n. 237.
2. Modarressi, *ibid.*, 99, 248.
3. On this date, see Modarressi, *ibid.*, 99, n. 244. The text of this volume utilised herein was downloaded from http://www.aqaed.info/book/75/indexs.html, 12 February 2010.
4. Al-Tusi, *Fihrist*, 93; al-Najashi, *Rijal al-Najashi*, 261–2.
5. The two were Sad b. Abdallah al-Ashari (on whom see n. 20) and Muhammad b. Yahya, from whom al-Kulayni narrated many texts. Thirty-six of these ninety-nine traditions had appeared in *al-Kafi*, twenty-nine in *Basair* and four in *al-Mahasin*.
6. Ali b. Babawayh, *Kitab al-Imama*, 13; al-Kulayni, *al-Kafi*, 1: 338. Ali b. Babawayh's reference in the volume (14) to the final number of the Imams as twelve reinforced other contemporary references discussed in the previous chapter, n. 25. See also Modarressi, *Crisis and Consolidation*, 102.
7. Chapter 23 contains miscellaneous texts.
8. Ali b. Babawayh, *Kitab al-Imama*, 25f; al-Saffar, *Basair al-Darajat*, 488, 486; al-Kulayni, *al-Kafi*, 1: 179–8.
9. Ali b. Babawayh, *ibid.*, 93.
10. Modarressi, *Crisis and Consolidation*, 97, n. 234, 102–3, n. 259. Cf. Amir-Moezzi, *The Divine Guide*, 13. On al-Numani, see al-Najashi, *Rijal al-Najashi*, 383–4. For a detailed discussion, see A. Newman, 'Between Qum and the West: The Occultation According to al-Kulayni and al-Katib al-Nu'mani', in F. Daftary (ed.), *Culture and Memory in Medieval Islam: Essays in Honour of Wilferd Madelung* (London, 2003), 94–108.
11. Muhammad b. Ibrahim, Ibn Abi Zaynab al-Numani, *Kitab al-Ghayba*, ed. and trans.M. J. al-Ghaffari (Tehran, 1363/1985), 26–53, esp. 30–1.
12. This total does not include, for example, the many unnumbered texts, especially in his lengthy introduction.
13. The next largest was chapter 14, with forty-eight traditions.
14. Al-Kulayni, *al-Kafi*, 1: 335–43.
15. Al-Numani, *Kitab al-Ghayba*, 242–7.
16. Al-Numani, *ibid.*, 253–4.
17. See, for example, al-Numani, *ibid.*, 274–5.
18. Al-Numani, *ibid.*, 278–80.
19. For an overview of the Buyids, see Kennedy, *The Prophet and the Age of the Caliphates*, 212–49. See also the sources cited n. 2 of Chapter 4.
20. On Sad, see al-Najashi, *Rijal al-Najashi*, 177–8; al-Tusi, *Rijal*, 431, 475; al-Tusi, *al-Fihrist*, 101. Sad also composed a work on sects. He is not to be confused with the Sunni scholar Abul-Hasan Ali b. Ismail al-Ashari (d. *c.* 935), who also authored a work in this genre (*Maqalat al-Islamiyyin*), and was the 'founder' of the Ashari school of theology. See W. M. Watt, 'Al-Ashari, Abu'l-Hasan', *EI2*. On both, see n. 7 of the Introduction.
21. On Ibn Qulawayh, see al-Najashi, *ibid.*, 123–4; al-Tusi, *Rijal*, 458; al-Tusi, *al-Fihrist*, 42–3. On *Kamil*, see al-Tihrani, *al-Dharia*, 17: 255. The edition of the text used herein is available at: http://www.rafed.net/books/doaa/kamil/index.html, accessed 12 January 2011.
22. See also the sources in the previous note. R. T. Mortel notes that a number of Husaynids were settled in Ikhshid Egypt in the early tenth century. See his 'The Origins and Early

History of the Husaynid Amirate of Madina to the End of the Ayyubid Period', *Studia Islamica*, 74 (1991), 64–5.

23. See n. 70 of Chapter 2.
24. Ibn Qulawayh, *Kamil al-Ziyarat*, 159f.
25. Ibn Qulawayh, *ibid.*, 165f, 191f, 207. One of the narrators of texts in chapter 71 came from a sayyid known to have been in Egypt. See Muhsin al-Amin, *Ayan al-Shia* (Beirut, 1983), 4: 154–6.
26. Ibn Qulawayh, *ibid.*, 288f, esp. 299, 292. See also the reference to al-Sahib b. Abbad's poetry to visitors to Karbala at n. 47.
27. Ibn Qulawayh, *ibid.*, 297.
28. The introduction to Ibn Babawayh, *Maani al-Akhbar* (Qum, 1361) 17f, provides the best dating of his whereabouts. See also M. J. McDermott, 'Ebn Babawayh', *EIr*; Akhtar, *Early Shiite Imamiyyah Thinkers*, 39f.
29. On the 962 date, see Ibn Babawayh, *Uyun Akhbar al-Rida* (Tehran, n.d.), at chapter 69. On the debates, see Akhtar, *ibid.*, 43. On Abul-Fadl, see Kramer, *Humanism in the Renaissance of Islam*, 241f.
30. See, for example, Momen, *Introduction to Shii Islam*, 173–5; Halm, *Shiism*, 43–4, 54–5. On the first apparent reference by Jafar b. al-Hasan al-Hilli, al-Muhaqqiq, (d. 1277) to these as 'the four books', see Chapter 6.
31. Al-Tihrani, *al-Dharia*, 22: 232f, 17: 245–6; Akhtar, *Early Shiite Imamiyyah Thinkers*, 49–50, who gives the total as 5,963; A. al-Fadli, *Introduction to Hadith, including 'Dirayat al-hadith' by al-Shahid al-Thani*, trans. N. Virjee (London, 2002), 82, who gives the total as 5,998. Cf. Amir-Moezzi, *The Divine Guide*, 158, n. 143. On these other compilations, see also A. Newman, 'The Recovery of the Past: Ibn Babawayh, Baqir al-Majlisi and Safawid Medical Discourse', *Iran: Journal of the British Institute of Persian Studies*, 50 (2012), 109–27. Ibn Babawayh's *Madinat al-Ilm*, although lost by the Safawid period, was said to be larger than *al-Faqih*. See al-Tihrani, *ibid.*, 20: 251–3.
32. On the title, see al-Tihrani, *ibid.*, 18: 137, 2: 283. Modarressi, *Crisis and Consolidation*, 254, includes *al-Hayra* in the title. The edition used herein is, in fact, entitled only *Kamal al-Din fi Timam al-Nima* (Qum, 1405/1363).
33. Of the sixty-six traditions cited in chapter 22, for example, twenty-seven were cited from his father, with the next largest number (twelve) being cited from Ibn al-Walid, on whom see below. Eighteen of chapter 21's twenty-three texts were collected from his father.
34. 'Today, I have perfected your religion and completed my blessings for you.'
35. Ibn Babawayh, *Kamal*, 2f, 16–17. The verse reads: 'This is of the news of the *Ghayb* (the unseen) which We reveal by Inspiration to you [O Muhammad]. You were not [present] with them when they arranged their plan together, and [also, while] they were plotting.'
36. Modarressi, *Crisis and Consolidation*, 145–67, 169f.
37. Ibn Babawayh's father is credited with one unnumbered tradition, for a total of sixty-six.
38. The remaining twenty-seven chapters in this section contained nine or fewer texts; twenty-one chapters contained four or fewer traditions.
39. Ibn Babawayh, *Kamal*, 512, 516–17.
40. 32:4: 'that thou mayest warn a people to whom no Warner has come before thee'; 34:45: 'And We gave them no books which they studied, nor did We send to them any Warner before thee.'
41. He cited 57:18, 'Know that Allah gives life to the Earth after its death. We have made clear to you the *ayat* (the signs)', and noted it was *al-qaim* who would do this.
42. Ibn Babawayh, *Kamal*, 656f, esp. 656–7, 666–7, 679–80.
43. Ibn Babawayh, *ibid.*, 649f. Cf. al-Kulayni, *al-Kafi*, 8: 310.

44. Ibn Babawayh, *ibid.*, 434f, esp. 440, 442, 443. Cf. *al-Kafi*, 1: 329–32; these traditions are conflicting and it is not always clear that the sightings occurred after the occultation.

45. Ibn Babawayh, *ibid.*, 424f, esp. 431, 432. Cf. al-Kulayni, *al-Kafi*, 1: 514–25, with thirty-one traditions. In *al-Kafi*, there are only a handful of references herein to Uthman b. Said and his son, later said to have been the Hidden Imam's first and second *safirs* (a term nowadays translated as 'ambassador') as *wakils* of the eleventh Imam (1: 329–30/1), but none to any of his three successors, who were Iraq-based contemporaries of al-Kulayni.

46. See n. 28 above. A text (2: 121) was collected from a Nishaburi perfumer in 962, while another (2: 159) was collected in Qum in 949. The edition of the text is Tehran, n.d.

47. Sindawi, 'Visit to the Tomb of al-Husayn', 247. See M. Pomerantz, 'A Shii–Mutazili Poem of al-Sahib b. 'Abbad (d. 385/995)', in B. Craig (ed.), *Ismaili and Fatimid Studies in Honor of Paul E. Walker* (Chicago, 2010), 131–50, for Mutazili poetry, as well as poetry on cursing Muawiya and extolling Ali.

48. Madelung, ''Abd al-Jabbar b. Ahmad', *EIr*. On Ibn Abbad, see M. Pomerantz, 'Ebn Abbad, Esmail', *EIr*; Cl. Cahen *et al.*, 'Ibn Abbad' *EI2*. Madelung, *Religious Trends*, 30, 90. See also Kramer, *Humanism in the Renaissance of Islam, passim*, esp. 259f. On the crackdown on Sunni and Shii traditionism, see Pomerantz; McDermott, 'Ebn Babawayh'. See also McDermott's discussion of Abd al-Jabbar's critique of the faith's reliance on traditions, in his *The Theology of al-Shaikh al-Mufid* (Beirut, 1978), *passim*, esp. 53f.

49. Ibn Babawayh, *Uyun*, 1: 154f. See also D. Thomas, 'Two Muslim–Christian Debates from the Early Shi'ite Tradition', *Journal of Semitic Studies*, 33 (Spring 1988), 53–80, based on Ibn Babawayh's *al-Tawhid*. The version of the second exchange given herein is much truncated.

50. 'Most assuredly, we will give victory to our messengers and to those who believe, both in this world and on the day the witnesses are summoned.' Ibn Babawayh, *Uyun*, 1: 179f.

51. Ibn Babawayh, *ibid.*, 1: 222f. The portion of sura 40 cited in the text is: 'Then we caused to inherit the Book those whom We have chosen of Our servants . . .'

52. Ibn Babawayh, *ibid.*, 2: 138f.

53. Ibn Babawayh, *ibid.*, 2: 167f.

54. Ibn Babawayh, *ibid.*, 2: 254f (esp. 256, 257–8, 260–1), 2: 267f. Al-Kulayni (*al-Kafi*, 4: 584f) had cited five traditions on the importance of visiting Tus, and Ibn Qulawayh (318–23) had collected thirteen traditions.

55. Ibn Babawayh, *ibid.*, 2: 278f, esp. 279, 285–6, 274–83.

56. The work was translated by A. A. A. Fyzee as *A Shiite Creed* (Calcutta, 1942) and a very slightly revised version (Tehran, 1999) is available at: http://www.wofis.com/Publications. aspx?bookID=4, accessed 19 May 2011. All quotations and page references herein to this text are from this edition. In a prefatory note (xxxix–xl) to the 1999 edition, the 978 date – on which see al-Tihrani, *al-Dharia*, 2: 226 – is disputed and it is argued the work post-dates material in Ibn Babawayh's *Amali*. McDermott ('Ebn Babawayh'), noting that this was the second of Ibn Babawayh's works in this genre, offers the 978–9 date for the third, the same *Amali*. On the terminology, see Ibn Babawayh, *Creed*, 28

57. Ibn Babawayh, *Creed*, 27–83, esp. 33. The eponymous 'founder' of Asharism, Abul-Hasan al-Ashari, died in 935–6, whereas Mutazili tendencies are generally said to be visible from the eighth century, in both Basra and Baghdad. See D. Gimaret, 'Mutazila', *EI2*.

58. Ibn Babawayh, *ibid.*, 61, 63. Ibn Babawayh allowed only that suras 93 and 94 and 105 and 106 might be combined: 'He who asserts that we [i.e., the Twelvers] say that it is greater in extent than this (the present text) is a liar (77).'

59. Ibn Babawayh, *ibid.*, 84–6.

60. Ibn Babawayh, *ibid.*, 93, 99–103.

61. On the Sunnis, see W. Hallaq, *A History of Islamic Legal Theories* (Cambridge, 1997).
62. 'O ye who believe! Obey Allah and obey the Messenger and those of you who are in authority.'
63. Ibn Babawayh, *Creed*, 105f.
64. Thus, for example, he included no texts on *al-jihad* or *al-amr* and *al-nahy*.
65. Although he did name some of the works he consulted – including al-Barqi's *al-Mahasin* and a text of Sad b. Abdallah himself – he noted that the volume comprised texts taken from well-known sources, each of which was itself a *marja*. He did not formally name *al-Kafi* as one. Ibn Babawayh, *Man la Yahduruhu al-Faqih*, ed. H. M. al-Khurasan, 4 vols (Najaf, 1378), 1: 2–4. See also Ibn Babawayh, *Maani*, 24. On the date of 983, see McDermott, 'Ebn Babawayh'. On the compilation itself, see al-Tihrani, *al-Dharia*, 22: 233, 17: 245–6.
66. Ibn Babawayh, *al-Faqih*, 3: 6.
67. Ibn Babawayh, *ibid.*, 4: 51.
68. Ibn Babawayh, *ibid.*, 1: 266–70, 274–8, 251.
69. Ibn Babawayh, *ibid.*, 1: 247f; al-Kulayni, *al-Kafi*, 3: 375–6.
70. Ibn Babawayh, *ibid.*, 1: 264; al-Kulayni, *ibid.*, 3: 377–8.
71. Ibn Babawayh, *ibid.*, 1: 320–4; al-Kulayni, *ibid.*, 3: 459.
72. Ibn Babawayh, *ibid.*, 2: 2–5, 15f. Cf. al-Kulayni, *ibid.*, 1: 539–43.
73. Ibn Babawayh, *ibid.*, 2: 22. Cf. n. 62 of Chapter 2.
74. Ibn Babawayh, *ibid.*, 3: 2–3.
75. Ibn Babawayh, *ibid.*, 3: 108. This tradition was later cited by al-Sharif al-Murtada in his essay on working for *al-sultan*. See Madelung, 'A Treatise', 29.
76. Ibn Babawayh, *al-Faqih*, ed. A. A. al-Ghaffari (Qum, n.d.), 2: 572f, 586–92, 594–8, 598, 600–18. See al-Kulayni, *al-Kafi*, 4: 575, 578; Ibn Qulawayh, *Kamil al-Ziyarat*, 274, 275.
77. On those involving prayer, see Ibn Babawayh, *al-Faqih*, 1: 47, 102, 164, 252, 262, 271, 290, 331, 341, 380, 382 – all 'new' to the collection. See also 2: 128. See al-Kulayni, *al-Kafi*, 2: 217; 2: 171, 305; 4: 323.
78. H. Modarressi, *An Introduction to Shii Law* (London, 1984), 35–6.
79. Modarressi, *ibid.*

CHAPTER 4

Majority and minority: rationalism on the defensive in the later Buyid period

Both academics who study the faith and the faithful themselves are well acquainted with scholars of the later Buyid period such as Muhammad b. Muhammad b. Numan, known as al-Shaykh al-Mufid (d. 1022), Ali b. al-Husayn, al-Sharif al-Murtada (d. 1044) and their student Muhammad b. al-Hasan al-Tusi (d. 1067). All three were based in Baghdad. All three are known for promoting, to varying degrees, recourse to human-derived tools of analysis and interpretation on a par with, or even to the relative exclusion of, the revealed texts in the interpretation of doctrine and practice. The works of all three comprise the bulk of the extant primary source materials produced in the remaining years of the Buyid period to the capture of Baghdad in 1055 by the Sunni Saljuks. Unsurprisingly, therefore, it is their 'voices' that are privileged in discussions of developments in Twelver doctrine and practice in this period.

The atmosphere in which these scholars lived and worked offered a set of external, but also internal, challenges that were very different from those that Ibn Babawayh and al-Kulayni faced. The latter have not been well studied to date. Re-examined in the context of such challenges, these scholars' writings in fact reveal that they both disagreed among themselves on issues of doctrine and practice, and also that their views were very much in the minority in the Twelver community at the time.

The Shia in Baghdad: a beleaguered community

By the Buyid period, Baghdad was a well-developed urban centre with a history of sectarianism. Nevertheless, the later Sunni-authored accounts of events in the life of the city in these years suggest that the Buyids only exacerbated that sectarianism. By contrast, the Sunni caliphs, especially al-Qadir (reg. 991–1031), are portrayed as defenders of Sunnism, and, especially, the traditionism of the Sunni 'popular' classes.

In the years immediately following the Buyids' arrival, sectarian tensions continued apace. From 946 to 961, Sunnis plundered the al-Karkh quarter, the Shii Bab al-Taq was struck by fire and further sectarian strife forced the government to send in troops and banish some Shia.

In this already tense atmosphere, in 947 the Buyid amir Muizz al-Dawla (d. 967) embellished the tombs of Imams Musa and al-Jawad at al-Kazimayn and, in 963, he is said to have permitted public commemoration of Imam al-Husayn's death.[1] Despite the resulting anti-Shii riots the next year, the Shia commenced the commemoration of Ghadir Khumm. Sunni elements again reacted negatively, but the amirs are said to have persisted. After Adud al-Dawla (d. 983) took Baghdad from his cousin, he ordered the refurbishment of the graves of Imam Ali at Najaf (where he himself was buried) and Imam al-Husayn at Karbala.

Hanbali-oriented, Sunni 'popular' responses were supported by the caliph. Riots in the 990s forced the cancellation of Muharram ceremonies, and in these years, also according to later sources, Sunnis began commemorating two events – including *Yawm al-Ghar*, when Abu Bakr stayed in a cave with the Prophet – that fell just after Ashura and Ghadir Khumm.

Muharram commemorations are reported in 1002 and 1015, and riots are reported in 1006–7 and from 1016 to 1018.

In 1017, al-Qadir banned discussion of Shii and Mutazili doctrines. In 1018, he denounced the Mutazili view that the Quran had been created, affirmed the caliphate of the first three caliphs and dismissed the preacher at the Shii Baratha mosque. In 1026, special taxes were imposed on al-Karkh and the army invaded the quarter. In 1029, the preacher at the Baratha mosque was replaced, and Shii elements stoned his replacement. In 1031, Sunnis blocked the path of Qummi pilgrims to Kufa, and later, with Turkish elements, attacked al-Karkh. In 1049, Ashura commemorations generated riots. In 1051, Sunnis attacked al-Karkh and the graves of Imam Musa and Imam al-Jawad at al-Kazimayn. In 1053–4, as the Sunni Saljuks approached, there are reports of further conflict inside Baghdad.[2]

Read carefully, the sources do suggest that grievances against the wealthy underlay some of the period's discontent. Hunger/famine, high inflation and attacks on public institutions and on the better off in Baghdad over the late tenth and early eleventh centuries are attested. Al-Karkh's Shii merchants were attacked, but so were commercial and court-associated administrative elements.[3]

Shii young men and *ayyarun* – a term loosely referring to groups whose codes of behaviour and actions resemble those of chivalrous groups[4] – are also portrayed as actively organising Muharram commemorations and promoting the idea of a Shii Quran, as was clearly attested by Ibn Babawayh in his *al-Itiqadat*.[5] Twelver elites were held responsible by the court and non-Shii elements for the actions of these 'popular' elements. Following clashes between Sunni and Shii *ayyarun* in 1003–4, al-Mufid, though uninvolved, was said to have been banished. In 1006–7, after Sunni elements massed to curse al-Mufid, al-Karkh-based groups then attacked the houses of two prominent Sunni jurists.

The occasion for the later disorder in fact appears to have been the appearance of a Shii version of the Quran, known as the 'Ibn Masud' recension. Sunni scholars are said to have ordered the text burned, and a Shii who insulted those responsible was arrested and ordered executed by the caliph. Al-Karkh's Shia then attacked Sunni quarters and shouted support for the Fatimid Shii caliph. The caliph sent Sunni bands into the Shii quarters. Shii 'notables and merchants' publicly apologised to the caliph. Although again uninvolved, al-Mufid was exiled from the city.[6]

In 1019, after further riots, al-Mufid was banished again. In 1025, popular elements set fire to al-Murtada's house and most of al-Karkh. In 1031, the house of a prominent al-Karkh merchant was set aflame.[7]

The Sunni sources suggest also that Shii 'popular' elements were not always enamoured of their elite co-religionists. In 1030, the caliph himself ordered al-Murtada to organise Muharram commemorations. The Shii population opposed this and riots are reported throughout the city.[8]

Although the later Sunni sources depict Buyid Baghdad as continuously wracked by sectarian conflict, in fact court-based patronage over the period insured that Baghdad and provincial courts and centres in modern-day Iran – Hamadan, Isfahan, Rayy and Shiraz especially, but also Nishabur and Bukhara – as well as Basra and Aleppo were all also centres of vibrant intellectual life.

Religious scholars and poets flocked to and travelled between these centres. They served as administrators and accompanied their patrons on their journeys and military ventures. These patrons included the amir Adud al-Dawla, viziers – including both the Shii al-Amid and al-Sahib b. Abbad, the latter a poet and the possessor of a large library in Rayy. These and other senior and provincial officials were active patrons of the intellectual classes. All these gathered Sunni, Shia (including Zaydis, Ismailis and Twelvers), Kharijites, Christians, Jews and Sabians for wide-ranging discussions on such varied subjects as poetry, astrology, grammar and, of course, the religious sciences.[9] The Buyid amir, Adud al-Dawla, owner of a magnificent library in Shiraz, is said to have visited a discussion group organised by al-Mufid himself.[10]

Al-Shaykh al-Mufid

Al-Shaykh al-Mufid, a member of a sub-clan of the Quraysh, was born *c.* 948–50, between Baghdad and Mosul. Brought to Baghdad and settled in al-Karkh, he studied with Ibn Qulawayh and Ibn Babawayh, and Shii rationalists such as Ibn Abil-Junayd. Al-Mufid attracted the attention of Adud al-Dawla and the caliph al-Qadir – al-Mufid was one of the Sunni and Shii scholars whom the caliph obliged to sign a 1011 document denouncing Fatimid claims to being descendants of Ali and was banished from the city when the Shii 'popular classes got 'out of hand' – as well as the court-appointed Alid *naqib*, the Musawi sayyid Abu Abdallah Muhammad (d. 957–8), and his son and successor, Abu Ahmad. The latter engaged al-Mufid to teach his sons al-Murtada (b. 967) and al-Radi (b. 970), who later succeeded their father to the post.[11]

Al-Mufid is best known for his defence of the faith against Sunnis such as the traditionist al-Baqillani (d. 1013), the Mutazili Qadi Abd al-Jabbar, Hanafi and Hanbali jurists, Sunni grammarians, as well as non-Twelver Shia such as the Zaydis.[12] His *al-Ifsah* (*The Plain Statement*)[13] and his *al-Fusul al-Ashara fil Ghayba* (*Ten Chapters on the Occultation*) reflect attention to such audiences.[14] His efforts signalled acceptance of Buyid attempts to rekindle the pro-Mutazili alliance of al-Mamun's day against the caliph's promotion of traditionism.

His interaction with fellow believers is, however, less well studied to date. Like the works of Ibn Babawayh, al-Mufid's works reveal both the extent of disagreement over matters of both doctrine and practice, and that to which al-Mufid's own methodology and interpretations were not, in fact, widely accepted within the community at the time.

In his *Awail al-Maqalat* (*The Principle Theses*) he refers to disagreements between Twelvers, whom he refers to as Imamis,[15] and Sunni and other Shii groups. But he also refers frequently to disagreements within the Twelver community. He agreed, for example, with the *fuqaha* and the traditionists that the Imams heard the angels speak without seeing them, but noted that the al-Nawbakhtis and others rejected this.[16] On the very real issue of authenticity of the Uthmanic Codex of the Quran, as his teacher Ibn Babawayh, al-Mufid agreed with the view that only 'interpretations and explanations' were missing from the extant text. But, he noted, the al-Nawbakhtis, some Twelver practitioners of *kalam*, *ahl al-fiqh* (legists) and others had disagreed.[17]

In his commentary on *al-Itiqadat*, al-Mufid condemned his own teacher's citing of traditions that censured *al-jadal* (dialectics) and its practitioners. He argued that, in fact, the practice of *al-kalam* (theology and theological debate) was required of those who were masters of the discipline such as, he noted, himself.[18] He criticised Qummi reliance on *ahad* traditions, and stated that some of Ibn Babawayh's views mirrored those of unidentified elements who accepted the principle of the transmigration of souls. This, he said, allowed Sunnis to accuse the Shia of *zandaqa* (atheism) and was the result of using traditions whose authenticity was not verified.[19]

In an effort to calm sectarian tensions, al-Mufid also objected to Ibn Babawayh's statement that all the Imams had been poisoned. The poisoning of Imam al-Rida 'cannot be confirmed', he said, and he described reports of the poisoning of other Imams as 'confused'. Al-Mufid also argued for the infallibility of the Imams, breaking both with such extreme Imami rationalists as the al-Nawbakhtis, who had denied that the Imams had performed miracles, and such Qummi traditionists as Ibn Babawayh's teacher Ibn al-Walid.[20] Al-Mufid also denounced Ibn Babawayh's system for dealing with problematic traditions.[21]

As to his understanding of the hierarchical nature of authority with the community, in *al-Fusul al-Mukhtara*, al-Mufid criticised those 'of the Sawad and outlying districts, the Bedouin, both Arab and Persian, and the common people' as having 'no obligation to know and reason upon proofs owing to their lack of *uqul* (wisdom)'.[22]

Al-Mufid's great work of *ahkam*, *al-Muqnia fil-Fiqh*, offers evidence of his claims for the authority of the senior clerics over matters of daily practice during the occultation, as well as of divisions within the community on these issues and, again, of the minority status of his own interpretations.

On the collection and distribution of *al-zakat* revenues, for example, without citing any supporting traditions, al-Mufid stated that if the Imam were absent, *al-zakat* should be delivered to whomever the Imam had appointed. If *al-sufara* – whom he did not identify – were absent, the people should deliver *al-zakat* to 'the trustworthy *fuqaha*' as they are 'more knowledgeable' as to its disposition.[23]

Al-Mufid noted four opinions within the community on what to do with *al-khums*' revenues during *al-ghayba*: that the obligation to pay these lapsed; that *al-khums* should be buried for the Imam (*al-qaim*) to recover when he reappeared; that there was a connection between the progeny of the family of the Prophet and the poor among the Shia, based on the principle of *istishab* (permission for the continuation of something already permitted); and that the revenue should be set aside for *Sahib al-Amr*. If the believer felt he might die before the Imam's reappearance, he is to give it

to someone whom he trusts insofar as his *aql* (wisdom)
and *diyanatihi* (his faith) to give it to the Imam . . .
or he commends it to someone who takes his place
in *al-thiqa* (trustworthiness) and *al-diyana* (faith)
until the Imam of the Age appears.

Without citing any further evidence, he said this was *awdah* (the more clear). He noted that the same question had been raised with respect to *al-zakat*. That tax was to be commended to someone who would convey it to those who deserve it.[24] Al-Mufid stopped short, however, of clarifying to whom he was referring.

In the short section on the implementation of *al-hudud*, al-Mufid declared that the Imams 'entrusted [their undertaking] to the *fuqaha* of their Shia when possible', if they were not afraid of *Sultan al-Jawr* (a tyrannous ruler). Fear caused the obligation to undertake these to lapse. Al-Mufid then explained that the Imams *fawwadu* (entrusted) the *fuqaha* to gather the community together for the five (daily) prayers, prayers on special occasions, and other prayers when they were able and to render judgements among believers. This, he said, was proven in the *akhbar* (traditions) – although he cited none – and judged correct by those who were knowledgeable.[25] The *fuqaha*, or those among them who were appointed by *Sultan al-Jawr* to render judgements, could render judgements contrary to the *hukm* (ruling) of the Imams only 'if they were compelled to do this, based on *taqiyya* and fear for the faith and oneself'. Only potential bloodshed of believers exempted one from this.[26]

Al-Mufid's answers to eleven questions posed to him from Sari, in Mazandiran, in his *al-Masail al-Sarawiyya* also reveal efforts to claim authority for senior clerics in the Imam's absence and to critique Twelver traditionism.

In one reply, al-Mufid stated that the individual was not permitted 'to decide for himself' if there were conflicts between the Quran, the *Sunna* (which, for the Shia included the Imams' traditions) and rational demonstration' until he had both 'knowledge of such matters and the skill in reasoning'. Lacking these, 'let him go to one who does know'. If the individual did act on the basis of his own judgement and was right he would not be rewarded. If he did so and was wrong, he would not be excused.

He criticised Ibn Babawayh[27] and the traditionists for citing *ahad* or otherwise untrustworthy traditions. These, he said, were not 'people of reason and investigation', nor were they 'in the habit of thinking out and discussing what they relate'.

He also critiqued others such as Ibn Abil-Junayd for relying both on Sunni methodology, including *qiyas*, and *ahad* traditions.[28] In a likely reference to the tradition reported via Umar b. Hanzala, al-Mufid referred to Imam Jafar's injunction concerning hesitation and explained that it meant that the layman should refer the matter in question to 'someone more learned than himself'. This expert, in turn, should employ rational proofs and avoid recourse to such tools as analogy. Al-Mufid named himself as one such expert, noting that he had 'given answers about many disputed traditions in questions that came to me from Nishabur, Mosul, Fars, and the district known as Mazandiran'.[29]

On the Uthmanic Codex of the Quran – also addressed in *Awail al-Maqalat* – he rejected *ahad* traditions on the matter. Here, as his teacher Ibn Babawayh, al-Mufid again held that the extant version should be accepted, but conceded that only the awaited *Mahdi* had the full text.[30]

Against the background of contemporary controversies over visitation to nearby shrines in this period, but in distinction from his teacher Ibn Qulawayh, in his *al-Muqnia* visitation to Karbala did not take any precedence over visiting other sites.[31] The same obtained with regard to visiting the Khurasan site of Imam al-Rida, to whose legacy his teacher Ibn Babawayh had devoted so much attention.[32] In al-Mufid's separate work on *ziyara*, *Kitab al-Mazar* (*The Book of the Shrine*) visitation to Imam al-Husayn, as well as Fatima and others of the Imams did attract merit, but – as in *al-Muqnia* – it is visitation generally that emerges as the focus of the work's attention, not that to any one site in particular.[33]

Further efforts by al-Mufid to downplay sectarian tensions are in evidence in his *Kitab al-Irshad* (*Book of Guidance*), completed sometime before 987–8. The volume was composed for an otherwise unknown petitioner who appears to have been either personally uncertain about, or facing questions about, the Imams and their lives.[34]

Volume 1 deals solely with the life of Imam Ali, including the manner in which the Prophet relied on Ali and designated him as his successor. These accounts were mainly drawn, if not by explicit citation, from early biographies of the Prophet by Ibn Ishaq (d. 768), al-Waqidi (d. 823), the historian al-Tabari (d. 923), who were all Sunnis, and the Iranian Shii Abul-Faraj al-Isfahani (d. 967), author of the famous *Kitab al-Aghani* and an associate of the Hamdanid Sayf al-Dawla (ruled to 967) and then the Buyid vizier al-Sahib b. Abbad.

Al-Mufid shows that Ali was the logical choice to be the Prophet's successor. He cites Ali's legal judgements, portraying him as equal to Daud (David) in his legal knowledge, and many of Ali's speeches. Rejected by such earlier 'extreme' rationalists as the al-Nawbakhtis, al-Mufid also cited the many miracles ascribed to Ali, including military accomplishments and a foreknowledge of events, including his own death. Al-Mufid documented many of these with reference to traditions.[35]

Volume 2 deals with the lives of the succeeding Imams, not as full biographies to be sure but – utilising traditions that were available in the above-named collections of Twelver traditions, especially *al-Kafi* – focusing on disputes on the line of succession and particular qualities for which they were noted. Al-Mufid noted documents inherited by the Imams from the Prophet and Fatima which were said to have contained the names of all twelve Imams, the Imams' possession of certain of the Prophet's weapons and statements of the Prophet as recorded by Ali. As Ali, so the Imams are endowed with foreknowledge and the performance of various miracles – again aspects of their personalities disparaged by others within the community.

If his descriptions of these aspects of the Imams' lives accorded with those of al-Saffar and al-Kulayni, unlike his own teacher Ibn Babawayh al-Mufid, again, records none as having been poisoned.

The birth of the twelfth Imam is firmly attested, again by reference to traditions. Al-Mufid does not address the occultation *per se*, but he does cite traditions on those signs that will foreshadow *al-qaim*'s return.[36]

Al-Sharif al-Murtada

Al-Murtada was born in 966, a descendant of Imams Ali and Musa. His grandfather, father and brother were *naqibs* of the city's community. His father lost his post as *naqib* in the middle of sectarian riots in the city, was imprisoned, along with other Shii notables, by Adud al-Dawla himself and lost all his property.

Al-Murtada's younger brother al-Radi (970–1015) was a student of Qadi Abd al-Jabbar, other Mutazili scholars and a Maliki *faqih* who gifted a house to him. Al-Radi held the respect of the caliph al-Qadir and, for his poetry, that of al-Sahib b. Abbad. Al-Radi lost the *naqib* post when he refused to apologise to the Abbasid caliph for an unflattering poem – indeed, some of his poetry explicitly challenged the legitimacy of both the Umayyads and the Abbasids.

Al-Radi is also known for his assembly of *Nahj al-Balaghah* (*The Path of Eloquence*) a compilation of sermons, letters and sayings of Ali on a wide variety of issues.

Al-Murtada became *naqib* after al-Radi. Both brothers were said to be enormously wealthy. Al-Murtada was said to have owned some eighty nearby villages, had a large school, supported many students – including some non-Muslim students of astronomy – and had a library of some 80,000 volumes.[37]

By comparison with al-Mufid, al-Murtada is generally understood as having adopted a more rationalist approach to the understanding, and defence, of the faith, in which he accorded the traditions little if any notice. In fact, he was known to have argued that all traditions were forged or *ahad*.[38] On such theological issues as the infallibility of the Prophet and the Imams he was therefore closer to Abd al-Jabbar and Basran Mutazilism than al-Mufid, although his *al-Shafi* (*The Unequivocal*) on the Imamate, was a critique of a work by Abd al-Jabbar.[39]

Al-Murtada was active in addressing matters of jurisprudence as well, approved of *ijma* (consensus) as a proof and held that believers had to follow the rulings of a trained legal scholar. His *al-Dharia* (*The Means*) was one very earliest, extant, systematic works on Twelver *usul al-fiqh* (principles of jurisprudence) in which he distinguished between key principles and processes of doctrine and those relating to jurisprudence.[40]

As al-Mufid, al-Murtada was much more involved in disputes with fellow Twelvers than has been noted to date. Close attention to certain of his works reveal both his efforts, like those of al-Mufid, to assert the authority of his views on issues of doctrine and practice, and also the presence of a range of views on these across the community.

His correspondence with elements of the community in Hamdanid-controlled Mosul, for example, attests that his views on matters of doctrine and practice were not always widely accepted.

In opening remarks to a reply to some 110 questions put to him from the Mosulis, al-Murtada critiqued the use of *qiyas* and *ahad* traditions by some in the community. Using these, he argued, some of the faithful might be inclined to accept anthropomorphism. He did approve of *ijma*, arguing that during the occultation in any gathering where not all the identities of all were known 'the Imam is as one whom we do not know'.

The replies that follow cover questions coming from Mosul on such issues as ablutions, prayer, *al-zakat*, *al-khums*, marriage, divorce, adultery, inheritance, theft and relations with *ahl al-kitab*.[41] That he noted he had replied to some of these questions before, in a 990 essay, suggests that he felt the Mosulis were wilful in their disagreement on a range of doctrinal matters.

Herein, for example, the Mosulis queried *muta* marriage. In reply, al-Murtada appealed to *ijma* and Quran 4:24, especially use therein of the term *istimta* (deriving benefit) that, in law, can refer only to an *iqd* (a special fixed-term agreement/contract) that did not involve 'pleasure'. He concluded that such marriage was practiced during the time of the Prophet. Absent a prohibition against it, the practice must be permissible.[42]

Occasionally, al-Murtada referred to the *tariqat al-ihtiyat* (the path of caution) as a proof. Thus, on *salat al-duha* (the voluntary supererogatory prayer organised in the morning, mid-morning or late morning, and valued among the Sunnis), al-Murtada declared that the prayer was '*bida* [innovation] and . . . not permitted'. His evidence? 'The path of caution and *ijma* together.'[43]

From Diyar Bakr came a series of queries, including one on the permissibility of the Friday congregational prayer if someone of whose faith there was uncertainty led it. This was a clear suggestion that such was already the practice in this far-off community, perhaps based on the tradition cited by Ibn Babawayh from his father in *al-Faqih* that cited *taqiyya* as a basis for praying with a non-Twelver prayer leader.

Al-Murtada's reply was brief but categorical: someone who does not meet the legal requirements cannot lead the prayer. He also ruled against performing the prayer if an Imami and an opponent led it together. Absent 'a just imam, or he whom the just imam *nasabahu* (has designated)', the noontime prayer was to be prayed.[44]

In his replies to the Mosulis and those in Diyar Bakr, al-Murtada also addressed some very basic issues related to the categories of items subject to *al-khums* and to its recipients. In the first case, again, he cited only *ijma* as evidence supporting his ruling. Al-Mufid had addressed *al-khums* and that al-Murtada also addressed such issues relating to *al-khums* in his later *al-Intisar* suggests continued disagreement within segments of the community on the processes relating to the tax.[45]

To be sure, these several works lacked references to the authority of the community's senior *ulama* as explicit as those of al-Mufid. In his more general *Jumal al-Ilm wal-Amal* (*Compendia of Knowledge and Practice*), al-Murtada was perfectly clear: it was 'best' to deliver *al-zakat* to the Imam 'and to his successors *al-naibin anu* (deputising on his behalf).' If this was not possible then 'the trustworthy *fuqaha*' should take delivery.[46] That he was not similarly explicit in his other writings on the subject above only further suggests al-Murtada's own sense that such claims were, or might prove, controversial in the communities in question.

Al-Murtada's 1026 essay on the permissibility of working for the established political institution was dedicated to a Twelver government official with whom he was on close terms. As cited in the essay, some of those opposing such service were clearly citing traditions. In his reply, al-Murtada argued that the Imams had permitted believers to hold office under *al-zalimun* (oppressors) and had permitted individuals in this situation to administer the *hudud*; he cited no traditions supporting this view. It was forbidden, he said also, to oppose the tenure in office of 'he whom *al-Imam al-Adil* [the Imam] appoints'. A pious person who accepted office under *al-Sultan al-Jair* (the tyrannous ruler) without duress was to be presumed to have done so for pious reasons. It was not permitted to oppose his tenure in office, and if he were seen to committing a usually reprehensible act, it was to be presumed he was doing so for good purpose.[47]

Al-Shaykh al-Tusi: blending revelation and reason

Muhammad b. al-Hasan al-Tusi was born four years after the death of Ibn Babawayh, in 995, in Tus, site of the tomb of the eighth Imam. He arrived in Baghdad *c.* 1017, aged about 23, and attached himself to al-Mufid and, at the latter's death in 1022, to al-Murtada. At al-Murtada's death in 1044–5, al-Tusi was appointed head of the capital's Imami community, and received an appointment in *kalam* from the Abbasid caliph. He studied with Sunnis and taught Sunni and Shii students alike. When the Saljuks entered Baghdad in 1055, the resulting sectarian riots engulfed al-Tusi's own house and various Shii libraries: thousands of texts are said to have been lost. Al-Tusi fled to Najaf, where he died in December 1067 and was buried.[48]

Al-Tusi is perhaps best known as the compiler of the last two of the 'four books' of the Imams' traditions completed before 1055. In fact, however, al-Tusi also authored works across a range of the religious sciences broader than any other Twelver scholar to this date. Al-Tusi, a student of these rationalist spokesmen for the community, recipient of the caliph's favour and an outsider, was certainly aware not only of sectarian tensions within the city, but also the challenges to his teachers' methodology and rulings coming from within the community. Al-Tusi's 'project' entailed the underpinning of his teachers' rulings by engaging with the Imams' traditions more actively than they.

The evolution in the manner of al-Tusi's recourse both to the traditions and to the rationalist methodology of his teachers can be traced in his opening remarks to his two collections of the Imams' traditions – *Tahdhib al-Ahkam* (*The Rectification of Rulings*), commenced after 1017 and completed after 1022; and *al-Istibsar* (*The Seeking of Insight*), his second collection of the traditions completed before al-Murtada's death in 1040 – as well as his *Uddat al-Usul* (*The Instrument of the Usul*), his discussion of Twelver jurisprudence, also completed before 1040.

Tahdhib contains some 13,600 traditions, fewer than *al-Kafi* but more than twice those in *al-Faqih*. *Tahdhib* was in fact a commentary on his teacher al-Mufid's *al-Muqnia* in which al-Tusi provided traditions in support of al-Mufid's rulings. As such, *Tahdhib* further suggests awareness by both al-Tusi and his teacher – who must have approved the project – of contemporary concerns with the original author's repeated failure to refer to the traditions in his rulings.

In his preface, al-Tusi made clear his intention to offer rulings by reconciling apparently inconsistent and contradictory traditions based on *ijma*, on discerning the original principles at work in these traditions, on their external elements and their implied meaning, or the falsity of the tradition or the weakness in the *isnad*.[49] That he soon abandoned citing full *isnad*,[50] tracing the tradition only as far back as earlier collections or books of the *usul*, underlined the object of the undertaking as the issuance of rulings. The principle of hesitation at points of doubt, established by al-Kulayni and seconded by Ibn Babawayh, was no longer applicable.

In opening remarks to *al-Istibsar* – with its approximately 6,000 texts, close to the number of those in *al-Faqih* – al-Tusi offered a system for the categorisation of the traditions much more developed than that in *Tahdhib*. Here he rejected reliance on traditions whose *isnad* was problematic – for example, *ahad* traditions – or did not conform to *adilla al-aql* (the rationalist proofs). The latter, he held, could, however, validate an otherwise *ahad* text. In the case of contradictory traditions, that of the 'more just' narrator was to be followed, or that narrated by the individual who has transmitted more traditions. *Ijma* was also cited. Absent again was reference to doubt and hesitation.[51]

The preface to *Udda* addressed the use of the revealed texts in a still more highly developed manner. Herein al-Tusi referred to various exegetical principles – non-Twelver in origin – needed to achieve proper understanding of the revelation. He also postulated a gap between those capable of the application of such tools and those incapable, and stated it was 'permissible' for the 'ordinary believer' to follow (using the term *taqlid*) the scholar. This, he said, was the view of the Basran Mutazila and 'most *fuqaha*'. He supported this statement not with traditions, but by noting that 'the common people among the Imamis' had always sought the opinion of the *ulama* and received rulings from them.[52] Elsewhere, following al-Murtada's definition of *ijma*, al-Tusi argued that, because the Imam was present in the community, albeit in occultation, if the opinion of every 'competent person' within the community who could have been the Imam at the time was ascertained, and if all of these agreed, then this constituted evidence as to the Imam's opinion.[53]

The traditions alone were thus not the ultimate repository of knowledge. They needed examination and interpretation by those trained in the techniques and application of the various disciplines to which he argued reference was necessary. Al-Mufid's recourse to the revelation had been limited. Al-Murtada had all but rejected any practical role for the revelation in delineating doctrine and practice. Al-Tusi called for re-engaging with the traditions, but only via the rationalist analytical tools that his two teachers had, in fact, delineated.

The rationalists and the *rijal*

The *isnad* of the Imams' traditions – that is, the list of all those who transmitted the text, beginning with the individual who had heard the statement from one of the Imams – was key to the reliability of the text itself. Neither al-Kulayni nor Ibn Babawayh had formally studied the *rijal* (literally, 'men', i.e., the narrators).[54]

Al-Tusi's concern with the tools to be applied to the traditions encompassed interest in the reliability of their narrators. He produced two works in this genre: an abridgement of al-Kashshi's work, which is all that remains of the original, and a volume on the companions of the various Imams. He also compiled a *fihrist* (index) of works written by key figures in the Twelver tradition to date.

In the process, al-Tusi did not shy away from passing judgement on the reliability of earlier figures. Those branded 'weak', 'corrupt', 'an exaggerator' included some whose names appeared in the *isnad* of traditions appearing in *al-Kafi*, for example. Some were now said to have given allegiance to Alids other than the twelve Imams themselves, particularly at the death of an Imam when succession was an issue. Some claimed special authority for themselves within the community. Others attributed special powers to the Imams, including the performance of miracles and foreknowledge of events, or claimed they themselves possessed such knowledge or that they were no longer obligated to perform such certain basic religious duties as prayer or fasting.

Ahmad b. Ali al-Asadi al-Najashi (d. 1058–9), who came from a family of prominent Shii scholars – his father had studied with Ibn Babawayh and an ancestor was a companion of Imam Jafar – also completed a work of biographies.[55]

Al-Najashi, from Kufa, was acquainted with Ahmad b. al-Husayn al-Ghadairi (d. 1058), another prominent figure in this field. The latter's father al-Husayn (d. 1020) had taught al-Tusi and al-Najashi and was himself a student of Ibn Babawayh, the latter's father and Ibn Qulawayh. His son's work in this genre addressed only those he deemed to be unreliable. Like al-Tusi, he did not mince his words, calling some 'liar', 'exaggerator', 'corrupt', 'fabricator of *hadiths*', or simply 'weak' or 'careless'. He did occasionally overturn earlier verdicts on some or note the reliability of others in some respects.[56]

Al-Tusi and the *ahkam/furu*

Al-Tusi's work with the traditions and the *rijal* laid the bases for rulings on key daily practices distinctive to the Twelver community offered in his works of *fiqh*, including *al-Nihaya* and his later *al-Mabsut* – both completed sometime after *al-Istibsar*, itself finished before 1040. His rulings were not always consistent, however, no doubt reflecting both the evolution in his own thinking, but very likely also the strength of alternate views within the community.

Across his several works of *fiqh* al-Tusi did consistently argue for the delegation of authority in judicial interpretation to those whom *Sultan al-Haqq* had given permission. In *al-Nihaya fi Mujjarad al-Fiqh wal-Fatawi* (*The Ultimate in Only Fiqh and Legal Rulings*), he said this meant the *fuqaha* when the *Sultan* (the Imam) could not do so themselves. In *al-Mabsut fil-Fiqh* (*The Detailed on Fiqh*), he carefully noted that such individuals must be knowledgeable in the Quran, the *Sunna* and *ijma, ikhtilaf* (the differences in rulings) and Arabic. As regards the Quran, the individual must be skilled in the appropriate exegetical principles.[57]

On the implementation of the *hudud*, in *al-Nihaya* al-Tusi at one point stated that these were to be implemented by those who undertook *ahkam*, not formally naming the *fuqaha*. He did allow that the individual could undertake some punishments.[58] Only elsewhere in the volume, in the section on *jihad*, did al-Tusi state that the Imami judge was also permitted and indeed authorised by the Imams to undertake *al-hudud* and *al-ahkam* in addition to exercising judicial authority *al-qada*.[59] In *al-Mabsut*, however, al-Tusi did not explicitly refer to the *fuqaha per se* or cite any formal delegation. He also noted that the individual could undertake the *hudud* in personal matters and the Imam in others.[60]

Al-Tusi's several discussions of Friday prayer during the occultation are especially noteworthy. For al-Mufid, the *fuqaha* could lead a variety of prayers, but not this prayer. In *al-Nihaya*, al-Tusi stated that the prayer was a religious obligation if the Imam or 'he whom the Imam designates' was present – echoing al-Murtada. Al-Murtada did not specify to whom he was referring and here al-Tusi himself did not make this clear. Elsewhere, in *al-Nihaya*, in discussing *jihad*, al-Tusi stated – only – that 'it is permissible' for the *fuqaha* to convoke this prayer and other prayers.[61] In *al-Mabsut*, he made no reference to the *fuqaha* as even being permitted to organise the prayer.[62]

On *zakat*, al-Mufid had stated that in the absence of the Imam or the *sufara*, the *fuqaha* were to handle *al-zakat* based on their being 'more knowledgeable as to its disposition' than someone who has no 'understanding of his faith'. Al-Murtada too was clear: the Imam, his *naib* or the 'trustworthy *fuqaha*' were to handle *al-zakat*.

Unusually in *Tahdhib*, and suggesting the contemporary controversial nature of the discussion, al-Tusi offered a comment on the matter before citing any of the Imams' traditions, and this not in the main section on *al-zakat*.

Herein he offered a schema of the line of authority after the Prophet that was much more detailed than that presented by al-Mufid and al-Murtada. In the Imam's absence, al-Tusi declared, the revenues should be delivered to 'his *khalifa*'. In the absence of the latter, they were to be given to *man nasabuhu fi maqamihi bi khassatihi* (he whom he appointed specifically in his place). In the absence of the *sufara*, to whom the preceding formula applied, it was 'obligatory to deliver it to *al-fuqaha al-mamunin* (the trustworthy fuqaha)', because, said al-Tusi, 'the *faqih* knows its place better than one who has no *fiqh* (knowledge)' – echoing Al-Mufid.[63]

In his later *al-Nihaya*, however, he stated that in the absence of the Imam or the latter's appointee, the revenues could be distributed directly to the recipients, although at such a time the shares of *al-muallafa qulubuhim, al-amilun* (the agents) and *fi sabil Allah/jihad* lapsed. This was because these depended upon the presence of the Imams or his appointee to carry out their functions. But, in the section on *zakat al-fitr*, the alms given at the end of Ramadan, al-Tusi stated that '[i]f there was no Imam it [*zakat al-fitr*] is delivered to the *fuqaha* . . . for them to distribute'.[64]

In *al-Mabsut*'s main section on *al-zakat*, al-Tusi backtracked. Herein he stated only that it was 'preferable' to deliver the revenues to 'the *ulama*' for distribution, though he did also note that the individual also could distribute these himself. As to *zakat al-fitr*, he maintained the retreat from his position in *Tahdhib*, stating only that it was 'recommended' that *zakat al-fitr* be delivered 'to the Imam or the *ulama*' for distribution as he/they saw fit. He added, however, that the believer could distribute it himself.[65]

Over the course of these works, al-Tusi also offered an increasingly detailed exposition of the categories of *al-zakat* recipients, to include such *masalih* (beneficial items) as the building of canals, mosques, assisting pilgrims, the *hajj* and holy warriors, and thus ensured the clergy a share in these revenues.[66]

Al-Tusi's discussions on *al-khums* also expanded on the categories of wealth subject to this tax.[67] As to its collection and distribution, al-Mufid had noted considerable disagreement on the issue, in regard to which he offered his own – clearly minority – preference.

In *Tahdhib*, al-Tusi in fact referred to his teacher's ruling. The traditions he then cited contained no specific statements by the Imams justifying al-Mufid's position. Al-Tusi himself made no further comment, either in support of al-Mufid's ruling or on the traditions with which he followed it.[68] Al-Mufid had also referred to three other views on its distribution during the Imam's absence.

By the time al-Tusi composed his *al-Nihaya* community views appear to have changed slightly. As al-Mufid, al-Tusi noted four opinions on the matter. Al-Mufid's third group was not mentioned in *al-Nihaya*. Al-Tusi's fourth group, with whose position al-Tusi agreed, held that the revenues were to be split into six, the first three of which were now the Imam's shares. These should be buried or entrusted to a trustworthy individual. The remaining shares were to be distributed among the appropriate recipients. This view incorporated elements of the views of al-Mufid's third group and his own position but did, ultimately, represent a retreat from the position of his teacher. This view, said al-Tusi, was in accord with caution.[69] Like al-Mufid's view, however, this was clearly a minority position within the community.

Al-Mufid and al-Murtada had made more subjective the conditions under with service to the political institution might be undertaken.

In *Tahdhib*, al-Tusi endeavoured to legitimise his teachers' positions on cooperation with the established political institution by citing more traditions reflective of this tendency.[70] In *al-Nihaya*, he ruled that an individual might accept an appointment to enforce the *hudud* from a *Sultan Zalim*,[71] in the belief that he is doing so with the permission of *Sultan al-Haqq* (i.e., the Imam) and that other believers must assist that individual. But, if service involved also practicing *taqiyya*, it must not extend to killing and he might accept remuneration for such service. That al-Tusi did not address the issue in later works suggests that he felt his point had been made and/or that the matter was less controversial than issues of Friday prayer and the religious taxes.[72]

With respect to the various rituals as they had developed to date, al-Tusi did devote some fifty-three chapters of texts to *ziyara* in his *Tahdhib*.[73] But, as al-Mufid's own work on such visitation, written in an atmosphere of sectarian tension, al-Tusi's more than 200 traditions cited here did not privilege visitation to any one of the Imams over any of the others, let alone *ziyara* to the Imams over *ziyara* to the Prophet himself. His later *al-Nihaya* and *al-Mabsut* contained no separate chapters on *ziyara* at all; *al-Nihaya* contained a section on the *hajj*, but *al-Mabsut* did not. *Al-Istibsar* contained no chapters on *ziyara*.

As to the earth of Imam Husayn's grave site, *Tahdhib* contains a few references to the *tin*, of which several refer to its curative powers.[74] This is noted once in *al-Nihaya*. There are no such references in *al-Istibsar* and two in *al-Mabsut*.[75]

Al-Mufid composed some three essays on Shii 'temporary marriage'. A generation later, however, al-Tusi either deemed it less worthy of attention or, perhaps as likely, was trying to downplay its significance. He collected some ninety references to this form of marriage in *Tahdhib*. Many of these came in those sections on prayer and the *hajj*, but some also appeared in the chapters on marriage, divorce and adultery.[76] Even the severe abridgement of *Tahdhib* that was *al-Istibsar* contained some sixty-eight traditions thereon and the issue had its own dedicated set of chapters.[77] There were also references to *muta* in *al-Nihaya*, where the subject merited its own chapter. But in his later *al-Mabsut* it merited but a handful.[78]

Al-Tusi and the occultation

Al-Tusi completed his work on the occultation *c*. 1055, the year Saljuks took Baghdad and twelve years before his own death.[79] It is not surprising that he undertook such a work only in his very later years, after he had completed research into and authored volumes on a range of the religious sciences broader than any other Twelver scholar to this date. His work across all these disciplines had prepared him to address the key theological 'problem' facing the Twelver community.

This single work on the issue of perhaps prime importance to the believing community may be said to embody his overall approach: he devoted special attention to the Imams' revelation – citing traditions from Ibn Babawayh's compilations, those of al-Barqi, al-Saffar, al-Kulayni and al-Numani, and as well as traditions first cited in his own two collections – but only as mediated by rationalist tools of interpretation.[80]

The result was the fullest, single explanation to this point of the nature of the Imamate, of the Imams as twelve in number, and of the two periods of the occultation as shorter and longer, with the former being that in which the Imam had communicated to the faithful via four named *sufara* – as distinct from named *wakils* – and the longer being that in which the community now found itself.[81] In the process, also, he cited the Imams' denunciations of Shii splinter groups, *wakils* who had been censured and such individuals as al-Hallaj and al-Shalmaghani who had ventured special claims for their own status in the community. He referred also to messages received from the Hidden Imam, to traditions on the Imams' miracles and the miraculous birth of the last Imam and to traditions that the time of the Imam's return was not fixed and the signs that would presage his return.

If the references to miracles was reminiscent and, in fact, relied on traditions extant in the collections of al-Saffar and al-Kulayni, it also built on his teacher al-Mufid's acceptance of these, over the objections of such rationalists as the al-Nawbakhtis. So too, the naming of the four *sufara* had clear implications for both the efficacy of the rationalist interpretation of Imami doctrine, and practice and the legitimacy of interaction between prominent members of the Twelver community and the non-Twelver political institution. The Imam's third agent was al-Husayn b. Ruh al-Nawbakhti (d. 937–8), a relative of Abu Sahl, who was himself well known both for his rationalist views and his close connections with the Abbasid court.[82]

In the end, al-Tusi's exposition of *al-qiyam* (the rising, i.e., the return of the Hidden Imam) postponed the establishment of justice on earth until his return. According to al-Tusi, the Imam would arise 'with a sword and do away with the kingdoms and vanquish each sultan, and establish *al-adl* (justice) and destroy *al-Jawr* (oppression)', but at a time as yet unknown to humanity. Al-Tusi included traditions that fear for his life had been the cause of the Imam's withdrawal from the community and was the chief impediment to his return, and argued that the time of the Imam's return was in Allah's hands and that this was a testing time for the faithful.[83]

Al-Tusi's formulations effectively accorded the occultation a semi-permanent status and mandated the reaching of an accommodation with an 'unjust' world until that time.

That al-Tusi also cited traditions in which the Imams branded as liars those who had set a time for the Imam's return does suggest that, as a century before, so in al-Tusi's own time some were expecting the Imam's imminent reappearance.[84]

Alternative visions: disagreements among the faithful

The suggestion that some were setting times for the Imam's return points this up as a point of contention within the contemporary community.

The disagreements in al-Tusi's time over *al-khums*, and their evolution since the time of al-Mufid, have been noted, as have disagreements – even between these three scholars themselves – on the Friday prayer.[85]

These were not the only such issues. In fact, based on the reported observations of contemporary non-believers, Twelver rationalist elements were probably still in the minority, or at least not all that visible, in the mid-eleventh century just as in the time of al-Mufid and al-Murtada.

Indeed, in his preface to *Tahdhib*, begun soon after his 1017 arrival in Baghdad, al-Tusi referred to the opponents of Imamism as noting the extent of disagreements within the community. Al-Tusi also noted that al-Mufid told him of a believer who, as result of 'confusion' resulting from *ikhtilaf al-hadith* (conflicts between the *hadith*), now 'followed the path of *al-taqlid* . . . without *basira* (discernment)', a clear reference to the rejection of rationalist tools of analysis as a valid means of interpreting doctrine.[86]

Likewise, in the introduction to *al-Mabsut*, completed after 1044, al-Tusi stated that non-Twelvers were accusing the Imamis of having no works of *furu* or *Masail* (issues in law) at all, of being merely *ahl al-hash* (interpolators) and *munaqada* (contradictors), and of denying the principles of *qiyas* and *ijtihad* without which the science of *furu* and *masail* could not exist.[87]

There was clearly enough truth in such observations to have struck a nerve. Even on the nature of judicial authority, al-Tusi refers to intra-faith disagreements. Thus, in *al-Mabsut*, on the issue of judgement, al-Tusi stated that if the *hakim* (judge) erred and it became clear that an earlier judge had erred, the *hukm* (ruling) was faulty, and he must reopen the case. Others, he said, held that if it became known that the judge had erred in a matter in which *ijtihad* was not permitted, such as if his *hukm* contradicted the Quran, the *Sunna* or *ijma*, his ruling was invalid. Still others held that the *hukm* was invalid only if it contradicted consensus, not the Quran or the *Sunna*.[88]

Also in this later work, al-Tusi stated that if the Imam chose an individual from among *ahl al-ilm* (the ulama) to be judge, it was incumbent on the individual to accept the charge. He noted, however, that some said that the individual was not obliged to accept.[89]

In his discussion of the characteristics required of a judge in *al-Mabsut*, al-Tusi referred to some in the community who permitted one who '*yuqallid* (follows previous rulings uncritically)[90] and renders judgements' to be a *qadi* – a distinctly populist interpretation that rejected any recourse to rationalist principles. Others held that only those judges who 'were of *ahl al-ilm wal-ijtihad* (those of learning and individual interpretation) . . . should be followed'. A third group maintained that believers should follow the decisions issued by an individual simply 'more learned' than oneself.[91]

Summary and conclusion

The history and development of the faith in the later years of the Buyid period is most often discussed with reference to the careers and scholarly contributions of a small handful of Baghdad-based Twelver scholars. Later, Sunni histories depict the capital in these years as beset by continuous, and violent, sectarian conflict, and these few Twelver scholars are seen as active in their defence of the faith against Sunni and non-Twelver Shii opposition and in the process, as predisposed to rationalist theology and jurisprudence.

In fact, however, as revealed in their own writings, these few scholars were as much, if not more, engaged in intra-Twelver disputation. These scholars' works attest to their efforts to assert their authority over, and make rulings on, doctrinal and practical matters based on their expertise in these sciences among the faithful in Baghdad and its environs, but also further afield. Although not as much information is available on the nature of those disagreeing with each of these scholars as is desirable, the methodological approaches used, and interpretations offered, by these scholars were very much in the minority at the time. In fact, a sort of Twelver pluralism, especially visible, for example, in the several discussions of the disposition of *al-khums* during the Imam's absence, may be presumed to have been the norm in these years, as it had been over the late ninth and tenth centuries. The query from Diyar Bakr on congregational prayer suggests some strands of this pluralism may also have entailed practical interaction with non-Twelvers.

The lines of demarcation between the beliefs and practices of the Twelvers, other Shi and even Sunni elements may have been becoming apparent in some instances, but in others these may not have been as finely and firmly understood and accepted among the faithful of the period as these several authors hoped. Also, although the doctrinal and practical aspects of the hierarchicalisation of the community that these several scholars were proposing is perhaps accepted as normative today, it was not understood as such at the time.

Elements of al-Tusi's blend of recourse to the revealed texts and rationalist discourse in particular may also be familiar today. Nevertheless, and in fact, these were offered in the context of the contemporary disquiet with the approaches and interpretations of his teachers and, in particular, their lack of reference to the traditions.

That al-Tusi's methodology and, especially, his *ahkam* interpretations varied over time, attests to his clear understanding of the degree of discomfort therewith within the wider community. Even his masterful work on the occultation, the product of finely honed use of revelation and reason and the basis of the normative understanding thereof today, suggests lingering uncertainty in some quarters, if not also, continued expectation of the Imam's imminent return.

Notes

1. J. Calmard, 'Imam Husayn in Popular Literature', *EIr*; M. Litvak, 'Kazemayn', *EIr*. See also n. 2 below.
2. The later the source, the more detailed the references to many of these events, although dates are not always agreed. These accounts are accepted less than critically by secondary-source authors. See McDermott, *Theology of al-Shaikh al-Mufid*, 16–22, citing Ibn al-Jawzi (d. 1201) and Ibn al-Athir (d. 1233); Kramer, *Humanism in the Renaissance of Islam*, 96–102, 50–2, 62–3, citing these and Ibn Kathir (d. 1373); Sabari, *Mouvements populaires à Bagdad*, 69, 108, 110, 70, 101, 85, 62f, 66f, 80f, 90, citing the same sources. M. Canard's earlier, 'Bagdad au IVe siècle de l'hégire (Xe siècle de l'ère chrétienne', *Arabica*, 9 (1962), 267–87, also depended heavily on such sources. See also Halm, *Shiism*, 46–8; M. Streck and J. Lassner, 'al-Karkh', *EI2*; Akhtar, *Early Shiite Imamiyyah Thinkers*, 81–2. See also such, more general, works on the Buyids as M. Kabir, *The Buwayhid Dynasty of Baghdad, 334/946–447/1055* (Calcutta, 1964), 201f and 214f, on some of the key sources on the period; J. Donahue, *The Buwayhid Dynasty in Iraq, 334 H./945 to 403 H./1012. Shaping Institutions for the Future* (Leiden, 2003), xiv–xv, 49–50, 101, 103, 277–8, 281, 283, 285–6 and, especially, 329–33.
3. Sabari, *Mouvements populaires à Bagdad*, 41–3, 62f, 66f, 80.
4. Fr. Taeschner, 'Ayyar', *EI2*; W. Hanaway *et al.*, 'Ayyar', *EIr*. See also M. Zakeri, 'Javanmardi', *EIr*.
5. Sabari, *Mouvements populaires à Bagdad*, 88, 90; McDermott, *Theology of al-Shaikh al-Mufid*, 19; Chapter 3, n. 58.
6. See the sources in n. 2 above, Akhtar, *Early Shiite Imamiyyah Thinkers*, 130; Howard's introduction to al-Mufid, *Kitab al-Irshad*, trans. I. K. A. Howard (London, 1981), xxvi–xxvii. On this recension of the Quran, see E. Kohlberg and Amir-Moezzi (eds.), *Revelation and Falsification. The Kitab al-qira'at of Ahmad b. Muhammad al-Sayyari* (Leiden, 2009), 7, n. 32, 17, 23, 44; McDermott, *ibid.*, 19.
7. McDermott, *ibid.*, 21; Sabari, *Mouvements populaires à Bagdad*, 81–5.
8. Sabari, *ibid.*, 110, citing Ibn al-Jawzi.
9. The Jewish communities, based near the Shii al-Karkh quarter, suffered from the attacks visited on their Shii neighbours. See Kramer, *Humanism in the Renaissance of Islam*, 75f. On Abul-Fadl and Ibn Abbad, see Kramer, *ibid.*, 261f, and the previous chapter.
10. Kramer, *ibid.*; McDermott, *Theology of al-Shaikh al-Mufid*, 9, 14.
11. For a still useful introduction to al-Mufid and his thought, see McDermott, *ibid.* See also Akhtar, *Early Shiite Imamiyyah Thinkers*, 79–122.
12. Momen, *Introduction to Shii Islam*, 79; Halm, *Shiism*, 49–50, McDermott, *ibid.*, *passim*. For a list of al-Mufid's writings, see McDermott, *ibid.*, 27ff; Akhtar, *ibid.*, 88f. McDermott on Al-Mufid's encounter with Mutazilism is still authoritative, although Akhtar does repay attention.
13. Al-Mufid, *al-Ifsah*, in *Iddat Rasa'il*, 2nd edn (Qum, n.d.), 1–163.
14. Al-Mufid, *al-Masail al-Ashara fil-Ghayba* (Qum, n.d.). See p. 28 therein for the various titles of this work.
15. Al-Mufid, *Awail al-Maqalat* including al-Mufid, *Tashih al-Itiqadat*, ed. A. S. Wajdi (Tabriz, 1370–1), 49. On *Awail*, see McDermott, *Theology of al-Shaikh al-Mufid*, 21.

16. Al-Mufid, *Awail al-Maqalat*, 66, 57–8, 102, 100, 58, 72–4, 75, 79, 80–7, 95–9, 110.
17. Al-Mufid, *ibid.*, 93–5. For a recent introduction to this issue, see Kohlberg and Amir-Moezzi, *Revelation and Falsification*, esp. 1–38.
18. Al-Mufid, *Tashih*, 201f. Arguably, the positions of teacher and student were not that far apart. Ibn Babawayh actually said (43) that such disputation 'is allowed *without restriction* to him who is well-versed' in the discipline.
19. Al-Mufid, *ibid.*, 207f. Ibn Babawayh, as seen, had denounced transmigration of souls. See Chapter 3, n. 58.
20. Al-Mufid, *ibid.*, 33, 238–41. In his *al-Irshad*, on which see below, al-Mufid lists only five of the Imams as having been killed: Ali, al-Hasan, al-Husayn, Musa and al-Rida.
21. Al-Mufid, *ibid.*, 245–8. These were outlined, in brief, in al-Mufid's *al-Muqnia*, on which see below.
22. Al-Mufid, *Al-Fusul al-Mukhtara* (Qum, 1396), 76-80. On 'Imami practitioners of *kalam* in Khurasan, Fars and Iraq', see *al-Fusul*, 76.
23. Al-Mufid, *Al-Muqnia fil-Fiqh* (Qum, 1417), 252.
24. Al-Mufid, *Al-Muqnia*, 285–6.
25. On the Friday congregational prayer in particular, see *Al-Muqnia*, 162–5, where there is no reference to the Imam or a deputy, *per se*, let alone the *faqih*, but a requirement that the prayer be performed if a suitable 'imam' was available.
26. Al-Mufid, *ibid.*, 810–12.
27. Al-Mufid's reference to Ibn Babawayh as deceased suggests the reply was composed after 991.
28. On al-Mufid and Ibn al-Junayd, see Modarressi, *An Introduction to Shii Law*, 35–9; McDermott, *Theology of al-Shaikh al-Mufid*, 305f.
29. Al-Mufid, 'al-Masail al-Sarawiyya', in al-Mufid, *Iddat Rasa'il*, 221–5. On Sari as the point of origin of these queries, see Saib Abd al-Hamid's introduction to the Qum 1413 edition. Thanks to Professor H. Modarressi for directing my attention to this reference.
30. Al-Mufid, 'al-Masail al-Sarawiyya', in *Awail al-Maqalat*, 225–6.
31. Indeed, in his section on the Imam (al-Mufid, *al-Muqnia*, 468–9), only three *hadiths* are cited, of which one had been cited in the earlier *Kamil* (chapter 69/6).
32. Al-Mufid, *ibid.*, 456f.
33. Al-Mufid, *Kitab al-Mazar* (Beirut, 1993/1414). Of the 800 traditions in *Kamil*, 69 per cent, involved visiting the third Imam, where of *al-Mazar*'s 136, only fifty-nine, 43 per cent, dealt with *ziyara* to the third Imam, the best times/dates for doing so and the properties of the site's *tin/turba*. Of the 136, ninety-seven, 71 per cent, had appeared in his teacher's *Kamil*. See also Sindawi, 'Visit to the Tomb of al-Husayn', 250–1, 253–4, for poetry composed in 1009 and 1036 on visiting the site and a 1038 poem of al-Murtada in which such a visit was spoken of as *fard* (an obligation).
34. Al-Mufid, *Kitab al-Irshad*. On the work itself see Howard's introductory remarks, xxi–xxxv.
35. Al-Mufid, *ibid.*, 229f. He did not offer sources for the traditions.
36. Al-Mufid, *ibid.*, 279–555.
37. S. Stetkevych, 'Al-Sharif al-Radi and the Poetics of Alid Legitimacy, Elegy for al-Husayn ibn Ali on Ashura', 391 AH', *Journal of Arabic Literature*, 38(3) (2007), 293–323; M. Djebli, 'al-Sharif al-Radi', *EI2*. On both men, see Akhtar, *Early Shiite Imamiyyah Thinkers*, 122f, 177f. See also W. Madelung, 'A Treatise of the Sharif al-Murtada on the Legality of Working for the Government (*Masala fi-l-amal maa al-sultan*)', *Bulletin of the School of Oriental and African Studies*, 43(1) (1980), 29.
38. Madelung, 'Imamism', 26; Kohlberg, 'Imamite Attitude', n. 70, 215.
39. See A. A. Sachedina, 'A Treatise on the Occultation of the Twelfth Imamite Imam', *Studia*

Islamica, 48 (1978), 109–24, a commentary and translation of an essay by Al-Murtada. See also Al-Murtada, *al-Shafi fil-Imama*, ed. F. al-Milani 4 vols (Qum, 1410) and another separate essay on the occultation, *al-Muqnia* (Qum, 1416).

40. For lists of al-Murtada's works, al-Tihrani, *al-Dharia*, 20: 329f; 5: 170f; 10: 173f. See also Akhtar, *Early Shiite Imamiyyah Thinkers*, 186–90.

41. Al-Murtada, *Jawabat al-Masail al-Mosuliyyat al-Thalitha*, in *Rasa'il al-Sharif al-Murtada*, ed. S. M. Raja'i, 1 (Qum, 1405), 201–13. The original questions are, in fact, infrequently cited, and so can only be inferred from the points made in the reply.

42. Al-Murtada, *Jawabat al-Masail al-Mosuliyyat*, 1: 237. Indeed, al-Mufid, clearly feeling the issue to be sufficiently controversial, composed several works on the marriage. See al-Tihrani, *al-Dharia*, 19: 66.

43. Al-Murtada, *ibid.*, 1: 221.

44. Al-Murtada, *Jawabat al-Masail al-Miyyafariqin*, in *Rasa'il al-Sharif al-Murtada*, ed. S. M. Raja'i, 1 (Qum, 1405), 271–2. Al-Mufid ruled similarly (*al-Muqnia*, 163), when he stated that the prayer 'lapsed' in this instance. There was no reference in either case to someone else being delegated to lead the prayer. On the tradition in *al-Faqih*, see Chapter 3, n. 69.

45. Al-Murtada, *Jawabat al-Masail al-Miyyafariqin*, 226–8; al-Murtada, *Al-Intisar* (Qum, 1415), 225–7.

46. Al-Murtada, *Jumal al-Ilm wal-Amal* in *Rasail al-Sharif al-Murtada*, ed. S. M. Raja'i, 3 (Qum, 1405), 81.

47. Madelung, 'A Treatise', 30. Among the traditions al-Murtada did cite was the 'atonement' tradition cited by Ibn Babawayh in *al-Faqih* (29, n. 29). See Chapter 3, n. 75. For a more detailed discussion on both al-Mufid and al-Murtada's views, see A. Newman, 'Minority Reports', in F. Daftary and G. Miskinzoda (eds), *The Study of Shi'i Islam. The State of the Field and Issues of Methodology* (London, 2013 (forthcoming)).

48. For an overview on al-Tusi, see Muhammad b. al-Hasan al-Tusi, *Kitab al-Ghayba*, eds A. al-Tihrani *et al.* (Qum, 1411), 7f. In English, see Akhtar, *Early Shiite Imamiyyah Thinkers*, 205f, which includes a list of al-Tusi's works (218f); C. Marcinkowski, 'Rapprochement and Fealty during the Buyids and Early Saljuks: The Life and Times of Muhammad ibn al-Hasan al-Tusi', *Islamic Studies*, 40(2) (2001), 273–96. On the Saljuks and the damage done to the Shii resources, see Akhtar, *ibid.*, 205, citing later sources, and n. 10 of the following chapter.

49. Al-Tusi, *Tahdhib al-Ahkam*, ed. H. M. al-Khurasan, 10 vols (Najaf, 1378/1959–1382/1962), 1: 2–4.

50. Al-Tusi did cite all pertinent traditions on a given subject – even apparently contradictory texts – and cited complete *isnad* – in most of the collection's first section, *Kitab al-Tihara* (ritual cleanliness). As he explained at the end of the work, he then realised the work would be too long. See al-Tusi, *Tahdhib*, 10: 4–5.

51. Al-Tusi, *Al-Istibsar*, ed. H. M. al-Khurasan, 4 vols (Najaf, 1375/1956–1376/1957), 2: 14–16.

52. Al-Tusi, *Uddat al-Usul*, ed. M. R. Ansari Qummi. (n.pl., 1376/1417), 2: 729–30. See also N. Calder, 'The Structure of Authority in Imami Shii Jurisprudence', unpublished PhD dissertation, School of Oriental and African Studies, 1980, 175–83, 212, 55.

53. Al-Tusi, *ibid.*, 2: 601f

54. Al-Barqi had compiled a *rijal* work. See Ahmad b. Muhammad b. Khalid al-Barqi al-Qummi, *al-Rijal*, ed. J. M. Urmawi (Tehran, 1342) (together with Ibn Daud's *Kitab al-Rijal*). A contemporary of al-Kulayni, Abu Amr Muhammad al-Kashshi, collected narratives on a number of transmitters of the Imams' traditions through the Imamate of Imam Rida. Al-Kashshi did not render any final judgements on their reliability. See A. A. Sachedina,

'The Significance of Kashshi's *Rijal* in Understanding the Early Role of the Shiite *Fuqaha*', in R. Savory (ed.), *Logos Islamikos. Studia Islamica in honorem Georgii Michaelis Wickens* (Toronto, 1984), 183–206.

55. Among those whom both scholars adjudged to be unreliable, but whose names appeared in *al-Kafi* and the earlier collections cited above, were the Kufan Muhammad b. Sinan (d. 835). See al-Tusi, *al-Fihrist*, 131, 143, 41–2; al-Najashi, *Rijal al-Najashi*, 115–16, 416, 328. See also Madelung, *Religious Trends*, 80; Modarressi, *Crisis and Consolidation*, 22, 28, 35, n. 101, 45. Another was Jabir b. Yazid al-Jufi (d. 745–6), on whom see al-Tusi, *al-Fihrist*, 45; al-Najashi, *ibid.*, 128–9; Kohlberg, 'al-Usul', 145; W. Madelung, 'Djabir al-Jufi', *EI2*; Modarressi, *ibid.*, 41.

56. See his *Rijal ibn al-Ghadairi* (Qum, 1422/1380). Both al-Najashi and Ibn al-Ghadairi, for example, condemned Muhammad b. Jumhur (al-Tusi, *al-Fihrist*, 146; al-Najashi, *Rijal al-Najashi*, 337; Ibn al-Ghadairi, *ibid.*, 92; Modarressi, *Crisis*, 22, n. 26). The traditions of Daud b. Kathir al-Taqi (d. after 816–17) were condemned by al-Najashi (156) and Ibn al-Ghadairi (134–5), but accepted by al-Tusi (*al-Fihrist*, 68). See also Kohlberg, 'al-Usul', 144–5.

57. Al-Tusi, *al-Nihaya fi Mujjarad al-Fiqh wal-Fatawi* (Beirut, 1390/1970), 300–3; Al-Tusi, *al-Mabsut fil-Fiqh*, eds M. T. al-Kashfi and M. B. al-Bihbudi, 8 vols (Tehran, 1387–1393), 8: 98–9, 96, 97.

58. Al-Tusi, *al-Nihaya*, 711, 722, 712, 732, 690–1, 692, 701, 723–4, 726–7.

59. Al-Tusi, *al-Nihaya*, 300–3

60. Al-Tusi, *al-Mabsut*, 8: 3–7, 4, 37, 11, 47, 48. See also 8: 12, 34, 36, 9, 13, 54.

61. Al-Tusi, *al-Nihaya*, 133, 302.

62. Al-Tusi, *al-Mabsut*, 1: 143–4, 147–9.

63. Al-Tusi, *Tahdhib*, 4: 90.

64. Al-Tusi, *al-Nihaya*, 184–9, 192. On the categories, see Chapter 2, n. 63.

65. Al-Tusi, *al-Mabsut*, 1: 252; 233. See also *ibid.*, 1: 240, 242.

66. Compare *al-Nihaya*, 184, and *al-Mabsut*, 1: 252.

67. Compare *al-Nihaya*, 196–8, and *al-Mabsut*, 1: 234–8.

68. Al-Tusi, *Tahdhib*, 4: 147–50.

69. Al-Tusi, *al-Nihaya*, 200–1. This is repeated in *al-Mabsut*, 1: 263–4.

70. Al-Tusi, *Tahdhib*, 6: 222–5.

71. Al-Tusi left such terms as *zalim* undefined, ignoring the definition of *jawr* offered by Ibn Babawayh. See *al-Nihaya*, 356.

72. Al-Tusi, *Tahdhib*, 6: 222f; *al-Nihaya*, 300–3. In *al-Mabsut* (8: 81–5), the issue is not addressed. None of the traditions in *Tahdhib* were cited in *al-Istibsar*, nor did he include a corresponding section in *al-Mabsut*.

73. Al-Tusi, *Tahdhib*, ed. S. H. al-Musawi al-Khurasan (Tehran, 1365), 6: 2f.

74. Al-Tusi, *ibid.*, 6 : 74–6.

75. Al-Tusi, *al-Nihaya*, 590; *al-Mabsut*, 1: 177, 186.

76. See, for example, *Tahdhib*, 5: 172f, 435f, 7: 248f, 8: 32f.

77. Al-Tusi, *Istibsar*, 3: 141f.

78. Al-Tusi, *al-Nihaya*, 489f; *al-Mabsut*, 4: 366, 5: 447, for example.

79. Al-Tusi, *al-Ghayba*, 1, does not identify the 'shaykh' to whom al-Tusi refers as asking for the book. Al-Tihrani (*al-Dharia*, 16: 79) rejected the assertion that this was his teacher al-Mufid. Akhtar (*Early Shiite Imamiyyah Thinkers*, 231) noted al-Tusi's own reference in the volume (112) to the year as 1055.

80. Al-Tusi, *al-Ghayba*, 43, 87, 95, 220, 224.

81. Ibn Babawayh had listed these names but not as the four, and only, *sufara per se*. Al-Mufid,

as seen, had used the term *sufara*, but left the term undefined. Al-Tusi's naming of these four as such seems to be the earliest written record of this formal designation. See the following note.

82. Herein (393) al-Tusi cited Ibn Babawayh's tradition in *Kamal* (431–2) naming the four who were now said to be the *sufara*. See Chapter 3, at n. 45.

83. Al-Tusi, *ibid.*, 199–200.

84. Al-Tusi, *ibid.*, 330, 335, 425f

85. In his *Quranic Hermeneutics. Al-Tabrisi and the Craft of Commentary* (London, 2011), 49, B. Fudge refers to al-Tusi, in his seminal *tafsir* (Quran commentary) work *al-Tibyan*, as noting that some Twelvers did not believe in the doctrine of *al-raja* (the return), that is, the resurrection of the dead prior to the Day of Judgement.

86. Al-Tusi, *Tahdhib*, 1: 2–33.

87. Al-Tusi, *al-Mabsut*, 1: 1–3.

88. Al-Tusi, *al-Mabsut*, 8: 101–2.

89. Al-Tusi, *al-Mabsut*, 8: 82.

90. See the reference by al-Mufid to such elements in his *al-Fusul al-Mukhtara*, and n. 22.

91. Al-Tusi, *al-Mabsut*, 8: 98–9.

CHAPTER 5

Betwixt and between: the Twelvers and the Turks

In the later Buyid period and the very early years after the arrival of the Sunni Saljuks in the area in the 1050s, the written record suggests that the Twelver scholarly community at least generally remained beholden to the legacy of the later Buyid period rationalists.

But the Saljuks' appearance resulted in the destruction of key Twelver resources in Baghdad, and, at least initially, removed the community and its elites from a position of prominence and favour by virtue of association with the political centre. Over the years from 1055 to the 1258 conquest of Baghdad by the Mongols, believers across the region were relatively more isolated from each other than they had been during the Buyid period.

The written record suggests that the Arab west remained home to many. But their fortunes were uneven over these years, to say the least. Among the elites some continued to follow al-Tusi's legacy. Others, to varying degrees, questioned that legacy and rationalist approaches generally, as did some popular elements.

To the east, in Iran, after initial Saljuk hostility to the faith, Shii activity experienced a marked resurgence, particularly over the twelfth century. Nevertheless, the Shia were in the minority on the plateau, caught between the Saljuks' pro-Hanafi agenda and the plateau's existing Shafii tendencies. Tradition-based discourse was valued among the 'popular' classes, but also, as in the Buyid period, sectarian distinctions could become blurred. Veneration of the Prophet's family in particular was widespread even among the Turkish newcomers to the area, and was becoming mixed with Sufi and Sufi messianic discourse. The plateau's scholarly elite, as in the later Buyid period, were attuned to rationalist discourse, were sensitive to sectarian tensions and maintained an accommodationist tone. They studied with Sunnis and – possibly encouraged by the lack of availability of pre-1055 Twelver sources in these years – utilised Sunni materials in their own work. Some sought out points of commonality between Sunni and Shii, for example, veneration for the Prophet's family.

The initial legacy

Exchanges between the Twelver elites of late Buyid Baghdad and the faithful elsewhere attest to the presence of communities in locations in modern-day

Lebanon, Syria and Egypt, as well as elsewhere in Iraq, for example, to the west. To the east, al-Tusi alone had students whose names suggest connections to Rayy, Qum, Nishabur, Gurgan, Qazwin and, further afield, Nasaf.[1]

Representative of these various pockets of the faith were such scholars as Taqi al-Din b. Najm al-Din al-Halabi (d. 1055), Sallar b. Abd al-Aziz al-Daylami (d. 1056–7) and Abd al-Aziz, known as Ibn al-Barraj (d. 1088).

Al-Halabi, by birth from Aleppo, studied with al-Murtada and al-Tusi, wrote a commentary on a *fiqh* work of al-Murtada and a work on Imami *usul*, taught Ibn al-Barraj and Sallar and was appointed to a post in his home town by al-Murtada. Born in Daylam, Sallar came to Baghdad and studied with al-Mufid, al-Murtada and, perhaps, al-Tusi as well. He was al-Murtada's personal representative in Aleppo. Sallar taught the sons of both al-Tusi and al-Halabi. Although he was a strong proponent of the use of *ijtihad*, and authored works on *fiqh* and *kalam*, Sallar nevertheless disagreed with some of his contemporaries on some specific points of *furu*. Ibn al-Barraj was born and grew up in Cairo. He studied with Sallar, al-Halabi and, perhaps, al-Mufid as well. Al-Murtada appointed him a *qadi* in Tripoli. At al-Murtada's death, he became al-Tusi's personal representative in the city.

Although there is little reliable information on actual practice, in matters of *fiqh*, at least, these scholars tended to follow their teachers: Sallar agreed with al-Tusi that the *fuqaha* might conduct various prayers, but, following al-Murtada, not the Friday prayer. Al-Halabi also stopped just short of formally allowing the *fuqaha* to do so during the occultation. Ibn al-Barraj also followed al-Murtada. As to *al-khums*, al-Tusi, al-Halabi and Ibn al-Barraj acknowledged different options for the collection and distribution of the text, and favoured a role for the *faqih*. Sallar, however, ruled that during the occultation the individual was permitted disposition over all its shares.[2]

The works of these and other scholars of the immediate post-al-Tusi generation merit further study for any insights they might contain concerning the state of the community in these years.

What is clear, however, is that the late Buyid period community was in disagreement over a number of issues of both doctrine and practice, and that the views on these of those scholars of this period best known today were clearly in the minority.

The arrival of the Saljuks
Whatever the course(s) the faith and the faithful might have taken to resolve these differences thereafter is a moot point, however.

In 1055, following on several decades of victories in the east, under Tughril (d. 1063) Saljuk forces – essentially under a commission from the caliphate to crush the Shii Buyids – crashed into Baghdad. Under Tughril's successor Alp Arsalan (d. 1072) they took Armenia, Georgia and, after defeating the

Byzantines at Manzikirt in 1071, seized nearly all of Anatolia. At the death of the latter's successor Malik Shah (d. 1092), whose first vizier was the famous Nizam al-Mulk (d. 1092), Saljuk territory came to be split among the family, with subdivisions in 'Rum', Syria, Iraq, Baghdad and Khurasan. Later succession issues and local risings caused further political fragmentation. The Saljuks were the Islamic power at the time of the First (1096) and Second (1147) Crusades.[3]

The Saljuks were Iranian in cultural orientation – Nizam al-Mulk and the famous Sunni philosopher/Sufi al-Ghazali (d. 1111) were both Iranians, for example – but also very Sunni in their faith. The vizier Nizam al-Mulk, in his famous *Siyatsatnama* (*Book of Government*), composed for Malik Shah, offered only very scathing views of the Shia, especially the Ismailis.[4]

Even before their capture of Baghdad, the Saljuks were noted for this hostility. In 1053, Tughril ordered the public cursing of Asharis and the Shia, for example. The Saljuk failure to halt the sectarian fighting that broke out in Baghdad following their conquest, and brought about the destruction of many Shii schools, mosques and libraries, only further attested to this.[5] Those elements of the community that could flee the city did so. Al-Tusi, who lost his home and library, fled to Najaf – where, at the time, only a small number of the faithful were based – and started a school. He died in Najaf in 1067.[6]

Nevertheless, the situation of the Shia did soon begin to improve. Tughril is said to have treated the Shia of al-Karkh well. Nizam al-Mulk repealed Tughril's public cursing of the Shia and Asharism. The vizier also looked after some sayyids and some Shia and enjoyed good relations with Shii ulama, even attending weekly sessions with some in Rayy. Malik Shah appointed a Twelver Shii to the vizierate, and he and Nizam al-Mulk visited the shrines in Iraq and Tus. Malik Shah's son and successor, Muhammad (1105–18), also appointed Twelvers with connections to Qum and Kashan to his service. Shiites were said to have been viziers in the reign of Ahmad Sanjar (1118–57), during which time Asharism was publicly condemned, as well as during the reigns of Sulayman Shah (1160–1) and Tughril III (1176–94). These Twelver officials are recorded as having made numerous donations to the tombs of the Imams and Fatimid sayyids in Mecca and Medina, as well as to sites in Baghdad and Rayy, Kashan and Sabziwar.

Perhaps more importantly, however, a ban by the same Malik Shah on the Shia building of mosques, schools and *khanaqah*s (Sufi retreats) was not carried out. Indeed, many Shii schools are recorded as being built in Khurasan, Mazandiran, Qum – where nine are cited – Aba, Sabziwar, Varamin and Kashan – with four – and to the west in Aleppo. Schools were also built in Rayy during the reigns of Malik Shah and his successors. Numerous private Shii private libraries are also mentioned, in Rayy, Isfahan and Sava, as well as across Iraq and Khurasan.[7]

Scattered pockets and lost resources

Nevertheless, from 1055 the Twelvers were very much less major 'players' at the political centre and on the region's spiritual and political scene than they had been under the Buyids. In the years from 1055 to 1258, the various pockets of believers scattered from west to east across the region were very much more on their own.

Appendix I suggests that in the fifth Muslim century, corresponding to the years 1009–1105, it was in Iran that the greatest amount of scholarly activity was being supported and carried out, especially in Tus/Nishabur as well as Rayy and Qazwin. To the west, there were clearly clusters of the faithful in Tripoli, Aleppo, Baghdad, Basra and Kufa. Evidence of movement between these is as, or perhaps more interesting, indicative of the extent to which those in these different pockets were actively aware of each other. There was certainly movement within these regions, but there is also evidence of movement across these, from Gurgan to Baghdad, for example, from Fars to Iraq to Aleppo, from Qazwin to Iraq, from Basra to Rayy, from Egypt to Baghdad, from Baghdad to Ghazna and Samarqand.[8]

In the sixth century, that is from 1106 to 1202, almost neatly corresponding to the twelfth century AD, the main clusters of Shii activity across the region were now overwhelmingly, and in very much greater numbers, located in Iran, especially in Rayy, Qum, Qazwin and Kashan, as well as the Nishabur/Tus/Bayhaq area. The sudden rise in Shii activity on the plateau may have been due to the infrastructural activity noted above. In any case, to the west, Baghdad in Iraq was experiencing something of a decline, while al-Hilla, Najaf and Kufa were beginning to become centres of activity. Aleppo remained a cluster. Bahrain now also appears as a centre of activity.

Evidence of movement within these several regions is present, but there is also evidence of movement across the region, for example, from Aleppo to Iraq, from Najaf to Rayy, from Jabal Amil in the Lebanon to Baghdad and, in the other direction, from Rayy and Daylam to Baghdad and two pilgrimages from Iran.[9]

Appendix II, however, suggests that access to the key pre-1055 texts, via copies of these being made and dated to the period between the 1055 and 1258 falls of Baghdad, was extremely limited.

Many manuscripts may have been lost initially during the Saljuk invasion and in the 1059 fire at a library in al-Karkh, when more than 10,000 works are said to have been destroyed.[10] To be sure, the students of al-Mufid, al-Mufid and al-Tusi may well have possessed personal copies of some, if not all, of their teachers' works, if not also earlier texts.[11] But that so very few copies of pre-1055 works across the range of Shii religious sciences – from the traditions, to *fiqh/furu*, to *tafsir* to theology and *rijal* – can be dated to the years between 1055 and

1258 suggests that much of what was lost in 1055 was not replaced. Over the two centuries following 1055 the scholar or student, perhaps especially those located in any of the smaller pockets of the faithful, searching for written guidance on matters of doctrine and practice would have had limited success.[12]

The opposition of such Buyid period scholars as al-Mufid, al-Murtada and al-Tusi to translating of the Quran and their privileging of Arabic in, for example, ritual prayer may well have further disadvantaged the Twelver 'narrative' to the east.[13]

The community in the west: Syria

In the Arabic-speaking lands to the west of the Iranian plateau the extant written legacy suggests a continued predisposition to rationalist discourse and analysis among those few scholars of the period best known today. Occasionally, however, both elite and non-elite, anti-rationalist discourse can be discerned.

During the Buyid period, to the west of Baghdad both the Hamdanids, of Mosul and Aleppo, and the Uqaylid 'states' are often held to have been 'Shii' in faith. Tolerance of Shii and especially some Twelver elements in their cities spoke more to their rulers' interest in broadening their appeal locally and to their (vain) hope of Fatimid support against their eastern enemies, than to any deep spiritual commitment to the faith. The Hamdanids had been *de facto* rulers of Mosul since 935, having previously been Abbasid vassals. The Buyids took Mosul in 979. Hamdanid forces had taken Aleppo in 944, but lost the city to the Ismaili Fatimids in the mid-eleventh century. Meanwhile, from Mosul the Uqaylids, who had been allies of the Mosuli Hamdanids, after acknowledging Buyid power, came to rule northern Iraq and parts of Syria until, in 1085, the Sunni Saljuks took the area.[14]

Shiism in Aleppo suffered further when the Zangids, the Saljuk-appointed rulers of Mosul, took the city in 1128. Thereafter, the city was on the frontline between Muslim and Crusader armies. The Shia sometimes sided with the latter against the former.[15]

Later Twelver sources note that, according to the Sunni historian Ibn Kathir (d. 1373), when the Ayyubid Salah al-Din (d. 1193) laid siege to Aleppo, the city's *wali* gathered its inhabitants together to urge resistance. In return for a promise of participation in this resistance, the city's Shia were granted the right to entrust their marriages and contracts to one Ibn Zuhra. They were also promised that the Shii quarter of the city would be renovated.[16] The account indicates not only the extent of the family's influence within the city, but also suggests that the fortunes of the city's Imami community had sunk to the point where they were not in control of many intra-community affairs and that their economic fortunes had also suffered.

Yaqut al-Hamawi (d. 1229) refers to several important Shii grave sites, and also to the issuance by local *fuqaha* of Shii fatwas. Jalal al-Din al-Rumi (d. 1273), in his *Mathnawi*, refers to mourning ceremonies in Aleppo commemorating the martyrdom of Imam al-Husayn,[17] although whether these were exclusively organised by or for Twelvers is not clear.

In Aleppo over these later years the work of scholars such as Hamza b. Ali b. Zuhra al-Halabi, Ibn Zuhra (d. 1189–90)[18] suggests the continued strength of al-Tusi's influence among the scholarly elite. Descendants of Imam Jafar al-Sadiq, the Zuhra family, were among the wealthy, well-known Imami families of Aleppo, and served as the *naqib*s of the Alid community.

Ibn Zuhra himself appears to have been a strong advocate of clerical author-ity and recourse to rationalism as a source of doctrine and practice. He authored treatises refuting Sunni traditionism and Asharism, and supporting philosophy and *muta* marriage. Clearly, Ibn Zuhra was confident enough to assert aspects of Twelver distinctiveness, but also aware of, and challenged by, the resurgence of Sunni traditionalist discourse being promoted by the centre in Baghdad, discussed below. Ibn Zuhra's balanced recourse to reason and the Imams' traditions paralleled that of al-Tusi, and seems to have produced few practical disagreements with his predecessors among the Imami rationalists over matters of religious practice.[19]

Resurgent traditionism in Baghdad

As suggested, Iraq's overall fortunes as a centre of scholarship were stable over the eleventh and twelfth centuries, even if activity in Baghdad experienced something of a decline. To be sure, very little is known of the many scholars of the period from the mid-eleventh to the mid-twelfth centuries. In the years from 1065 to 1173, however, Sunni Shii clashes are again reported in the city by the later Sunni sources.[20]

In the years thereafter, the forty-seven-year reign of the caliph al-Nasir (1180–1225) was crucial. Al-Nasir is known for his efforts to crush Saljuk power. He invited the Khwarazmshahs to attack the Saljuks from the east, which they did, defeating and killing Tughril III in 1194 and extending their authority over a large part of the Iranian plateau. The caliph is then said to have urged the Mongols to check Khwarazmshah power.

Closer to home, in the interest of promoting Islamic unity and enhancing his own power as caliph, al-Nasir encouraged compromise between Sunni and Shii elements with a blend of *futuwwa*[21] and *tassawuf* (popular mysticism), along with criticisms of philosophy and support for the study of the *hadith*.

In the process, he also reached out to the Shia, who may have comprised as much as half of Baghdad's population in these years. Al-Nasir embellished and enlarged the *Ghaybat Mahdi* in Samarra, the site where the twelfth Imam is said to have gone into concealment, even as he also deflected obvious Alid criticisms of the legitimacy of the Abbasid caliphate., These moves seem to have enjoyed support among some Twelvers in the city.[22]

One contemporary Twelver scholar of the day was Ali b. Musa al-Husayni al-Hilli (d. 1266), Ibn Tawus. The Tawus family tree stretched back to Imams al-Hasan and al-Husayn via Imam Musa, and included a connection to al-Tusi. Ibn Tawus was born in al-Hilla in 1193, and after study there spent some fifteen years in Baghdad. He returned to al-Hilla in the early 1240s, resided in Najaf, Karbala and Samarra and returned to Baghdad in 1254–5.

Ibn Tawus was on good terms with the penultimate caliph al-Mustansir (*reg.* 1226–42), who provided him with accommodation and acceded to his requests to support astrology. He turned down an offer from al-Mustansir to become the capital's *naqib*, and rejected the caliph's request for him to issue fatwas and to act as emissary to the approaching Mongols in the late 1230s. His return to al-Hilla followed by residences elsewhere after al-Mustansir's 1242 death, were, Ibn Tawus admitted, efforts to withdraw ever further from Baghdad society.

In Baghdad, Ibn Tawus married the daughter of the Shii vizier and was friendly with Ibn al-Alqami (d. 1258), vizier to the last Abbasid caliph al-Musta-sim (*reg.* 1242–58) and his family. He was present in the capital at the Mongol conquest of Baghdad in 1258.

Ibn Tawus' return to Baghdad underlines the resurgence of Twelver presence and influence in Baghdad, and the city's renewed reputation as something of a centre of scholarship.

Indeed, in his recreation of Ibn Tawus' 'library', Kohlberg lists some 670 works, all in Arabic, to which Ibn Tawus refers as having accessed directly, that is, that he owned, or indirectly, via borrowing or reading in another library, in the course of his own scholarship. He, at least, was able to locate, if not obtain, copies of a number of key pre-1055 works of Twelver scholarship, as listed above,[23] even if so few further copies of these were produced in these two centuries.

Ibn Tawus did, for example, have access to a 942–3 copy of Ibn Babawayh's *Maani al-Akhbar*, a copy of al-Mufid's *al-Muqnia* made in the author's own lifetime, a 1064 copy of al-Tusi's *Ikhtiyar*, the abridgement of al-Kashshi's *rijal* work, as dictated by al-Tusi, and a 1078–9 copy of al-Tusi's *Kitab al-Ghayba*.

Nevertheless, it is not clear that Ibn Tawus had access to complete copies of the works from which he quoted. Also, there are no references to works such as al-Saffar's *Basair*, *al-Imama wa al-Tabsira* of Ibn Babawayh's father, al-Mufid's *al-Mazar*, al-Tusi's *al-Khilaf* (a work on disputation), or Ibn al-Ghadairi's work on *rijal*. Complete copies of al-Barqi's *al-Mahasin* seem not to have been available from this time.[24]

Ibn Tawus shared the criticisms of al-Tusi and his legacy voiced by his own teacher Warram b. Amir Fawaris (d. 1208), and the latter's Rayy-born teacher Mahmud b. Ali al-Razi al-Himmasi (d. after 1187) (on both of whom see further below), among others. In his *Kashf al-Mahajja*, written in 1251–2, Ibn Tawus warned his son against the 'ignorant followers' of the descendants of al-Tusi, and mentioned that Warram had told him that his own teacher al-Himmasi had criticised many as uncritical followers of each other and earlier scholars.

Ibn Tawus, in fact, turned away from *fiqh*, composing but one work in this genre. In a work composed in the early 1250s, he explained that all such questions were a matter of dispute and he did not wish to offer erroneous rulings. In *Kashf*, he noted that he felt that such rulings might be shown to be unsubstantiated and be construed as based on a personal desire for worldly authority. His aim, he said, was to work with the traditions, even *ahad* traditions, and leave *ahl al-nazar* (the people of speculation) to offer rulings. Ibn Tawus also rejected *kalam* and Mutazilism that, he said, offered beliefs that were not certain and could be refuted. Man knew Allah by virtue of Allah's granting that knowledge, not by recourse *to nazar*. Mutazilism, he held, introduced doubt and confusion. People needed only to be taught about the Prophet and the Imams.[25]

At the same time, Ibn Tawus was attentive to popular practice. In his *al-Aman*, a volume on travel, for example, he placed special emphasis on visiting the grave sites of the Imams. That of Imam al-Husayn came in for particular attention, as did the curative powers of the *turba* (earth) therefrom, and its ability to prevent fear. In *al-Aman*, he also noted the import of marking Shii days of commemoration, special prayers and other popular practices. He also valued such popular practices as casting lots to divine the future, talismans and even astrology.[26]

Ibn Tawus' scepticism of rationalist tendencies was shared by, and perhaps reflected that of, some 'popular' elements within Baghdad's Twelver community. 'Popular' association with and affinity for the traditions is revealed by an encounter between a Twelver rationalist named Ahmad b. Abd al-Aziz al-Baghdadi, a contemporary of the Mutazilite Ibn Abil-Hadid (d. 1257), and an unnamed preacher during the reign of al-Nasir. The latter's efforts to create Sunni–Shii unity, and to challenge rationalist discourse in the process, have been noted. The preacher is described as versed in '*hadith* and *rijal*' and well known for his 'rebuking of *ahl al-kalam*, and especially the Mutazila and *ahl al-nazar*, *ala qaida al-hashwiyya* (on the basis of the *hashwiyya*[27] methodology). He is said to have attracted crowds comprising both the common people and the notables of the city. Although the account, perhaps unsurprisingly, described the preacher as a 'renegade' from the Shia, the local Shii community, clearly still considering him one of their own, was sufficiently exercised that 'a group of the Shii leaders' selected an individual – the above-named Ahmad – to challenge the preacher. A subsequent public gathering, described as overflowing, rapidly deteriorated into sectarian fighting. The preacher made his way to safety. The sultan ordered the crowd be dispersed, but had Ahmad – not the traditionist preacher – jailed.[28] Spurred on by the caliph's own traditionist agenda, it is not surprising that the preacher and his ideas were more popular in the city, and their support more important to the authorities, than the rationalist discourse of Amad b. Abd al-Aziz.

The community in al-Hilla: the critique of al-Tusi

Not far away, the *tabaqat* literature suggests that al-Hilla was beginning to establish itself as a centre of Twelver scholarship, if only in the later twelfth century.

Al-Hilla's history as a site dates to perhaps as early as 1006, though it is usually said to have been founded *c.* 1101–2. In the later Buyid period al-Hilla had been under the domination of the Shii Banu Mazyad tribe, with the approval of the Buyids. The city fell to the Saljuks in 1150, and its final independence from Baghdad ended in the 1160s.[29]

The al-Hilla-based scholar of these years best known among both later Twelver and Western scholars is Muhammad b. Mansur, Ibn Idris al-Hilli (d. 1202). He was a contemporary of al-Himmasi, discussed below, and the two men knew each other's work.[30] Among Ibn Idris' students were both a member of the Zuhra family – Ibn Idris was a contemporary of Ibn Zuhra and exchanged *ijazat* ('permissions' from one scholar to another authorising the latter, for example, to narrate/teach the former's work) with him – and a scholar with connections to the Jabal Amil region of modern-day Lebanon.

Though, as noted below, al-Himmasi was also critical of al-Tusi's legacy and the community's over-reliance thereon, Twelver and Western scholars often characterise Ibn Idris as the first Twelver scholar to have presented detailed, polemical criticisms of al-Tusi.[31]

In fact, Ibn Idris did offer challenges to al-Tusi's methodology and rulings on matters of *ahkam*. But in the process he did not stray that far from rulings on these offered by other, earlier Twelver rationalists.

Thus, in his multi-volume work on *furu al-Sarair*, his position on Friday prayer was the same as that of Sallar: the *fuqaha* might lead the people in other prayers, but not the Friday congregational prayer. Ibn Idris was as equivocal as to the extent of the authority permitted the *fuqaha* on other issues as earlier scholars, for example, allowing *al-zakat* revenues to be distributed by the donor himself.

He did, however, retreat on the matter of the implementation of *al-hudud* during the occultation. Ibn Idris criticised as based on *akhbar al-ahad* al-Tusi's ruling, and, by implication that of al-Murtada as well, that an official appointed by an unjust ruler to implement *al-hudud* might do so if he felt that thereby he was applying the Law, that he was doing so with the permission of the Hidden Imam, and that believers were obliged to assist such an individual in the performance of his tasks. Remaining true to these scholars' jurisprudential rationalism, however, he argued that based on *ijma* only, the Imams themselves might implement the *hudud*. In fact, on such issues as relations between believers and the government, comprising *al-qada* and *al-hudud*, Ibn Idris generally agreed with most of the positions adopted earlier either by al-Tusi or such others as al-Murtada, Sallar and Ibn al-Barraj.[32]

To the extent that al-Tusi emerges as more a collector of traditions than a reliable *faqih*, he was arguably a stalking horse for Ibn Idris' comments on the state of the community in his day, as Ibn Babawayh had been for al-Mufid. If Ibn Idris did retreat on certain of the prerogatives of the *fuqaha* during the absence of the Imam, he did so in the service of a more radical rationalism than that proposed by al-Tusi, which produced rulings more akin to those of al-Mufid and al-Murtada and their rationalist students and successors.[33]

Moreover, Ibn Idris praised al-Tusi's *tafsir* work *al-Tibyan*, on which he himself did a commentary, and offered apologies for what he said were errors in al-Tusi's *al-Nihaya* by arguing that al-Tusi made such errors because he was so keen in mind and preoccupied with his writing. Overall, in fact, Ibn Idris characterised al-Tusi as always 'truthful'.[34]

Other rationalists of this period clearly attempted to utilise the revelation in an effort both to support rationalist interpretations of Imami doctrine and practice and to bolster the legitimacy of the faith within the Islamic pantheon of sects.

Yahya b. al-Hasan al-Hilli, Ibn al-Batriq (d. 1203), for example, was interested in both speculative theology and the *hadith*. Born in al-Hilla, Ibn al-Batriq lived there for a while before moving to Aleppo, Baghdad and Wasit, where he finally settled. In his *al-Umdah min Sihah al-Akhbar* (*The Support, from the Correct of the Akhbar*) on the Imamate of Ali, he utilised nearly 1,000 Shii and non-Shii traditions.[35] His recourse to the Sunni revelation can only have helped to reinforce the legitimacy of Twelver discourse located as it was within the Sunni-dominated political institution.

Populism on the Iranian plateau

The *tabaqat* literature does suggest that over the eleventh and twelfth centuries the Iran-based centres of the faith experienced very considerable growth.

The presence of such pockets, as well as the infrastructural work done in these years, are confirmed in *Kitab al-Naqd* (*The Book of Criticism*), a work written between 1164 and 1171 by one Abd al-Jalil al-Qazwini at the request of a Rayy-based Twelver *naqib* in response to an attack on the faith by a Shii convert to Sunnism.[36] Al-Qazwini identifies key centres of the faith extant in his time as located in the Jibal (a term for northwest Iran or 'Persian Iraq'), in Rayy, Varamin, Qazwin, Ava (Aba), Qum and Kashan – from whence Ahmad Sanjar's Shii viziers apparently hailed. He also refers to the towns of Sari and Arim in Mazandiran, Astarabad, Gurgan and Dihistun and, further afield, in Khurasan, which was still mainly Sunni, Sabziwar, Tus – site of Imam al-Rida's tomb – and Nishabur.

Al-Qazwini also notes the extent of the faith's bases among particular vocational groups. These included the weavers in Qum, Kashan and Varamin, for example, but also the cobblers in Rayy, donkey drivers in Sabziwar and among hatters, tanners and sword-makers in Ava.[37]

To be sure, over the period the Mazandiran-based Bawandid rulers were Twelvers – and may well have been the very first genuine Twelver Shii dynasty – and so did look after both Twelver and Zaydi elements. But relations with both local elements and the Saljuks, such as Sanjar, were uneven. As vassals of the Saljuks, the Bawandids had an uneven political-military history over the Saljuk period.[38]

Nevertheless, the Shia were in the minority. Shafii Sunnism was the area's dominant persuasion at the start of this period. The Saljuk agenda, however, called for the imposition of Hanafism, which they had long espoused, and, in the process, the downgrading of Ashari traditionism. In fact, in 1142–3, prominent Shafii scholars in Rayy were forced to sign documents repudiating Asharism. The next year, Asharism was condemned publicly in Baghdad. Two years later anti-Ashari moves were announced in Hamadan. Sultan Masud (1134–52) sent a Hanafi preacher to Isfahan, and his anti-Ashari activities provoked riots. The same preacher did the same in Qazwin, at the time a Shafii centre. Even the Turkish soldiers sent to enforce these edicts are said to have been fanatical in their devotion to crushing Asharism.

Clashes between Shafii and Hanafi elements were not uncommon. In Nishabur, in 1158 – before Ibn Tawus' birth in 1193, but within the lifetimes of Ibn Zuhra and Ibn Idris – Shafiis used as an excuse their three years of feuding with the Shia to burn down a Hanafi school. Eventually, eight Hanafi and seventeen Shafii schools were destroyed. These years also witnessed Shafii–Hanafi riots in Marv, Balk and, in the 1200s, in Isfahan as well as Rayy and Nishabur.[39]

In this atmosphere al-Qazwini and, presumably also, the Razi *naqib* who asked him to compose the work, were at special pains to reject the claims voiced by the former Shii that the Shia condemned all other Muslims. Distancing himself from certain 'unorthodox' elements within Shiism,[40] al-Qazwini variously branded these elements as Akhbari, *ghali* and *hashwi* or, at times, all of these at once. That he composed *al-Naqd* in Persian – whereas most of the Twelver theological and legal literature in this period was composed in Arabic – suggests his perception, if not also that the *naqib*, of the immediacy of the problem and the consequent need to make this point to as wide an audience as possible.

There is no adequate means of delineating the beliefs of his target groups as fully as might be desirable. Certainly, al-Qazwini's equating of Akhbarism with *ghuluw* would only have rendered the former all the more problematic and accentuated his portrayal of the latter as heterodox. Al-Qazwini's appeal to Mutazilism and rejection of traditionism – a confluence of interests with the Saljuk agenda – highlighted the potential for some common ground between Sunnis and Shia at the elite level, in opposition to 'extreme' traditionism. As cited by al-Qazwini, the latter extended to the extreme veneration of Ali, polemics against the companions of the Prophet and a litany of 'unorthodox' practices, including, for example, starting the Ramadan fast two days before the start of the month and ending it two days before its end.[41] The convert also complained, for example, that the Shia engaged *manaqib khwanan*, preachers who publicly recited the merits of Ali – as, in fact, did similar preachers for the Sunni figures.[42]

Such discourse and clashes suggest that at times lines between these Sunni groups and between Sunni and Shii, if not necessarily Twelver Shii *per se*, could be distinct and understood as such on the ground. Other evidence suggests these lines could also become blurred.

Various Shii tombs, such as that of the son of the fifth Imam Muhammad al-Baqir in Kashan, or that of the Hasanid Abd al-Azim in Rayy, the shrine of Imam Rida's sister Fatima in Qum and sites in Ava and Qazwin are said to have been visited by Shii and Sunni alike. Al-Qazwini records that even Sunnis accepted the tradition that a visit to the tomb of Imam al-Rida in Tus was held to be equivalent to seventy pilgrimages to Mecca.

In Isfahan, Baghdad, Hamadan, Rayy and perhaps other Sunni conurbations as well, Muharram – seemingly the most quintessential and distinctive of Shii, if again, not distinctly Twelver, rituals – was even commemorated by Sunnis who did not shy away from cursing the Umayyads.[43]

There is evidence also of the spread of forms of Imamism among 'rank and file' Saljuk elements. Al-Qazwini's interlocutor complains that every *saray* of the Turks was populated by at least ten or fifteen 'Rafidis'. There were also said to be Shia among the secretaries of the court's administrative organs: now even the chamberlains, doorkeepers, cooks and valets were professing 'Rafidis'. Turks, Sunni and Shii, are also said to have participated in Ashura commemorations. It was widely held that the Turks' arrival in the region would inaugurate those processes leading to the return of the *Mahdi* himself.[44]

Widespread, non-sectarian veneration of Ahl al-Bayt generally is further attested, and was no doubt only further encouraged, by the number of imam-zadas – shrines believed to be a tomb of a descendant of one of the Imams – that appeared on the plateau over the period to 1258. A site in Tabas dates to 1057, shortly after the fall of Baghdad. There were also constructions in Rayy, for the Hasanid Abd al-Azim, as well as in Isfahan, Nishabur, Kashan, Sojas, Qazwin, Gurgan and Varamin. In the twelfth and early thirteenth centuries, there were further constructions in Luristan, Qazwin, north Tihran, Shushtar, Qum, Kashan, Damawand and Hamadan. Further work was also undertaken at the Qum shrine of Imam Rida's sister Fatima in this period as well, though the original work dated to the ninth century. A site at Quchan is identified with the Khwarazmshahs.[45]

The influence of Alidism generally and the veneration of the Imams – which also had some appeal for Christian elements – was widespread to the northwest as well. In eastern Anatolia, great spiritual ferment among the tribal elements, waves of whom had been sweeping into the region since the Saljuk period, was fast becoming the norm. The Saljuks had exploited these to draw support from the Byzantines. By the mid-thirteenth century, Anatolia was heavily populated by these Turkic peoples. The *babas*, spiritual leaders, who travelled with the Turkmen tribes coming west, promulgated a heady mixture of traditional Turkic shamanism, Alidism, Imamism and messianism throughout the region, themselves drawing on the discourse of such figures as Ahmad Yasawi, the twelfth-century central Asian mystic, and his adherents, with their strange costumes, stories of miracles and wandering minstrels. The latter had more influence among such elements than contemporary urban mystics and philosophers.

In Khurasan, the Qalandariyya movement, with its sometimes extreme Alid theology and secret practices, assumed importance in this period.

Later in the period, the mystic figure known as Haji Biktash (d. 1270s), supposedly born in Khurasan and said to have been a follower of Yasawi, became involved with the Baba Ishaq movement in Anatolia. The latter erupted in 1239–40, challenging both the Rum Saljuks and urban mystics and philosophers. These repeatedly defeated forces sent against them until they were finally suppressed. Though executed in 1241, Haji Biktash is said to have lived on thereafter.[46]

Even contemporary, but 'higher' Sufi orders of the day venerated the Imams. Thus, Rumi, born in Balkh but dying in the Rum Saljuk capital of Qunya, and his order and his attachment to Shams bespoke veneration for Imam Ali.[47]

The plateau's elites

If the Saljuks grew more tolerant of the Twelvers – if not the Ismailis – this was certainly facilitated by elements of the plateau-based scholarly elite being attuned to the widespread Alid sympathies abroad among Shii and Sunni at the time, being critical of over-reliance on traditions, in line with the Saljuk's anti-Ashari tendencies, even as they were willing and able to get along with both Sunni elements and the political establishment. In this these scholars reprised the accommodationist tendencies of earlier generations of Twelver rationalist scholars.

Where little information is available for scholars in the Arab West over the years from the mid-eleventh to the mid-twelfth centuries, the careers and contributions of those Iran-based clerics of the period best known today – Abu Ali Fadl b. al-Hasan al-Tabrisi (d. 1154), Muhammad b. Ali, Ibn Shahr Ashub (d. 1192), Qutb al-Din Said b. Hibatallah al-Rawandi (d. 1178) and Mahmud b. Ali al-Himmasi al-Razi (d. early thirteenth century) – reveal an active awareness of, and an accommodationist engagement with, the complex spiritual dynamic that prevailed in the area. To be sure, some were also clearly sufficiently concerned with the latter to seek out opportunities outside the region.

Al-Tabrisi[48] is best known as author of the tafsir work *Majma al-Bayan* and

Ilam al-Wara. He spent most of his life in the Khurasan area, passing some years in Tus before moving to Sabziwar in 1128–9. Khurasan was Sunni, but there were pockets of Shia scattered throughout the area. Al-Tabrisi, however, studied with both Sunni scholars and Shii scholars of Khurasan, Mazandiran and Qum. His work reflects knowledge of, and debt to, Sunni discourse and methodology, but also veneration for, and appreciation of, the special role of Ahl al-Bayt and an acknowledgement of the potential compatibility of both.

Bayhaq was home to a family of prominent, originally Zaydi, sayyids with whom al-Tabrisi was connected by marriage and to one of whom he dedicated his *Majma al-Bayan* (*The Meeting Place of the Explanation*). The work was completed in 1142, most likely in Sabziwar. *Majma* is notable for its relatively few citations of earlier Twelver *tafsir* works other than al-Tusi's *Tibyan*. *Majma* is work beholden to, if not patterned on, al-Tusi's own deference to Sunni argumentation and sources, tolerance of Sunni Mutazilism, and attention and reference to a wide range of Islamic religious sciences.[49]

Al-Tabrisi's *Ilam al-Wara* (*The Mark of the Mortals*) – on the lives of the Prophet, Ali and the other Imams through to the twelfth Imam – was written for one of the Bawandid rulers. *Ilam*, probably completed in Tus, is also notable for its citations of both Sunni and Shii sources. As such, in an area overwhelmingly Sunni in orientation, the work further attests to tendencies among Twelver rationalist elements now, as earlier in Baghdad, to engage with non-Shii materials in order to seek common ground, for example, in and thereby encourage and legitimise the veneration of the Imams. To be sure, the relative dearth of pre-1055 Shii materials may have been a factor as well.

Love for the Prophet and his family, especially his grandsons, dominates the work. Considerable attention is given to Karbala and the dramatic nature of the events of the day, the sky raining blood, for example. Traditions available in al-Kulayni and Ibn Babawayh were cited, as were traditions found in *Basair*, which had promoted a more miraculous portrayal of the Imams. Indeed, there are references to the Imams' possession of other texts such as *Mashaf Fatima*. Special importance is given to visitation to the grave of Fatima in Qum as well.[50]

Al-Tabrisi himself taught later scholars such as Ibn Shahr Ashub, the *rijal* scholar Muntajab al-Din (d. *c.* 1189) and Qutb al-Din al-Rawandi.

Ibn Shahr Ashub was from Mazandiran. He also studied with Sunni scholars, including the Mutazili al-Zamakhshahri (d. *c.* 1143), al-Tabrisi and al-Rawandi, others based in Sabziwar/Bayhaq and Tus, and those with connections to Gurgan and Nishabur – where he spent some forty years. Ibn Shahr Ashub moved west in *c.* 1151, studying in Rayy and Isfahan. He then spent some ten years in Baghdad, attracting the attention of the court and being invited to preach. He then travelled to Aleppo. There he taught members of the Zuhra family and remained until his death.[51]

He is perhaps best known for his *rijal* work *Maalim al-Ulama*. This work, of

more than 1,000 entries, pales by comparison with the works in this genre of
al-Tusi and al-Najashi, let alone that of al-Kashshi. Ibn Shahr Ashub's entries
are usually no more than a line, if but a phrase. By contrast, al-Najashi's 1,200+
entries are often rich with biographical information and evaluation, as are the
nearly 900 entries in the *Fihrist* of al-Tusi, to say nothing of al-Tusi own *rijal*
work of over 6,400 entries on the companions of the Imams. In fact, however,
other than passing references in his opening remarks, Ibn Shahr Ashub does not
formally cite al-Tusi or Ibn al-Ghadairi and mentions al-Najashi only once.

Ibn Shahr Ashub probably completed his multi-volume *Manaqib Al Abi Talib*
whilst in Baghdad. In his introduction, he gives some hint of the state of relations
between Sunnis and Shiis in the realm generally, if not Baghdad in particular,
in the midst of caliphal backing for traditionism. He found the Shia reticent to
take up the challenge to Sunni animosity towards Ali, his Imamate and that of
the Imams, their *ilm*, and the different sects that abounded.

Tellingly, however, this contribution, in the *manaqib* tradition, privileged
recourse to both Sunni and Shii sources especially where, for example, they
agreed on a tradition. The former included works from the Sunni traditionist Muhammad b. Ismail al-Bukhari (d. 870) to al-Ghazali and a broad range
of Sunni *tafsir* works. The latter included work by al-Tabrisi, but also such
pre-1055 works as al-Mufid's *Irshad*, works by al-Murtada and al-Tusi, Ibn
Babawayh's *Kamal*, *al-Tawhid* and *Khisal*, and, to a very limited extent, al-
Kulayni, al-Saffar and al-Barqi – suggesting their continued availability, if only
indirectly, in Baghdad. Ibn Shahr Ashub carefully notes, however, that while his
work is based on the revealed sources, he applies rationalist analytical tools to
this material.[52]

The *rijal* scholar Muntajab al-Din, Ali b. Ubayd Allah Babawayh also hailed
from the plateau. A descendant of the well-known Babawayh family of Qum
and Rayy, he spent time in Isfahan, Qazwin, Baghdad and al-Hilla, where
he met Ibn Idris. He also journeyed to Khwarazm, Tabaristan, Kashan and
Nishabur. As those named above, he also studied with a large number and wide
range of scholars, including Hanafis in Rayy, a Hanbali in Baghdad, and a
Zaydi.

He completed his work before 1195–6 at the request of a *naqib* in Rayy. The
some 550 entries include citations of a number of late Buyid, but especially eleventh and twelfth-century scholars from across the region. The entries, as those
of Ibn Shahr Ashub, are usually quite short. He also does not systematically cite
his sources.[53]

Al-Rawandi was also a native Iranian, born in a small village between
Kashan and Isfahan. A student of al-Tabrisi, he authored several commentaries
on *al-Nihaya*, a commentary on al-Tusi's short *al-Jumal wal-Uqud* and works of
fiqh, *kalam* and the traditions.

Al-Rawandi's interests might appear to have run counter to the main currents of late Buyid Imami rationalism as they were on offer in this period. He was apparently critical of philosophy: his traditions' collection *al-Kharaij* dealt with the miracles of the Imams and was cited by later critics as containing 'extreme' traditions. He did cite texts traceable to al-Saffar, as well as al-Kulayni and al-Mufid, and some that feature in all three. There are also traditions that could be found in Ibn Babawayh's several compilations – such as *Uyun*, *Kamal*, *Maani*, *al-Tawhid* and his *Amali* – as well as *Ilam*. He did not devote any special attention to the events at Karbala, and included just a few texts on *ziyara* to the grave of Imam al-Husayn and the medicinal properties of the earth therefrom. He also authored a work in which he described some ninety-five points of dispute between al-Mufid and al-Murtada.[54]

His 1167 *Fiqh al Quran* was a collection of Quranic verses arranged in the order of a *fiqh* work, to which he added the comments of Twelver and non-Twelver scholars, and traditions, as well as his own. The work reveals al-Rawandi to have followed both the broad rationalist interpretive principles and many of the specific points of law established in the late Buyid period. In his very short introduction to this work, for example, al-Rawandi described *ijma* as a 'definitive proof mandating *ilm* owing to the presence of the infallible one [the Imam] who does not permit error'. In his discussion of *al-zakat*, if not elsewhere, he confirmed his understanding of the importance of the role of the *fuqaha* during the occultation and of their position as next in line of authority after *al-sufara*. He, as al-Tusi, did allow the donor to distribute *al-zakat* among the recipients in a later chapter. But, echoing Buyid-period commentators, he did privilege the role of the *faqih* 'because *al-faqih* knows its distribution better than someone who possesses no *fiqh*'. He did not specifically address the question of Friday prayer during the occultation: in line with al-Murtada and Sallar, he stated only that the prayer was obligatory on condition of the presence of '*al-Sultan al-adil* or he whom he appoints'. This text does not include any reference to Karbala or *ziyara* to that site, or any others at all and only brief references to *muta* marriage.[55]

Al-Himmasi al-Razi followed a slightly more emphatic rationalist approach. Born near Rayy in Iran, he later travelled to Iraq, including Najaf/Karbala and al-Hilla, and returned to his home town to became a teacher a school built, in part, by the Bawandids, with whom Tabrisi had also had connections.[56]

In this anti-traditionist atmosphere, al-Himmasi debated with Ashari scholars and was apparently supportive of the theological vision of al-Murtada. His rationalist proclivities are clearly evident in elements of his polemic. He was opposed to *al-taqlid*, in the context of an uncritical over-reliance on the traditions, and he criticised post-al-Tusi generations as having followed uncritically both al-Tusi and each other, and thus failing to be true *mujtahidin*. Al-Himmasi also criticised al-Tusi – perhaps as suggested above, one of the first of this generation to do so, before Ibn Idris – for relying on traditions that al-Himmasi himself alleged were *ahad*.[57]

Summary and conclusion

The arrival of the Sunni Saljuks on the scene in the 1050s was the occasion of the destruction of key Twelver resources in Baghdad, and did, as importantly, remove the Twelvers and, especially, their elites from their position of pre-eminence at the Buyid court and, concomitantly, across the region as well. If the Saljuks did not single out Twelvers for persecution, nevertheless, the faithful were a minority scattered across the region and generally without access to key works of the faith produced prior to 1055.

The written record suggests that the Arab west remained home to many, although those active from the mid-eleventh to the mid-twelfth centuries are not well known today. The fortunes of those pockets were 'uneven' over these years, to say the least, even as rationalist methodology remained dominant among elites. As their late Buyid predecessors, these maintained affiliations with the Saljuk political institution. As represented by these scholars, some, such as Ibn Zuhra, followed al-Tusi's legacy. Some, such as Ibn Tawus, raised questions about the over-emphasis on rationalist methodology, and remained 'in touch' with the 'popular' classes, some of whom shared an aversion to the officially sponsored anti-traditionist discourse. Others, such as Ibn Idris, queried al-Tusi's methodology, the uncritical approach to al-Tusi's legacy adopted by many and some of al-Tusi's rulings, but did not fundamentally challenge the rationalist methodology of the late Buyid period scholarly elite.

In these years sites on the Iranian plateau were the major centres of activity across the region. There, the Saljuks were actively promoting anti-traditionist Hanafism and the Shia could be caught in the middle between the Saljuks' agenda and the plateau's existing Shafii tendencies.

The written record suggests the presence of traditionist-based discourse especially among the 'popular' classes, but also that sectarian distinctions could become blurred. Indeed, Shii-style veneration of the Prophet's family in particular was widespread even among the Turkish newcomers to the area, and was becoming mixed with Sufi and Sufi messianic discourse.

The plateau's scholarly elite were mainly rationalists. There was visible support for a professionalised hierarchy within the community, first in evidence in the middle and especially later Buyid period. But these scholars were also attuned to the region's contemporary, very complex religious discourse. In this they were perhaps encouraged by the Saljuk's anti-traditionist agenda, as well as the distinct lack of availability of Twelver sources, and many studied with Sunni scholars, and were cognisant of and willing to utilise Sunni materials in their own work. Some seem to have sought out points of common belief between Sunni and Shii, focusing, for example, on a common love for *Ahl al-Bayt*.

Notes

1. On al-Tusi's students, see Akhtar, *Early Shiite Imamiyyah Thinkers*, 209f.
2. On these scholars, see, for example, A. Pakatchi and S. Umar, 'Halabi, Abul-Salah', *EI2*; E. Kohlberg, 'Halabi, Abu al-Selah', *EIr*. See also such later Shii biographical dictionaries as that of Abdallah Afandi (d. 1717), *Riyad al-Ulama*, 5 vols (Qum, 1401), 1: 99–100; 2: 438–9; 3: 136; Muhammad Baqir al-Khwansari (d. 1895), *Raudat al-Jannat*, eds M. T. al-Kashfi and A. Ismaililiyan, 8 vols (Tehran and Qum, 1390–1392), 2: 111, 113, 115; 2: 370–2; 4: 202–4. See also Abd al-Aziz, Ibn al-Barraj, *Sharh Jumal al-Ilm wal-Amal*, ed. K. M. Shanachi (Mashhad, 1974), 123, 131; al-Hasan b. Yusuf al-Hilli, al-Allama (d. 1325), *Mukhtalaf al-Shia* (Tehran, n.d.), 2: 169; 2: 36. On Ibn al-Barraj, see also R. Gleave, 'Shii Jurisprudence during the Seljuq Period', in S. Mecit and C. Lange (eds), *The Seljuqs. Politics, Society and Culture* (Edinburgh, 2011), 221.
3. On the Saljuks, see C. E. Bosworth *et al.*, 'Saldjukids', *EI2*. More recently, see A. Peacock, *Early Seljuq History. A New Interpretation* (London, 2010); Mecit and Lange (eds), *The Seljuqs*.
4. D. Durand-Guédy, *Iranian Elites and Turkish Rulers. A History of Isfahan in the Saljuq Period* (London, 2010), 142f. See also C. Hillenbrand, 'The Power Struggle Between the Saljuqs and the Ismailis of Alamut, 487–518/1094–1124: the Saljuq Perspective', in F. Daftary (ed.), *Medieval Ismaili's History and Thought* (Cambridge, 1996), 205–20; Peacock, *Early Seljuq History*, 99, 119–21.
5. Chapter 4, n. 48, and n. 10, below.
6. Marcinkowski, 'Rapprochement and Fealty', 285; Akhtar, *Early Shiite Imamiyyah Thinkers*, 211; Madelung, *Religious Trends*, 26f.
7. A. Bausani, 'Religion in the Saljuq Period', in J. A. Boyle *et al.* (eds), *Cambridge History of Iran, vol. 5: The Saljuq and Mongol Periods* (Cambridge, 1968), 248; Madelung, *Religious Trends*, 33, 85; J. Calmard, 'Le chiisme imamite en Iran à l'époque seljoukide d'après *le Kitab al-naqd*', *Le monde iranien et l'Islam*, 1 (1971), 56–8, 62, 60–1; M. Moazzen, 'Shiite Higher Learning and the Role of the *Madrasa-yi Sultani* in Late Safawid Iran', unpublished PhD dissertation, University of Toronto, 2011, 22–3, 37f, citing Abd al-Jalil Al-Qazwini, *Kitab al-Naqd*, ed. Jalal al-Din Husain Urmawi (Tehran, 1371/1992), 473, 12, 47–8, 163–4, 170–1; Peacock, *Early Seljuq History*, 120. See also D. G. Tor, 'Sovereign and Pious', in S. Mecit and C. Lange (eds), *The Seljuqs. Politics, Society and Culture* (Edinburgh, 2011), 51.
8. Al-Tihrani, *Tabaqat* (Qum, n.d.), second/fifth century AH, 62, 83, 68, 101, 158, 183, 184.
9. Al-Tihrani, *ibid.*, 2/6: 19, 57, 193, 11, 581, 149f, 128, 242–3. For cross-border movement in the seventh century, see 3/7: 136–7, 17, 19, 158, 162–3.
10. See Akhtar, as cited in n. 48 in Chapter 4. See also M. T. Yaghoubi and A. Montazerolghaem, 'The Shia of Baghdad at the time of the Abbasid caliphate and the Seljuk Sultanate (447–575 AH)', *Journal of Shia Islamic Studies*, 6(1) (2013), 64–5, citing Ibn al-Athir. See also R. Gleave, 'Shii Jurisprudence', 205–6, also citing later sources; H. al-Hilli, *al-Hilla wa Atharuha al-Ilmi wal-Adabi* (Qum, 1432/1390/2011), 29, citing no supporting sources.
11. Al-Tihrani himself records the copying of a few pre-1055 works, mainly those of al-Tusi, in this period. For the latter century, see, for example, al-Tihrani, *Tabaqat*, 6: 43, 81, 88-89, 159, 188, 245, 291, 327–8, 337. On copies of *Amali* of Ibn Babawayh, al-Mufid's *Irshad*, and the *rijal* works of al-Kashshi and al-Najashi, see 13–14, 341, 250, 177, 310, 261.
12. See Appendix II. As noted therein, the recorded dates of copies are always Hijri dates and the listing are organised by known death dates of the authors.
13. The Sunni Hanafi school – favoured by the Saljuks – was distinctly more flexible with regard to the use of the 'vernacular', on the Iranian plateau in particular. See T. Zadeh,

The Vernacular Qur'an. Translation and the Rise of Persian Exegesis (Oxford, 2012), 232–6, 127–31. See also 53f, 69f, 108f.

14. Kennedy, *The Prophet and the Age of the Caliphates*, 267f, 297f. See also M. Canard, 'Hamdanids', *EI2*.

15. J. Sauvaget, 'Halab', *EI2*; C. E. Bosworth, 'Saldjukids', *EI2*.

16. Afandi, *Riyad al-Ulama*, 2: 203, 208, albeit giving the date 507/1113; al-Khwansari, *Raudat al-Jannat*, 2: 374, 376. See also n. 18.

17. Yaqut al-Hamawi, *Mujam al-Buldan* (Beirut, 1397/1977), 2: 282–4; W. Akhtar, 'An Introduction to Imamiyyah Scholars, Major Shii Thinkers of the Fifth/Eleventh Century', *Al-Tawhid*, 4(4) (1407), and n. 38, available at: http://www.al-islam.org/al-tawhid/scholars.htm, accessed 15 October 2011.

18. Later generations of Imami biographers often made errors with Ibn Zuhra's name, suggesting, that information on Imami scholars writing between 1055 and 1501, and living in the scattered Imami communities of this period, was not always available to later and contemporary scholars. See, for example, Afandi, *Riyad al-Ulama*, 5: 358, where he identified him Abdallah b. Zuhra and said he had studied under al-Allama al-Hilli (2: 207). Ibn Kathir's reference in this account was most likely to Hamza's father, since Hamza himself was not born until 1117.

19. Al-Khwansari, *Raudat al-Jannat*, 2: 375; 6: 269.

20. Yaghoubi and Montazerolghaem,'The Shia of Baghdad', 64–5, citing Ibn al-Athir and Ibn al-Jawzi.

21. On the *futuwwa*, associations loosely based on chivalrous codes of conduct, and the link between 'popular' Sufism and the *futuwwa*, see M. Zakeri, 'Javanmardi', *EIr*.

22. A. Hartmann, 'Al-Nasir Li-Din Allah', *EI2*; Zakeri, 'Javanmardi'. See also Durand-Guédy, *Iranian Elites and Turkish Rulers*, 282–3.

23. On Ibn Tawus life and career see Kohlberg, *A Medieval Muslim Scholar at Work*, esp. 1f.

24. Kohlberg, *ibid.*, 79–81, 241. Kohlberg noted (351) that Ibn Tawus cited the Imams' traditions from only two books of al-Tusi's *Tahdhib* and that Ibn Tawus cited passages not available in published editions of Ibn Babawayh's *Uyun* (378–9), that he also cited passages from al-Mufid's original *Awail* that are not extant (130–1) and that the same applied to al-Tusi's *Amali* (112). Of the 670 works to which he did have had access, Kohlberg notes (78) that some 220 titles are Sunni works. On the dates of some, see 84f. A recent survey suggests no copies of Ibn al-Ghadairi's *rijal* work were made from 1055 to this period. See *Rijal Ibn al-Ghadairi*, 18.

25. Kohlberg, *ibid.*, 18–23. See also 376. See also al-Khwansari, *Raudat al-Jannat*, 7: 161, 4: 326; al-Tihrani, *al-Dharia*, 18: 58. Kohlberg suggests (22) that in his privileging of the traditions, his rejection of *kalam* and Mutazilism, and his aversion to *fiqh*, Ibn Tawus' views were akin to the Akhbaris of the Safawid period.

26. Ali b. Musa, Ibn Tawus, *al-Aman min Akhtar al-Asfar* (*The Safety from the Dangers of Travels*) (Qum, 1409), 47, 162. See also Kohlberg, *ibid.*, 22–3 and, on the work on *ziyara*, 46–8.

27. A term used by rationalist scholars to refer to traditionists. See Ed., 'Hashwiyya', *EI2*; A. S. Halkin, 'The Hashwiyya', *Journal of the American Oriental Society*, 54 (1934), 1–28.

28. Al-Amin, *Ayan*, 3: 5f.

29. G. Makdisi, 'Notes on Hilla and the Mazyadids in Medieval Islam', *Journal of the American Orientalist Society*, 74 (1954), 249–62. See also H. al-Hilli, *al-Hilla wa Atharuha*, 18f.

30. Afandi, *Riyad al-Ulama*, 5: 31; al-Khwansari, *Raudat al-Jannat*, 7: 160; H. al-Hilli, *ibid.*, 31f. If there were myriad other al-Hilla-based scholars before Ibn Idris, they are not discussed by H. al-Hilli.

31. See, for example, Y. al-Bahrani (d. 1772), *Luluat al-Bahrayn* (Najaf, 1969), 276–7. See also

Momen, *Introduction to Shii Islam*, 89; H. al-Hilli, *aibid.*, 34, 36; N. Calder, '*Khums* in Imami Shii Jurisprudence from the Tenth to the Sixteenth Century, AD', *Bulletin of the School of Oriental and African Studies*, 45(1) (1982), 41. Later scholars incorrectly claimed Ibn Idris was actually related to al-Tusi. See al-Bahrani, *Luluat*, 278; al-Khwansari, *Raudat al-Jannat*, 6: 276–9. See also Afandi, *Riyad al-Ulama*, 5: 31. This error either arose from wishful thinking or is another example of the poor quality of the information about the scholars of this period available to contemporary and later generations of scholars.

32. Ibn Idris, *al-Sarair al-Hawi li Tahrir al-Fatawi* (*The Encompassing Secrets in the Editing of the Fatwas*), 3 vols (Qum, 1410), 1: 492f, 458–9; 2: 21–7.

33. On Ibn Idris' use of *ijma* and other principles of rationalist principles, see *al-Sarair* 1: 19, 92, 96, 100, 103, 118.

34. Al-Tihrani, 4: 225, 6: 31; al-Khwansari, *Raudat al-Jannat*, 6: 220, 218; al-Bahrani, *Luluat*, 297. See also Gleave, 'Shii Jurisprudence', 221f.

35. Afandi, *Riyad al-Ulama*, 5: 354–9; al-Bahrani, *ibid.*, 283, n.26, 285, n. 27; al-Khwansari, *ibid.*, 8: 196–7. See also al-Tihrani, second/sixth century, 337–8. Another scholar of this period, 'Abd Allah, son of Jafar Duryasti, a traditionist, came to Baghdad in 1170 and returned to Rayy after some years, dying there after 1203. See R. Jafariyan, 'Four Centuries of Influence of Iraqi Shiism on Pre-Safawid Iran', available at: http://www.al-islam.org/mot/iraqishiism, ch. 3, accessed 31 December 2012.

36. Calmard, 'Le chiisme imamite en Iran', 43–67; Madelung, 'Abd al-Jalil Razi', *EIr*; Halm, *Shiism*, 57f.

37. Calmard, *ibid.*, 52–3.

38. Madelung, 'Al-e Bavand', *EIr*; Madelung, *Religious Trends*, 85; Fudge, *Quranic Hermeneutics*, 29.

39. Madelung, *Religious Trends*, 35–7. See also Peacock, *Early Seljuq History*, 100f.

40. Indeed, al-Qazwini refers to a volume he had composed on the virtues of Aisha, the wife of the Prophet, with which no Sunni might find fault. He cited another of his works in which he proved that the Shia, in fact, esteemed certain important Muslim figures. Interestingly, as Madelung notes, the list thereof included the founders of Mutazilism. See Madelung, 'Imamism', 21; R. Gleave, *Scripturalist Islam. The History and Doctrines of the Akhbari Shii School* (Leiden, 2007), 17–25.

41. Gleave, *ibid.*, provides the best coverage of al-Qazwini's scattered criticisms of the Akhbaris. Not long thereafter, the Sunni Fakhr al-Din al-Razi (d. 1210), an adherent of both Shafiism and Asharism, in his monumental *Usul al-Mahsul* referred to Akhbaris among the Imamis as relying only on reports traceable to the Imams – a 'definition' of Akhbarism only implied by al-Qazwini. These, al-Razi said, had been the majority of the earliest Shia. See Gleave, 25–7.

42. M. Mahdjoub, 'The Evolution of Popular Eulogy of the Imams Among the Shia', in S. A. Arjomand (ed.), *Authority and Political Culture in Shi'ism* (Albany, NY, 1988), 54–79, esp. 55–7.

43. Mahdjoub, *ibid.*, 68–70; Calmard, 'Le chiisme imamite en Iran', 64.

44. Calmard, *ibid.*, 49–50, 64–6.

45. P. Varjavand *et al.*, 'Emamzadeh', *EIr*.

46. H. Algar, 'Bektash, Haji', *EIr*; C. Cahen, 'Baba Ishaq, Baba Ilyas, Hadjdji Bektash et quelques autres', *Turcica*, 1 (1969), 53–64; J. Birge, *The Bektashi Order of Dervishes* (London, 1937), 23–32.

47. M. Mazzaoui, *The Origins of the Safawids. Shiism, Sufism, and the Ghulat* (Wiesbaden, 1972), 59–60, n. 3.

48. He is not to be confused with his contemporary, the author of *al-Ihtijaj*, Ahmad b. Ali, Abu Mansur, al-Tabarsi (d. *c.* 1223).

49. Fudge, *Quranic Hermeneutics*, 34, 37–9, 49. See also the introduction to al-Shaykh al-Tabrisi, *Ilam al-Wara*, 2 vols (Qum, 1417), 1: 18.

50. Fudge, *ibid.*, 29f. See also M. Pierce, 'Remembering the Infallible Imams, Narrative and Memory in Medieval Twelver Shiism', unpublished PhD dissertation, Boston University, 2013; al-Tabrisi, *Ilam*, 1: 536.

51. See the introduction to his *Maalim al-Din* (n.pl., n.d.), by Muhammad Sadiq Bahr al-Ulum, 1–36.

52. Ibn Shahr Ashub, *Manaqib Al Abi Talib*, 3 vols (Najaf, 1376/1956), 1: 3f, 223, 225, 236, 256, 315, 332, 339, 302, 14

53. Muntajab al-Din, *Fihrist Muntajab al-Din*, ed. Jalal-Din Urmawi (Qum, 1366), 8f, 399.

54. Al-Rawandi, *al-Kharaij wal-Jaraih*, 3 vols (n.pl., 1409), 2: 292f; 1: 380; 2: 768; 1: 443; 2: 872–3. See also Afandi, *Riyad al-Ulama*, 2: 419, 423–4; al-Bahrani, *Luluat*, 340, n. 4, 305–6; al-Khwansari, *Raudat al-Jannat*, 4: 7–8. Errors were also made by later scholars concerning al-Rawandi's name; some even suggested he had studied with al-Mufid. See, for example, al-Tihrani, *al-Dharia*, 7: 145–6; Afandi, *ibid.*

55. Al-Rawandi, *Fiqh al-Quran*, 2 vols (Qum, 1397–99), 1: 4; 1:228–229, 236–237, 219; 1:133–134, 135; 2: 94f, 104f, 1: 267f, 194, 320f. See also al-Tihrani, 6: 295.

56. Later Twelver biographers disagreed over this man's details as well. According to Afandi (*Riyad al-Ulama*, 5: 203), he was born in al-Hims, that is, modern-day Syria. Al-Nuri (d. 1902), however, quoted the earlier Safawid-period scholar Shaykh Baha' al-Din, known as Shaykh Bahai (d. 1621), that he was born near Rayy in Iran. Al-Nuri agreed with Afandi, as did al-Khwansari. See al-Husayn b. Muhammad al-Nuri, *Mustadrak al-Wasail*, 3 vols (Tehran, 1382), 477–8; al-Khwansari, *Raudat al-Jannat*, 7: 158f; al-Bahrani, *Luluat*, 348, n. 22. See also Gleave, 'Shii Jurisprudence', 207.

57. Al-Khwansari, *Raudat al-Jannat*, 7: 161, 160, 159.

CHAPTER 6

The Mongol and Ilkhanid periods: the rise and limits of the school of al-Hilla

The century or more following the fall of Baghdad to the Mongols and the killing of the last Abbasid caliph, like the later Buyid period, has been viewed by scholars and the faithful alike mainly via the careers and contributions of a precious few – in this case, Jafar b. al-Hasan al-Hilli (d. 1277), known later as *al-Muhaqqiq* (the researcher), and his nephew al-Hasan b. Yusuf al-Hilli (d. 1325), later called *al-Allama* (the most learned).[1]

As in 1055, so the 1258 fall of Baghdad resulted in widespread destruction of the community's resources. Twelver scholars did win recognition by the Mongol and Ilkhanid political establishment, as they did with that of the Saljuks. But actual Twelver influence was quite probably more limited than later Twelver accounts suggest.

The larger community remained fragmented and scattered across the region, the availability of key, early primary sources remained problematic and the onset of a marked decline in scholarly activity across the region, but especially in Iran, that would last until the fifteenth century is particularly notable.

Missing is the post-1258 equivalent of al-Qazwini's *Kitab al-Naqd*, with its insights into the situations of the non-elite believers – the majority in any age – across parts of the region at least. Indeed, what remains for later generations, admittedly and once again, are the written texts of these several elites. Read carefully, however, these, as earlier texts, reveal a degree of equivocation on a variety of issues that attests to disquiet within the community as to the specific interpretations of their authors, these authors' efforts to assert their authority over the community more generally and, also as prior to 1258, the continuation of Twelver pluralism in matters of doctrine and, especially, practice.

The fall of Baghdad and the rise of al-Hilla

The destruction visited on the scholarly community of Baghdad during the Mongol conquest of the city seems to have rivalled that of the Saljuk conquest. As to the Shia, Baghdad's Shii quarter of al-Karkh was plundered and the shrine at al-Kazimayn was destroyed, both probably owing to sectarian fighting. The overall loss of Shii materials, some key items among which were already, for Ibn Tawus anyway, no longer directly accessible, was arguably the greater as these were less dispersed than corresponding Sunni materials.[2]

Al-Hilla had been, as already seen, a Twelver centre before 1258. According to Twelver sources, the survival and, thus the subsequent rise in the fortunes of al-Hilla in the aftermath of the fall of Baghdad, owed itself in no small part to one of the Tawus family.

A nephew of Ibn Tawus, one Majd al-Din, along with the father of al-Allama, are said to have met Hulagu Khan (d. 1265) before he invaded Baghdad and to have recounted to the Mongol conqueror a prophecy of Imam Ali that fore-told that Hulagu would end Abbasid rule. He also sent a large sum of money to Hulagu and dedicated a work to him. Thus, it is said, he saved al-Hilla from destruction, although in fact the town's surrender to the Mongols probably also made a good bit of difference. Mongol troops were also sent to protect Imam Ali's grave site at Najaf, and Karbala was also spared destruction.

Ibn Tawus, born in al-Hilla, may also have had some role in the saving of his home town. He was caught in Baghdad during Hulagu's entrance into the city. According to his own account, at a meeting of all the city's scholars convened by Hulagu shortly thereafter, he was the only one who, when presented with Hulagu's request for a ruling on whether it was preferable to serve a just non-believing ruler or an unjust Muslim, affirmed the former. At that the others in attendance agreed, but Ibn Tawus and some 1,000 followers were escorted to al-Hilla.[3] Ibn Tawus, in Najaf in 1259, was back in Baghdad in 1260, having accepted an appointment by Hulagu as the city's Alid *naqib*. He was the made *naqib* of all Iraq in 1262–3.[4]

Other members of the Al Tawus also enjoyed connections to the Mongols. A son of Ibn Tawus was briefly *naqib* of both Baghdad and Najaf, and his own son was nominated to be *naqib*. Majd al-Din's brother Ahmad b. al-Hasan (d. 1304) led the *hajj* on several occasions. As to al-Hilla, the connection between the town and the Al Tawus also included that of Ibn Tawus' third brother, Ahmad (d. 1274–5). It is said that he was brought to Hulagu by Nasir al-Din al-Tusi (d. 1274) – a sympathiser with Twelver Shiism, if not himself an acknowledged Twelver – and was gifted a large estate in al-Hilla and died there in 1274–5. He was a teacher of al-Allama. He was the first to offer the formal classification of the Twelver traditions into the four categories of *sahih* (correct), *hasan* (good), *muwaththaq* (trustworthy) and *daif* (weak). With his death, however, the entire remaining male line of the Al Tawus came to an end.[5]

It was in al-Hilla, in 1205, a half-century before the arrival of Hulagu, that Jafar b. al-Hasan, al-Muhaqqiq, was born. From an established scholarly family, al-Muhaqqiq spent most of his life in the town. He had close ties to both contemporary and earlier moderate rationalist Twelver scholars. He studied under his father, as well as a member of Al Zuhra family and Muhammad b. Nama al-Hilli (d. 1239–48), a student of Ibn Idris. As his predecessors among the rationalists of the later Buyid period, al-Muhaqqiq was not at all opposed to involvement with the political institution. Indeed, he established connections with various officials at the Mongol court, including Nasir al-Din al-Tusi. Al-Muhaqqiq also dedicated his *al-Mutabar*, a work on *usul*, to an Imami official at court. His students included those with affiliations both to al-Hilla and also to such other pockets of the community as Abi, Sham (i.e., greater Syria) and Kufa.[6]

The Mongols were not uninterested in Shiism, if not Twelver Shiism in particular. In this period, for example, Ghazan (1295–1304) visited the Iraqi shrine cities and may have had coins struck bearing Shii-type inscriptions. Ghazan also maintained an interest in the family of the Prophet, for example, by establishing hostels for sayyids.[7]

Indeed, in the years immediately following 1258, the Mongols were also witness to the popular veneration for the family of the Prophet's family visible across the plateau, especially in the preceding centuries. In these years imamzadas were established at Shahsavar, Burujird, sites in Qum, Qazwin, Sava, Khuzistan, Varamin, Isfahan, Hamadan, Ishtihard, Nurabad (Fars), Shahrida (Isfahan), Tabriz, Sabziwar, Gilan, Kashan, Amul and Kilardasht. Work was also done on the shrine in Rayy and on another site in Rayy and a site in Bistam.[8]

Al-Muhaqqiq's nephew, al-Allama was born in al-Hilla in 1250, and was of the same Banu Asad tribe of which the town's founders, the Banu Mazyad, were a sub-clan. He witnessed the arrival of Mongols in the region and, as noted, his father apparently assisted in al-Hilla's formal surrender, thereby sparing the town. Al-Allama studied under a series of scholars, including his father and his uncle al-Muhaqqiq, members of the Al Tawus, other al-Hilla-based scholars and Nasir al-Din al-Tusi himself. He also studied under Shafii, Kufa and Baghdad-based Hanafi scholars, and debated with the great Shafii Ashari scholar, Abdallah al-Baydawi (d. *c.* 1286). He did spend time in al-Hilla, but also in Baghdad and Maragha, site of al-Tusi's famous observatory. His students hailed from Medina, Gurgan, Amul, in Tabaristan, from among Al Zuhra and other Aleppans as well as from the Jabal Amil region of the Lebanon. Several sources note that he became head of the Imami community in al-Hilla.[9]

Al-Allama himself spent much of the mature period of his career in Baghdad, but, more travelled than his uncle Jafar, *c.* 1309 he settled at the court of the Ilkhanid sultan Uljaitu (d. 1316), especially in the capital of Sultaniyya, near modern-day Qazwin. There it is said that he won a measure of tolerance for the faith. He debated with Sunni scholars at court. His later role in the conversion of the Khan to the Twelver faith is recounted, usually at length, in the major Shii biographical dictionaries.[10] According to these accounts, the sultan ordered the *khutba* throughout the realm to be read in the name of the twelve Imams, and had coins struck bearing the names of the Imams.[11]

Whatever the case, al-Allama did dedicate a number of works to Uljaitu. His

Kashifat al-Haqq (*The Unveiling of the Truth*), written at the sultan's request, was a description of the differences between himself and a Sunni cleric with whom he had debated at court in the presence of the sultan. Al-Allama also composed *Minhaj al-Karama fil-Imama* (*The Manner of Nobility on the Imamate*), on the Imamate in general, the proof of the Imamate of Ali and the twelfth Imam in particular, and the invalidation of the rule of the first three caliphs. In his dedication, al-Allama described the sultan as 'the kings of kings of the Arab and Persian peoples'. His *Nahj al-Haqq* (*The Path of Truth*), also dedicated to the Khan, was a similarly basic work on the faith. In both works he cited a tradition attributed to Imam Ali that al-Allama interpreted as predicting the coming of the Mongols, and added that it was based on this text that al-Hilla had surrendered to the Mongols – according to al-Allama, this was the same text Ibn Tawus had cited to Hulagu. Al-Allama also wrote a short work on Imami *ahkam* in response to questions put to him by Uljaitu, and an essay on prayer and ablutions for a vizier at court.[12]

Twelver sources also suggest that after the sultan's conversion to Imamism, al-Allama began to receive assistance from the sultan for the propagation of the faith and was constantly present at court or with the sultan during his travels. By the latter half of his career, even non-Twelver sources record that al-Allama had become extremely wealthy.[13]

The state of the community

If activity at al-Hilla generally and that of the Al Tawus and, especially, that of the two Hillis was so extensive, Appendix II suggests that no great recovery of pre-1055 texts occurred over this period beyond, perhaps, the production of copies for individual use.[14]

No copies of *al-Mahasin*, *Basair* or *Kamil al-Ziyarat* are recorded, and but three copies of *al-Kafi* are attested. All of Ibn Babawayh's works seemingly disappeared. The same applies to the several works of al-Mufid and al-Murtada. Some of al-Tusi's works seem to have been more accessible: his *tafsir* work *al-Tibyan* fared the best, and there are a very few copies of *al-Mabsut* and *al-Istibsar* dated to this period. His *rijal* works and those of his contemporaries, however, 'disappear' over the thirteenth and fourteenth centuries.

In the twelfth century Iran-based pockets of the faith had predominated in the region. With the rise of al-Hilla on the intellectual 'map', for each of the next two centuries the situation between Iran and Iraq was more balanced. As suggested in Appendix I, for the thirteenth century – the years that included the 1258 fall of Baghdad to the Mongols – there is a very marked decline in Iran-based scholarly activity that lasted until the sixteenth century. Pending detailed study, it might certainly appear that this decline could be attributed to the Mongol invasion and its aftermath. Certainly, Qum, for example, is said to have suffered terribly during the invasion, and its numbers for this century are markedly lower than for the previous century.

Whatever the cause(s), in the thirteenth century Iraq is associated with a very modest rise in numbers over the previous century. Of the Iraqi sites, the largest cluster is associated with al-Hilla – which experienced a large increase over the previous century – making it the largest centre in the region, although Baghdad was not far behind.[15] Bahrain and Aleppo are accorded eleven.

As for movement between regions, in the thirteenth century scholars travelled from the Hijaz to Baghdad and remaining there, from Isfahan to Baghdad in the 1230s, from Zanjan to al-Hilla, Tabriz to Najaf, from Ramalla to Aleppo, from Tabriz to Najaf, and also before 1258, from al-Hilla to Damascus, to Aleppo and to Egypt.[16]

Taken together the overall figures for activity across the region – if not absolutely accurate – are quite a lot lower than for the previous century, mainly owing the Iranian decline.

Over the fourteenth century, al-Hilla's prominence, and that of Iraq generally, grew further, followed by Aleppo and Jabal Amil, such that, again, together the scholars associated with these regions dwarfed those identified with all the sites in Iran taken together. To be sure, Iran does enjoy a slight edge over Iraq, though the difference is small, especially if the numbers attested are taken as indicative and not absolute. Across the century Iran-based figures can also be seen to have gone to al-Hilla, India, Aleppo, Kufa and Damascus. A Yemeni came to Mosul and an Aleppan travelled through Khurasan but returned home.[17] But for this century, as for the previous one, even if, as suggested, the figures cannot be taken as absolute, the overall numbers of active Twelver scholars remain low. If al-Hilla's numbers expanded in these years, however, the city never became as great a centre of scholarship in this period as some Iranian sites had been in the twelfth century.

The jurisprudence of al-Hilla: cautious advances I

Just as al-Muhaqqiq and al-Allama were on good terms with the secular authorities of their times, as were their late Buyid period rationalist predecessors, so each argued for a rationalist form of jurisprudence. The latter necessitated a hierarchical structure of authority within the community during the occultation and, as it had in the past, an especially politically quietist/accommodationist form of theology and practice. Their *ahkam* formulations, however, reveal a cautious and sometimes hesitant, if not also equivocal, manner that, together with their frequent recourse to the traditions, suggests that their views and their authority more generally were contested within the community. Yet again, it appears that the rationalist elites' interpretations were in the minority.

In his *fiqh* work *al-Mutabar* (*The Contemplation*), al-Muhaqqiq accepted the need for a class of scholars specialising in rationalist interpretations of issues related to *fiqh* as empowered to deal with problems for which no revelation was deemed relevant. He also argued that when rendering a ruling, the mufti was 'talking with the tongue of his [Allah's] law'. But he noted also that although the law was full of uncertainties, scholars – that is, the *fuqaha*, whom he said were needed in times when new problems presented themselves and were 'the heirs of the Prophet' – should be careful that these doubts and uncertainties did not invalidate the judicial process.[18]

Al-Muhaqqiq re-adopted a view on the use of *akhbar al-ahad* of al-Tusi – thus repudiating Ibn Idris – that those of such traditions that had been accepted by the *fuqaha*, or could be certified as validly linked to an Imam, were valid sources of the law.[19] He also argued for *ijma* as a *hujja*, as it was based on the presence of the Imam himself among those whose opinion formed the consensus.

But he also acknowledged there was always a good possibility that there had been dissent as well as agreement on a given issue. Therefore, there was not always certainty as to the Imam's presence among the scholars of the past. In these and other instances, unlike those of his predecessors such as al-Mufid and al-Murtada, he was at pains to cite support from the Quran and the Imams' traditions.[20]

Al-Allama is well known for having divided the community into *mujtahid* (legist) and *muqallid* (lay believer), and maintaining that it was incumbent on the latter to follow the former even if the *mujtahid* made an error. The very act of the following even a mistaken ruling absolved the lay believer of any sin. Also, the mistaken *mujtahid* would suffer no penalties for his mistake. In any case, as well, a ruling lapsed with death of *mujtahid*; thus, only the rulings of a living *mujtahid* were to be followed.[21] But in the course of making such points, there were interesting nuances thereto.

Thus, in the process of arguing for the principles, in his *Mabadi al-Wusul* (*The Starting Points of the Arrival*), a work on *usul al-fiqh* completed sometime before 1305–6, he also provided some detail as to the sources of jurisprudence: the ulama deduce *ahkam* from generalities of the Quran and the *Sunna*, entailing knowledge of some 400 verses from the Quran and the relevant traditions, to which were to be applied the various rationalist principles of jurisprudence, such as *al-baraa al-asliyya* (the presumption of permissibility). The scholar must have ability in Arabic[22] and must also be knowledgeable in such associated disciplines as the science of *rijal*, for example. Here, too, even as he formally accepted the principle of *ijtihad* – where those before him had equated it with Sunni *qiyas* (analogy) and had rejected it – al-Allama did so cautiously, noting that a *mujtahid* might be qualified to exercise *ijtihad* in some areas of the law but not others.

He also referred to and accepted the classification system for the traditions as developed by Ibn Tawus' brother Ahmad. He accepted the use of *akhbar al-ahad*, but not, however, if the text in question was a source of *ilm* (definitive knowledge). He, as others, accepted the principle of recourse to *ijma* as a proof if there was evidence of the view of the Imam: in effect, solving the issue of dissent raised by his uncle.[23]

In his 1297 *Kashf al-Murad* (*The Discovery of the Intention*), al-Allama reiterated the necessity and, indeed, the obligation of the faithful to adhere to Mutazilite rationalist ethics. Good and bad were intellectually derived principles. In an advance over the late Buyid rationalists and even the great Mutazili scholar Abd al-Jabbar himself, al-Allama provided details of the division of *hasan* (good) actions into four sub-divisions. These were *mubah* (permitted actions), where no blame attaches to the performance of the action in question, or lack thereof; *wajib* (obligatory), for which one received blame if one failed to perform the action, and praise if one did; *mandub* (commended), performance of which won praise, but no blame was attached if it was not performed; and, *makhruh* (reprehensible), neglect of which was praiseworthy, but performance of which was blameworthy.[24]

The Hillis and the *Ahkam*: cautious advances II

In their works on *fiqh*, both Hillis accepted the parameters of the Imami *furu* established by al-Mufid, al-Murtada and al-Tusi. They further defined the characteristics of the *faqih*, endowed him with even greater authority over community affairs and made additional provisions for accommodation with the ruling political institution.

Their discussions on questions involving personal and community practice, nevertheless, exhibit some caution and equivocation, careful attention to the revelation and clear acknowledgement of extant, alternative interpretations.

Thus, in respect of *al-qada*, in his famous *Sharai al-Islam* (*The Laws of Islam*), completed in 1272, al-Muhaqqiq stated that in the absence of the Imam, judging could be undertaken by a *faqih* who is '*al-Jami l'l-Sifat al-Mashruta fi-l'-Fatwa* (possessing the necessary characteristics for [delivering] the legal ruling)'. He was one of the earliest scholars to employ this particular phrase, even if he did not define these characteristics herein.

Perhaps sensing he was on shaky ground with such a statement, he substantiated the ruling by citing referred to the delegation tradition transmitted via Abu Khadija from Imam Jafar. The text in question, however, cited the Imam as directing the community to designate their own judges. In his later abbreviation of this work, *al-Mukhtasar al-Nafi* (*The Useful Abbreviation*), however, al-Muhaqqiq closed off any potential 'public' input into this process, stating that 'the designation of *al-awwam* (the common people)' was 'not sufficient'.[25]

As for al-Allama, in his *Qawaid al-Ahkam* (*The Bases of the Rulings*), completed c. 1300–1, he was even firmer on this latter point. He noted that the assumption of judicial authority stemmed from the permission of the Imam or his *naib*, not the designation of the community. He said that during the occultation the judgement of the *faqih* who was *al-Jami li Sharait al-Ifta* (the *faqih* possessing the characteristics for issuing legal rulings) was to be followed.

Al-Allama defined these characteristics, in some detail, as including ability in the various rationalist principles of jurisprudence as well as Arabic. In a clear reference to those less literate, both literally and especially in the rationalist religious sciences, al-Allama stated that memorisation of the sources themselves was insufficient without the ability to perform such deduction. Knowledge of earlier rulings was not necessary, he noted. In his briefer 1277–8 *Irshad al-Adhan* (*The Guide to the Intellects*), he uses the same terminology.[26]

Both men noticeably retreated from any of the late Buyid period references to the role of the *faqih* and the Friday congregational prayer, as well as the implementation of legal punishments, even if not consistently so.

Al-Muhaqqiq's preference for the performance of the prayer and its being lead by a *naib* of the Imam, for example, is clear in *Sharai*. However, the *faqih* is not formally identified as such. Indeed, in his later abbreviation, reference to the *naib* is missing, though his preference for the prayer's performance was still clear.[27]

Al-Allama, in discussing the prayer across several works of *fiqh*, made no formal provisions for the prayer's performance in the occultation. Indeed, in *Tahrir al-Ahkam* (*The Editing of the Rulings*), completed before 1299–1300, he stated that in the absence of the Imam or his *naib*, *ijma* required that the obligation lapse, a position similar to that of al-Murtada, Sallar and Ibn Idris. The *fuqaha*, he said, were able to gather the people together for all the prayers except the Friday prayer.[28] In his later *Mukhtalaf al-Shia* (*What is Disputed of the Shia*), completed between 1300 and 1309, however, he made provision both for the conduct of all the prayers and the implementation of *al-hudud* by the *fuqaha* during the occultation of the Imam. He said that the prayer was obligatory, on the basis of *ijma* – thus dismissing Ibn Idris' objections to the use of *ahad* traditions on the prayer. He did not address the issue directly in his *Irshad*.[29]

As to the *hudud* on the occultation, al-Muhaqqiq in *Sharai* stated that the *fuqaha* were permitted to undertake both the *hudud* and the *ahkam*, just as they were permitted *al-hukm* (judgement) among the people with the authority of *Sultan al-Waqt*, that is, the Imam. The people, he added, were obliged to assist them, suggesting that this was not always the case in his own time. In his later abbreviation, he retreated. Here he stated only that 'it is said' that 'the *fuqaha* undertake *al-hudud* during the occultation if they are trustworthy, and the people are obliged to assist them'.[30]

Al-Allama, indeed and yet again, was quite definitive on the matter of *al-hudud* during the occultation: in both his *Tahrir* and *Qawaid*, for example, he stated that the *fuqaha* were to undertake this task. Indeed, in *Tahrir*, he added the necessity of the *fuqaha* possessing '*sharait al-hukm*' during the occultation and prohibited *taqlid* (following) of earlier rulings. He made the same point in his *Irshad*.[31]

As to *al-zakat*, al-Muhaqqiq mainly followed the understandings laid down by al-Tusi as to the categories of recipients of the revenues. The individual could distribute *zakat* revenues, but it was preferable for the funds to be given to the Imam and obligatory if he requested it. No merit was attained if the donor distributed the funds. He did, however, note that some held the opposite view. In both works, he stated that if the Imam were absent then the trustworthy *faqih* should receive *al-zakat* for distribution, as he knew its destination – a ruling familiar from the later Buyid period.[32]

Al-Allama adhered to the expanding of categories of recipients of *al-zakat*, as per al-Tusi and al-Muhaqqiq. But, in contrast, he held that during the time of the Imam's presence in the community the revenues could be delivered to him or to the recipients directly. During the occultation, in something of a retreat from al-Muhaqqiq's more absolute position, in *Qawaid* al-Allama noted it was recommended that the funds go the trustworthy *faqih*. The donor could distribute the revenues directly. But, he stated, delivery of *zakat* to an intermediary during the occultation was the only means by which the donor could gain *ijza* (reward) for his donation. In *Tahrir*, *ijza* could be gained by direct distributions of the funds.[33] In his discussion on *zakat* in *Irshad*, al-Allama stated only that it is 'desirable' during the occultation that the *faqih* be given the tax for distribution. On the *zakat* paid at the end of Ramadan, he ruled that it was best if the 'Imam, his *naib* or the *faqih*' have a role, apparently not equating the latter two figures.[34]

In his extensive discussion of the issue in his work on *khilaf* (disagreements), however, he came very closed to reversing himself. Here he stated that *ijza* could be obtained only by delivering *al-zakat* to the *wakil* (agent), and that the latter could demand *al-zakat* from the donor, even if the donor had distributed *al-zakat* among the recipients himself. From other references in this work it is clear that the *wakil* referred to the *safir*, but al-Allama did fail to reiterate that the *faqih* replaced the latter during the occultation. Al-Allama stopped just short of formally asserting the dominance of the *fuqaha* over the process of the collection and the distribution of *al-zakat*.[35]

The same applied with respect to the distribution of *al-khums* during the absence of the Imam. In *Sharai*, al-Muhaqqiq stated only that 'the individual who possessed *al-hukm* by right of *al-niyaba* is obligated to assume authority over the disposition of the Imam's share'. If his intent was perhaps clear he, just as had al-Allama on *al-zakat*, stopped just short of naming the *faqih* as such. In *al-Mukhtasar*, curiously, however, he ignored the issue of the occultation altogether.[36]

Al-Allama offered different rulings on the distribution of *al-khums* during the absence of the Imam. In *Tahrir*, he noted a variety of options as extant. He agreed with those who ruled that during the occultation all the shares should be distributed among all the recipient categories, a view in accord with al-Muhaq-qiq's earlier ruling. This view, said al-Allama, was obligatory in the period of the Imam's presence within the community, and in the occultation it was *al-aqrab* (the closer). Whoever had the right of *hukm* by virtue of *al-niyaba* was to assume responsibility for the distribution of the Imam's shares among the recipients. In *Tahrir*, however, he did not specify how the remaining shares were to be distributed during the occultation. In *Qawaid*, he stated that the donor could choose between entrusting *al-khums* so that it would be given to the Imam, or giving half of it to the appropriate recipients and safeguarding the remainder, that is, the *Imam's* shares, or distributing it all. *Al-hakim* was to supervise the actual distribution.[37] In both instances, al-Allama did not take that final step to identify the *naib/hakim* as the *faqih*. Indeed, his discussion on *al-khums* in his *Irshad* contains no reference to the receipt or distribution of the revenues at all.[38]

In his *Mukhtalaf*, al-Allama offered yet another view. The six shares must be divided into halves. The last three categories of recipients may be given their shares, though he did not specify by whom. The Imam's shares should be protected until the Imam's return, or else entrusted to a *thiqa* (a trustworthy person), and from one *thiqa* to another until, at the Imam's return when these could be given to him.[39] This view was in accord with that of al-Tusi in *al-Nihaya*, but represented a change in al-Allama's views in both *Tahrir* and *Qawaid*. The *faqih* was, again, not formally mentioned.

One's understanding of the Hillis' views and rulings on the role of the *fuqaha* in these very basic daily activities of the community clearly very much depended on which of their works one had to hand. If one had access to several or even all of these works of both scholars, let alone all of al-Allama's works in this genre,[40] confusion was certainly possible.

Al-Hilla, the traditions and the *rijal*

Al-Muhaqqiq is said to have been the first scholar to refer to 'the four books' of the Imams' traditions as such.[41] Al-Allama is known to have completed works both on the traditions and on the *rijal*. Tellingly – for al-Allama's own legacy – of these, as will be noted further below, none of the former are extant. Of the latter, only one remains, that entitled *al-Khulasa* (*The Summary*). Even in the opening to the latter, al-Allama is clear as to the importance of reference to the textual revelation and of attention to the *rijal* literature to determine if the tradition related was reliable or not.[42]

Another al-Hilla-based scholar of this period, al-Hasan b. Ali, known as Ibn Daud (d. 1307), also completed a *rijal* work, with over 2,400 entries. He and al-Allama had studied together with al-Muhaqqiq, and Ibn Daud was also a student of Ahmad b. Musa al-Tawus.[43] Neither this work nor al-Allama's *al-Khulasa*, with its 1,779 entries, equalled the 6,400+ entries of al-Tusi's work on the Imams' companions, to be sure. But each contains more entries than those of Ibn Shahr Ashub (1,000+) and Muntajab al-Din (553).

The *fawaid* (sing. *faida*, addendum) in the works of al-Allama and Ibn Daud also reflected much greater attention to, and interest in, the genre than that exhibited by earlier contributors to the genre. Among al-Allama's addenda is one critiquing al-Tusi and Ibn Babawayh in their citations of *isnad* and their own recitations of their links to each. Ibn Daud included individual sections on earlier figures who had been members of such 'sects' as the Waqifis, Fathis, Zaydis, Kaysanis and the *ghulat*.

Each clearly had access to copies of key earlier works in genre. In his entries, al-Allama refers to earlier works such as those of al-Kashshi, al-Barqi, Ibn al-Ghadairi, al-Tusi, al-Najashi and Ibn Shahr Ashub. Ibn Daud's sources were as extensive.[44] Compared with Ibn Shahr Ashub and Muntajab al-Din, al-Allama and Ibn Daud seem to have felt they were reviving the science of *rijal* for those unschooled in it, and, perhaps especially, those without access to the earlier texts. To the extent that the latter was true, it would confirm the limited availability of such earlier texts among their contemporaries.

Alternative discourses

The Hillis' various rulings on matters of practice noted above do, if only indirectly, suggest that alternative views on such issues were abroad in the community. There are also occasional direct references to such views, as noted in the case of al-Muhaqqiq's views on *al-zakat*.

Al-Muhaqqiq addressed his *fiqh* work *al-Mutabar*, composed after his *Sharai* and *al-Mukhtasar*, to an Imami scholar and official at court. Herein he warned the latter against *al-hashwiyya* and *al-muqallida*, who might 'cheat you in order to attract you into their ignorance'.[45] These, he noted in a commentary on al-Tusi's *al-Nihaya*, accepted *akhbar al-ahad* – which, of course, both he and al-Allama did as well – while others within the community rejected all such traditions.[46] As to the Friday congregational prayer, in both his *fiqh* works, al-Muhaqqiq referred to a group that had forbidden the performance of this prayer during the occultation.[47] As to the distribution of *al-khums* during the occultation, al-Muhaqqiq disagreed with al-Tusi and ruled that all of *al-khums* should be distributed among the recipient categories, including the Imam's shares. Nevertheless, he listed four other opinions put forth within the community concerning the distribution of *al-khums* in the Imam's absence. These included the three views al-Tusi noted in *al-Nihaya*, and al-Tusi's own choice, to preserve the Imam's share for his return and distribute the remainder among the legitimate recipient categories. In *Tahrir*, al-Allama also listed various opinions on what to do with *al-khums* in the occultation.[48]

The introductions to several of al-Allama's *fiqh* works offer evidence of alternative discourses and direct evidence of challenges to the authority of the *faqih* generally and of himself specifically. In his 1289 *Muntaha al-Matlab*, he decried the influence of the *hashwiyya*. He also noted his own reliance herein on al-Mufid and al-Tusi, and criticised the people of his age as beholden to emotions and holding false beliefs.[49] In his *Tahrir al-Ahkam*, he called for respect for those who are engaged in teaching, that voices should not be raised against him, that there should be no talking over him, that he should be defended against gossip and that his students should not associate with his enemies.[50] He opened his *Tadhkira al-Fuqaha* (*The Message of the Fuqaha*), another work of *fiqh* completed between 1303 and 1321, with a strong statement on the importance of the role of the *fuqaha*, their role in transmitting the law of the Prophet, their being the repository of the *fatwas* of the Imams and heirs of the prophets: 'Everyone is required to follow their paths.' Absent is any suggestion that the expertise of the *mujtahid* might be limited to certain disciplines and not others.[51] In his 1304 *usul* work, *Nihaya al-Wusul ila Ilm al-Usul* (*The Ultimate of the Arrival to the Science of the Usul*), al-Allama criticised the Akhbaris for relying on *akhbar al-ahad*, and scholars like al-Tusi for having accepted such *ahad* traditions. He cited al-Murtada as the only example of a figure who had challenged the legitimacy of recourse to such traditions as a source of knowledge.[52]

As to practical issues, in both *Tahrir* and *Qawaid*, in his sections on prayer, al-Allama noted, as had al-Muhaqqiq, the presence of dissent within the community over the legitimacy of the congregational prayer during the occultation of the Imam.[53] In *Tahrir*, al-Allama also rejected the claim of some who argued that an illiterate might serve as reader at the prayer service.[54] In his *Mukhtalaf*, he also noted disagreement within the community on issues related to *al-khums*. His reference here to Sallar as representative of those who ruled that all items of *al-khums* were permitted to believers during the occultation, and his listing of the different options concerning *al-khums* during the occultation as listed by al-Mufid, suggests these views also had found expression within the contemporary community. Al-Allama also noted that some scholars ruled that the Imam's shares were also to be divided among the recipient categories,[55] a view corresponding to that of al-Muhaqqiq.

Summary and conclusion

For discussions of developments in the faith over the Mongol and early Ilkhanid periods, scholars of Twelver Shiism have, if perhaps necessarily, privileged the written works of the smallest of handfuls of scholars to date – chiefly the two Hillis.

In fact, however, the contributions of both Hillis, as those of others of the scholarly class, need to be set against a broader background of developments.

The community remained fragmented across the region, and the availability of key early texts, already problematic, only worsened with the destruction that befell Baghdad at the Mongols' capture of the city in 1258.

The data suggests that overall scholarly activity across the region began to decline in this period. Iran-based activity declined markedly and, relatively, activity to the west of the plateau began to overtake that in Iran. Al-Hilla does emerges as something of an outpost or at least an exceptional centre of rationalist Twelver scholarly activity over these years. But elsewhere in Arab lands there was also activity.

Any connections enjoyed by the Hillis with the political establishment in this period were limited and probably exceptional. Indeed, with the Mongol conquest over – Ibn Tawus having died less than ten years after the fall of Baghdad, and Nasir al-Din al-Tusi, if a Twelver, a decade later – Mongol/Ilkhanid interest in Shiism, if not Twelver Shiism, was considerably less than that of Shii scholars in the Mongols and Ilkhanids. Uljaitu's 'conversion' likely meant more to al-Allama – let alone to later generations of Twelver scholars – than it did to 'the convert' himself.

To the extent that anything is known about the actual state of the community, the Hillis' biographies and contributions do repay attention. Al-Allama, as those among the previous period's scholars, studied with Sunnis, and both Hillis were adherents of the rationalist approach identified with al-Murtada and al-Mufid, and further refined by al-Tusi. In the process, both Hillis, but al-Allama especially, projected the further differentiation of the faith's senior scholars from the lay faithful, the further enhancement of their authority over the interpretation of matters of doctrine and practice, and recourse to a longer, more detailed list of skill sets – all bespeaking an interest in the increasing professionalisation of the *fuqaha*.

Nevertheless, in their works of *fiqh* neither consistently or unequivocally advanced the authority of the *faqih* as the Imam's *naib* over day-to-day matters of both personal and community practice markedly beyond that on offer in the works of earlier generations. Their legacy was, potentially, confusion.

Al-Allama refers also to challenges to the authority both of the *faqih* generally and his own personally. These, in addition to disagreement over the *ahkam*, were, no doubt, factors in the Hillis' evident caution and equivocation.

Once again, the views of those scholars best known today, rationalists all, were most probably in the minority in their own time.

Notes

1. See, for example, Momen, *Introduction to Shii Islam*, 94–6; Halm, *Shiism*, 63–7.
2. Kohlberg, *A Medieval Scholar*, 80. Of the 670 works to which Ibn Tawus had access, some 220 of which were Sunni in origin (Kohlberg, 78), Kohlberg notes (87) that more than a third are now not extant. Many of the city's libraries were destroyed during the Mongol

sack. Kohlberg notes that after the death of Ibn Tawus' second son in 1312 (18), Ibn Tawus' own library disappeared (80).

3. Kohlberg, *ibid.*, 15, 10–11; S. Schmidtke, *The Theology of al-Allama al-Hilli (d. 725/1325)* (Berlin, 1991), 10–11, citing al-Allama himself.

4. In a 1264 note Ibn Tawus opined that he – as a descendent of Imam Musa – might be the one referred to in a tradition from Imam Jafar that foretold that the destruction of the Abbasids would be followed by the rule of a member of *Ahl al-Bayt*. He died in Baghdad in 1266. Kohlberg, *ibid.*, 11–12.

5. Kohlberg, *ibid.*, 15–18. See Halm, *Shiism*, 60–1; H. Daiber, 'al-Tusi, Nasir al-Din', *EI2*.

6. H. al-Hilli, *al-Hilla wa Atharuha*, 39–50. See also Afandi, *Riyad al-Ulama*, 1: 103–4; al-Bahrani, *Luluat*, 227–35, 227, n. 1; al-Tihrani, *al-Dharia*, 1: 178. Later Twelver biographers recount that al-Tusi attended a *majlis* of al-Muhaqqiq in al-Hilla itself, and that the former acknowledged al-Hilli's scholarship and his rank of *mujtahid* in the community. Al-Tusi was said to be the instigator of the final fate of the last Abbasid caliph, helped along by the Shii vizier at the time, Ibn al-Alqami. On the meeting between al-Tusi and al-Hilli, see Mazzaoui, *Origins of the Safawids*, 24–7, 83. On the essay said to have been written by al-Hilli for al-Tusi, see al-Amin, *Ayan*, 4: 89f.

7. Mazzaoui, *ibid.*, 39; al-Amin, *ibid.*, 9: 120f.

8. Varjavand.

9. The best English-language discussion on al-Allama is found in Schmidtke, *Theology of al-Allama al-Hilli*, 9f. In Arabic, see H. al-Hilli, *al-Hilla wa Atharuha*, 51–72. See also Afandi, *Riyad al-Ulama*, 1: 359, 384–5; al-Bahrani, *Luluat*, 211, 223–6; al-Khwansari, *Raudat al-Jannat*, 2: 278–9. On al-Allama's students, see also Schmidtke, *ibid.*, 35–40.

10. See, for example, al-Bahrani, *ibid.*, 224–6; al-Khwansari, *ibid.*, 2: 279; al-Amin, *Ayan*, 5: 396f. Many of these accounts relied heavily on a conversion account offered by Hafiz Abru (d. 1429–30). See Mazzaoui, *Origins of the Safawids*, 22, n. 1. Mazzaoui (38, 40) notes the accounts of the conversion but, in any case, suggested that, although interested in Islam, the Mongols 'remained essentially foreign to what was going on along (sic) the religious level'. Indeed, before he, apparently, converted to Shiism, the Khan had been, initially, a Buddhist, a Sunni Hanafi and then a Shafii. In this period most of those living in urban settings on the plateau remained Sunnis.

11. Afandi, *Riyad al-Ulama*, 1: 361; al-Bahrani, *ibid.* On al-Hilli at court, see also Schmidtke, *ibid.*, 23–32.

12. On these works see al-Bahrani, *ibid.*, 224–5, 218, n. 51; al-Khwansari, *Raudat al-Jannat*, 2: 275, 284, 281; Mazzaoui, *Origins of the Safawids*, 28–30; al-Tihrani, 24: 416.

13. Mazzaoui, *ibid.*, 27, n. 5, citing contemporary correspondence.

14. These included works cited by al-Tihrani – again, not absolute but indicative figures – and include copies of works by al-Tusi (*Tabaqat*, third/seventh century: 43–4, 52, 103), *al-Kafi* (36, 183) and works by Ibn Babawayh, al-Murtada, Ibn al-Barraj and Sallar (105, 115, 184, 113).

15. On notable figures buried in the Kazimayn in this period, see M. H. Al Yasin, *Tarikh al-Mashhad al-Kazimi* (Baghdad, 1967/1387), 50f. On Qum, see the following note.

16. Al-Tihrani, third/seventh century: 136, 17, 158, 19, 105, 118, 134, 135, 162–3. Qum remains on this list, although it had suffered badly in the initial Mongol invasion of the plateau. In 1284–5, sixty years after those attacks, the city was reported to be in ruins and to have remained so during the reign of the Ilkhanid Uljaitu (*reg.* 1304–16). See A. K. S. Lambton, 'Qum. The Evolution of a Medieval City', *Journal of the Royal Asiatic Society*, 2 (1990), 328–9. The number of scholars associated with the city over these years, relative to the twelfth century, does seem to corroborate the historical account.

17. Al-Tihrani, third/eighth century: 43, 44–5, 123, 186–7, 209–10, 240, 195.
18. Jafar b. al-Hasan al-Hilli, al-Muhaqqiq, *al-Mutabar*, 2 vols (n.pl., 1364), 1: 19, 22
19. Al-Muhaqqiq, *ibid.*, 1: 29.
20. Al-Muhaqqiq, *ibid.*, 1: 31. For an English-language discussion, see Calder, 'The Structure of Authority', 228, 196–7; A. A. Sachedina, *The Idea of the Mahdi in Twelver Shiism* (Albany, NY, 1981), 140–1.
21. Calder, *ibid.*, 102–4, 230–41, 218–19, 221, 324; Sachedina, *ibid.*, 213, n. 7. See also Madelung, 'Authority', n. 26; Halm, *Shiism*, 66–7.
22. See Chapter 5, n. 13. On the Hillis' predisposition against the vernacular see Zadeh, *The Vernacular Qur'an*, 128–9. See also the text below at n. 26.
23. Al-Hasan b. Yusuf al-Hilli, al-Allama, *Mabadi al-Wusul* (n.pl., 1404), 243–4, 203f, 215–16, 195. On the date of this work, see Schmidtke, *Theology of al-Allama al-Hilli*, 66.
24. Calder, 'The Structure of Authority', 219–20, citing *Kashf*. On the date, see Schmidtke, *ibid.*, 50.
25. Al-Muhaqqiq, *Sharai al-Islam* (Najaf, 1389/1969), 4: 67–9; Al-Muhaqqiq, *al-Mukhtasar al-Nafi* (Najaf, 1383/1964), 283–4. For the tradition, see al-Kulayni, *al-Kafi*, 7: 412; Ibn Babawayh, *al-Faqih*, 3: 1; al-Tusi, *Tahdhib*, 6: 219. On the date of *Sharai*, see al-Tihrani, *al-Dharia*, 13: 48. On the text of the tradition, see also Chapter 2, n. 52.
26. Al-Allama's listing of the *sharait* included: ability in the Quran, the *Sunna*, *ijma* and *khilaf* (disagreement), *adilla al-aql* (the rationalist proofs) – *al-istishab*, *al-baraa al-asliyya* and others – Arabic, *usul al-qawaid*, *usul al-fiqh* and the conditions of al-*burhan* (evidence). See al-Allama, *Qawaid al-Ahkam*, 2 vols in 1 (Qum, n.d.), 2: 200–2. See also his *Irshad al-Adhan*, 2 vols (Qum, 1410), 2: 138. On the date, see Schmidtke, *Theology of al-Allama al-Hilli*, 63.
27. Al-Muhaqqiq, *Sharai*, 1: 94–100; al-Muhaqqiq, *al-Mukhtasar*, 61–2.
28. Al-Muhaqqiq, *Tahrir al-Ahkam*, 2 vols. in 1 (Mashhad, n.d.), 1: 43. On this date see Schmidtke, *Theology of al-Allama al-Hilli*, 63. See also al-Allama, *Qawaid*, 1: 36, 45.
29. Al-Allama, *Mukhtalaf al-Shia*, 1: 108–9; al-Allama, *Irshad*, 1: 257–9. On the date see Schmidtke, *ibid.*, 62; al-Tihrani, 3: 378–9, 30: 219.
30. Al-Muhaqqiq, *Sharai*, 1: 344–5; al-Muhaqqiq, *al-Mukhtasar*, 143.
31. Al-Allama, *Tahrir*, 1: 157–8; al-Allama, *Qawaid*, 1: 118–19; al-Allama, *Irshad*, 1: 353.
32. Al-Muhaqqiq, *Sharai*, 1: 164–5; al-Muhaqqiq, *al-Mukhtasar*, 87–8.
33. Al-Allama, *Tahrir*, 1: 67; al-Allama, *Qawaid*, 1: 57–9. See also Calder, 'Zakat', 476.
34. Al-Allama, *Irshad*, 1: 288, 291.
35. Al-Allama, *Mukhtalaf*, 2: 21.
36. Al-Muhaqqiq, *Sharai*, 1: 184; al-Muhaqqiq, *al-Mukhtasar*, 90–1.
37. Al-Allama, *Tahrir*, 1: 75; al-Allama, *Qawaid*, 1: 62–3. Cf. Calder, 'Khums', 43–4.
38. Al-Allama, *Irshad* 1: 292–4.
39. Al-Allama, *Mukhtalaf*, 2: 37–40.
40. For a list of al-Allama's legal works, see Schmidtke, *Theology of al-Allama al-Hilli*, 62–5. As she notes, some of these are missing.
41. Amir-Moezzi, *The Divine Guide*, 20, n. 86.
42. Al-Allama noted that earlier shaykhs had many works in this genre, but that many of these were long and others were too brief. In this volume, he said he did not intend to cite all their works or their biographies – these would be covered in his larger *Kashf al-Maqal fi Marifat al-Rijal* (*The Discovery of the Proposition on the Knowledge of the Rijal*). The latter is lost. See al-Allama, *Khulasat al-Aqwal* (*A Summary of the Statements*) (n.pl., 1417), 43–4. See S. Abd al-Aziz al-Tabatabai, *Maktabat al-Allama al-Hilli* (Qum, 1416), 166, 118f. On *Kashf*, see al-Tihrani, 10: 133. See also Schmidtke, *Theology of al-Allama al-Hilli*, 68–9.

43. Al-Hasan b. Ali, Ibn Daud, *Rijal Ibn Daud*, ed. S. Muhammad Sadiq, Al Bahr al-Ulum (n.pl., 1392/1972), introduction, 5–7.
44. See, for example, Ibn Daud, *Rijal*, 25f.
45. Al-Muhaqqiq, *al-Mutabar*, 22.
46. M. T. Danishpazhuh (ed.), *Catalogue méthodique, descriptif et raisonné des manuscrits concernant la tradition, les principes de la jurisprudence et le droit musulman de la Bibliothèque de l'Université de Téhéran don de M. le professuer Meshkât*, 6 vols (Tehran, 1330–1335), 5: 2002–4; Calder, 'The Structure', 229–30.
47. Al-Muhaqqiq, *Sharai*, 1: 98; al-Muhaqqiq, *al-Mukhtasar*, 62.
48. Al-Muhaqqiq, *Sharai*, 1: 184. See also al-Tusi, *al-Nihaya*, 200–1.
49. Al-Allama, *Muntaha al-Matlab* (n.pl., 1412), 3–12. On the date, see Schmidtke, *Theology of al-Allama al-Hilli*, 64.
50. Al-Allama, *Tahrir* (n.pl., 1420), 1: 31f, 34f.
51. Al-Allama, *Tahdkira al-Fuqaha* (n.pl., n.d.). 1: 3–4. On the date, see al-Tihrani, 4: 43f; Schmidtke, *Theology of al-Allama al-Hilli*, 64.
52. Calder, 'The Structure', 231; al-Khwansari, *Raudat al-Jannat*, 6: 284; Danishpazhuh, *Catalogue méthodique*, 5: 1742–6.
53. Al-Allama, *Tahrir*, 1: 43; al-Allama, *Qawaid*, 1: 36.
54. Al-Allama, *Tahrir*, 1: 53.
55. Al-Allama, *Mukhtalaf*, 2: 37–40. See also *Tahrir*, 1: 75

CHAPTER 7

The severest of challenges

Previous existential challenges to the faith can be associated with specific dates – 1055 and 1258, for example, may be said to have been military-political challenges: libraries were lost and scholars were scattered as the result of specific conquests.

Over the nearly two centuries from the death of al-Allama al-Hilli in 1325 to the capture of Tabriz by the Safawids in 1501, the faith faced an existential challenge of a very different sort. Over these years the faith faced the prospect of slow absorption into the plethora of messianic, heterodox Sufi-style movements that had their origins in earlier periods, but may be said to have peaked across the region in these centuries. To make matters worse, the scholarly centres of the faith were still based to the west, far from, and thus not engaging actively with, these millenarianist movements. The continued limited availability of both key older and even more recently composed texts in these years, coupled with the continued low level of scholarly activity across the region, but in Iran especially, where many of these movements had their greatest influence, can only have further hindered any effective response to this challenge.

By the late 1400s, little if anything of the legacy of the late Buyid period's rationalist discourse was at all discernible across the region.

The state of the faith in the fourteenth century

Al-Allama died in al-Hilla in 1325 and was buried in Najaf.

Despite his apparent success in converting Uljaitu, the Mongols did not suddenly adopt and promote any form of Shiism, let alone Twelver Shiism, as their official faith. At the death of Uljaitu's successor Abu Said in 1335, the Ilkhanid polity as any sort of a unified political entity collapsed. In its place arose localised entities such as the Jalayirids, based in western Iran and Iraq, including Baghdad; the Chubanids, based in Azerbaijan; and the Muzaffarids, based around Isfahan. These and, further east, the Sarbadars, based in Sabziwar, the Kartids, in Herat, and the Injuids in Fars – the latter both former Ilkhanid vassals – all achieved some visibility on the scene until the arrival of Timur in the region in the later 1300s.

To the west, the Mamluks had stopped the Mongols' further advancement at the 1260 battle of Ayn Jalut, north of Jerusalem. A formal treaty reached between the Mamluks and Abu Said thereafter finally settled conflict between the two. In the aftermath of the latter's death the Mamluks seized territory along the eastern Mediterranean coast and the hinterland.[1]

Over these years, scholarly activity generally continued reduced and the Iranian plateau's position as the location of many important clusters of the faithful, as represented by the number of scholars associated with such sites, continued to slip compared with pockets in the Arab west. Thus, in the fourteenth century Iran is accorded some seventy-one, a less than significant rise over the numbers for the previous century, with clusters – all in the single figures – in Qum, Shiraz and Kashan, and the area around Nishabur/Tus. These are much more scattered than in the previous century, even as the figures suggest a continued low level of activity.[2] Nearly the same number are seen to be associated with Iraq, with thirty-three at al-Hilla; as in the previous century far outshining any other single locale, Iraqi or otherwise. Thirteen are associated with Jabal Amil in the Lebanon, a considerable increase over the previous century; sixteen are connected with Aleppo; six with Bahrain; and four with the Hijaz. Perhaps further representative of such trends over the fourteenth century, Iran-based figures can be seen to have gone to al-Hilla, India, Aleppo, Kufa and Damascus. A Yemeni came to Mosul, an Aleppan travelled through Khurasan and returned home.[3]

As to the availability of key sources, as seen in Appendix II, the situation also continued to be problematic. For pre-1055 texts, even if individuals may have had, or had access to, copies of such works, their widespread availability became quite dire.

Even the works of the more recent scholars were only unevenly available in this period. Thus, some copies of al-Tabrisi's *Majma al-Bayan* were extant. Works by al-Rawandi were in short supply and Ibn Idris' *al-Sarair* may be said to have disappeared. Perhaps more importantly, and tellingly, the availability of the works of the two Hillis was quite uneven over each of the two centuries following al-Allama's death. Copies of al-Muhaqqiq's two main works were not in great supply, although there were a few of *al-Mukhtasar*. As to al-Allama's works, of his *fiqh* contributions, his *Qawaid* might be said to have been widely available, as were, if to a lesser extent, his *Tahrir, Irshad* and, much less so, his *Mukhtalaf*. But his *Tadhkira* and *Muntaha* may be said to not to have been available. Of his three works on *usul* only *Nihaya* might have been available, with six copies, the same number as his *Kashf*. His *rijal* work *Khulasa* was not available, nor was his short theological work *al-Bab al-hadi ashar*, although, because of its 1928 English translation, it is relatively well known today.[4]

Many of al-Allama's other works were, in fact, very soon lost for good. Six of some seven works on the traditions of the Imams were lost, as was his major work on *rijal, Kashf al-Maqal*. Of another work on theology, *Nihayat al-Maram*, only four incomplete manuscript copies are known today. His philosophical works, works on grammar and his two works of *tafsir* also disappeared.[5] Even the number of what might be termed 'personal copies' of some of these works was still small.[6]

In these years scholars began composing commentaries (*sharh*, pl. *shuruh*) and marginalia (*hashiya*, pl. *hawashi*) on texts, but few, if any, of these are recorded for works completed before 1258, perhaps further attesting to issues of availability. Even for post-1258 works, such as those of the Hillis, the situation was uneven. Few such works were written on al-Muhaqqiq's works of *fiqh*.[7] Al-Allama's *fiqh* works attracted more such attention than his other works, but only unevenly. Thus, three commentaries and six marginalia were composed on his *Qawaid*, although of the latter one each was done by the author himself and his own son. His *Irshad* also attracted attention, with four commentaries and marginalia each, of each of which, however, his son contributed one. His other *fiqh* works did not attract such notice, and of his non-*fiqh* works only his *Tahdhib*, an *usul* work, was the subject of commentaries, with five *shuruh* – one done by his own son – and two marginalia. Of three *shuruh* on his *Mabadi*, two were done by his son and one by a nephew.[8]

From west to east: the Shia in greater Syria/Lebanon

The *tabaqat* literature suggests a notable rise in the numbers of clerics' associated with the Lebanon in this century, particularly the Jabal Amil area, the westernmost territory of the region. In this period it was home to one of those Twelver scholars so well known in Western and Shii sources, Muhammad b. Makki al-Amili, Ibn Makki (d. 1384), later called *al-Shahid al-Awwal* (the first martyr).

Shii tradition traces the origins of this community to Abu Dharr al-Ghifari, a companion of Ali who was exiled to the area by the caliph Uthman. It does seem that Tripoli and Sayda (Sidon) were home to Shii elements as early as the eighth century. During the Buyid/Hamdanid period, as noted, there were Twelver Shii scholars, students of the Baghdad elite, in the region's major cities. The eleventh-century Ismaili traveller Nasir Khusraw said that Tyre and Tripoli were mainly Shii in his time, there being many mosques there and houses and sites built like *rabatat*. Early thirteenth-century Damascus was said to be home to various Shii groups. The chronicler Ibn al-Athir (d. 1233) notes Shiites in the Ramalla area and Damascus, and in the later 1200s Jizzin, in the Jabal Amil area of Lebanon, was also said to be Shii.[9]

As to Damascus, there were very few overtly Twelver elements living there. During the later Mamluk period, a *qadi* was burned alive for his alleged 'rafidi' views, even as the authorities offered official protection for the Muharram commemorations in the city. To be sure, the latter perhaps attests to the manner in which, as elsewhere in the region, Sunni and Shii alike found meaning in the commemoration of the tragedy.[10]

When the Mamluks took the city from the Crusaders after the 1291 siege of

Acre, they were harsh on the Shia in the region generally. The Druze, Nusayris and Twelvers in the Kisrawan, in the mountains above Beirut, were also forced out of the area into the Biqaa valley.[11]

If there were Shii scholars in the Jabal Amil region of what is now southern Lebanon before the twelfth century, however, they are not known. But when Salah al-Din invaded the area there were Shia in Aleppo and in some areas of Jabal Amil. In his 1324 sojourn in the region, Ibn Batuta speaks of 'rafidi' elements, as identified by the distinctive style of their ablutions. Indeed, Amilis are recorded among the students of Ibn Tawus, al-Muhaqqiq and al-Allama.[12]

Born in Jizzin, in the Jabal Amil, in 1333, less then a decade after the death of al-Allama in 1325, Muhammad b. Makki's (d. 1384) career demonstrates the extent to which in this period Arab Twelver scholars were aware of other pockets of the community in Arab lands, but avoided sojourns further east. Although from a clerical family, and although a prominent al-Hilla-associated scholar had settled in Jizzin from Aleppo in the later 1200s, Ibn Makki clearly perceived the limits of his world: as at least two earlier scholars had done, he made his way to al-Hilla. There he studied with al-Allama's son and a member of the Aleppan Zuhra family, among others. He thence moved to Karbala, to Jerusalem and then Mecca, which he reached in the mid-1350s. He was back in Jizzin c. 1357, teaching.

Although he is credited with the establishment of Twelver Shii scholarship in the Jabal Amil region, as many of his Shii predecessors Ibn Makki, during a sojourn in Baghdad, studied with a number of Sunni scholars. In Damascus, while he was known to be a Shiite, he was not openly anti-Sunni and even studied with a Rayy-born Shafii scholar who also had studied with al-Allama.[13]

But the atmosphere in the area was not always so tolerant. A 1363 edict caused many Shii elements in Beirut and Sidon to renounce their faith, and between 1343 and 1379–80, several 'rafidis' – one apparently from al-Hilla and another from the Karak area of the Biqaa valley – a Shirazi and a Christian were executed. All were said to have expressed distinctly Alid sentiments.[14]

In this atmosphere, some seventy or more former Shia of the Jabal Amil region denounced Ibn Makki. At his 1384 trial, presided over by Maliki, Shafii and Hanafi judges, it was clear, however, that it was Ibn Makki's alleged public rejection of Abu Bakr, Umar and Aisha, along the lines of the cursing that had resulted in the other executions mentioned above, that was at issue. In his account Ibn Makki's student al-Miqdad al-Suyuri (d. 1423) attests that his teacher rejected the charges and, at one point, even claimed to be a Shafii. Nevertheless, the guilty verdict was unanimous.

There is no evidence that Ibn Makki's correspondence with the Sarbadars in Iran, discussed further below, was directly at issue in his trial. To be sure, the Sarbadar's earlier Sufi–Shii messianism and the few very Shii Sarbadar coins minted in this period might have reminded the authorities in greater Syria of the Shii populations in their own midst and caused worry that the approach of Timur might further stir them. Perhaps these trends and events also informed the decision to execute Ibn Makki, as those others from the 1350s to the 1380s, to cow the local Shia.

Certainly, in any case, in combination with the 1363 edict, in this atmosphere some renounced their faith and turned against such of the elites as Ibn Makki. Indeed, their denunciation of Ibn Makki may have been an opportunity for such elements to prove their recently adopted anti-Shii tendencies.[15]

Ibn Makki's writings

Perhaps unsurprisingly given his association with al-Hilla, Ibn Makki remained faithful to the basic parameters of rationalist Imami theology, jurisprudence, and *ahkam*.

His well-known work of *fiqh*, the very short *al-Lumaa al Dimashqiyya* (*Damascene Flashes*) completed between 1380 and 1382, reveals him also to have been in agreement with the broad practical rules for community life laid down by his rationalist predecessors. Thus, Ibn Makki called *al-qada* the province of the Imam or his *naib*, and stated that in the occultation it was to be undertaken by *al-Faqih al-Jami li-Sharait al-Ifta*, the phrase used by al-Muhaqqiq and al-Allama.[16]

Ibn Makki completed only a portion of his *Dhikra al-Shia fi Ahkam al-Sharia* (*The Recollection of the Shia as Regards the Rulings of the Law*) two years before his 1384 execution, that is, after having completed *al-Lumaa*. Herein he reiterated the basic hierarchical division of the community between the *mujtahid/mufti* and the *muqallid* derived from the delegation tradition transmitted via Umar b. Hanzala. He also enumerated some thirteen qualities as required of a *faqih*, in effect defining the *sharait* referred to in *al-Lumaa*. These included his faith; his *adala* (justness); knowledge of, for example, the Quran, the *Sunna*, *ijma*, *kalam*, *usul*, language (Arabic); the exegetical pairs of analysis; and biography. The *faqih* was also required to understand from the texts what was 'the required end' if there was no *qarina* (link through the individuals to an Imam) and the 'end intended' if there was. A good memory was also a necessity. He here also noted that during the occultation there was always a *mujtahid*.[17]

In his discussions on Friday prayer, Ibn Makki offered varying rulings. In *al-Lumaa* he stated that the prayer was not to be performed 'unless with the Imam or his designee, even if he is a *faqih*, as long as gathering together is possible during the occultation'. Here, he seemingly equated *al-naib* with the *faqih*, where earlier scholars had, at times, described the *faqih* as the former's successor.[18] In *Dhikra* he went as far as to state that the Imam's permission to do so was required, but then also stated that such permission did exist and that, since the *faqih* dealt with other such issues, he could undertake this as well. As throughout this text, however, in this matter Ibn Makki was careful to cite supporting traditions.[19]

On *al-zakat* he retreated from al-Allama's requirement that it be delivered to *faqih* during the occultation, noting only that 'it is said, this is obligatory'.[20] As to *al-khums*, the appropriate shares were to be given to the Imam 'if he were present, or to his *nuwwab* [plural of *naib*] if [the Imam were] absent, or to be safeguarded'.[21] He, as the Hillis, did not mention the *faqih per se*.

Ibn Makki's separate work on *ziyara* does devote considerable attention to visitation to Imam al-Husayn, but not out of line with visitations elsewhere.[22]

Interestingly, perusal of his incomplete *Dhikra* does suggest that his travels had afforded him access to a broad range of very early and more recent sources, although perhaps only indirectly and/or in part. Those whose works are cited include al-Rawandi, Sallar, Ibn al-Barraj, Ibn Idris and al-Murtada. Al-Murtada's works cited include some of his essays as well as his *al-Intisar*. Ibn Makki also refers to al-Mufid's *al-Muqnia*. He also cited traditions that were available in both of al-Tusi's collections, *al-Faqih*, *al-Kafi*, al-Numani's volume on the occultation and even *al-Mahasin* and *Basair*.[23]

The Shia of the Hijaz

The Shia from across the region, such as Ibn Makki, did travel to the Hijaz, for the pilgrimage, of course, but apparently also for scholarly reasons.

Over this period Hasanid, Zaydi Shiism was pre-eminent in Mecca. The Meccans gave their allegiance to the Fatimids from the later tenth century, but attempted to balance this with associations with the Abbasids, who pressurised them to abandon various distinctly Shii practices and who enjoyed the support of the city's Grand Sharif. The Hasanid 'Hawashim' achieved unified control over the city in 1062 and remained in control until 1200–1.

After the fall of the Fatimids, Salah al-Din achieved at least nominal control over the city in 1173, but failed to persuade the Meccans to abandon their Zaydism. The Mamluks, after they took the Hijaz in the 1260s, did succeed in pressuring the Sharifs to renounce Zaydism. However, this was a political move and never resulted in any persecution of Zaydis. The Mongols and the Mamluks sparred over the city, and by the 1320s Zaydism had been restored in Mecca, with Zaydi prayers being delivered at the Grand Mosque. Although in 1353 a Zaydi imam was beaten to death on Mamluk orders, in the following century the city's Hasanids were known for their Zaydism. From the fifteenth century, a rise in known affiliations with Sunni scholars suggests local sharifs were distancing themselves from their forbearers' Zaydism.[24]

The Husaynid line, descended from the fourth Imam, Zayn al-Abidin, held sway in Medina. Although they pledged allegiance to the Fatimids, they also struggled to maintain some independence. Their efforts were moderately successful during the eleventh and twelfth centuries, although they were able repel Meccan incursions. In the later twelfth century, the Husaynid Sharif is reported to have been a close associate of Salah al-Din. In the early thirteenth century, the Medinans repelled further Meccan attacks. The Twelver Shii *khutba* was recited in the city until 1284 when the Mamluks installed a Sunni Imam. It is worth noting that both cities benefited greatly from Ismaili Fatimid patronage.[25]

Millenarianism on the plateau

To the east, the naturally decentralising tendencies that became established in the aftermath of the death of the Ilkhanid Abu Said in 1335 only further encouraged the spread of the popular, very heterodox blend of Sufi–Shii millenarian discourse that had long been present in the region.

In these years, for example, Ala al-Din al-Simnani (d. 1336) was a member of the Kubrawi brotherhood based in northeastern Iran, whose 'founder' Kubra (d. *c.* 1221), of Khwarazm, apparently perished during the Mongols' westward advance. In 1286, after a mystical experience that caused him to abandon government service, family and property, Simnani became identified with an extreme form of veneration for Ali, *Ahl al-Bayt* and the twelfth Imam. Yet, bespeaking the fluidity of such discourse common to the region in these years, he – like the Kubrawiyya generally – does not seem to have been a Twelver *per se*.[26]

In the Mazandiran/Sabziwar area, Shaykh Khalifa (d. 1335) and his successor Shaykh al-Hasan Juri (d. 1342) were more militant. The former preached the imminent return of the twelfth Imam, a message that attracted the support of bazaar elements, tradesmen and craftsmen. It was not attractive to Sunni elements, who killed him. Juri continued to spread the message in the Nishabur/Tus area, and enjoyed support from a base similar to that of his predecessor. His discourse was more radical than that of the rising Sarbadar movement with whom he allied to fight off the Kartids of Herat, and in which struggles he was killed. A pupil of Juri who was a Husayni descendant of Imam Zayn al-Abidin, and himself a Shii darwish, was the father of the 'founder' of the Shii Marashi dynasty. From 1361 he maintained an independent position along the Caspian until the arrival of Timur.[27]

Where the region's earlier proto-Shii 'states', such as the Bawandids, had been more traditionally dynastic and court-centred, the Sarbadar 'state' came to reflect, uniquely, the fusion of the contemporary messianic Shii–Sufism of the region with a political structure.

Based in Sabziwar, the Sarbadars had been a force in Khurasan since the 1330s. Some of their early rulers had preached a Sufi messianic discourse, if not any formal Twelver Shii message, reflecting the discourse of Sufi darwish elements. The latter reflected association with traditional *akhi/futuwwa* tribal-based movements that flourished in the region over the period. Indeed, early Sarbadar military victories owed much to the presence of such elements with the movement.[28] With the accession of Ali Muayyad (*reg.* 1364–86), if Sunnism continued to be the official faith, the names of Ali and of the Imams began to feature on coins. The darwish messianism was downplayed. At the appearance of Timur on scene in 1381, however, Ali surrendered immediately and, at Timur's 'request', abandoned all Shii tendencies.[29]

It was Ali who initiated a correspondence with Ibn Makki to the west, inviting him to come to Khurasan. In yet another example of the poor state of information about figures in the years between 1055 and 1501, some later Twelver sources suggest that Ibn Makki, already in jail, composed his famous *al-Lumaa al-Dimashqiyya* and dispatched it back to Ali with the latter's messenger within a matter of days.[30] In fact, however, Ali had abandoned his Shii affiliations *c.* 1381, several years before Ibn Makki's 1384 execution. It seems more reasonable to date their correspondence as early as Ali's 1361 accession and, perhaps, during Ibn Makki's residence in Baghdad. As to the text itself, other Twelver sources refer to copies of the text as extant as early as 1380.[31]

If Ibn Makki came to know of it, Ali Muayyd's subsequent easy abandonment of any commitment to the faith might well have confirmed the validity of his decision not to set off for Khurasan.[32]

Dissent in Ibn Makki's time

As noted, references in Ibn Makki's works attest to dissent on issues even within the faith's scholarly community. In *Dhikra*, for example, he noted criticisms that both al-Muhaqqiq and al-Allama had claimed *ijma* where in reality there had been none, and himself argued for recourse to a form of *ijma* based solely on the absence of dissent.[33]

There were also named scholars in this period who were disenchanted with rationalist scholarship. One such was al-Hasan b. Sulayman al-Hilli, known to have been active between 1356 and 1399 and who had studied with Ibn Makki in 1356. Author of an abridgement of *Basair al-Darajat*, he was deeply critical of al-Mufid and al-Tusi for having failed to acknowledge the superiority of the Imams over all other prophets except Muhammad and of these scholars' recourse to rationalist interpretations. Altogether more confrontational in tone, al-Hilli also claimed traditions reinforcing the fact of the falsity of the Uthmanic Codex had been dropped from earlier collections.[34]

A contemporary, Rajab b. Muhammad al-Bursi (d. 1411), author of *Mashariq al-Anwar al-Yaqin fi Kashf Haqaiq Israr Amir al-Muminin* (*The Orients of the Lights of Certainty concerning the Secrets of the Commander of the Faithful*), completed *c.* 1367, and *Mashariq al-Aman* (*The Orients of Safety*), completed in 1398–9, stands out for having purposely resettled in the east in this period. A native of al-Hilla, *c.* 1368, some four years after the accession of the Sarbadar Ali Muayyad, aged about 26, al-Bursi settled in Tus. He seems to have practised a form of Shii Gnosticism that is 'high' Sufism. His apparent elevation of the person of Ali to that on offer in traditions available in *Basair* itself and his understanding of the pre-creational existence of both the Prophet and Imam Ali, were not popular in al-Hilla at the time or among later commentators. His clear reliance on the Andalus-born mystic Ibn Arabi (d. 1240, in Damascus) only encouraged criticism.[35]

The Iranian Shii Sayyid Haydar Amuli (d. after 1385) was perhaps also in this tradition. After study in his home town of Amul, in Mazandiran, he travelled to Astarabad and Isfahan before returning home to undertake service with the local ruler. The latter's murder in 1349 coincided with Amuli's abandonment of this career for a Sufi-style path. He visited the Shii shrines in Iraq and, via Jerusalem, undertook the *hajj*. He then went to Iraq where in Baghdad he studied with under al-Allama's son Muhammad (d. 1370). He then settled in Najaf. Amuli searched for affinities between aspects of the faith and Sufism, with the Imams as guides for the faithful and for those seeking a mystical path. Amuli was critical both of those who had reduced the faith to a series of legalisms and of Sufis who could not see that the Imams had been the precursors of this form of mystical inquiry. In the process, he may be said to have offered a Shii variant on the ideas of Ibn Arabi.[36]

The age of the Timurids

In 1387, Timur (d. 1405) and his armies took Isfahan and moved on areas near Qum in the early 1390s, only to take Georgia and Armenia in the next few years. Timur then invaded the Indian subcontinent in 1398. Returning from that campaign, he renewed his westward march, defeating the Mamluks, taking Aleppo, Damascus and Baghdad and defeating the Ottomans near Ankara in 1402.

After Timur's death in modern-day Kazakhstan, his youngest son Shah Rukh (d. 1447) eventually succeeded him, but mainly ruling over the plateau and the eastern territories. To the west, the Qara Quyunlu (Black Sheep) Turkmen, whom Timur himself had defeated, expanded eastward, taking Baghdad in 1410 and, thereby, finally ending the Jalayarid dynasty of whom they had initially been vassals. The Qara Quyunlu ruler Jahan Shah (d. 1467), who made his capital at Tabriz, made peace with Shah Rukh, but at the latter's death moved further east to take central and southern Iran, and even Oman in the Persian Gulf.

In 1467, Jahan Shah was crushed by an Aq Quyunlu (White Sheep) Turkmen force led by Uzun Hasan (d. 1478). The latter had been Timur's ally against the Ottomans and had been gifted the area around Diyar Bakr. At Jahan Shah's death soon after, the Aq Quyunlu defeated Timur's great-grandson Abu Said (d. 1469), and commenced the taking of Iraq, areas on the plateau into Khurasan and the Persian Gulf coast. Uzun Hasan was himself defeated by

Ottoman forces in 1473 and, following his death, his son and successor Yaqub (d. 1490) was unable to hold the realm together.[37]

The fifteenth-century community

For the fifteenth century, al-Tihrani's *tabaqat* suggests still further concentration of scholarly activity outside the Iranian plateau. Over the period, the geographical associations of the largest number of scholars do suggest connections to sites in Iran, the northern regions in particular. Overall, the figure of those based in Iran is even lower than for the previous century. Second, in a notable rise over the previous centuries, is the region of Jabal Amil. Iraq slips to third, with a lower figure for those associated with al-Hilla. Fourth is eastern Arabia and the Persian Gulf, rising to double figures in this century. The region of Syria also declined in this century, and Herat and India now appear as centres of activity.

Of the Iranian scholars who moved about in this period, four (two from Rayy and one each from Astarabad and Qum) went to Najaf. One from Mazandiran went to the Jabal Amil region, and a Lahiji was identified as living in India. A further two, one from Mashhad/Tus and another identified with Kashan, are in Iraq. A Herati died in Quhistan. A Bahraini scholar went to India via Rayy and then came to Najaf, another went to Iran via the Jazair marshlands of southern Iraq, and yet another was in Astarabad. In the Lebanon, an Amili scholar, an ancestor of the well-known Safawid period scholar Shaykh Baha' al-Din (d. 1621), journeyed all over the region to the west of the Iranian plateau, and another figure went to Arab Iraq. During the reign of Shah Rukh the *naqib* of Iraq and Khurasan left Najaf to settle in Sabziwar, where his descendants remained. Another Iraqi went to Aleppo. A Syrian went to Yazd. A number of the clerics of the century are recorded as having been in contact with the established political authorities of the period – the Jalayirids and the Timurids.[38]

The concomitant continued poor accessibility of key texts in the faith's written legacy, even indirectly commentaries and marginalia, over the fifteenth century has been discussed.

The Shia of the Gulf

The eastern Arabia/Persian Gulf region, with which some twenty-one scholars in this period – thirteen with ties to the Bahrain region alone – were associated, makes the region the fourth largest cluster of Shii scholarly activity over the century.

The region as a whole was traditionally associated with pearling and, in the oases especially, date production. In the early fourteenth century, Ibn Battuta noted that al-Ahsa produced the most dates in the world. The region also sat on the spice trade routes from south and east Asia through to Europe.

In the fourteenth century, the Ismaili Jarwanids ruled the Bahrain area. They were extremely tolerant of Twelver tendencies and scholars in the region. In the mid-fifteenth century, these gave way to the Sunnism of the Banu Jabr. Shii-style Friday prayers were ended, Sunni judges were appointed and the Shia were put under pressure to convert.

As noted above, in this period also a Bahraini scholar went to India via Rayy and then came to Najaf; another went to Iran via the Jazair region and yet another was in Astarabad. Traditionally, however, aspiring scholars from these areas had travelled to Iraq, especially al-Hilla, for their training, studying with al-Allama, for example, and later Ibn Makki. In the fifteenth century, despite the shift in rule and faith, and the efforts taken against the faith, the region continued to produce scholars who continued to move north for further study. Thus, Ibn Fahd al-Hilli, on whom see below, was a student of a Bahraini scholar and taught Sayyid Muhammad Nurbakhsh (d. 1464), whose father was from the al-Qatif region of eastern Arabia. Ibn Abi Jumhur al-Ahsai (d. 1496), also discussed below, studied with his father in the region, but then he went on to Najaf and taught there and in Iran; he visited his homeland in 1488.[39]

Coming the other way, the father of Shaykh al-Husayn b. Muflih (d. 1526) was a prominent cleric from the Basra area who settled in the region. He was, apparently, quite wealthy – as suggested from his pilgrimage and visits to the Iraqi shrine cities nearly every year.[40]

The renewal of the millenarian challenge

To the east, the political turmoil across the region over these years was matched by, and can only have encouraged, the range of both quietist and but also militantly pantheistic, messianic and egalitarian Sufi orders and other heterodox spiritual movements whose polemics often exhibited a distinctly Shii, antiestablishment tone. These included movements such as the Hurufis, influential from Khurasan to Anatolia and Syria, the Nurbakhshis in southwestern Iran and the Mushasha in southern Iraq.

The Hurufi movement, for example, was associated with Fadlallah al-Astarabadi (d. 1394), a sayyid and the son of a *qadi*, and enjoyed a following among artisans. As other such movements, the Hurufis venerated the fourteen 'innocents' – Muhammad, Fatima and the twelve Imams – and identified them with letters of the alphabet and parts of the body. They rejected the legitimacy of current rulers, said there was a curve in revelation over human history, and argued that the appearance of Muhammad as the last of the prophets inaugurated processes that would usher in a more perfect age in which current rulers, all illegitimate and unjust, would be swept away.

In the early fifteenth century also, the chief of the Nasqshbandi order, whose 'founder' was Baha al-Din Naqshband of Bukhara (d. 1389), declared that, on the basis of a dream, a disciple of his, Muhammad Nurbakhsh (1393–1464), born in northeast Iran, was the *Mahdi*. He abandoned Shafiism, espoused by many of region's Sufi orders, for Shii *fiqh*. His very heterodox spiritual discourse also referred to Jesus coming down from the sky as light. Coins were minted in his name in Kurdistan. Those of the Naqshbandiyya who accepted him and his Shiism came to be called the Nurbakhshiyyah.

In Wasit, in Iraq, sometime after 1436, Sayyid Muhammad b. Falah (d. 1461), born in Wasit, declared himself *Mahdi* and had coins minted bearing the names of the twelve Imams. He is said to have attracted the attention of tribal elements in the nearby southern Iraqi marshlands who endowed him with special abilities, if not also divine status. His Mushasha forces seized Basra, Huwayza and Wasit, and in 1454 they entered Najaf and al-Hilla. Though defeated in battle by the Qara Quyunlu in 1456–7, the Mushasha seized territory along the eastern coastal area of Arabia – including the oases of al-Qatif and al-Ahsa – and northward to Kirmanshah and Fars. In 1478, they reached Baghdad.[41]

The range of imamzadas completed in these years across the region also attests to the continued strength of popular veneration for the family of the Prophet generally, if not a profound understanding of, and commitment to, the distinctive doctrines and practices of the Twelver faith in particular.

Thus, work was done on several sites in Qum and in Simnan, as well as Isfahan, at a site where the mother of Jahan Shah Qara Quyunlu was also buried, nine sites across Mazandiran, one of which was for to a local Marashi sayyid, Rayy, Dizful, Gurgan, Luristan, Burujird, Qum, Bumhen, sites in and near Tehran, and Yazd.[42]

In the midst of this turmoil, and the continued very uneven access to the faith's written legacy, some Iran-based clerics were leaving the plateau for sites further west in this period. Others were interested in more esoteric forms of inquiry.

Ibn Abi Jumhur al-Ahsai (d. 1496), from eastern Arabia, travelled widely throughout the region, visiting the Jabal Amil area, Najaf, Tus, the Hijaz and al-Hilla – in some cases several times. Ibn Abi Jumhur was influenced by such diverse, esoteric disciplines as the Illuminationism of the Iran-born al-Suhrawardi (d. 1191), the mystical – not to say Sufi – inquiry of Ibn Arabi and the metaphysics of Ibn Sina (d 1037). In this he followed the paths of Maytham b. Ali al-Bahrani (d. 1280) and Haydar Amuli. While some contemporary sources charged him with Akhbari tendencies, his works, in fact, rather exhibit clear interest in, and reference to, the rationalist religious sciences.[43]

One scholar was associated with the Mushasha movement in southern Iraq. Ibn Fahd al-Hilli (d. 1437) was a student of students of both Ibn Makki, including al-Suyuri, and al-Allama's son Muhammad, and generally followed their lines of thought. It was one of Ibn Fahd's students – the Wasit-born sayyid Muhammad b. Falah (d. 1461) – who spearheaded the Mushasha risings. In fact, Ibn Fahd and the sayyid each married into the other's family. Ibn Falah is said also to have sat in for his teacher in the latter's lessons.[44]

Indeed, and perhaps unsurprisingly, the discourse of the region's more successful polities in this period openly identified with such discourse, speaking to tribal and other elements associated with the strength of such feelings for the Imams as part of the fusion of Sufi–Shii discourse across the region.

Timur had claimed divine approval for his rule, and his discourse evoked associations that attested to the importance of his own Turco-Mongol constituency. But he and his immediate successors were also known for their patronage of Shii shrines and Shii families. Shah Rukh's wife Gawhar Shad (d. 1457) undertook the construction of the mosque, named after her, at Imam al-Rida's shrine that was completed in 1418. The later Timurid ruler of Herat, al-Husayn Bayqara (d. 1506), attempted to have the *khutba* read in the name of the Imams.[45]

To the west the Qara Quyunlu rulers Aspand (d. 1445) and his brother Jahan Shah openly identified with the region's very heterodox, especially tribe-based, spiritual discourse. The latter's poetry praised Ali, and his coins featured the names of the caliphs on one side and those of the Imams on the other. He also had his mother buried at an imamzadas in Isfahan. Jahan Shah's brother attempted to declare the Twelver faith to be the realm's official faith. The 'universalist discourse' of the Aq Quyunlu ruler Uzun Hasan, who defeated Jahan Shah in battle in 1467, improved on Jahan Shah's message. The Shii dimensions thereof are reflected in mosque inscriptions in which Uzun Hasan was called 'the just Sultan' and 'the just Imam', terms that in Twelver Shii discourse that could identify him as the returned twelfth Imam. The great Persian Sunni Naqshbandi Sufi poet Jami (d. 1492), invoking an earlier religio-political legitimacy associated with holy war and raids on the infidel, described Uzun Hasan, who wore Sufi-style darwish dress at public audiences, as 'Sultan of the *ghazis* (holy raiders)'. Such notions facilitated the re-alignment of Qara Quyunlu member tribes under his leadership following the 1467 defeat.[46]

Indeed, in his identification with, and struggle for the 'hearts and minds' of, the Turkic elements, Uzun Hasan also identified with such discourses as were espoused by various of the region's Sufi orders. Among these, Uzun Hasan deemed the Safawids, based at Ardabil, to be of sufficient importance that he married his sister and his daughter to Junayd (d. 1460), a direct descendant of the order's founder Shaykh Safi al-Din (d. 1344), and to Junayd's son Haydar (d. 1488), respectively. One of Haydar's three sons from this marriage was Ismail, born in 1487.[47]

Summary and conclusion

Across the region in the fourteenth and fifteenth centuries, the faith was under a different challenge, which was arguably greater than those presented by the arrivals of the Saljuks and Mongols.

The faith's key written sources, even those completed a scant century before, remained largely inaccessible over these years. What remained of the legacy of the rationalist variant of the faith remained largely confined to the Arabic-speaking lands, particularly Iraq and the Lebanon. The level of scholarly activity continued to be limited, and there and to the east, if for different reasons, the fate of the faith was uncertain, while internal disagreements – as evidenced by the anti-rationalist and Sufi-style discourse of such figures as al-Hasan al-Hilli, Rajab al-Bursi and Haydar Amuli – flourished.

To the east, over these years post-Ilkhanid political fragmentation, the Timurid invasion and subsequent further political disintegration only encouraged the spread of a plethora of Sufi–Shii messianic discourses and movements. Some, such as the Sarbadars and the Mushasha took on 'statist' forms, and some in the Twelver scholarly tradition may have been attracted to these. The discourse of the region's post-Timurid tribal-based polities also reflected and encouraged the messianism rife among the very Turkmen tribes on whose political and military power these 'states' were based.

Altogether by the end of the fifteenth century, if traces of what is taken as normative Twelver doctrine and practice today, let alone in late Buyid Baghdad, had not quite disappeared the written record suggests they were very few and very far between.

Notes

1. The complex political history of this period has yet to be written. The discussion in *The Cambridge History of Iran, vol. 6: The Timurid and Safawid Periods*, eds P. Jackson and L. Lockhart (Cambridge, 1986), although dated and very detailed, is still useful.
2. In these years Qum is said to have recovered slightly from earlier ravages only to suffer again at the arrival of Timur. See Lambton, 'Qum', 328–30.
3. Al-Tihrani, third/eighth century: 43, 44–5, 123, 186–7, 209–10, 240, 195.
4. Al-Allama, *al-Bab al-hadi ashar*, trans. W. E. Miller (London, 1928).
5. Schmidtke, *Theology of al-Allama al-Hilli*, 73, 51, 54–5, 58, 70, 72, 68. As already noted, Ibn Tawus' library was lost after the death of his son Ali in 1312. See Kohlberg, *A Medieval Scholar*, 18, 30.
6. For the ninth Islamic century/fifteenth century AD, al-Tihrani lists copies of al-Muhaqqiq's *Sharai* (fourth/ninth century: 10, 16, 38, 43, 82, 106), works by al-Allama (10, 45, 62, 76, 100, 103, 151, 153), but very few copies of earlier works (Ibn Babawayh: 100; al-Tusi: 100).
7. Al-Tihrani, *al-Dharia*, 6: 106f; 13: 47049, 316f.
8. Al-Tihrani, *ibid.*, 14: 17f; 6: 169f; 13: 165f; 6: 54; 14: 52. There are no commentaries or

marginalia for his *Muntaha al-Wusul, Kashf al-Murad* or his *Nihaya*. As to his short *al-Bab al-Hadi Ashar*, two *shuruh* were done in this period (al-Tihrani, 13: 117f). There were no commentaries or marginalia on his surviving *rijal* work (al-Tihrani, 6: 82f).

9.   Muhsin al-Amin, *Khitat Jabal Amil* (Beirut, 1961), 75–86, 90, 365–6. See also R. Abisaab, 'Shiite Beginnings and Scholastic Tradition in Jabal Amil in Lebanon', *Muslim World* (1999), 4f.

10. S. Winter, 'Shams al-Din Muhammad ibn Makki "al-Shahid al-Awwal" (d. 1384) and the Shiah of Syria', *Mamluk Studies Review*, 3 (1999), 156.

11. Y. Nakash, *Reaching for Power* (Princeton, 2006), 30; S. Winter, *The Shiites of Lebanon under Ottoman Rule, 1516–1788* (Cambridge, 2010), 62.

12. Al-Amin, *Khitat*, 71. Al-Amin (77f, 252) does argue that there must have been some earlier presence, given the nearby Twelver pockets. For Shia in this period, see 91, 347, 360. See also Abisaab, 'Shiite Beginnings', 12f.

13. S. Winter, 'Shams al-Din Muhammad', 149–50, 156–9, 164–6. Winter (152, 166–7) notes that even Ibn Taymiyya (d. 1328), who blamed Shiism for the Mongol invasion and urged the Mamluks to attack the Shia of Kisrawan, carried on a discourse with al-Allama. Ibn Makki possessed a copy of Ibn Babawayh's *al-Faqih* that he gave to his daughter. She and his wife were said to have been recognised as *mujtahida* in some areas of *ahkam* (Winter, 159).

14. Winter, 'Shams al-Din Muhammad', 167–71. For an account of Ibn Makki's trial, see Winter, *ibid.*, 171f.

15. Winter (*ibid.*, 162) also suggested that Ibn Makki's opposition to the popular Sufism of the wandering 'dervish' sort so common throughout the region in these years may also have encouraged these renegade Shia to denounce him.

16. Ibn Makki, Muhammad al-Amili, *al-Lumaa al-Dimashqiyya* (Qum, 1387/1967), 3: 61–93, esp. 67.

17. Ibn Makki, *Dhikra al-Shia fi Ahkam al-Sharia*, 4 vols (Qum, 1419), 1: 39–63, 44.

18. Ibn Makki, *al-Lumaa*, 1: 657–72, esp. 662.

19. Ibn Makki, *Dhikra*, 4: 100, 104–5.

20. Ibn Makki, *al-Lumaa*, 2: 11–62, esp. 53. Cf. Calder, '*Zakat*', 476–7.

21. Ibn Makki, *al-Lumaa*, 2: 65–83, especially 82. Cf. Calder, '*Khums*', 44.

22. Ibn Makki, *Kitab al-Mazar* (n.pl., 1410), esp. 114–88, which is chapter 4 of a total of eight chapters and a lengthy conclusion.

23. Ibn Makki, *Dhikra*, 1: 59, for example.

24. R. T. Mortel, 'Zaydi Shiism and the Hasanid Sharifs of Mecca', *International Journal of Middle Eastern Studies*, 19(4) (1987), *passim*, esp. 464.

25. Mortel, 'The Origins and Early History', esp. 75–6.

26. J. Baldick, *Mystical Islam* (London, 1989), 94–5; H. Algar, 'Kobrawiyya II. The Order', *EIr*; J. van Ess, 'Ala-al-Dawla Semnani', *EIr*.

27. H. Algar, 'Iran IX. Religion in Iran (2), Islam in Iran (2.2) Mongol and Timurid Periods', *EIr*; J. Calmard, 'Marashis', *EI2*; Halm, *Shiism*, 71–2.

28. To be sure, a coin minted in Tus in 1357 bore the inscription 'Sultan Muhammad the Mahdi', a clear reference to the twelfth Imam and perhaps an indication of a belief in his imminent return. See J. M. Smith, *The History of the Sarbadar Dynasty, 1336–1381 AD and its Sources* (The Hague, 1970), 196–8, 76f, 131–2, 77, 80, 144–8, 139–41, 159–66.

29. Smith, *ibid.*, *passim*; C. Melville, 'Sarbadarids', *EI2*; J. Aubin, 'La fin de l'état sarbadar du Khorassan', *Journal Asiatique* (1974), 95–118.

30. Afandi, *Riyad al-Ulama*, 5: 190, Muhammad b. al-Hasan, al-Hurr al-Amili (d. 1693), *Kitab*

Amal al-Amil, 2 vols (Baghdad, 1385), 1: 181–3. See also S. A. Arjomand, *The Shadow of God*, 70–1, 290, n. 16; Momen, *Introduction to Shii Islam*, 99, 319–20; Halm, *Shiism*, 71.

31. Al-Bahrani, *Luluat*, 146–8; al-Amin, *Ayan*, 10: 59f.

32. See also n. 15 on Ibn Makki's opposition to popular Sufism.

33. Ibn Makki, *Dhikra*, esp. 1: 49f. See also Calder, 'The Structure', 197–8.

34. See al-Tihrani, *al-Dharia*, 20: 182–3, 1: 247, 17: 52, 4: 54, 1: 91–2; al-Khwansari, *Raudat al-Jannat*, 2: 293–4.

35. B. T. Lawson, 'A 14th Century Shii Gnostic, Rajab Bursi and his *Mashariq al-Anwar*', in *Islamic Philosophy Yearbook*, 1 (Moscow, 2009), 422–38. See also Amir-Moezzi, *Le guide divin*, 152, n. 86; al-Tihrani, *ibid.*, 21:34; Afandi, *Riyad al-Ulama*, 2: 205, 306–7, 309; al-Hurr al-Amili, *Kitab Amal*, 2: 117-18; al-Khwansari, *ibid.*, 3: 337–8, 340–2. Al-Khwansari, commenting on al-Bursi's influence among the popular elements, described the latter as 'duller than cattle'.

36. E. Kohlberg, 'Amoli, Sayyed Baha' al-Din', *EIr*; J. van Ess, 'Haydar-i Amuli', *EI2*.

37. These events are addressed in *The Cambridge History of Iran, vol. 6: The Timurid and Safawid Periods*, eds P. Jackson and L. Lockhart (Cambridge, 1986).

38. Al-Tihrani, *Tabaqat*, fourth/ninth century: 23, 63, 41, 55, 48, 98, 121–2, 7–8, 1, 119–20, 153, 81–2, 95–6, 42, 13, 24, 80, 38, 103. See also fourth/tenth century: 86; fifth/eleventh century: 278–9.

39. Al-Tihrani, *Tabaqat*, fourth/ninth century: 7–8, 1; fourth/tenth century: 86.

40. J. Cole, 'Rival Empires of Trade and Imami Shiism in Eastern Arabia, 1300–1800', *International Journal of Middle East Studies*, 19(2) (1987), 179, 180–1, On Nurbakhsh, see S. Bashir, 'The Imam's Return: Messianic Leadership in Later Medieval Shiism', in L. Walbridge (ed.), *The Most Learned of the Shia* (Oxford, 2001), 21–33.

41. On all these and other movements such as that of Shaykh Badr al-Din in western Anatolia and *Ahl al-Haqq* in Kurdistan, see I. P. Petrushevsky, *Islam in Iran*, trans. H. Evans (London, 1985), 260–4, 291–300; Baldick, *Mystical Islam*, 71–7, 94, 96, 100–4, 111. Useful contributions on individual movements include Birge, *The Bektashi Order*, 32f; H. Norris, 'The Hurufi Legacy of Fadlullah of Astarabad', in L. Lewisohn (ed.), *The Legacy of Medieval Persian Sufism* (London, 1992), 87–97; S. Bashir, 'Enshrining Divinity: The Death and Memorialisation of Fazlallah Astarabadi in Hurufi Thought', *The Muslim World*, 90 (2000), 289–308; Bashir, 'The Imam's Return'; T. Graham, 'Shah Nimatullah Wali, Founder of the Nimatullahi Sufi Order', in Lewisohn (ed.), *The Legacy*, 173–90; B. G. Martin, 'A Short History of the Khalwati Order of Dervishes', in N. Keddie (ed.), *Scholars, Saints, and Sufis* (Berkeley, CA, 1978), 275–305; H. Algar, 'Naqshbandis and Safawids: A Contribution to the Religious History of Iran and Her Neighbors', in M. Mazzaoui (ed.), *Safawid Iran and Her Neighbors* (Salt Lake City, UT, 2003), 7f; Mazzaoui, *Origins of the Safawids*, 67–9.

42. Varjavand.

43. Afandi, *Riyad al-Ulama*, 5: 50–1; al-Bahrayni, *Luluat*, 166–7; al-Khwansari, *Raudat al-Jannat*, 7: 30–3; Modarressi, *An Introduction*, 52, n. 3; Cole, 'Rival', 181f; S. Schmidtke, 'New Sources for the Life and Work of Ibn Abi Jumhur al-Ahsai', *Studia Iranica*, 38 (2009), 49–68; A. al-Oraibi, 'Rationalism in the School of Bahrayn: A Historical Perspective', in L. Clarke (ed.), *Shiite Heritage* (Binghamton, NY, 2001), 331–44, esp. 331–6.

44. J. H. Shubbar, *Tarikh al-Mushashaiyin va Tarajim Alaihim* (Najaf, 1385/1965), 15–24, 215, 28–30, 32; Mazzaoui, *Origins of the Safawids*, 67–9.

45. Mazzaoui, *ibid.*, 63–6; J. Aubin, 'Notes sur quelques documents Aq Qoyunlu', *Mélanges Louis Massignon*, 1 (Damas, 1956), 123–47. In these years, the Jalayarids embellished the Kazimayn, site of the tombs of Imams Musa and al-Jawad, in Baghdad. Timur visited after his arrival in Baghdad. See Al Yasin, *Tarikh al-Mashhad*, 52–3.

46. J. Woods, *The Aqquyunlu. Clan, Confederation, Empire*, rev. edn (Salt Lake City, UT, 1999), 82–3, 89, 102–3, 105–9, 259, nn 77–9. On Jahan Shah, who also claimed divine approbation for his rule and also displayed interest in Shiism, see V. Minorsky, 'Jihan Shah Qaraquyunlu and his Poetry', *Bulletin of the School of Oriental and African Studies*, 16(2) (1954), esp. 281; a descendant of Jahan Shah founded the Shii Qutb Shah dynasty in India in 1481. See also J. Calmard (ed.), 'Les rituels shiites et le pouvoir. L'imposition du shiisme safawide: eulogies et malédictions canoniques', in *Études Safawides* (Paris/Tehran, 1993), 113. On Aspand, see also Shubbar, *Tarikh al-Mushashaiyin*, 215. The Qara Quyunlu ruler Yusuf (d. 1420) visited the Kazimayn (Al Yasin, *ibid.*, 54). See also Newman, *Safavid Iran*.

47. Woods, *The Aqquyunlu*, 9, 83–4, 107, 150, 211; V. Minorsky [C. E. Bosworth], 'Uzun Hasan', *EI2*; G. Sarwar, *History of Shah Ismail* (Aligarh, 1939), 24f, 30f, 94–5.

CHAPTER 8

Shiism in the sixteenth century: the limits of power (and influence)

In 1501, the first Safawid shah Ismail I (d. 1524), at the head of a coalition of Turkic tribal elements – noted for their twelve-coned red headgear, in homage to the Imams, and so called the Qizilbash (red head) – captured Tabriz. Within some ten years Safawid forces reached Herat, securing lands previously held by some eight different rulers.

For historians of Iran, the Safawid period is that in which Persian became increasingly used across a wide range of genres, including religious writings. It is also the period when Iran may be said to have assumed the geographical contours with which it is associated today. The period also has long been notable for its many and diverse artistic, architectural and literary accomplishments.

For students of Twelver Shiism, however, it is Ismail's establishment of the faith as his realm's official religion that marks the period out for its importance. From this period study of the evolution of Twelver Shiism and of Iran's becoming a modern nation-state becomes so intertwined that the history of, and developments in, the one are often seen mainly, if not solely, in relation to the other.

In reality, however, by the end of the sixteenth century, the faith had yet to become firmly established either at the Safawid court or among the realm's populace. The longevity of the Safawid project itself was also repeatedly open to serious question over these years.

In these very same years, Twelver Shiism also found a foothold in southern India, albeit for very different reasons, although by the century's end that presence also appeared as limited and tenuous as that in Iran.

It would seem that the Arabic-speaking lands to the west of Iran remained at the core of Shii activity, despite the arrival in the area of the Sunni Ottomans. Together with even the patronage on offer in the Indian subcontinent, these as well as well as eastern Arabian and Gulf sites were clearly perceived as active and viable centres of community life and scholarly activity over the century by those who were unsure of the Safawid association with the faith.

The scattered pockets

Based on the *tabaqat* literature, in the sixteenth century, as the previous century, the number of Iran-based scholars was greater than those associated with other sites. Whether owing to better reporting on scholars in this period[1] and/or an absolute increase the actual number of Iran-based scholars, that number does rise dramatically in these years, with noticeable growth in the number of those scholars linked to the north and to Khurasan, along with Shiraz, Kashan and Isfahan. As in the previous century, however, the much smaller region of Jabal Amil comes a very strong second, with numbers greater than the previous century. Iraq's centres come third, also as the previous century: Najaf grows in number, while al-Hilla declines. Fourth in both centuries was the region of eastern Arabia. India features more prominently this century than the last century, and both Herat and Yemen also make appearances.

As, or perhaps more, interesting is the traceable movement of scholars between these sites. Such movement suggests that scholars continued to understand all these sites as viable centres of scholarship and/or patronage.

Thus, in addition to the scholars named elsewhere in this chapter, and over and above movement within these regions, a Gilani visited Cairo, and an Astarabadi journeyed to the shrine cities where he studied al-Hilli's *Sharai* with Ali al-Karaki (d. 1534), on whom see below, in 1516 and then settled in Kashan. Other Iranians also visited Iraqi sites, including Najaf. Three Iranians visited Istanbul. A Kashani, a Tabasi and a Bahraini are each recorded as being in India. A Shirazi convert is reported as being at the court of the Nizam shahs in the Deccan. The son of another scholar is recorded as having been to India and returned. A *qadi al-askar* (military judge) during the reign of Tahmasb travelled to India and then returned to Khurasan where he became a teacher. Two other Iraqi scholars went to India. A scholar born in Medina moved to Jabal Amil where he had a son. A Basran settled in Shiraz. During the reign of Ismail's son and successor Tahmasb (*reg.* 1524–76), a Baghdadi judge who had journeyed to Kashan, Shiraz and Tabriz gained the post of *qadi al-askar*. A Bukharan went to India.[2]

Further attesting to the activity at, and viability of, these various Iranian and non-Iranian centres is the copying of manuscripts noted by al-Tihrani in his volume for this century, even if there is no way to be certain that the copies in question survived to be among those counted for Appendix II. Most of those copyists who can be identified seem to have had associations with Iran.[3]

But scholars associated with the Jabal Amil region as well as Iraq, especially Najaf, Bahrain/al-Ahsa and the Hijaz were also involved in the copying of texts.[4] Copies of some of the key works of the faith produced by pre-Buyid and Buyid scholars can be associated with specific communities across the Shii world. Of earlier scholars, *al-Kafi* was copied by those associated with Jabal Amil and Najaf. A Bahraini produced a copy of *Qurb al-Isnad* by al-Himyari (d. after 910), and a work by Ibn Babawayh was copied in this period by a scholar associated with Najaf.[5] Works by al-Tusi copied in Iraq in this period included his *Tahdhib al-Ahkam*. A Najafi produced a copy of al-Najashi's *rijal* work. Works by al-Mufid were also copied by those associated with Najaf and

Bahrain. A copy of al-Kashshi's *rijal* was produced by a figure associated with Jabal Amil.[6]

The written legacy

The sixteenth century has been said to have witnessed something of a revival of interest in the Imams' traditions.[7]

In fact, however, and in spite of the copying activity going on across the region, in most respects the general availability of 'key' pre-1501 Twelver texts in this century remained little changed over the previous century, with a few important exceptions.

As Appendix II suggests, of works produced up to the early tenth century, only *al-Kafi* experienced any greater availability in this period, but only in the latter half of the century, when a record twenty-eight copies were produced. This is a figure so high as to suggest statistical significance even if the exact number cannot be taken as absolute. Ibn Babawayh's many collections continued generally to be unavailable, but of al-Tusi's two collections, as *al-Kafi*, his *Tahdhib* experienced marked growth in available copies over the two halves of the century, from six to twenty-eight. *Al-Istibsar* witnessed a similar pattern, even if the actual numbers are not as significant. Al-Tusi's other works, however, remained relatively inaccessible over this period, as did the works of al-Mufid and al-Murtada. Only the latter's *al-Intisar* achieved a level of statistical significance across the entire Shii world. There are no commentaries or marginalia on all these pre-1055 works produced over the sixteenth century.

As for post-1055 works, overall there were precious few copies of those made either, with several notable exceptions. Al-Tabrisi's *Majma* experienced an *al-Kafi/Tahdhib*-like growth in availability from the first to the second half of the sixteenth century. Works by al-Rawandi and Ibn Idris may be said to have been unavailable. Al-Allama's *Qawaid* was especially accessible over both the fifteenth and sixteenth centuries, for example, while his *Irshad* was accessible over the entire sixteenth century. Al-Allama's *Tahrir* and *Mukhtalaf* achieved such status only later in the century, as his *usul* work *Tahdhib*. Al-Muhaqqiq's *Muarij* and *al-Mutabar* nearly disappeared. Commentaries and marginalia in al-Muhaqqiq's *Sharai* and his *al-Mukhtasar* are noted.

Commentaries and marginalia on al-Allama's *Qawaid*, *Irshad* and, to a lesser extent, his *Tahrir* are recorded. There were no commentaries or marginalia authored for his *Tadhkira* or *Mukhtalaf*.[8]

As to al-Allama's non-*fiqh* works, his *usul* work *Tahdhib* attracted attention, but not his *Nihaya* or *Mabadi*. His *rijal* work *Khulasa* did attract marginalia, but not his theology work *Kashf al-Murad*. By contrast, up to the end of the seventeenth century some twelve commentaries were produced on his very short *al-Bab al-Hadi Ashar*, including six in the sixteenth century itself, and one marginalia.[9]

Finally, Ibn Makki's *al-Lumaa* and his *Dhikra* were not widely available until the latter half of the sixteenth century. There are two commentaries in this period cited for *al-Lumaa*, and one marginalia done before. There are none of either cited for *Dhikra*.[10]

Of the numbers of commentaries and marginalia produced on these works produced in the sixteenth century, however, it was the same very small number of scholars, inside or outside Iran, who were actively engaging with all these texts. Indeed, as will be suggested, these commentaries and marginalia were the vehicles by which some of these few offered their major advances in *fiqh*. As per Appendix IV, those whose names figure so consistently as authors of these commentaries and marginalia – al-Karaki, Ibrahim al-Qatifi, Shaykh Zayn al-Din and his student, Shaykh al-Husayn – were all Arab scholars. Of these four, only al-Karaki relocated to newly-Shii Safawid Iran early in his career. Al-Qatifi and Shaykh Zayn al-Din pointedly did not, and the latter's student, Shaykh al-Husayn, only came to Iran later in his career.[11]

Iran in the first Safawid century: a failure to take hold

It is perhaps not surprising that by century's end the faith was not all that well established either at the Safawid court or among the realm's populace. In fact, Safawid religious discourse over this period was not distinctly, or even solely, Twelver in nature.

The Safawid order was 'founded' by Shaykh Safi al-Din as a quietist and Sunni Sufi order. By the time of Junayd and Haydar, however, the order had been transformed by an influx into its ranks of Turkic tribal elements. The order's discourse was now marked by the very combination of radical Sufi millenarian and also an extreme, messianic veneration for Ali and the Imams that was sweeping the region, coupled with a proactive military strategy. Indeed, both Junayd and Haydar died in battle. This combination of messianic discourse and military action distinguished the Safawids from the region's two earlier tribal statelets, the Qara Quyunlu and Aq Quyunlu. In the wake of Aq Quyunlu military defeats that contributed to that polity's disintegration, member tribes' allegiance shifted to the Safawids.

In 1499, Ismail left Lahijan, where he had been hidden by supporters after Haydar's death, for Syria and Asia Minor. Along the way he picked up additional followers. In 1501, after two successful battles, the second against a small Aq Quyunlu contingent, Ismail entered Tabriz, the capital of the Il-al-Khanids, Jahan Shah Qara Quyunlu and Uzun Hasan Aq Quyunlu, his own grandfather.

Although as ignorant of the finer points of Twelver doctrine and practice as most of those in his immediate entourage,[12] Ismail did have some experience of Zaydi Shiism as a youth in Lahijan. This experience perhaps sparked an awareness that references to himself as *al-Imam al-Adil al-Kamil* (the perfect, the just Imam) or *al-Sultan al-Adil* (the just Sultan) could allude both to his status as the political successor to his grandfather Uzun Hasan, to whom similar terms had been applied, but also, in Twelver tradition, to himself as the now-returned twelfth Imam.

In these early years too, the Safawids also laid claim to their sayyid status. This encouraged Ismail's identification as the Hidden Imam and equated the Safawids with the sayyid founders of the region's other egalitarian and millenarian movements as the Hurufis, Nurbakhshis and the Mushasha.[13]

'Popular' tales of the day also portrayed Ismail as the returned Abu Muslim. The latter, head of the Khurasan-based Arab armies that founded the Abbasid state, was said by some to have gone into hiding. He would reappear to establish justice in the world.[14]

Ismail's poetry reveals the heterodox nature of these and other discourses surrounding him. On the one hand, that poetry identified him as Ali and Ali's 'adherent', the twelve Imams, if not also the now returned Hidden Imam and Allah himself. On the other hand, the young shah was also projected as at one with the chief figures of the native Tajik Persian cultural legacy, such as Khusraw, Rustam and Alexander.[15]

Ismail's complex, heterodox discourse attested to the shah's aspiration to 'universalist' rule over the region's Turkic tribal levies and the settled Tajik elements. The latter, after nominal conversions to the new faith, provided the Safawids with the very administrative expertise that the latter's Sunni fathers and grandfathers had offered the region's earlier Sunni political establishments.

It was this very heterodox discourse, together with marriage alliances, grants of land and court positions, that kept the alliance of Turk and Tajik united in support of the larger Safawid polity in the face of a series of existential military-political challenges. These included the disastrous defeat at the hands of the Ottomans at Chaldiran in 1514 – after which the Ottomans fortunately moved southwest, to Egypt, rather than east – and, more importantly, two prolonged civil wars at the death of Ismail in 1524 and Tahmasb in 1576. Each of the latter two especially saw great swathes of Safawid territory lost to the Sunni Ottomans on the west and Sunni Uzbegs to the northeast, as Turk and Tajik forces at the Safawid centre struggled to realign themselves around, and thus attain paramount influence over, successive shahs.

But this heterodoxy could not have reassured any great numbers of the contemporary, usually urban-based, Twelver scholarly elite. As Ibn Makki had avoided the Sarbadars, so in fact over this period no large numbers of established Arab Twelver scholars can be shown to have relocated to Safawid territory.[16]

To be sure, the Safawid centre did make efforts to strengthen the position of the faith in the realm. In the years after Chaldiran, Ismail and others at court were especially attentive to the veneration of the Imams. Ismail himself undertook improvements to various religious shrines and buildings in this period.[17] His Mawsillu tribal wife, Tajlu Khanum (d. 1540), endowed the farms, gardens and villages she owned around Varamin, Qum and Qazwin to the shrine of Fatima in Qum.[18] Tahmasb made several pilgrimages to the shrine of Imam al-Rida in Mashhad/Tus. He also approved the Marashi sayyids as overseers of a key shrine in Qazwin and repaired and/or embellished a number of religious sites.

Others at court, including other members of the Safawid house, Turk and Tajik elites, also publicly supported the faith. A sister of Tahmasb made important donations to the Iraqi shrine cities, and at her death in 1564 another sister was buried in Karbala. In Isfahan in 1566–7, an Afshar chieftain built a canal from the nearby Zayanda Rud to the Masjid-i Ali and appointed the city's *Shaykh al-Islam*, the Arab Ali Minshar al-Karaki, as supervisor of its *waqf*. The latter attests to a working relationship between some Twelver clerics and members of the tribal military-political elite.[19]

During the reign of Tahmasb also, work was done on *imamzada*s in Hamadan, Bumhen, Shiraz, Ray, Mazandiran, Shimiran, Nur, Bawanat, Kashan, Qazwin, Tabas, Yazd and Varamin. Local elements also were clearly supportive of this more popular manifestation of the faith, as attested by an Isfahani grain merchant's dedication in 1539–40 of the revenues from a local orchard to the *imamzada* of Harun-i Wilayat. To bolster his credibility among the 'popular' classes, Tahmasb was also a prominent patron of Muharram ceremonies. A sister of the shah was said to have been left unmarried for the Imam, and a horse was also saddled and ready for his return.[20]

Nevertheless, during the reign of Ismail II (1576–7), the first of Tahmasb's sons to succeed his father, it quickly became clear that Sunnism was still very much a force in the realm. In Qazwin, by this time the Safawid capital, enormous crowds attended the distinctly Sunni preaching of Mirza Makhdum Sharifi (d. 1587). The latter was a Shirazi judge descended from one of the many Tajik elites who had nominally converted to the realm's new faith. He was appointed joint *sadr* (the realm's chief religious official) by Ismail II and his supporters. This appointment bespoke an effort to re-establish Sunnism in the realm, or at least to reach out to the many recent converts to Twelver Shiism to achieve a reconciliation between Sunnism and Shiism as a means of bolstering Ismail II's own domestic legitimacy in the midst of the second of the century's civil wars. That this move was defeated by another, stronger, alliance of Turk and Tajik elements owed itself less to any profound commitment to or understanding of Twelver Shiism than it did to political manoeuvring.[21]

Among the populace, too, the level of commitment to, and understanding of, the faith's distinct doctrines and practices also remained minimal. Indeed, the years following Ismail II's death in 1577 witnessed the rising of several pseudo-Ismails, described as *qalandar*s (darwishes), unattached to any recognised Sufi order. Such movements had, in fact, been visible also during the 1574 illness suffered by Tahmasb, two years before his death. These, who appeared after 1577 were said to have enjoyed widespread support, especially among native Iranian Tajiks across the plateau – in Luristan, Fars, Khuzistan, Hamadan, Gilan and Khurasan. One even originated in the Ardabil area, the birthplace of the Safawid Sufi order. The broad, apparently non-Qizilbash, tribal support these risings also enjoyed, among Kurds and Lurs especially, suggests a renewed interest in the militant Sufi dimension that was a feature of early Safawid spiritual discourse.[22]

During the ten-year rule of Ismail II's successor Khudabanda, Tahmasb's eldest son, the court resumed its efforts to identify Twelver Shiism as the realm's established faith and the person of the shah with, as chief spokesman for and defender of, the faith.[23]

In 1587, a Qizilbash-Tajik faction enthroned Khudabanda's son Abbas. His rule was not accepted by other Turk and Tajik factions, and both the Ottomans and Uzbeks only added more chunks of Safawid territory to those they had seized since the death of Tahmasb.

More importantly, however, non-Twelver spiritual discourse continued to flourish in these years, and was, indeed, encouraged by the accession itself. Some Sufi elements challenged Abbas I's identity as *pir* (leader of the Sufi order), implying that the still-living Khudabanda remained the head of the Safawid Sufi order. In 1592–3, Sufis in Lahijan, from whose ranks Ismail I had drawn support, also questioned the Abbas' identity as the present *pir*.[24] In 1590, several years after Abbas' enthronement, local clerics crushed a rising by a Shiraz-based Nuqtawi poet, whom Tahmasb had blinded in 1565. Two years later, a Nuqtawi darwish rose up in Qazwin. The darwish, from a family of refuse collectors and well-diggers, was popular there, as well as in Sava, Kashan, Isfahan, Nain and Shiraz, towards the end of Tahmasb's reign. Nuqtawi elements said that 1593 was the year a Nuqtawi who enjoyed unity with Allah would assume power. This preaching apparently was popular among both the Turks and Tajiks. Indeed, following the crushing of the rising, an amir of the Ustajlu tribe – an original member tribe of the Qizilbash coalition – and other Qizilbash elements were among those executed.[25]

Too, twice in the years after 1590 the Mushasha Arabs of lower Iraq, known for their overt Twelver associations, moved to assert their independence, even occupying Dizful.[26]

If by the end of the century Shiism had yet to find a firm footing among both the plateau's elite and 'popular' elements, the association of the Safawids with the faith also generated much unease within the Shii clerical class.

In the first fifty years after Tabriz, Ali al-Karaki, associated with the Karak Nuh region of Lebanon, was one – early in his own career and early in the reign of Ismail – of the few who came to court. But his identification with the Safawid Shii project generated opposition both inside and outside the realm.

During al-Karaki's lifetime, the Bahraini cleric Ibrahim al-Qatifi, on behalf of himself and other Arab Twelver scholars, criticised al-Karaki's acceptance of remuneration from the court. [27] After al-Karaki's death, the Lebanese Shaykh Zayn al-Din Amili and his student and associate Shaykh al-Husayn al-Amili – both of whom had in fact had secured teaching positions in the Lebanon at the time, after having presented themselves as Shafii scholars – offered criticisms of al-Karaki's legacy.[28] Shaykh al-Husayn's departure to Iran and even Zayn al-Din's sudden execution by the Ottomans in 1558, several years after a 1555 peace treaty with the Ottomans, failed to spark any mass exodus of Arab Shii clerics to Safawid territory.

Al-Karaki's more important, and longer lasting, scholarly contribution was his formulation of the concept of the *faqih* as *naib amm* (general deputy) of the absent Imam, in contrast to the term *naib khass* (special deputy). The latter term referred to contemporaries of the Imam designated by the latter to undertake only specific functions or named activities in the community; the term perhaps also referred to the four *safirs*.[29] Reference to *niyaba amma* (the general deputy-ship) implied, in theory, the final dropping of any limits to the exercise of the Imam's prerogatives by the *faqih*. Al-Karaki utilised the term in a 1510 rebuttal of the criticisms of al-Qatifi and others over his service to, and acceptance of, remuneration from Ismail and in discussing the issue of Friday prayer in his 1527 *Jami al-Maqasid*, an unfinished commentary on al-Allama's *Qawaid*.[30] In fact, in 1532, during the very early years of Tahmasb's reign, as the civil war raged and Ottoman forces continued their attacks, a *firman* was issued designating al-Karaki *naib al-Imam*.

Nevertheless, as a further indication of the lack of both court and popular support for the faith, soon after al-Karaki's death two years later, his several projects to establish the faith in Iran – including the institution of Friday prayer throughout the realm – seem to have been abandoned.[31]

Shaykh Zayn al-Din never came to Iran. He and his student Shaykh al-Husayn also publicly repudiated some of al-Karaki's rulings after the latter's death. But in his 1549–50 commentary on Ibn Makki's *al-Lumaa* Zayn al-Din did utilise the term with reference to his stipulation of the involvement of the *faqih* as the deputy of the Imam, and being in possession of all his authority, in the collection and distribution of *al-zakat* during the occultation.[32]

At the Safawid court al-Karaki's loyal service to the Safawids, through the Chaldiran defeat and the civil war that followed Ismail's death, was remembered. Thus, when they came to Iran, Ali al-Karaki's own son, for example, was honoured at court, as was the son of one of al-Karaki's daughters, Sayyid al-Husayn (d. 1592–3). In *c.* 1552, nearly twenty years after the death of his grandfather and five decades after Tabriz, the latter came to Iran. As a mark of particular favour, Sayyid al-Husayn was appointed Ardabil's Shaykh al-Islam.

After a 1559 essay for Tahmasb, in which he argued for the legitimacy of the *faqih* leading Friday prayer during the occultation – the position for which both Shaykh Zayn al-Din and Shaykh al-Husayn, who held no *faqih* was necessary, had criticised his grandfather – Sayyid al-Husayn was invited to the newly designated capital of Qazwin. There, *c.* 1563, he was appointed the capital's Shaykh al-Islam, replacing Shaykh al-Husayn. The latter, in post since *c.* 1557, had restored Friday prayer following its discontinuation some two decades before, following Ali al-Karaki's death.[33]

Sayyid al-Husayn's gaining of this post probably owed itself to his grandfather's proven record of service to a younger Tahmasb. Certainly, the finer points of their debates on Friday prayer, as the finer points of the 1532 *firman* declaring Ali al-Karaki *naib al-Imam*, were little understood by the Turk and Tajik elites, let alone the mass of the population, many of whom were still clearly committed to more heterodox discourses.

In the event, Shaykh al-Husayn was then appointed *Shaykh al-Islam* in Mashhad and then in Herat, before asking permission from Tahmasb to perform the pilgrimage with his son. He was allowed to do so, but permission for his son Shaykh Bahai (d. 1621) to accompany him was refused. Al-Husayn did go to Mecca, arriving in 1576. Instead of returning to Iran, he settled in Bahrain where he died soon after. In a letter he wrote to his son, he advised Bahai that he could be wealthy in India or be pious in Bahrain, but could be neither in Iran.[34] With that, he effectively repudiated his two decades of residence and government service in Iran.

The Lebanon

Although the *tabaqat* data suggests there may have been fewer scholars associated with the Lebanon in this period than Iran, the Jabal Amil region especially, proportional to their respective sizes, there was a greater concentration of Twelver scholars associated with the Lebanon over this century than with Iran.

Not as much is known of the Shii population of the region over these years as might be desirable. After defeating the Safawids at Chaldiran, the Ottomans moved southwest. The Shii Baalbak-based Harfush clan surrendered to the Ottomans when they arrived in the area in 1516 and, though there were anti-Ottoman risings in 1518 and 1520, they provided archers to the Ottomans in 1568.

As early as 1526, the Ottomans were aware of the presence of distinctly Twelver communities in their midst, as Syrian pilgrims went to the shrines in Iraq and they knew of revenues coming to those shrines from Iranian pilgrims.[35] The Ottomans were also no doubt aware of the Shii *ashraf* in the Lebanon/ Syria region. The Zuhra Shia of Aleppo were still a force, and the al-Murtada family had been *naqib*s of Baalbak since Mamluk times when they moved into the Karak Nuh area of the Biqaa.

Indeed, by this period the growth of *waqf* and the establishment of shrines in the region suggest that the wealth of the Karak Nuh area may have been growing. Elsewhere in the area over this century there were mosques built in Juba and Hawla.[36] There are also concentrations of Twelver scholars reported in the Jabal Amil areas of Nabatiyah, Aynath, Mays – where, mid-century, some 400 students are reported to have been attending a newly established school – as well as Jizzin, Juba and Karak Nuh in the Biqaa.[37] Schools were established in each of the last two in these years.[38]

Scholars of these regions did continue to travel throughout the Shii world. They are not, however, seen to be emigrating to Safawid Iran in any discernibly large numbers either in the immediate aftermath of the faith's establishment in Iran or even after the 1558 execution of Shaykh Zayn al-Din, most likely a one-off incident and not part of any official Ottoman anti-Shii policy.[39] Indeed, Shaykh Zayn al-Din's own son al-Hasan (d. 1602–3) and his relative and associate Sayyid Muhammad, (d. 1600) did move east, but only as far as Iraq's shrine cities. Although both were students of Zayn al-Din's own student Shaykh al-Husayn, they did not follow the latter's lead and relocate to Iran, given their fears of being pressed into government service in Iran.[40] As noted, even Shaykh al-Husayn later regretted his subsequent service to Shah Tahmasb.

The *tabaqat* literature does allow the tracing of the movements out of the region of some eleven scholars over the century. Three went to Iraq, but only six – including Ali al-Karaki, Shaykh al-Husayn and Sayyid al-Husayn and the ancestor of Baqir al-Majlisi – are recorded herein as having gone to Iran. One each went to Damascus and Cairo.[41]

Nevertheless, and overall, it seems that over the period the situation for the Lebanese Twelver scholarly community was not deemed dire enough, nor was the Safawid situation generally or, more specifically, deemed sufficiently better to encourage any large numbers to relocate.

Arab Iraq: still viable after all these years

The third most active site in these years was Iraq. This included Najaf, al-Jazair, in southern Iraq, and al-Hilla. If Najaf's numbers rose over the previous century and al-Hilla's numbers declined, the overall figures bespeak the presence of an active scholarly community at the Iraqi sites.

The Ottomans and Safawids in fact vied with each other to identify themselves with the shrine cities. Their patronage may well have accounted for that growth, or at least ensured some stability.

Both Najaf and Karbala depended upon water from the Euphrates. Ismail, after his capture of the area in 1508, ordered the redigging of a canal for Najaf and made endowments to the servants of the two shrines in the city. Repairs were also ordered to the shrine of Imam Musa. The shah also visited Karbala and ordered embellishments to the shrine of Imam al-Husayn and made donations. He also visited al-Hilla. Tahmasb visited Karbala in 1527 and ordered that a canal be built from al-Hilla to the city. Both shahs were also attentive to Samarra.[42]

In 1534, after having captured Arab Iraq from the Safawids during the civil war that followed Ismail's death in 1524, the Ottoman sultan Sulayman visited Kufa, al-Hilla and the shrines. He ordered repairs to the shrines and that the shrine attendants were to be paid from the city's treasury. When Salim II (*reg.* 1566–74) visited, he ordered an aqueduct built. In 1573, a saray for pilgrims was built in Karbala. The Ottomans ordered work done in Najaf in 1574–5, 1576, 1583 and 1587. The Manarat al-Abd was built in 1574–5. In 1583, Murad III ordered the Baghdad governor to undertake work at the Karbala shrine, and further infrastructural work was done in 1591. Even local officials visiting the area took care to visit Najaf and Karbala.[43]

The Safawids may have lost the territory, but they did not lose interest in the cities in these years. As noted, one of Tahmasb's sisters made important donations to the shrines, and another was buried in Karbala. Ottoman records suggest that in the early 1570s, at least, there were appointed figures reciting from the Quran and meeting processions bearing corpses from Iran to be buried near the holy precincts, with their heads being directed towards Ardabil, that is, not, as ritually prescribed, toward the Hijaz.[44]

In the years 1565–85, the Ottomans were very concerned with the presence of pro-Safawid tribal 'Qizilbash' elements in Ottoman territory, just as the Porte was aware of overt pro-Safawid activity at the shrines as sponsored by Tahmasb. In Mosul in 1574, Muharram ceremonies generated some concern. From the 1560s, but especially in the years after Tahmasb's 1576 death, anti-Sunni activity was perceived to be on the increase in the empire, particularly among tribal elements, owing to Safawid influence. In these years a false shah Ismail is reported as having risen. In 1579 and 1580, risings by 'rafidis' are reported.[45]

Towards the end of the century, water was again said to have become an issue for both of the shrine cities, and Najaf's population is said to have dwindled markedly.[46]

Nevertheless, as noted, the shrines were still clearly understood as active in these years, and preferable to Iran. Shaykh Zayn al-Din's son al-Hasan and Sayyid Muhammad, as noted, studied there – avoiding Iran – with Abdallah al-Yazdi (d. 1573) and Ahmad al-Ardabili, both of whom had resettled there from Iran.[47]

The Shia in the Hijaz and the Gulf

At least from the end of the Mamluk period or the early Ottoman period – the Ottomans took the Hijaz in 1517 – leading families of the Prophet's descendants in both cities were either Shiites or at least cultivated ties with Shiites of other regions, patronising laudatory works by Shiite scholars on the descendants of the Prophet. They also benefited from gifts, donations, and endowments from Arab Shiites and from pilgrims with ties to the Shiite polities in Iran and the Deccan.[48]

In these years, indeed, there was enough of a community in the area, and their position was sufficiently precarious, that they could feel the impact of Safawid policy: they complained of harassment there when, as noted, al-Karaki composed his 1511 treatise on the legality of cursing the Sunni caliphs. There was certainly still something of a community in Mecca when Shaykh Zayn al-Din reached the city in the 1550s.[49]

During the reign of Tahmasb, to be sure, three scholars associated with Yemen were in or came to Qazwin, apparently in fear of the Ottoman presence in the region.[50]

But unease with Safawid Shiism still remained. From the Hijaz a prominent father and son, when decamping from the region, elected to go to India. The former, Sayyid Ali b. al-Hasan Shudqum al-Madani (d. 1552), was in fact the *naqib* in Medina. In India, he became associated with the Nizam Shahs in the Deccan, and made no effort to associate with the Safawids. His son al-Hasan (d. 1591) later also resigned as *naqib*, came to India and also became associated with the Nizam Shahs. Although he journeyed through Iran in the 1550s and met Tahmasb in 1556, al-Hasan died in India.[51]

In these years, even the Gulf Shia continued to be more aligned with the north than with Iran-based Shiism. Following the Safawid capture of Baghdad and the shrine cities in 1508, the Mushasha leadership had pledged fealty to Ismail I and gifts were exchanged. The later murder of the joint rulers of the confederation by the new Safawid governor of Shushtar, most likely on Ismail's orders, provoked an outburst among followers of the Mushasha. Basra and al-Ahsa experienced especially violent anti-Safawid outbursts.[52]

In the Persian Gulf in this period, the routing of the Asian spice trade via Hurmuz to Europe took on added importance. In 1515, the Portuguese seized Hurmuz and reintegrated it into their trade network – based regionally in Goa, in western India – as that network extended around the Cape of Good Hope, which they had rounded in 1488. In 1521, a combined Portuguese–Hurmuzi force took Bahrain and stationed Portuguese troops there.

The Ottomans took the port city of Basra in 1536 and reached al-Ahsa in 1550. The Portuguese checked that advance and, in the process, sacked the eastern Arabia town of al-Qatif in 1552. Thereafter, however, a stalemate obtained between the two forces: the Portuguese tried to redirect the land trade in spice and pearls to their own Gulf-based vessels, and the Ottomans worked to ensure that the Shii landlords of al-Qatif and al-Ahsa lost their lands. The Ottomans' 1550 effort to seize Bahrain failed, but they encouraged a rebellion in eastern Arabia by the Banu Khalid, who subsequently enjoyed considerable autonomy in their proxy struggles against the Portuguese.

In their struggle with the Safawids over the spice trade, the Ottomans closed the pilgrimage route from eastern Arabia through the 1590s. The later 1500s experienced a revival in the spice trade through the region, in the midst, or perhaps because, of this standoff. But when the eastern Arabic–Hijaz routes were reopened, the Ottomans made sure Twelvers in the region were excluded from taking part.

Owing to its geographical position, and the local and regional standoffs, local scholarship flourished and retained some independence in both movement and, therefore, also in relation to trends in scholarship in both Iraq and Iran.[53]

The eastern Gulf area continued to be associated with a large number of scholars. Of these, several were associated with al-Ahsa and al-Qatif.

As to the Bahrain area generally, of the eighteen listed, two were in Yazd and one studied with al-Karaki and became his representative in Yazd. None of the others, however, seems to have enjoyed any Iran connections. One was in India in 1582, and a sayyid is identified with his own school on the island itself.[54] Of the five identified as associated with al-Ahsa, one is said to have been Mashhad during the reign of Tahmasb, but there is no indication of any longer-term stay or any connection to the court.[55] For al-Qatif, three scholars are listed; Ibrahim al-Qatifi did travel to Najaf and al-Hilla, and to Mashhad, where he met and debated with al-Karaki; thereafter he returned to Iraq. Neither of the others, one being al-Qatifi's teacher and the other his own son, had any Iran connections.[56]

As to lively debates featuring some intellectual distance from, for example, Iran-based trends in scholarship, Sayyid al-Husayn b. al-Hasan al-Ghurayfi al-Bahrani (d. 1592), from a village in the south of the main island of Bahrain, wrote a work forbidding the emulation of *mujtahids*.[57] To be sure, rationalist approaches also continued to exist. Shaykh Daud b. Abi Shafiz, a theologian, litterateur, philosopher and polymath who had his own school, wrote on logic in the tradition of al-Farabi. He debated with al-Ghurayfi and Shaykh Zayn al-Din's student Shaykh al-Husayn al-Amili when the latter settled in Bahrain. There is some suggestion that Shaykh al-Husayn's interest in the traditions stimulated local discussion. There is no record that either al-Ghurayfi or Shaykh Daud had any Safawid connections.[58]

The Deccan 'states': more Shiism from above

The years in which Shiism was formally established in Iran also witnessed the establishment of the faith in three of the five Deccan 'states'. The prospects for their longevity and the popularity of the faith could not have seemed any more promising there than for Iran, however.

There had been Twelvers in the Indian subcontinent since the fourteenth century, but, as in the west, in these years veneration for the Prophet's family was mixed with certain Sufi, if not also Sunni, beliefs. The arrival of followers of Simnani, a Sunni who nevertheless venerated the Family, and of the son of Nimatallah Vali (d. 1431), together with the arrival of sayyids from Shii Sabziwar in Kashmir from the later 1300s gave these beliefs fresh momentum.[59]

In the south central area of Indian, there had been some Twelvers present in the Bahmani 'state' (1347–1528), whose break up gave rise to the five Deccan polities. These included a Shirazi, who helped Persianise the court such that the Bahmanis venerated the Prophet's family even if they were not necessarily Shia.

As in Safawid Iran, official professions of Shiism in three of those five Deccan realms preceded any profound commitment to, and understanding of, the faith's very distinctive doctrines and practices by political elites or society at large.

Based in Gulcunda, in southern India, near Hyderabad – then a centre of the diamond trade and sword production – the Qutb Shahi polity was one of the three. The Qutb Shahs are said to have owed their origins to a Qara Quyunlu figure born in Hamadan, Sultan Quli Qutb al-Din (d. 1543). Fleeing Iran when the Aq Quyunlu took the plateau, Sultan Quli arrived in Delhi in the late 1400s and then moved to southern India. In *c.* 1510, he seized Gulcunda. In 1512, some eleven years after Qizilbash forces had taken Tabriz and two years after Ismail had taken Herat, Sultan Quli formally declared the Twelver faith that of his own, considerably, smaller realm.

As the first Muslim 'state' in India and, perhaps encouraged as much by the origins of its founder as by a need to attract allies, the Qutb Shahi polity was a very 'Persian' entity – even Noruz was celebrated there. It was also a very cosmopolitan centre of scholarship and learning, drawing literati from Iran, especially, but also from Arabic-speaking lands and central Asia.

But the early association of the realm with the faith was as limited as that of the Safawids. Not only had its ruler only recently arrived on the scene, but early Qutb Shahi history was also as problematic as that of the Safawids. In 1543, Sultan Quli's son Jamshid (d. 1550) succeeded his father, after assassinating him and blinding his own brother, a potential claimant to the throne. Jamshid's son, aged 7, died less than a year later.

Sultan Quli's brother Ibrahim (d. 1580) succeeded him and ruled for nearly three decades. He was attentive to both local and Arabo-Persian cultural norms. But he also warred with the two nearby Shii polities. He did organise an alliance with them against a neighbouring Hindu state. But, after defeating the Hindus in 1565, the three Shii 'states' resumed their hostilities.

For some, however, the Qutb Shahs offered better prospects than the Safawids. In 1581, Mir Muhammad Mumin, an Astarabadi sayyid and former tutor to a son of Tahmasb, arrived in Gulcunda, fleeing the turmoil of the Safawid civil war. He stayed some twenty-five years. This was during the reign of Muhammad Quli (*reg.* 1580–1612), and only now were efforts to establish and popularise Shiism commenced. These included the building, *c.* 1591, of the Charminar mosque. In 1593, five years after Abbas I's accession in Iran, work commenced on an *Ashur khana*, a dedicated building for commemorating the events at Karbala, with an Husayni *alam* (standard). A Shii cemetery was established and villages were established in the area with mosques and *Ashur khana alams*. Hindus were assisted in converting and ceremonies were established not only for the Prophet's birthday, but also such very Shii, if not necessarily Twelver, occasions as Ghadir Khumm and even such Persian ones as Noruz.[60]

Based in nearby Bijapur, to the west, the Adil Shahi sultanate, the second of the Deccan's Shii realms, was founded by Yusuf Adil Shah (1489–1510), an Ottoman Turk with ties to Ismail I. Shiism was formally established there in 1502, the year after Ismail took Tabriz.

Realpolitik played as much, if not more, of a role in this association as any profound understanding of the faith. It was in the hope of some assistance against local opponents that the Adil Shahs recognised the Safawids as their sovereigns. Some Iranian and Shii figures did appear on the scene and, as in Gulcunda under the Qutb Shahs, the outward signs of the faith were officially encouraged: the early caliphs were cursed, for example, and Muharram was commemorated.

But local nobles were allowed to follow whatever faith they desired and most of the military were Hanafis. Sunni–Shii riots were also frequent.

In fact, the Shii affiliation also was not assured. Yusuf's immediate successor, the regent, restored Sunnism. Yusuf's son Ismail then restored Shiism, and ties with Ismail I in Iran were encouraged to the point where Adil Shah soldiers apparently wore the Qizilbash twelve-coned hat. Ismail's son Ibrahim (1534–58) re-instituted Sunni practices. Shii allegiances were restored under his successor Ali (1558–80), only to be discarded under Ibrahim II (1580–1626).

Sometime in this period the 'state' and the shah exchanged embassies, suggesting that Safawid Iran saw the Adil Shahs as political-military counterweights to growing Mughal power.[61]

North of the Adil Shahs, in Ahmadnagar, the third Deccan Shii 'state', the Nizam Shah polity was founded by one Shah Tahir (d. *c.* 1545–9) who, fleeing from Ismail I's anti-Ismaili policies, arrived in Goa in 1520. He reached Ahmadnagar in 1522. Having converted to Twelver Shiism, he convinced the local ruler Burhan (1508–53) to adopt the faith as that of his realm. This Burhan did in 1537.

There was widespread popular opposition to this move. Nevertheless, funds were thereafter sent to Karbala and Najaf, and Shah Tahir sent letters to Tahmasb. And, at his death in 1553, Burhan's body was sent to Karbala for burial.

Shiism is said to have flourished in the area until 1586 when the faith was dis-established, in the process of which many foreigners and Shia were killed. The faith was briefly re-established in the early 1590s, but remained influential only among elites. Embassies were exchanged with the Safawids, but soon after the accession of the Mughal Akbar (*reg.* 1556–1605) the Mughals commenced putting an end to the realm's independence.[62]

The political elites of all three Deccan polities certainly hoped that the Shii connection would attract Safawid support to aid them in their battles with their Muslim and Hindu rivals, and the Mughals to the north. The Deccan elites retained their affections for Persian culture and veneration of the Imams, works on which were increasingly appearing in the new language of Urdu. But most Muslims remained Sunnis and the masses remained Hindu.[63] Aside from some outward signs of commitment to faith, the finer details of the faith's doctrines and practice did not penetrate mass consciousness over the period – much as was the case in Iran in these same years.

Nevertheless, some Iranian poets, artisans and, especially a number of Shii scholars, did come to the Deccan and Mughal India in these years, mainly in search of patronage.[64] Further afield, as noted, even the Shii Shudqum al-Madanis, prominent members of the Hijazi community, in leaving Arabia, preferred association with the Deccan rather than with Iran.[65]

Further north, Humayun (d. 1556), the son of the founder of the Mughal polity – the Timurid Babur (d. 1530) – had been helped by the Safawids to regain his throne in 1555. Northern India experienced some limited contact with Shiism, and Iranian immigration, over the century. In Kashmir, in the late sixteenth century, the Chak clan formally adopted Shiism. In 1589, Humayun's son Akbar used Sunni reaction to this move as an excuse to add the region to his growing empire. Although Iranians did serve in many capacities during Akbar's reign,[66] he tolerated but did not promote Shiism. Shii scholars were invited to debate Sunnis at court, and when a Sunni mullah attacked a Shii mullah the Sunni was executed. Sunnis perceived Shii influence as growing, and some were concerned at the presence of ranking officials who were Iranians.[67]

Summary and conclusion

Over the period scholarly activity featured in all of the region's several Shii pockets. On balance, however, despite the arrival of the Sunni Ottomans, the Arabic-speaking lands remained at the core of Shii activity. Together with the patronage on offer in the Deccan, these offered alternatives to association with Safawid Shiism, with which, clearly, a number of established scholars had reservations.

Indeed, absent hindsight, over the latter years of the sixteenth century the future of the Safawid polity itself, let alone the realm's association with the faith, could only have seemed quite precarious. The faith had some following among some elites, even if aspects of doctrine and practice were not well understood, at least for 'political' reasons. Among the population at large, however, the millenarianism that brought the Safawids to power remained widespread. In India, what commitment to, and understanding of, the faith there was remained limited to the elites. But if their continued independent existence was as problematic as that of the Safawids, the absence in the Deccan of the heterodoxy of the Iranian plateau was not. That absence may well have been a factor in the decision of some to come to the Indian subcontinent.

Nevertheless, again, when the fortunes of the faith remained at a very low ebb, two important developments over the period stand out.

The first was the elaboration of the concept of *niyaba amma* (general deputy-ship) among Amili scholars. That the terminology as it appeared in such early writings of Ali al-Karaki was so quickly 'mirrored' in the works of Shaykh Zayn al-Din suggests that the concept itself – or at least the general understanding that, given the continuing absence of the Imam, the authority of the *faqih* should expand – had been in the making for some time.

As importantly, if only towards the latter half of the century, efforts to recover some of the faith's heritage, as embodied in key pre- and some post-1055 and still pre-Safawid scholarly texts, were now visibly underway.

Both developments would prove to be useful in a new series of challenges that would mark the Shii experience in the seventeenth century, in Iran in particular.

Notes

1. The marked rise in interest in *rijal* in the later Safawid period is discussed in Chapter 9.
2. Al-Tihrani, *Tabaqat*, fourth/tenth century: 41, 48–9, 8, 48, 48–9, 95, 250, 100, 276, 134, 145, 223, 23, 136, 277, 38, 108, 61, 217, 238, 210–11, 11, 149, 211, 182–3, 86. Further movements are discussed below.
3. Al-Tihrani, *ibid.*, 2, 5, 12, 29, 37, 46, 57, 69, 105, 110, 119, 121, 157, 158, 169, 177, 178, 181, 185, 194, 208, 224, 229, 232, 234, 237, 251, 260
4. Al-Tihrani, *ibid.*, 14, 148, 153, 212, 227, 18, 36, 38, 150, 153, 172, 223, 239–40, 258, 262, 267, 9, 60, 61, 86, 98, 131, 146, 203, 229, 269, 276, 227.
5. Al-Tihrani, *ibid.*, 69, 157, 239–40, 153–4, 268, 9. There were even copies being made of contemporary works. These included works by Ibrahim al-Qatifi (d. after 1539), on whom see further below, in Najaf and al-Hilla (262, 267), Ali al-Karaki in al-Hilla and Bahrain (e.g., 9, 61, 68, 262; al-Tihrani, *al-Dharia*, 15: 1702) and Shaykh Zayn al-Din al-Amili (d. 1558) in Bahrain (61).

6. A copy of a work by al-Allama was produced by a Bahraini. See al-Tihrani, ibid., 98, 57, 18, 177, 54, 269, 150, 276, 12, 227, 232.

7. See D. Stewart, 'The Genesis of the Akhbari Revival', in M. Mazzaoui (ed.), *Safawid Iran and Her Neighbors* (Salt Lake City, UT, 2003), 174–9. Stewart (175–6) cites Shaykh Zayn al-Din al-Amili's 1545 dream in Sivas in which al-Kulayni complained to him and his student Shaykh al-Husayn (d. 1576) of the poor condition of copies of his *al-Kafi*. The dream points to a realisation of the poor state of the Shii *corpus* of traditions to the west of Safawid Iran.

8. Al-Tihrani, *al-Dharia*, 13: 316f; 6: 106f; 14: 57.

9. Al-Tihrani, *ibid.*, 14: 17f, 6: 169f; 13: 141f, 6: 32f; 13: 73f, 6: 14–18; 13: 165f, 6: 54; 14: 52; 6: 82; 13: 117f, 4: 83f.

10. Al-Tihrani, *ibid.*, 14: 47–51, 6: 190.

11. Ahmad al-Ardabili (d. 1585), Iranian by birth, in fact left Safawid territory for the Iraqi shrine cities and was critical of Ali al-Karaki's Safawid involvements. A. Newman, 'The Myth of the Clerical Migration to Safawid Iran: Arab Shiite Opposition to Ali al-Karaki and Safawid Shiism', *Die Welt des Islams*, 33 (1993), 108, n. 90.

12. Indeed, Hasan Rumlu, who completed his *Ahsan al-Tawarikh* in 1577 wrote that when Ismail decided to establish the faith in Iran, there was no book immediately available which delineated the tenets of the faith. A copy of the first volume of a *fiqh* work entitled *Qawaid al-Islam* and ascribed to al-Allama al-Hilli was eventually located, however. The title cited is not listed among al-Allama's works, but it may well be his *Qawaid al-Ahkam*, of which, as has been suggested, a fair number of copies were extant. Hasan Beg Rumlu, *Ahsan al-Tawarikh* (Tehran, 1357), 86. See also Mazzaoui, *The Origins of the Safawids*, 6. For a more detailed discussion of sixteenth-century Iran, see Newman, *Safavid Iran*.

13. Z. V. Togan, 'Sur l'origine des Safawides', *Mélanges Louis Massignon* 3 (Damas, 1957), 345–57. On use of the term *al-imam al-adil* as a reference to the Imam by al-Murtada, see Chapter 4, at n. 47. See also Newman, 'The Myth', 71, n. 13 for a discussion of the ambiguity of the term. See also n. 23 below. For an early reference to *imam adil*, see also Chapter 2, n, 58.

14. For the Biktashis, Abu Muslim was the link between the Prophet, Ali and the later Imams. Qizilbash elements apparently venerated that order's eponymous founder Hajji Biktash who, like Ismail himself, had a Christian mother. See Birge, *The Bektashi Order*, 33–69.

15. V. Minorsky, 'The Poetry of Shah Ismail I', *Bulletin of the School of Oriental and African Studies*, 10 (1942), 1006a–53a, esp. 1042a, 1043a, 1044a, 1047a, 1048a. See also W. Thackston, 'The Diwan of Khatai: Pictures for the Poetry of Shah Ismail', *Asian Art*, 1(4) (1988), 37–63.

16. See Newman, 'The Myth'; D. Stewart, 'Notes on the Migration of Amili Scholars to Safawid Iran', *Journal of Near Eastern Studies*, 55(2) (1996), 81–103.

17. See R. Hillenbrand, 'Safavid Architecture', in *The Cambridge History of Iran, vol. 6: The Timurid and Safavid Periods*, eds P. Jackson and L. Lockhart (Cambridge, 1986, 767–8; H. Naraqi, *Asar-i Tarikhi-yi Shahristanha-yi Kashan va Natanz* (Tehran, 1348/1969), 399.

18. See M. Szuppe, 'La participation des femmes de la famille royale à l'exercice du pouvoir en Iran safawide au XVIe siècle (Première Partie)', *Studia Iranica*, 23(2) (1994), 250–1; M. Szuppe, 'La participation des femmes de la famille royale à l'exercice du pouvoir en Iran safawide au XVIe siècle (Seconde Partie)', *Studia Iranica*, 24(1) (1995), 71.

19. H. Modarressi Tabatabai, *Bargi az Tarikh-i Qazwin* (Qum, 1361), 21–2, 23–5, 28, 42, 64–70, 121f, 147–50; Rumlu, *Ahsan al-Tawarikh*, 184; S. Blake, *Half the World. The Social Architecture of Safavid Isfahan, 1590–1722* (Costa Mesa, 1999), 170; L. Hunarfar, *Ganjinah-i Asar-i Tarikhi-i Isfahan* (Isfahan, 1344), 362. On Ali Minshar, who may well have come to Iran from India, see Newman, 'The Myth', n. 94.

20. J. Calmard, 'Shii Rituals and Power, II', in C. Melville (ed.), *Safawid Persia* (London/ New York, 1996), 139–90, esp. 142–3; M. Membré, *Mission to the Lord Sophy of Persia (1539–1542)*, trans. with Introduction and Notes by A. H. Morton (London, 1993), 43, 25–6; Modarressi, *Bargi*, 22, 60f, 148f; Hillenbrand, 'Safawid Architecture', 6: 770; Varjavand. Safawid iconography over this period was, if Alid, not necessarily distinctly Twelver in nature. See, for example, C. Gruber, 'When *Nubuvvat* Encounters *Valayat*', in P. Khosronejad (ed.), *The Art and Material Culture of Iranian Shiism* (London, 2012), 46–73, and the other chapters on this collection which trace the Sufi roots of some of this Alid iconography.

21. See R. Stanfield, 'Mirza Makhdum Sharifi: A 16th Century Sunni *sadr* at the Safawid Court', unpublished PhD thesis, New York University, 1993; R. Johnson, 'Sunni Survival in Safawid Iran: Anti-Sunni Activities during the Reign of Tahmasb I', *Iranian Studies*, 27(1–4) (1994), 127–33; S. Gholsorkhi, 'Ismail II and Mirza Makhdum Sharifi: An Interlude in Safawid History', *Iinternational Journal of Middle East Studies*, 26(3) (1994), 477–88.

22. R. Savory, 'A Curious Episode of Safawid History', in C. E. Bosworth (ed.), *Iran and Islam* (Edinburgh, 1971), 461–73, citing Munshi, *History of Shah Abbas*, 1: 401f.

23. A 1578 inscription in Isfahan's Congregational Mosque, the year of his accession, referring to him as 'the most just . . . Sultan . . . the Shadow of Allah'. The city's Shah Zayd Imamzada was built in 1586, the same year that mosques in Shiraz were repaired. See Hillenbrand, 'Safawid Architecture', 6: 773–4; Hunarfar, *Ganjinah-i Asar-i*, 164–5, 389–91, 134–5; Blake, *Half the World*, 150.

24. Savory, 'A Curious Episode', 469; R. Savory, 'The Office of Khalifat al-Khulafa under the Safawids', *Journal of the American Oriental Society*, 85 (1965), 501.

25. I. Ishraqi, '"Noqtaviyya" à l'époque safawides', in A. Newman (ed.), *Society and Culture in the Early Modern Middle East. Studies on Iran in the Safawid Period* (Leiden, 2003), 347-8; K. Babayan, 'The Waning of the Qizilbash: The Spiritual and the Temporal in Seventeenth Century Iran', unpublished PhD dissertation, Princeton University, 1993, 46–6; I. Munshi, *History of Shah Abbas the Great*, trans. R. M. Savory, 3 vols (Boulder, CO, 1978–1986), 2: 649–50; A. Amanat, 'The Nuqtawi Movement of Mahmud Pisikhani and his Persian Cycle of Mystical-materialism', in F. Daftary (ed.), *Medieval Ismaili History and Thought* (Cambridge, 1996), 290f; Newman, *Safavid Iran*, 17n21.

26. Shubbar, *Tarikh al-Mushashaiyin*, 101–4, 216–17; al-Amin, *Ayan*, 9: 42f.

27. Newman, *Safavid Iran*, 24, 37–38; Newman, 'The Myth', 78–94, 96–104. Twelvers in the Hijaz complained they were suffering from al-Karaki's 1511 essay promoting the cursing of the first three caliphs in Iran. See al-Bahrani, *Luluat*, 153; al-Khwansari, *Raudat al-Jannat*, 4: 362; al-Amin, *Ayan*, 8: 208f; al-Tihrani, *al-Dharia*, 24: 250–1

28. On these criticisms, especially regarding Friday prayer, see below. See also D. Stewart, 'Husayn b. Abd al-Samad al-Amili's Treatise for Sultan Suleiman and the Shii Shafii Legal Tradition', *Islamic Law and Society*, 4(2) (1997), 168f; D. Stewart, 'The Ottoman Execution of Zayn al-Din al-Amili', *Die Welt des Islams*, 48 (2008), 342; Winter, *The Shiites of Lebanon*, 23–6. Shaykh al-Husayn, on whom see below, also opposed al-Karaki's cursing of the first three caliphs. See R. J. Abisaab, *Converting Persia. Religion and Power in the Safawid Empire* (London, 2004), 34.

29. Calder, 'Zakat', 479–80. See also E. Kohlberg, 'The Development of the Imami Shii Doctrine of Jihad', *ZDMG*, 126(1) (1976), 64–86, esp. 83.

30. Newman, 'The Myth', 85.

31. Newman, 'The Myth', 100–3. The *firman*, so technical as to suggest it was in fact drafted by al-Karaki himself (Newman, 101), is translated by S. A. Arjomand (ed.) in his 'Two

Decrees of Shah Tahmasp Concerning Statecraft and the Authority of Shaykh Ali al-Karaki', in *Authority and Political Culture in Shiism* (Albany, NY, 1988), 250–62.

32. Calder, 'Zakat', 478–9. On the date of this work, see Stewart, 'The Execution', 323. On the other challenges to al-Karaki by Shaykh Zayn al-Din and Shaykh Husayn, see Newman, 'The Myth', 91f, 105f.

33. D. Stewart, 'Polemics and Patronage in Safawid Iran: The Debate on Friday Prayer during the Reign of Shah Tahmasb', *Buletin of the School of Oriental and African Studies*, 72(3) (2009), 425–57. See the discussion on the prayer in the next chapter.

34. Newman, 'The Myth', 108, n. 90; D. Stewart, 'The First Shaykh al-Islam of the Safawid Capital of Qazwin', *Journal of the American Oriental Society*, 116(3) (1996), 389–90.

35. Winter, *The Shiites of Lebanon*, 45f, 15f; C. Imber, 'The Persecution of the Ottoman Shiites According to the *muhimme defterleri*, 1565–85', *Der Islam*, 56 (1979), 271. A 1589 treatise called for cooperation between Sunni and Alawi.

36. Winter, *ibid.*, 26–7, 43f; al-Amin, *Khitat*, 177, 275. See also M. Salati, 'Toleration, Persecution and Local Realities: Observations on the Shiism in the Holy Places and the Bilad al-Sham (16th–17th centuries)', *Convegno sul Tema La Shi'a Nell'Impero Ottomano*, Rome, 15 April 1991 (Rome, 1993), 121–48.

37. Al-Amin, *ibid.*, 362–3. Al-Khwansari (*Raudat al-Jannat*, 7: 3) referred without criticism to mention by al-Hurr al-Amili of a funeral in the Jabal Amil area during the time of Shaykh Zayn al-Din that was attended by seventy mujtahids. If the accuracy of such figures is problematic, they are suggestive of activity in the region and, perhaps also, how many senior scholars did not emigrate to Safawid territory in this period. See also al-Amin, 74.

38. Abisaab, 'Shiite Beginnnings', 16–17.

39. Al-Amin, *Khitat*, 365–6. Stewart provides the most detailed account of this event. See his 'The Ottoman Execution'. See also Winter, *The Shiites of Lebanon*, 24. On these villages and their scholars, see the following passages in al-Amin's *Khitat* cross-referenced, where possible, with the reference, by volume and page, in his *Ayan al-Shia*. For Nabatiyah: 136, 8: 127; 11–12, 2: 584f; for Mays: 6, 2: 195; 17, 245, 10: 113; 39, 4: 131; 165–6, 363; for Jizzin: 213, 229, 9: 424; for Karak: 57, 5: 34; 71, 119, 122, 153, 160, 163; for Juba: 11, 6, 51, 89, 97, 7: 310, 102, 122. 12, 147–9, 8: 151, 8: 188; 148, 8; 241; 212, 10: 208, 8: 333. Shaykh Zayn al-Din was well known enough to attract a student from Lahijan (Stewart, 33).

40. Newman, 'The Myth', 107–8.

41. Al-Tihrani, *Tabaqat*, fourth/tenth century: 10, 14, 149, 155–6, 62, 71, 73, 147–8, 158, 90, 148, 149, 90.

42. A. al-Azzawi, *Tarikh al-Iraq bayn al-Ihtilalayn*, 8 vols (Baghdad, 1935–56), 3: 337, 341. The last apparent attention to this water issue was paid in the Mongol period when, in 1263, the local governor ordered a canal to be built from the river to the city. See Y. Nakash, *The Shiis of Iraq* (Princeton, 1995), 19; al-Tihrani, *ibid.*, third/seventh century: 97–8; Al Yasin, *Tarikh al-Mashhad al-Kazimi*, 55–84; A. Northridge, 'The Shrine in its Historical Context', in I. Panjwani (ed.), *The Shia of Samarra* (London, 2012), 63.

43. Al-Azzawi, *ibid.*, 4: 29, 34–5, 49, 114, 119f, 129f, 36–7; al-Amin, *Khitat*, 275. See also Newman, 'The Myth', 104.

44. Imber, 'Persecution of the Ottoman Shiites', 246f.

45. Imber, 'Persecution of the Ottoman Shiites', 251.

46. Nakash, *The Shiis of Iraq*, 19.

47. Newman, 'The Myth', 107–8, esp. 108, n. 90. On al-Ardabili, see n. 11.

48. Stewart, 'The Ottoman Execution', 339. On a family of *naqib*s in Medina, see al-Tihrani, *Tabaqat*, fourth/tenth century: 52–3.

49. Notes 27, 28; Stewart, 'The Ottoman Execution', 326–7.

50. Al-Tihrani, *Tabaqat*, fourth/tenth century: 170, 174, 236.

51. Al-Tihrani, *ibid.*, 167–88, 52. See also Afandi, *Riyad al-Ulama*, 1: 236–43; al-Amin, *Ayan*, 5: 175. In 1575, al-Hasan received an *ijaza* from Shaykh al-Husayn al-Amili. See al-Tihrani, *al-Dharia*, 2: 87.

52. Shubbar, *Tarikh al-Mushashaiyin*, 216–17, 85–7. Shubbar (86, n. 2) gives 1518 as the year of the execution.

53. Cole, 'Rival', esp. 182f. See also J. Mandaville, 'The Ottoman Province of al-Hasa in the Sixteenth and Seventeenth Centuries', *Journal of the American Oriental Society*, 90(3) (1970), 486–513. The Ottomans built a mosque in al-Ahsa in 1554, probably not a Shii one. See al-Azzawi, *Tarikh al-Iraq*, 4: 284, who notes the remission of local taxes to Istanbul.

54. On these, see al-Tihrani, *Tabaqat*, fourth/tenth century: 120; 274–5; al-Amin, *Ayan*, 10: 289; al-Tihrani, *ibid.*, 61, 262, al-Amin, *ibid.*, 10: 204. On the others, see references in al-Tihrani (fourth/tenth century) and al-Amin, as follows: 47, 4: 615; 47, 4: 615; 75, al-Tihrani, *al-Dharia*, 2: 238, al-Amin, *ibid.*, 6: 116; 83; 98, al-Tihrani, *al-Dharia*, 15: 1702; 120–1, 7: 469; 128, 154, 8: 206; al-Tihrani, 196, al-Tihrani, *al-Dharia*, 24: 423; 262, 10: 204; 276.

55. Non-Iran-based scholars, including al-Qatifi himself, did visit the shrine, but did not remain in Safawid territory. See al-Tihrani, *Tabaqat*, fourth/tenth century: 1, who, according to al-Amin (2: 23) was of the seventeenth century. See also 144–5; 213–14, 203, 274).

56. On the dates for al-Qatifi's Iran trip as between 1508 and 1510, see Newman, 'The Myth', 83. See also al-Tihrani, *Tabaqat*, fourth/tenth century: 3, 37, 159.

57. Al-Tihrani, *al-Dharia*, 6: 151, 16: 68, 15: 70; Cole, 'Rival', 186. The text generated a number of marginalia, as listed here. See also 13: 337 on his other works. On his family and his sons, two of whom spent all their time in Arab lands, and the other of whom travelled quite a bit, including Iran, but mainly throughout Arab lands, see al-Amin, *Ayan*, 5: 470.

58. Al-Amin, *ibid.*, 6: 366, 383–4; Cole, 'Rival', 186; al-Oraibi, 'Rationalism in the School of Bahrayn'.

59. S. A. A. Rizvi, *A Socio-intellectual History of the Isna Ashari Shiis in India*, 2 vols (Canberra, 1986), 1: 247–341, esp. 1: 157f, 166; Baldick, 94–5. See M. Ahmed, 'The Shiis of Pakistan', in M. Kramer (ed.), *Shiism, Resistance and Revolution* (Boulder, CO, 1987), esp. 276. For an overview, see J. Cole, 'Conversion III. To Imami Shiism in India', *EIr*; J. Cole, *Roots of North Indian Shiism in Iran and Iraq. Religion and State in Awadh, 1722–1859* (Berkeley, CA, 1988), 22–4.

60. Rizvi, *ibid.*, 1: 155, 303–19; J. N. Hollister, *The Shia of India* (London, 1953), 120–5.

61. Rivzi, *ibid.*, 1: 262–81; Hollister, *ibid.*, 112–17.

62. Rizvi, *ibid.*, 1: 281–92; Hollister, *ibid.*, 117–20. His brother also came to India (al-Tihrani, *al-Dharia*, fourth/tenth century: 38).

63. Cole, *Roots of North Indian Shiism*, 24.

64. S. Dale, in his 'A Safawid Poet in the Heart of Darkness: The Indian Poems of Ashraf Mazandarani', *Iranian Studies*, 36(2) (2003), esp. 199–200, points to relative wealth and corresponding 'scale of patronage' as a reason for poets' migration to India. See also M. Haneda, 'Emigration of Iranian Elites to India During the 16th–18th Centuries', in M. Szuppe (ed.), *L'héritage timouride. Iran–Asie centrale–Inde XVe–XVIIIe siècles* (Tashkent/Aix-en-Provence, 1997), 135. See also Newman, *Safavid Iran*, 35, n.71.

65. A. Ahmad, 'Safawid Poets and India', *Iran*, 14, (1976), 128. Artists who came to Gulcunda included a calligrapher each from Shiraz and Bahrain. On letters exchanged with Shah Tahir, see Rizvi, *A Socio-intellectual History*, 1: 289–90. See also al-Amin, *Ayan*, 6: 22.

66. S. Subrahmanyam, 'Iranians Abroad: Intra-Asian Elite Migration and Early Modern

State Formation', *Journal of Asian Studies*, 51 (1992), 340–63, also reviews the history of the Deccan 'states' and Iranian employment there and among the Mughals.

67.   Rizvi, *A Socio-intellectual History*, 1: 166f, 214–19, 232–3, 234–41; Hollister, *The Shia of India*, 141–50.

CHAPTER 9

The past rediscovered and the future assured: Shiism in the seventeenth century

The story of Shiism in the seventeenth century would appear to be very much an Iranian story.

At the accession of Abbas I in 1587, both the place of the faith in Iran and, indeed, the longevity of the Safawid house itself were both questionable. It is only in the seventeenth century – and the later seventeenth century in particular – that the institutionalisation and the popularisation of the faith throughout the country can be witnessed. These processes occurred against the background of, and were encouraged by, a series of profound external political-military and, especially also, internal spiritual challenges. By century's end Iran was so firmly Shii that the association of the area with the faith outlasted the 1722 'political' end of the Safawid dynasty at the hands of the Afghans.

Nevertheless, the region's other centres of the faith remained active and, to varying degrees, independent of Safawid influence over the period. The fortunes of some – the Deccan sites were now were incorporated into the Sunni Mughal empire – experienced downturns, but by the end of the century all continued to be percerived as self-sufficient and viable.

The scattered pockets

The *tabaqat* work of al-Tihrani, summarised in Appendix I, suggests that over the eleventh Islamic century, that is, from 1592 – five years after Abbas I's formal accession – to 1688, Iran, including, especially, sites such as Isfahan, Mashhad, Shiraz and Kashan, was the region with which by far the most scholars of the period enjoyed some association. But if the numbers for Iran reflect an exponential increase over those for the previous century, so do those for other regions in the Shii world, from Lebanon in the far west, through Iraq to the Hijaz and eastern Arabia and into the Indian subcontinent.

Dateable movement and scholarly activity between all these, even if the numbers are limited, does suggest that at the time all these sites were perceived as viable centres of activity over the century. Scholars whose *nisba* suggests an Iranian connection travelled to India, Iraq, the Hijaz and eastern Arabia, and Bahrain; Iraqis travelled to Iran, India and the Gulf/Hijaz. Amilis went to Iran, but others travelled to Iraq, the Hijaz, India and Herat. One stayed in the region, serving as a judge in Baalbak. Those based in the Hijaz and eastern Arabia travelled to Iran, India and Iraq. A Bahraini went to India, but came back to Isfahan. Another went to Isfahan, studied with the same Shaykh Bahai, and returned to Bahrain where he was 'the first' to work with the traditions.

Some of these scholars moved through several sites: one went from Iraq to Isfahan and then on to Mecca; another moved from India to Isfahan to Khurasan; and another is said to have travelled through the Hijaz, Yemen, Ajam (Iran), India and then back to Iraq. Two moved through Iran to India. Another went from Mecca to Mashhad and then to Hyderabad, another went from India to the Hijaz, and another was in Najaf and then moved to Isfahan. A doctor and a legist with the *nisba* al-Karaki, a critic of *ijtihad*, was based in Isfahan, but then travelled to Hyderabad and died there in 1665. An Indian scholar is recorded as having gone to the Hijaz.[1]

Evidence of scholarly activity is also attested by manuscript copying. Such activity was occurring across the region. Al-Tihrani records that thirteen works of al-Tusi were copied in Iran, as were four copies of *al-Kafi*, nineteen of works by Ibn Babawayh, and one copy each of *Basair* and *al-Mahasin*. Iran also produced copies of works by al-Mufid, Ibn al-Ghadairi, Ibn Daud, Ibn Tawus, al-Muhaqqiq and al-Allama.[2]

But copies of three works of al-Tusi were also made in Iraq, as was *al-Kafi*, and three copies of works by Ibn Babawayh. *Basair* was copied in Najaf. Iraq also produced two copies of works by Ibn Tawus, as well as one each by al-Muhaqqiq and al-Allama. Two works of al-Tusi were copied in Bahrain, as were a copy of *al-Kafi* and of a work by Ibn Babawayh. Bahrain also produced a copy of al-Kashshi's *rijal*. Three copies of works by Ibn Babawayh were made in the Hijaz. Mecca produced a copy of al-Mufid's *Irshad*, and Indian sites produced copies of works by al-Murtada, al-Muhaqqiq, al-Allama and Ibn Makki.[3]

The written legacy

Appendix II suggests that in the early years of the eleventh century, that is, from 1592 to 1640, although the sites of the copying are not clear, overall the popularity of and access to a broad range of the faith's key texts, especially pre-1055 works, remained limited, in some instances as limited as over the entire previous century.

By contrast, the latter half of the eleventh Islamic century, from 1641 to 1688, witnessed an exponential increase in the availability of a broad range of these items, and discernible growth in the production of commentaries and marginal comments thereon. If the data is not absolutely accurate, the figures are certainly indicative of the scale of the increase in the availability of copies of these texts in the later years of the century. This is true of nearly all the works surveyed even if, in some cases, the actual numbers are small.

The pattern applies especially to the 'four books' of the Imams' traditions, the several other pre-Buyid collections and many of Ibn Babawayh's other compilations. The same is the case for works by al-Mufid, al-Murtada and others of al-Tusi's works, even if, in most cases, the numbers are small. The same applies to a range of post-1055 works, including the *fiqh* works of al-Muhaqqiq and al-Allama.

The period also is well known for the production of commentaries and marginalia. Appendix IV suggests that while the number of such commentaries and marginalia was small, in the years between 1592 and 1688, works of both genres became markedly more prominent. Overall, however, it was the works of which so many copies were made that were also were those subject to commentaries and marginalia. Thus, 'the four books' attracted particular attention, as did the *fiqh* works of al-Muhaqqiq and al-Allama. In at least one case there were more copies of these commentaries/marginalia on the post-1055 works of *fiqh* in circulation over the period than, apparently, of the original.[4]

Appendix III suggests that the seventeenth century was witness also to a rise in the scholarly interest in *tabaqat/rijal*. If Shaykh Zayn al-Din and his student Shaykh al-Husayn, spurred on by their interest in the traditions, were the first to address issues in *ilm al-diraya* (the science of the contextual study of the *hadith*) in the tenth/sixteenth century,[5] it was only in this century and in Iran that works in the genre become visible.

The dynamics of Shiism in seventeenth-century Iran

Most of the authors of these *shuruh*, *hawashi* and *rijal* works were based in Iran at the time. The sites of the vast copying activity documented in Appendix II are not clear. But that the preponderance of copying activity noted by al-Tihrani occurred in Iran suggests that most of those copies referred to in Appendix II were also produced in Iran.

It was not just copying, commentaries and *rijal* works that experienced such growth in later Safawid Iran. A renewed interest in the Imams' traditions themselves is also attested. Just as the pre-1055 period 'produced' its three Muhammads, compilers of 'the four books' of the Imams' traditions, this period of Safawid history is also known for its 'three Muhammads'. These were Muhammad b. al-Murtada, Fayd al-Kashani (d. 1680), Muhammad b. al-Hasan, al-Hurr al-Amili (d. 1693) and Muhammad Baqir al-Majlisi. Al-Kashani completed his *al-Wafi*, still largely unexplored by scholars in the field, by 1658; al-Hurr completed his *Wasail al-Shia* by 1677; and by 1670 al-Majlisi had finished some volumes of his *Bihar al-Anwar*, although it was only completed by his students after his death in 1699. Al-Hurr came to Iran from the Lebanon later in his life, but the other two were born there.[6]

It is often suggested that a renewed interest in the Imams' traditions in the seventeenth century in particular, and the rise of Akhbari–Usuli 'debates' as the chief, if not also the defining, spiritual polemic of Safawid Iran was down to the efforts of Muhammad Amin al-Astarabadi (d. 1626–7), who in 1622, having studied in Najaf and Shiraz before moving to Mecca, completed his *al-Fawaid al-Madaniyya*.[7] To be sure, Muhammad Amin – citing al-Allama himself – referred to the long-stated understanding of the faithful as being divided into Akhbaris and Usulis, singled out al-Allama, especially, for having divided the community into *mujtahid* and *muqallid*, and criticised such scholars as Ibn Makki, Ali al-Karaki, Shaykh Zayn al-Din and Shaykh Bahai for adopting Sunni Mutazila principles and ignoring the traditions.[8]

But the period is also noted for the growing use of Persian by the scholarly classes, across nearly all genres of the religious sciences and also for the translation of important Shii works from Arabic into Persian; for an expansion in philosophical inquiry and its reconciliation with aspects of Twelver Shiism via the works of scholars such as Mir Damad (d. 1630–1), Ali al-Karaki's grandson via marriage to a prominent Astarabadi sayyid family, Shaykh Bahai and, especially, their associate Sadr al-Din al-Shirazi, Mulla Sadra (d. 1640).[9] The century also witnessed an extraordinary increase in the number of mosques, schools and *imamzada*s – with sites such as Isfahan, in particular, but also Qum, Shiraz, Mashhad and Kashan becoming centres to which aspiring Iranian and non-Iranian scholars came to study – and for the expansion and 'popular' incorporation of rituals associated with the faith especially, for example, Muharram.

Iran: the external and internal challenges

The broad range of the developments in Iran sketched above occurred against the background of a series of external military and internal socioeconomic and, particularly, spiritual, challenges over these years.

In his earliest years, Abbas I (d. 1629) faced challenges both from the Ottomans and Uzbegs, who had clawed away at Safawid territory since his grandfather Tahmasb's death in 1576, and from family members, and their Turkish and Tajik allies, seeking to replace him on the throne.

Concomitant with, and no doubt encouraged by, these, Abbas' early years also witnessed on-going spiritual turmoil, including the questioning of, and challenges to, Abbas by Sufi, tribal and Tajik elements. In the seventeenth century these only continued. Thus, in 1614–16 arose another group of Lahijani Sufis as did, in 1619–20, a group led by Gilani sayyids, one of whom one proclaimed himself the deputy of the Hidden Imam. At Abbas' death and on the accession of his eldest son Shah Safi (*reg.* 1629–42), as the Ottomans and the Uzbegs again invaded, messianic outbursts occurred in Gilan and Mazandiran. In 1631, concomitant with a violent court-based coup, a darwish of the Afshar tribe, one of the original Qizilbash tribes, married to the daughter of a Safawid general, proclaimed himself *Sahib al-Zaman*.

In these years, two further sets of crises also gripped the realm. From 1617, scholarly essays note artisans and craftsmen as abandoning their professions for popular Sufi movements. Beginning *c.* 1626 and over the next two decades, a series of some twenty essays attacked the messianic veneration of Abu Muslim (d. 754), the Iranian Alid agent of the Abbasid movement in Khurasan, thereby attesting to the widespread popularity of the Abu Muslim legends on the urban scene.

Over these years also, the English and Dutch East India companies, whose presence Abbas I encouraged both for commercial reasons and to encourage the Euopean powers to ally with him against the Ottomans, commenced export of specie to other sites in their trading networks from mid-century. The specie outflow accentuated food shortages and inflation. These, in turn, most affected the urban middle and, especially, lower middle classes, and only further encouraged interest in alternative, particularly, Sufi-style and millenarian spiritual discourses and practices. Further essays in the later years of the century challenging the orthodoxy of the latter in particular, attest to the continued, and growing, strength of these movements. The centre weathered the Ottoman and Uzbeg incursions over these years – agreeing with the Ottmans the 1639 Zuhab treaty that lasted until the fall of Isfahan in 1722 to the Afghans. But efforts to combat the growing specie export, whose effects were exacerbated by a series of plagues, famines and other natural calamities, came to nought, with the result that spiritual tensions grew apace.[10]

The perceived scale of these extermal challenges to Safawid rule is attested by Abbas' relocation of the capital to Isfahan and by the renovation of the city's old square, but, more importantly, the work on a new square and its embellishment with major 'secular' and commercial infrastructure.

The perceived scale of these spiritual challenges to Safawid rule, especially early in the century, is attested by the scale of Abbas' patronage both of the religious infrastructure and the religious classes. New religious buildings figured prominently as part of Abbas' relocation of the Safawid capital from Qazwin to Isfahan, the renovation of the latter's traditional square and also the development of the new square.[11] Key Arab and Iran-based Twelver clerics were also encouraged to become close associates of the court. The former included Lutfallah al-Maysi al-Amili (d. 1622–3) and Abdallah al-Shushtari (d. 1612–13), both Arab émigrés, for each of whom the shah built a school. The court's clerical entourage also included Mir Damad and Shaykh Bahai. Abbas also married a number of his daughters into Tajik sayyid families as his father had married into the Marashi sayyid family.[12]

Both, while also interested in philosophical inquiry, were also active in their efforts to expand the authority over doctrine and practice of the senior cleric trained in the rationalist religious sciences – the *mujtahid* or *faqih* – during the Imam's absence. Bahai was an active proponent of *ijtihad*. Building on the principle of 'general deputyship', Bahai argued for greater clerical control over *al-zakat* and *al-khums*, for example. Mir Damad argued, as had his grandfather Ali al-Karaki, that the *faqih* was needed to lead the Friday congregational prayer in the occultation.[13] The scale of unrest over Abbas I's reign was so great, however, that in the early 1600s strident denunciations of Shaykh Bahai's alleged Sufi tendencies forced him to resign from his court-appointed post as Isfahan's *Shaykh al-Islam*. Sadra was also denounced for alleged 'popular' Sufi tendencies.[14] In later years, Abbas delegated clerical associates of the court to monitor the activities at the capital's coffee houses and to preach sermons or lead prayers along more acceptable lines. As part of this process, Mir Damad, Shaykh Bahai and some of their students such as Muhammad Taqi al-Majlisi (d. 1659), father of Muhammad Baqir, composed Persian-language religious primers on various, basic aspects of Twelver doctrine and practice.[15]

Abbas' reign saw the embellishment of two *imamzada*s in Isfahan and new ones built across the realm. The shah himself visited the Mashhad shrine of the eighth Imam some twelve times and made many endowments to it.[16] The court also encouraged Muharram commemorations and commemoration of the death of Imam Ali in 661, the Iranian New Year and *ayd-i qurban*. Part of the latter, commemorating Ibrahim's willingness to sacrifice his son, involved the procession of a camel chosen for ritual slaughter, which was the subject of great popular celebration and occasionally also violent anti-Sunni outbursts.[17] Abbas' successor Safi ordered improvements to shrines, his vizier Saru Taqi commenced building two new mosques in the capital and the court continued to sponsor 'popular' religious practices, especially Muharram commemorations. Some of these included self-mutilation.[18]

Subsequent successions proved to be peaceful affairs. But the Sufi–anti-Sufi polemics continued to generate even more discord, being fuelled further by the on-going specie and other crises.

Pre-Safawid sources, Persian and the anti-Sufi polemic

Two spiritual polemics of the period illustrate the extent to which the faith itself became increasingly firmly embedded in Safawid society over the course of the seventeenth century, as witnessed by the growing use of Persian, but also the extent to which scholars were making increasing use of the copies of a growing range of previously inaccessible pre-Safawid texts and thereby further stimulated the production thereof.

Broadly speaking, the anti-Sufi polemic, the indirect source of information about the growing Sufi presence on the urban scene in this period, expressed itself in two waves. The first, from the late 1620s to the mid-1650s, included the some twenty essays directed mainly against the messianic veneration of Abu Muslim, against urban-based storytellers for promoting the tradition and defending the Tajik sayyid Mir Lawhi (d. after 1672). Mir Lawhi had attacked Taqi al-Majlisi for his alleged public association with the Abu Muslim tradition and claimed that he had been physically assaulted by al-Majlisi's supporters. The second wave, which lasted through the latter years of the century, focused on named Sufi groups and various unorthodox doctrines and practice.

Over these years, authors of both sets of polemics made increasing use of both of the Imams' traditions and also of Persian, use of which, as noted, as a vernacular had long been frowned upon. The recourse to Persian on such a scale suggests that the authors of these texts, and their target audiences, were the very urban, popular classes among whom the Abu Muslim tradition was making some headway. The former attests to the growing availability of the Imams' traditions and support for their increasing availability over the period from the 1640s, as shown in Appendix II.

The Persian-language *Sahifat al-Rishad*, composed by the otherwise unknown Muhammad Zaman (d. 1631), a descendant of Imam al-Rida, is thought to have been the first of the anti-Abu Muslim essays in this period. The four-page essay highlighted but a few traditions on Abu Muslim cited from unnamed but 'reliable, trustworthy' books. The author offered a Persian translation of each and denounced those who attend the gathering of 'storytellers' in which Abu Muslim was venerated, citing in support a further tradition from Imam Jafar.[19] In his 1633 Persian-language *Izhar al-Haqq*, Ahmad Alawi, student and son-in-law of Mir Damad, drew special attention to a tradition from *al-Faqih*, which he also translated, in which the Prophet stated that those in the line of Abbas were oppressors.[20] Taliqani, author of the longer *Khulasat al-Fawaid*, also written in Persian, and who, like Mir Lawhi and Ahmad Alawi, had studied with Mir Damad, also cited traditions of the Imams, but from a wider range of sources, including texts from many sources that he named – *al-Kafi*, and, notably, Ibn Babawayh's *al-Faqih, Uyun Akhbar al-Rida* and *Amali*.[21]

Mir Lawhi himself probably authored a fourth essay in this tradition, also in Persian, *Salwat al-Shia*, between 1641 and 1650, as the discourse was beginning to shift to attacks on certain named, and very unorthodox, practices allegedly undertaken by Sufi groups. The latter ranged from abandoning prayer and fasting, to 'dancing' and 'singing', to sexual immorality. Mir Lawhi made particular use of works by al-Mufid, al-Allama and the traditions cited therein, a tradition cited from *al-Kafi* and others from unnamed sources.[22]

In his later Persian-language essay refuting Sufism and listing certain heretical Sufi doctrines and practices Muhammad Tahir (d. 1687) – a native of Shiraz who had studied in Najaf, but returned to Iran in mid-century – made ever greater use of the traditions. One thousand copies of this text were said to have been in circulation in the capital. An attack on singing in the first volume of a work by Shaykh Ali al-Amili (d. 1691) dating to 1662 and his later Arabic-language essay 'al-Siham al-Mariqa' which criticised *ghina* (singing), is notable for its citations of the traditions taken from named, very early sources. Indeed, the great grandson of Shaykh Zayn al-Din, Shaykh Ali, who was settled in Iran by about 1632, opened both of these works with a tradition, in *al-Kafi*, in which Imam Jafar quoted the Prophet as saying:

> After me will come people who chant the Quran
> in the chanting of singing and wailing and monastic
> practices. Following them is not permitted and their
> hearts and the hearts of those who follow them are
> turned inside out.[23]

Sometime prior to 1676–7, Muhammad Baqir al-Sabziwari (d. 1679) penned an Arabic-language response to an unnamed opponent of singing that is replete with citations of the traditions of the Imams, if mainly those available in *al-Kafi*.[24]

In the later years of the century, al-Hurr al-Amili, the compiler of *Wasail al-Shia* who arrived in Iran in the early 1660s, made at least three contributions to the anti-Sufi polemic. All three were more moderate in tone than some of the above-cited works in the anti-Sufi polemic. All three were in Arabic, suggesting his immediate intended audience was his fellow clerics. All three privileged both the Imams' traditions as well as a range of older texts. He opened the second of these, his 1665 book, *Al-Ithnaasharriya fi Radd al-Sufiyya* (*The Twelve, on the Response to the Sufis*), noting that he had been asked to address again the meaning of the text in *al-Kafi* on Quran chanting that he had addressed in a 1662 essay. In the process of quoting the Imams as condemning Sufism, he also cited traditions from the widest range of Ibn Babawayh's works cited to date, as well as al-Tusi's *Tahdhib*. He also cited statements from a range of well-known earlier and Safawid period Twelvers. These included al-Mufid, al-Murtada, al-Tusi, as well as more recent figures such as al-Allama, Ali al-Karaki and his son, Shaykh Bahai and even his own father – all condemning broader aspects of Sufi doctrine and practice.[25] Al-Hurr's was the widest range of pre-Safawid sources cited in the polemic to this date.

Pre-Safawid sources, Persian and Friday prayer

The second of the two great spiritual debates – that over Friday prayer – also illustrates both the extent to which reference to the pre-1501 texts, including the Imams' traditions, and, again, the use of Persian grew over the seventeenth century especially. The debates also suggest that an interest in the traditions and even opposition to *ijtihad*, as not having been countenanced in the Imams' traditions, did not preclude adherence to a very hierarchical notion of authority within the community during the Imam's continued absence.

The legitimacy of Friday prayer during the occultation had been controversial prior to 1501, as noted. Prior to 1501, however, the issue had not generated any number of dedicated essays.[26] By contrast, over the entirety of the Safawid period, some ninety separate essays on the subject appeared. Of these, eighty were composed in the seventeenth century.[27]

Of the essays composed in the sixteenth century, one, two and three, respectively, were composed by Ali al-Karaki, Shaykh al-Husayn al-Amili and his teacher Shaykh Zayn al-Din; all were composed in Arabic.

From early on, Ali al-Karaki had argued for the *takhyiri* (optional) position on the matter. In his 1515 Arabic-language essay on the prayer, he stated the need in the occultation for *al-Faqih al-Jami lil-Sharait* (the *faqih* possessing the qualifications) to lead the prayer. Al-Karaki did not formally use the term *al-naib al-amm*, but instead referred to the *faqih* as having been appointed *ala wajh kull* (generally). In support he cited a truncated form of the tradition of Umar b. Hanzala and *ijma*, citing al-Tusi, al-Halabi, al-Muhaqqiq, al-Allama and Ibn Makki.[28]

Al-Karaki's erstwhile critic Shaykh Zayn al-Din was perhaps the first to advocate the *ayni* position in this period, if not in Shii history, in an essay composed in 1555. This argument – a reversal of that held in his commentary on Ibn Makki's *al-Lumaa* and earlier works – held that the prayer was an obligation on the individual that should be performed in the occultation because it had been carried out when the Imams were present within the community. The prayer leader could, some maintained, be appointed by the secular authority, but no specific role was delineated for the *faqih* in the prayer. The Shaykh cited numerous traditions, though usually without naming their sources. Of the traditions he cited available in al-Tusi's collections, many had been cited in *al-Kafi* and *al-Faqih*. He also referred to earlier works of *fiqh* by al-Murtada and al-Tusi.[29]

Shaykh Zayn al-Din's student Shaykh al-Husayn, in both a *c.* 1556 dedicated essay on the subject and in his already-cited 1563 essay *al-Iqd al-Husayni*, dedicated to Shah Tahmasb, also advocated the *ayni* position. In the latter, he challenged al-Karaki's claim of *ijma* for the *takhyiri* position, noting the contradictions in the works of both al-Allama and Ibn Makki.[30] Instead, he scoured the revealed texts – the Quran, the traditions of the Prophet and also those of the Imams – for evidence that mandated the prayer's performance irrespective of the presence or absence of a *mujtahid/faqih*, and regardless of what any earlier scholars had said. To be sure, he did also cite the *ijma* of the ulama that the prayer should be performed. Now in Safawid territory, he was also careful to refer to the power and authority of the shah.[31]

Neither the *takhyiri* nor the *ayni* position challenged clerical authority *per se*. Indeed, Shaykh Zayn al-Din, as noted, used al-Karaki's formulation of the *faqih* as *al-naib al-amm*, to allot to the *faqih* key roles in managing *al-zakat*.

In the next century the Safawid court, in the face of continued millenarian risings, moved firmly to establish the faith throughout the realm. The posts of

Imam Juma (leader of the Friday prayer), *Shaykh al-Islam* (chief religious figure in a city) and *sadr* were court appointments.[32] Most who wrote on the prayer argued for the *ayni* position,[33] but, as in the sixteenth century, even advocates of the *takhyiri* position, such as the court associate Mir Damad, supported the hierarchical structure of authority in the community during the occultation.

In this century, however, as the anti-Sufi polemic, so in the argumentation over Friday prayer, both Persian, the traditions and pre-Safawid texts played a discernibly greater role.

Mushin Fayd al-Kashani, son-in-law of Mulla Sadra, had argued for the *ayni* position as early as 1619 in a general *fiqh* work.[34] In 1645, he also penned a Persian-language essay on the subject, with a 'popular' audience in mind, and in 1647 an Arabic-language essay, that is, addressed to his colleagues. In the latter, al-Kashani criticised *ashab al-ray wal-ijtihad* (the proponents of opinion and independent reasoning) for their insistence both on the presence of *al-faqih* in his capacity as *naib* and the concept of *al-idhn al-amm* (the general permission).

He detailed the lack of supporting evidence in the Quran, in the Imams' traditions and in *ijma*, and cited evidence that the prayer was to be performed whatever the circumstances. He also cited a broader range of works than those cited in the previous century. Thus, he cited *al-Kafi*, Ibn Babawayh's *al-Faqih* and *Amali* and the traditions of al-Tusi, whose pro-*ijtihad* position was clear. He also referred to and criticised discussions on the issue by al-Tusi, al-Mufid, al-Murtada, Sallar, al-Halabi, Ibn Idris, Ibn Zuhra, al-Muhaqqiq and al-Allama – citing some of his *fiqh* works and *Nihaya* – and such Safawid period scholars as Shaykh Zayn al-Din and Taqi al-Majlisi. He also referred to extant disputes over *ijma* between Akhbaris and Usulis.[35]

In 1654, al-Kashani accepted Abbas II's invitation to come to Isfahan and act as the capital's Friday prayer leader in order to ameliorate the capital's spiritual tensions;[36] this was the same year as Taqi al-Majlisi was asked to prepare a Persian translation of *al-Faqih*. Al-Kashani accepted, but soon resigned due to the widespread opposition that arose. As described by al-Kashani himself, opponents included both those opposed to the performance of the prayer, those who opposed *ijtihad* and those who disagreed with al-Kashani's own close association with court. In a 1666 essay, he declared that he now believed that the prayer could be abandoned if performing it encouraged division, rebellion, contrariness and mutual hatred. In 'such instances', he noted, 'the Imams also abandoned it'.[37] In the event, it seems that in this period the prayer was again discontinued, at least in the capital, at least for a time.

Further essays were penned on the subject, taking the *ayni* and *takhyiri* positions, in both Persian and Arabic, suggesting that the target audiences were both clerical and 'popular'.[38]

The same Baqir al-Sabziwari who composed the 'moderate' essay on singing, an essay in which he argued for accommodation with the political establishment,[39] also authored an essay each in Arabic, for his scholarly colleagues, and in Persian, for 'mass' consumption, in favour of the *ayni* position.

Al-Sabziwari's essay in Arabic, for example, supporting the *ayni* position, drew both on earlier works of *fiqh*, the 'four books' and other of Ibn Babawayh's collections such as *Khisal* and *Amali*, as well as works by al-Mufid, al-Tusi – *al-Nihaya*, *al-Mabsut* – al-Muhaqqiq, al-Allama, Shaykh Zayn al-Din and even Sunni works.[40]

In 1675, the same Muhammad Tahir who had participated in the anti-Sufi polemic and was, like Shaykh Zayn al-Din and al-Kashani, a proponent of the *ayni* position on the Friday prayer, penned a Persian-language essay on the subject criticising Hasan Ali al-Shushtari (d. 1664–5). Abbas I had built a school for the latter's father Abdallah (d. 1612–13), who had held the *ayni* position. Hasan Ali opposed performance of the prayer and had composed an essay in Persian on the subject.

Muhammad Tahir offered text-based evidence for the *ayni* position and that there was no need for a *mujtahid*, in the process citing from, or referring to, a range of sources – collections of the Imams' traditions and works of *fiqh* and *usul* – slightly more diverse than those cited by al-Kashani two decades earlier. These included each of the 'four books', al-Barqi's *al-Mahasin* and Ibn Babawayh's *Amali*, essays by al-Murtada, al-Mufid, al-Tusi's *Khilaf*, works by al-Halabi, Ibn Zuhra, al-Tabrisi, al-Allama and more recent works such as Shaykh al-Husayn's *al-Iqd*.

Like al-Kashani, Muhammad Tahir was a critic of *ijtihad*. Beyond the issue of the prayer herein, he went on to argue against there being a *mujtahid*, let alone *ijtihad* or *taqlid*. *Ijtihad*, he said, as defined by the Usulis involves *dhann*, which is invalid. The Akhbaris, he said, always held the *ayni* position because this is what is attested by the Imams' traditions. On the prayer itself, he noted that earlier scholars, such as al-Allama in his *Nihaya* and al-Jurjani (d. 1413), had referred to Akhbaris and the Usulis, that the former had been companions of the Imams and recorded their traditions. These, Muhammad Tahir said, had argued for the *ayni* position as it reflected the Imams' traditions, in none of which was there any reference to the phrase 'on the condition of the presence of the Imam or his *naib*' in reference to the prayer. Such scholars as al-Mufid, al-Murtada and al-Tusi, he said, had adopted false, Sunni Mutazili ideas, such as *ijma*.[41]

While Muhammad Tahir and al-Kashani, both proponents of the *ayni* position, disagreed about the bases of legal rulings and opposed *ijtihad*, both upheld the hierarchical division of the community into scholar and non-scholar and the necessity of the latter to defer to the former.

Al-Kashani involved the *faqih* in the administration of *al-zakat*, and upheld the *faqih*'s involvement in the administration of *al-khums* 'by right of *al-niyaba*'.[42] The same Muhammad Tahir, who was later appointed Qum's *Shaykh al-Islam*, wrote in the same 1675 essay on the prayer that:

> the common people of this faith in this period, on questions and
> rulings are to refer to the *fuqaha* who are the agents, bearers and
> narrators of the *ahadith* of Ahl al-Bayt and act on the basis of their
> transmission and information.

and referred to, but did not cite, supporting traditions.[43]

Rising above the polemics: Baqir al-Majlisi and the traditions

Although the accessions of the subsequent two shahs passed smoothly the
domestic spiritual turmoil did not abate and was, in fact, fuelled by continuous
natural calamities into the mid-1690s. The understandable on-going appeal of
Sufi-style messianism is attested by the continuation of the anti-Sufi polemic into
Shah Sulayman's reign (*reg.* 1666/8–1694).

In 1687, the year Muhammad Tahir died and eight years after Sabziwari's
death, the court appointed Taqi al-Majlisi's son Muhammad Baqir al-Majlisi as
Isfahan's *Shaykh al-Islam*.

The traditions assembled by al-Kashani in *al-Wafi* and al-Hurr in *Wasail*
were organised into chapters along the lines of works of *fiqh*. Baqir al-Majlisi's
magnum opus *Bihar al-Anwar*, parts of which he had completed by 1670, is a
compendium of traditions on a wide variety of subjects and includes many
texts and much material believed to have been lost and/or, especially, of which
precious few copies had been produced to that time. Indeed, the project both
benefited from and encouraged both the contemporary 'recovery' of the early
compilations of the Imams' traditions and other early texts. Sections of *Bihar*
that he did complete before his death reveal his contribution to the 'rediscov-
ery' in this period of the many compilations assembled by Ibn Babawayh, for
example.[44] *Bihar* also included a substantial number of traditions from Ibn
Qulawayh's *Kamil al-Ziyarat*, the text of Muntajab al-Din's *Fihrist* and a host of
ijazat.[45] Al-Majlisi did not simply 'copy and paste' large numbers of traditions
from these earlier compilations into the corresponding sections of *Bihar*. Rather,
he critically selected those that most effectively supported his own, larger, very
contemporary agenda that privileged focus on the Imams as a means of damp-
ening down the period's spiritual tensions.[46]

To that same end, al-Majlisi also actively used Persian to address matters
of both belief and practice for lay believers. He is credited with some forty-
eight books in Persian, on such varied topics as the lives of the Prophet, Fatima
and the Imams, traditions on customs and behaviour, and the visiting of Shii
shrines. Many of these works were based on, or were shorter versions of, the
Arabic-language *Bihar* itself.[47] In this al-Majlisi was contributing to the production of Persian-language 'primers' on various matters of doctrine, a practice first

undertaken on such a large scale by earlier clerical associates of the court in response to the domestic spiritual disquiet of the later 1500s and early 1600s.

Other family members and many of his students were also actively engaged in aspects of al-Majlisi's project. Several family members penned both commentaries and marginalia of a number of key pre-Safawid texts, for example, as noted in Appendix IV. Two of al-Majlisi's students – Abdallah Afandi and Muhammad b. Ali al-Ardabili (d. 1699–1700) – produced important works of *rijal*, as did a nephew of al-Majlisi and al-Majlisi himself.[48]

Taken together, however, al-Majlisi's work in particular – *Bihar* remained incomplete at his death – bespoke an effort to strike a middle ground between the contemporary spiritual extremes by focusing firmly on the traditions and persons of the Imams themselves, as the ultimate sources of knowledge on all matters of doctrine and practice.

Al-Majlisi thereby challenged contemporary polemics focusing on alternative messianic personages, reinforced the position of senior clerics, including himself, as delegated by the Imam to interpret issues of jurisprudential and theological import, and to undertake such matters of daily practical import to the community as the conduct of Friday prayer and the collection and distribution of religious taxes during the occultation, and firmly linked these clerics to, and thereby legitimised, the broader Safawid project.

The latter days of the Safawids

Simultaneously with the sponsorship of this focus on the Imams, Shah Sulayman's court continued, and expanded on, its role as chief promoter of all manner of 'popular' religious practices, including Muharram ceremonies and ensuring these, especially, were festivals of elaborate 'public entertainment' as well as 'devotional' in nature. Elaborate ceremonies were also mounted in the provincial capitals. Yazid and the Ottomans were also cursed. Lavish banquets were organised for events such as Ghadir Khumm – marking the Prophet's designation of Ali as his successor. The shah himself also embellished several of the capital's *imamzadas* and other 'popular' religious sites. Court retainers and associates and even middle-class elements and guilds followed suit.[49]

With the construction over these years of a series of 'secular' buildings that also projected political legitimacy (such as the capital's Hasht Bihist palace), the deaths of Muhammad Tahir, al-Hurr al-Amili, Mir Lawhi and Shaykh Ali al-Amili, in the years following al-Majlisi's appointment as *Shaykh al-Islam* the vociferousness of the polemics against 'popular' Sufi tendencies began to abate such that these are harder to trace. Foreign travellers consistently report Sulayman's popularity and, at his death in 1694, the realm experienced its smoothest transition to date to his successor.[50]

To be sure, specie outflow and natural disasters continued to feature over the reign of Shah Sultan al-Husayn (*reg.* 1694–1722). These encouraged agitation in the capital and some provinces, and Uzbeg, Baluch, Mughal and Afghan raiding around Qandahar.

It was in this context that the court the centre also continued to enhance its public association with the faith. Shah Sulayman's body, as those of Safi and Abbas II, was sent to the shrine at Qum for burial, with prompting from al-Majlisi. The latter played a prominent role in both the ceremonies marking Sulayman's burial and Sultan al-Husayn's accession. The new shah issued a *firman* (a royal decree) banning wine, ordering the destruction of all wine in the royal wine cellars, and forbidding other excessive practices and displays. Female family members are identified with a mosque and school dating to 1703.

In 1704–5, six years after al-Majlisi's death and ten years after his own accession, the shah commenced the building of the Chahar Bagh School, bazaar and a three-storey saray complex, located along the eastern side. The original *waqf* deed was dated to 1706 and the school was officially inaugurated in 1710–11, simultaneous with, and in the aftermath of, the 1706 food riots in the capital, Uzbek attacks the same year, and many personnel changes at the central and provincial levels undertaken in response to these crises.

The entire complex, this period's most spectacular project, was paid for, in the tradition of Timurid, Turkish and Safawid female patronage, by the shah's mother.

But, as importantly, other elites and non-elites – including doctors, merchants and small craftsmen – made similar contributions to the religious infrastructure. Thereby these various groups affirmed their commitment both to the centre and, more importantly for the present study, the faith itself.[51]

The other centres: Iraq and the shrine cities

Over this century the shrine cities of Najaf, site of the tomb of Imam Ali, and Karbala, site of the tombs of Husayn and his half brother al-Abbas, are usually said not to have been in the best of straits. A contemporary Portuguese source noted that by 1604 Najaf was in ruins and home to but 500 souls, the canal dug by the Ottoman Salim II having dried up. Karbala was said to have been in the same condition.[52]

But the number of scholars associated with Iraq, and Najaf especially, and the level of manuscript copying over the century, noted above, nevertheless suggest a continued level of activity over the period.

Indeed, Safawid patronage over the century continued apace. The Safawids lost control of the area in 1534, and in the next century held Iraq only from 1623 to 1638. Before, during and after that time, if perhaps only to assert their position in the Shii world, they did not forget the shrines. Abbas I dedicated a substantial portion of the income of Isfahan's royal saray, built in 1603, to the male and female sayyids both of Najaf and Medina. A 1608 *waqf* dedicated items to the shrine in Najaf. After capturing the area, Abbas visited the shrines and ordered a new canal built from al-Hilla. This was said to have dried up, but he also ordered that work be done at al-Kazimayn. In 1629, Indian rulers are said to have paid for a new wall around the city. Further improvements were ordered to the Najaf shrine in 1631. Shah Safi visited al-Hilla and the shrine cities, distributed funds among local religious officials and oversaw work on the Imam Ali mosque.[53]

The Shia did suffer at the Ottoman reconquest. The much damaged shrine of a Sufi saint was repaired with monies from the sale of lands seized from Twelvers. Residents of Iranian origin were said to have been killed and al-Kazimayn to have been plundered.[54] A canal built by the Ottomans in the early 1680s to bring water to Kufa was not extended to Najaf.

But the Safawid court did continue to favour the Imam Ali shrine in the mid-century, and in 1714–16 the court also added to endowments for Najaf and funded stipends as well.[55] Both Abbas I and Sultan Husayn were also attentive to Samarra's al-Askari mosque, which contained the tombs of the tenth and eleventh Imams.[56]

Scholars continued to arrive in the area. Muhammad Tahir, a native of Shiraz, spent his formative years in Najaf, before returning to Iran. That both he and Shaykh Ali al-Amili – who arrived in Iran in the 1630s – were hostile to Muhammad Amin al-Astarabadi, to philosophical inquiry and 'popular' Sufism suggests that their sentiments were shared to the west in those years. Baqir al-Majlisi's sister married an Iranian scholar who had been based in Najaf, the Tajik sayyid Muhammad al-Shirwani (d. 1687–8); the marriage brought the al-Majlisi family a sayyid connection. Baqir al-Majlisi's future student Nimatallah al-Jazairi (d. 1701) visited Karbala and met with scholars there in the 1660s.[57]

The Lebanon

This period of Lebanon's history is marked by conflict and war at the local and regional levels, as well as conflict with the Ottoman authorities. But the roots of those involving the Shii Hamadas, for example, in fact mainly involved Ottoman manipulation of their enemies. There is no strong evidence that the Ottomans saw the local Shia as linked to Safawid Iran, with which, in any case, the Ottomans enjoyed peace after 1639. The apparently sectarian clashes between the Shia of the Baalbak area and local Druze and Christian elements, and even Jabal Amil itself, were rooted in local dynamics.[58]

Thus, there was no overt sectarian need to leave the region. In the early years of the seventeenth century, a member of the great Shii Harfushi clan left the region for Iran, for example, but only after trying to stay in Syria for as long as he could; he died in Iran in 1649. Another is recorded as dying in Tus in 1169.

Others seem to have stayed, despite local clashes recorded for 1670–1 and 1686.[59] Records attest that there were scholars present in the region in 1625 and 1656, that private libraries were still extant, that scholars came to the region, for example from Iraq *c.* 1699, and that infrastructure was being extended.[60]

Eastern Arabia and the Hijaz

Eastern Arabia and the Persian Gulf also continued to be the site of some activity in these years.

Al-Ahsa, nominally under Ottoman control, was in fact under the control of the local Sunni Arab tribal elements, the Banu Khalid. By the 1640s, the pilgrimage route from this region to the Hijaz had been re-opened, but the Ottomans continued to harass Shii pilgrims fearing the growth of Safawid influence. The Banu Khalid did maintain some degree of independence from both Baghdad and, especially, Istanbul. By the 1670s, the Banu Khalid had taken the Ottoman garrison at al-Ahsa.

Further east, the Safawids seized the island of Bahrain in 1602, and in 1622, in a joint expedition with the British, took Hurmuz, the Portuguese centre of operations in the region. Thereafter, the Safawids struggled to assert their influence over Bahraini Shiism. The *ayni* position on the prayer that prevailed in Iran in the seventeenth century became established here as well, and the shah's name was cited in the prayer.

Also, travel between the island, the larger region and Iran was common. Bahrainis were trained by Safawid court-based elites. Some stayed in Iran. Others returned to serve as appointed officials on the island, for example. On the island itself also, the Safawids established a judgeship, suggesting a greater vocational stratification here, as in Iran. To be sure, as noted, however, some local ulama also continued their Qutb Shah associations.

The area supported landed and merchant elements. Their wealth, plus the religious taxes on the traditional pearling trade, with some Safawid support, financed religious education and a local infrastructure.[61]

In the Hijiaz, clearly movements to and from the area noted above suggest that a community was still extant there. Indeed, as noted, Abbas I dedicated a substantial portion of the income of Isfahan's new royal saray to the male and female sayyids in Najaf and Medina, and others followed suit.[62] During his reign as well, Safawid authorities were keen to assist central Asian Sunni pilgrims on their way to the Hijaz. In the early years of the century, Muhammad Amin al-Astarabadi and the latter's teacher Muhammad b. Ali al-Astarabadi (d. 1619) were in the Hijaz, the latter for some considerable years. Shaykh Ali al-Amili, great-grandson of Shaykh Zayn al-Din, had been in Mecca before settling in Iran sometime in the early 1630s. Manuscripts were also being produced in the area.

Later in the century, Abbas II had to correspond with the authorities in

Mecca to facilitate the movement of Iranian pilgrims in this period. Safawid endowment of *waqf* to the Husaynids in the Hijaz continued apace, and during the later years of century the court was especially attentive to Hijazi sayyids who visited Isfahan, even as the court may also have been keen to limit pilgrimage to the Hijaz to limit the outflow of specie.[63]

The interest of the Hijazi Shia in Safawid support can only have been heightened by the 1677 murder of a descendant of Muhammad Amin al-Astarabadi in Mecca, a massacre of other Shia in the city in the same year, and other attacks and indignities suffered by Iranian pilgrims and the Shia in general. These, and the specie outflow issue, certainly contributed to an emphasis on the importance of Iran-based centres of pilgrimage, *pace* such works as Baqir al-Majlisi's 1667 Persian-language work on visitations, *Tuhfat al-Zair*.[64] Nevertheless, at least one Amili cleric was living in Mecca from 1662 to 1727.[65]

And, as noted, Hijazi clerics are also recorded as travelling elsewhere, even as far as India, as they had in the previous century.

The Indian subcontinent: winding up the Deccan

In India, the Deccan Shii kingdoms were brought under Mughal control over this century, gradually at first in some cases, and then finally and physically in all cases. But this did not always stop Shii migration to these areas, attesting to their being perceived as centres of activity over the period.

On the southwest coast of India, the Nizam Shahs – whose affinity with Shiism in the later 1500s was inconsistent anyway – received an embassy from Abbas I. Perhaps fearing Safawid interference, in 1633 Shah Jahan (*reg.* 1627–58) formally annexed the region. In this period also, the Adil shahs and the Safawid shah also exchanged embassies – further suggesting that Iran still saw these polities as possible counterweights to growing Mughal power. As with the Nizam Shahs, Shah Jahan forced the Adil Shahs to pay tribute from 1636. In 1686, Awrangzib (*reg.* 1658–1707) formally annexed the state.[66]

Mughal suspicions of the Qutb Shahs must also have run high. A Safawid delegation that arrived at Hyderabad in 1603 was feted. The mission did not secure the daughter of the Qutb Shah ruler as a wife for Abbas I, as intended, but the embassy did return to Iran laden with presents. The Qutb Shahs sent an embassy to Iran 1616, and in 1621 and 1634–5 further embassies from Iran were received.

In 1636, Shah Jahan forced them also to abandon their overt Shii affiliations – especially mention of the Safawid shah in the Friday prayers. Sunni Islam was made the official faith. Thereby they were effectively brought under Mughal control. The Mughals occupied Hyderabad in 1687. By the last quarter of the century Hyderabadi and other Deccan Shii notables were settled in Delhi.[67]

In their heyday, however, the Qutb Shahs were, however, known for their wealth and their multiculturalism: the realm's Sufis, Sunnis, Shia and Hindus co-existed, and the centre lavishly patronised the traditions and institutions of all. The Qutb Shahs favoured the Twelver faith in particular – being well-known patrons of Muharram commemorations – but their multicultural agenda also saw them try to 'Indianise' Shii rituals such that Hindus and Sunnis could participate without abandoning their own faiths. Even the traditional Muharram poetry, the *marsiya*, was set to traditional Indian tone patterns.[68]

In these years the Qutb Shahs were also well known as patrons of the faith. Muhammad Amin al-Astarabadi, for example, composed his Persian-language 'Danishnama-i Shahi' for a Qutb Shah ruler. The son of the sister of Shaykh Bahai became an envoy to the Safawids, returned to Hyderabad and was appointed to a prominent post. A *faqih* from Aynath in the Jabal Amil region travelled through Iran, where he studied with Bahai, but moved on to Hyderabad and won a court post, dying there in 1645, some years after the 1636 dis-establishment of the faith. Others who came to the area included a Bahraini, a Husayni sayyid from Karbala in 1686, other Amilis, a Tabrizi and a sayyid from Astarabad. An Ardistani who arrived in 1634 became quite wealthy, via merchant activities, enjoyed ties to the English East India Company and built a palace for the queen mother. The Qutb Shah sultan sent revenues from local villages via this man to Najaf and Karbala.[69]

As to the Mughals to the north, after the reign of Akbar (d. 1605) at least some Shia are said to have practiced *taqiyya*. Some did not. The Iranian sayyid, Nurallah al-Shushtari, of the Marashi sayyids who had settled in Shushtar, left Iran during the chaos following Tahmasb's death and arrived in 1585. Avoiding the Deccan, he secured a judgeship in Lahore. After the accession of Jahangir (*reg.* 1605–27), well known for his refutations of Mirza Makhdum Sharifi and a Sunni critic of al-Allama, Nurallah's opponents engineered his downfall. In 1610, Jahangir sanctioned his execution.[70] Also during Jahangir's reign, in Kashmir Sunni–Shii riots are reported in 1620s, after Shii cursing of the Sunnis, with these continuing into the later 1600s.[71]

However, Jahangir did also appoint Iranians to court positions. One such, Muhammad Amin, was a member of the well-known Shahristani sayyid family of Isfahan, with connections by marriage to the Safawid house. He had initially served the Qutb shah court, but was dismissed at the death of Sultan Muhammad Quli in 1612. He returned to Iran, but was invited by the Mughal emperor to return in 1617–18, and died there 1637. Muhammad Amin was well known also for his patronage of the Shia in the Deccan and his financial support of family members in Iraq.[72]

During the reign of Shah Jahan, Iranians also came to court. Ali Mardin, a former Safawid commander, was governor of the Punjab in 1639–40; a son was governor of Kashmir in the 1660s. Muharram ceremonies are reported in Lahore *c.* 1635.

Awrangzib is noted for having been very hostile to the local Shia – in 1668 he banned Muharram processions because of the riots caused by different groups of mourners – but was tolerant of Iranians. Several Iranian ulama came to India during his reign, including several members of the al-Majlisi family, one of whom became a favourite of the sultan.[73]

And further east

From Gulcunda Iranian merchants travelled to Siam, modern-day Thailand, and its capital Ayutthaya. Persian influence had been present there at least from the mid-fourteenth century. Iranian merchants may well have controlled trade in this region in these years: Persian was the language of commerce as far east as Malaysian Malacca, until it was taken by the Portuguese in 1511.

A large Iranian community seems to have been based in sixteenth-century Thailand. The Malay Sufi poet Fansuri (*fl.* late sixteenth century), born in Ayutthaya, spoke Persian. He had not been to Iran, although he did seem to have visited Iraq and may have been a Shiite. In *c.* 1602, a Qummi was the capital's first, court-appointed *Shaykh al-Islam*, and perhaps introduced the faith into Thailand in this period. By the early seventeenth century, and together with Iranian Shia coming from Hyderabad itself, Iranians may have constituted the majority of Muslims in the kingdom. An Astarabadi who arrived in the kingdom *c.* 1650 became prominent at court. Persian cultural influence at court is said to have been marked. In the 1660s, the court sent an embassy to Hyderabad, and in 1669 and in the 1680s embassies were sent to Iran. In 1684, the Thais appealed for naval aid against local enemies, and in 1685 Shah Sulayman sent an embassy. In these same years a French traveller noted court-sponsored Muharram processions in the city, and a large number of local converts to Islam – among young and old, men and women. Following the death of the king in 1688, however, this interest in, and patronage of, things Iranian and Shii seems to have declined.[74]

Sufi orders coming from the Hadramawt in Yemen and south India brought Islam to the Malay–Indonesian Archipelago in the thirteenth and fourteenth centuries. The Shii-style stories surrounding important Shii figures called the *Hikayat* literature may date to the next century. One, that of Muhammad al-Hanafiyya, tells of the struggle of this son of Imam Ali with the Umayyads. The heterodoxy of Fansuri's mystical discourse – he is said also to have been fluent in Arabic – did allow for considerable attention to the Imams, if not Twelver Shiism in particular.

During the later sixteenth century, Fansuri's brand of this discourse found a place in the Aceh region of Sumatra, which rose to trading prominence in the area after the 1511 Portuguese conquest of Malacca. It is said that a mid-seventeenth-century king in Aceh had Shii tendencies, although the establishment of Shafiism later in the century checked any possible spread of the faith.[75]

Summary and conclusion

The true establishment of the Twelver faith in Iran in this period occurred against the background and in response to a series of challenges that can only be described as existential in scale. These challenged both the longevity of the realm itself and the place therein of the Twelver faith.

Following the death of Abbas II in 1666, the French Huguenot Jean Chardin, in his description of Isfahan and its suburbs in this period, noted the capital city's thousands of palaces, forty-eight 'colleges', 162 mosques, 1,800 'spacious caravansarays', and 'really fine bazaars', and drew comparisons between the Iranian capital's population and that of London. If anything, Chardin's count of the religious buildings that dotted the city may have been low.[76]

In the remaining half century before the opportunistic fall of the capital to the Afghans in 1722 many more such religious edifices of all sorts were established and embellished both in Isfahan and elsewhere throughout the realm, funded by a range of donors, from the court and its associated elites down to merchants and craftsmen. Isfahan, but also cities such as Qazwin, Kashan, Qum, Shiraz and Mashhad were now established centres of Twelver scholarship that supported an ever-expanding network of teachers and students. After centuries in which so very few copies of the faith's key pre-1501 and even pre-1055 texts had been accessible on any wide scale, many of these had been recovered. A variety of religious positions were well established across the realm, and the scholarly elite, even if they disagreed among themselves on certain matters of practice, had closed ranks on the division in the community between *faqih/mujtahid* and lay believer and the necessity of the latter to refer to the former. Such distinctively Twelver ceremonials as Muharram were now part of popular ritual life.

By 1722, the Shii aversion to the vernacular was a thing of the past, and Persian was in widespread use both for all manner of religious works, as well as teaching and preaching, given prominence initially as part and parcel of efforts to influence the 'popular'. As in the past, so well into the seventeenth century, the community did not always follow the course charted for it by the elite, as evidenced by the several strands of opposition that forced al-Kashani's resignation as Isfahan's Friday prayer leader, let alone the on-going Sufi polemic. Nevertheless, by the end of the century the existential scale of such internal spiritual challenges appears to have lessened. The popular unrest that marked the later years of Sultan Husayn's rule was of a seemingly more political/economic nature, and less of the spiritual nature that was so very visible in the years after Tahmasb's death and into the reign of Abbas I and his several successors.

By 1722, as compared with 1587, the year of Abbas I's accession by a faction of Turks and Tajiks, Iran was a very Shii nation and was, as such, now the 'centre' of the faith across the region.

As Iran rose in prominence, so the formal affiliation of the Deccan 'states' with Twelver Shiism came to an end. The faith itself did not subsequently disappear from the Indian 'map', however, as attested by the continued influx of Iranians and even Shii clerics who came to the region over the period and growing signs of the faith's popularisation. The Iraqi shrines also continued to be, and were seen to be, centres of scholarly activity over the century, as were the Lebanon and eastern Arabia. Even the Hijaz remained on the 'map', although certainly the 1670s massacre must have taken its toll.

Notes

1. See, for example, al-Tihrani, *Tabaqat*, 5: 388, 126, 501, 410, 326, 236, 185, 385, 42, 522, 122, 25, 148, 402. On the doctor, see also al-Hurr al-Amili, *Kitab Amal al-Amil*, 70–4, and the limited notice of his work by al-Tihrani in *al-Dharia*, 25: 167.
2. Al-Tihrali, *al-Daharia*, 5: 159, 163, 186, 587, 197, 305, 312, 360, 375, 381, 432, 598; 152, 208, 405, 476, 530; 486, 249, 259, 301, 315, 347, 357, 335, 426, 428, 429, 440, 233, 282, 229; 305, 325, 426, 318, 305, 333, 423, 519, 330, 195, 285, 355, 335, 438.
3. Al-Tihrani, *ibid.*, 5: 476, 621, 563, 582, 617, 454, 298, 180, 178, 154, 265, 346, 404, 323, 311, 301, 350, 417.
4. See, for example, Appendix II on Ibn Makki's short *al-Lumaa* and Shaykh Zayn al-Din's commentary thereon entitled *al-Rawda*. *Masalik al-Afham*, Shaykh Zayn al-Din's commentary on al-Muhaqqiq's *Sharai*, was nearly equally as accessible in the second Safawid century as the original. Al-Allama's *Qawaid* was slightly more popular than al-Karaki's commentary *Jami al-Maqasid*, while his *Irshad* consistently outshone Shaykh Zayn al-Din's commentary thereon, *Raud al-Jinan*.
5. Stewart, 'The Genesis', 174–9; n. 7 of Chapter 8. On *ilm al-diraya*, see A. al-Fadli, *Introduction to Hadith*, 45f.
6. Al-Tihrani, *al-Dharia*, 25: 13–14; 4: 352–4. On *Bihar*, see Kohlberg, 'Behar al-Anwar', *EIr*. *Maladhdh al-Akhyar*, al-Majlisi's multi-volume collection of the Imams' statements, organised by *fiqh* chapters, has been published (Qum, 1408/1987), but has yet to be critically addressed by the field.
7. Newman, 'The Nature', 15(2), 250–3 reviews the conventional understanding of Muhammad Amin's legacy. More recently, Gleave (*Scripturalist Islam*, xviii, 32–6) also privileges the role of *al-Fawaid* in this process. See also E. Kohberg, 'Akhbariyya', *EIr*; W. Madelung, 'Akhbariyya', *EI2*; R. Gleave, 'Akhbariyya and Usuliyya', *EI3*; E. Gheisari and J. Qasemi, 'Akhbariyya', *EI3*. See also Momen, *Introduction to Shii Islam*, 117–18, 222–5; Halm, *Shiism*, 92f.
8. Muhammad Amin al-Astarabadi *al-Fawaid al-Madaniyya*, ed. R. al-Rahmati al-Araki (Qum 1424), 30, 37, 175, 37, 91, 132, 93, 97, 50, 520, 78, 117, 123, 129, 173–5, 180, 230, 305, 361, 363–4, 375, 396, 479, 556f, 317, 573. On his mention of Ibn Babawayh's *Madina al-Ilm*, see 130.
9. On the sixteenth-century roots of this inquiry, see R. Pourjavady, *Philosophy in Early Safawid Iran. Najm al-Din Mahmud al-Nayrizi and His Writings* (Leiden, 2011). On Mulla Sadra, see, for example, S. Rizvi, *Mulla Sadra and the Later Islamic Philosophical Tradition* (Edinburgh, 2013).
10. See Newman, *Safavid Iran*, esp. 50f.
11. Blake, *Half the World*, 15–27. Interestingly, in this period, Abbas I's chronicler Iskander Beg Munshi (d. 1633), referring to several thousand Hazaras in Afghanistan who fought

with the Uzbegs against Abbas I, stated that the majority of the Hazara population of Afghanistan was now Twelvers. S. A. Mousavi, *The Hazaras of Afghanistan. An Historical, Cultural, Economic and Political Study* (Richmond, 1998), 74, giving an incorrect reference to Munshi. See Iskander Beg Munshi, *History of Shah Abbas the Great*, trans. R. M. Savory, 3 vols, (Boulder, CO, 1978–1986), 60, 759, 899.

12. Hunarfar, *Ganjinah-i Asar-I*, 594; Munshi, *History of Shah Abbas*, 1: 236, 238; 2: 1146, 1187, 1234–5, 1261, 1302, 1320.

13. On Bahai, who also undertook a series of missions and tasks for Abbas I, see A. Newman, 'Towards a Reconsideration of the Isfahan School of Philosophy: Shaykh Bahai and the Role of the Safawid Ulama', *Studia Iranica*, 15(2) (1986), 175f, 179f; A. Newman, 'The Nature of the Akhbari/Usuli Dispute in Late-Safawid Iran. Part Two: The Conflict Reassessed', *Bulletin of the School of Oriental and African Studies*, 55(2) (1992), 250–61, esp. 258–9.

14. On Sadra's withdrawal to Kahak, see A. Newman, 'Fayd al-Kashani and the Rejection of the Clergy/State Alliance: Friday Prayer as Politics in the Safawid Period', in L. Walbridge (ed.), *The Most Learned of the Shi'a* (New York, 2001), 38. On Sadra, see nn. 9, 15.

15. Bahai's *Jami-i Abbasi*, a *fiqh* work, though unfinished at his death, is such an example, but these works also included some Persian-language texts on key rituals such as the hajj. See al-Tihrani, *al-Dharia*, 22: 258. On this work by Bahai, see Newman, 'Towards a Reconsideration of the Isfahan School of Philosophy', esp. 190f. On the aversion of earlier generations of scholars to the use of the vernacular, see Chapter 5, n. 13; Chapter 6, nn. 22, 26. On a Persian-language poem by Sadra on Imam Ali, see M. A. Amir-Moezzi, 'The Warrior of *Tawil*: A Poem about Ali by Mulla Sadra', in M. A. Amir-Moezzi, *The Spirituality of Shii Islam* (London, 2011), 307–37.

16. Varjavand.

17. Newman, *Safavid Iran*, 59; Calmard, 'Shii Rituals', 143–54; B. Rahimi, 'The Rebound Theatre State: The Politics of the Safawid Camel Sacrifice, 1598–1695 C E', *Iranian Studies*, 37(3) (2004), 451–78; B. Rahimi, *Theatre State and the Formation of Early Modern Public Sphere in Iran* (Leiden, 2011), 199, 221.

18. Newman, *ibid.*, 78; Rahimi, *ibid.*, 229f.

19. Muhammad Zaman b. Muhammad Jafar al-Rizawi, 'Sahifat al-Rishad', in R. Jafariyan (ed.), *Miras-i Islami-yi Iran*, 2 vols (Qum, 1374), 2: 268–72.

20. Ahmad Alawi, 'Izhar al-Haqq', in *ibid.*, esp. 263.

21. Abd al-Mutlab Taliqani, *Khulasat al-Fawaid*, in *ibid.*, esp. 273, 278, 284, 290, 295, 296.

22. Mir Lawhi [?], 'Salwat al-Shia, in *ibid.*, esp. 353. 348, 349, 351, 352–3.

23. Al-Kulayni, *al-Kafi*, 2: 614.

24. Al-Sabizwari's citations include many traditions from *al-Kafi*. See al-Kulayni, 6: 431–6, 2: 614; 5: 119–20; 4: 41. These essays, and the traditions cited therein, and their authors' clear references to contemporary practices, are discussed in A. Newman, 'Clerical Perceptions of Sufi Practices in Late Seventeenth-Century Persia: Arguments Over the Permissibility of Singing (Ghina)', in L. Lewisohn and D. Morgan (eds), *The Heritage of Sufism, vol. 3: Late Classical Persianate Sufism: the Safawid and Mughal Period (1501–1750)* (Oxford, 1999), 135–64, esp. 141, 150, 152–3, 157, 158. 161; A. Newman, 'Sufism and Anti-Sufism in Safawid Iran: The Authorship of the "Hadiqat al-Shia" Revisited', *Iran: Journal of the British Institute of Persian Studies*, 37 (1999), 95–108.

25. Al-Hurr's several contributions and the myriad traditions cited therein are discussed in A. Newman, 'Clerical Perceptions of Sufi Practices in Late 17th Century Persia, II: al-Hurr al-Amili (d. 1693) and the Debate on the Permissibility of Ghina', in Y. Suleiman (ed.), *Living Islamic History. Studies in Honour of Professor Carole Hillenbrand* (Edinburgh, 2010), 192–207.

26. See the list of these in al-Tihrani, *al-Dharia*, 15: 62–82.
27. Al-Tihrani, *ibid.*; R. Jafariyan (ed.), *Davazda Risala-yi Fiqhi darbara-yi Namaz-i Joma* (Qum, 1423/1381/2003), 70–95. These figures do not reflect other venues that post-1501 scholars may have used to express a view, in general works of *fiqh*, for example, as scholars had done prior to 1501.
28. Al-Karaki cited the shorter form of the text, available in al-Tusi's *Tahdhib*, not the earliest and fullest version available in *al-Kafi*. Al-Karaki explained that term *hakim* therein referred to the *faqih* as having been appointed by the Imams as their *'naib* in all of that which is delegated'. See Ali al-Karaki, 'Risala fi Salat al-Juma', in Jafariyan (ed.), *Davazda*, 110.
29. Shaykh Zayn al-Din al-Amili, 'Risala fi Salat al-Juma', in Jafariyan (ed.), *Davazda*, 137–81. That the Ottomans did the prayer, see Newman, 'The Myth', 79.
30. Stewart, 'Polemics', 437f.
31. Al-Husayn b. Abd al-Samad, al-Amili, *al-Iqd al-Husayni (al-Tahmasbi)*, ed. S. Jawad al-Mudarrisi al-Yazdi (Yazd, nd), 31f. See also his other essays on the prayer as cited in al-Tihrani, *al-Dharia*, 15: 288–9. See also Stewart, 'The First', esp. 4f, 23–30. On Shaykh al-Husayn restoring the Friday prayer, see Newman, 'Towards', 170, n. 17, and also Stewart, *ibid.*, 8, 14, 29.
32. On these posts see W. Floor, 'The *sadr* or Head of the Safavid Religious Administration, Judiciary and Endowments and other Members of the Religious Institution', *ZDMG*, 150, (2000), 461–500; R. Jafariyan, 'Mashaghal-i Idari-yi Ulama dar Dawlat-i Safawi', in *Din va Siyasat dar Dawra-yi Safawi* (Qum, 1370/1991), 75–118.
33. Of the ninety essays on the prayer composed over the period, forty-eight advocated the *ayni* position, of which forty were composed in this century.
34. Muhsin Fayd al-Kashani, *Mafatih al-Shara'i* (Beirut, 1388/1969), 1: 21–3, completed in 1632–3, citing his earlier *Mutasim al-Shia*.
35. Muhsin Fayd al-Kashani, *al-Shihab al-Thaqib* (Beirut, 1980), 8–10, 84, 27, 40, 55, 56–7, 66–7, 90–1 and *passim*. Several years after his arrival in the capital, in 1657, al-Kashani completed his major *akhbar* collection, *al-Wafi*, in which he further documented his argument on Friday prayer during the occultation. See *Kitab al-Wafi* (Qum, 1404), vol. 2 (ad *Abwab Fadl al-Salat*), 168f. On al-Kashani, see also Newman, 'Fayd'.
36. For the text of Abbas II's *firman* to al-Kashani, see I. Afshar (ed.), *Tarikh-e Kashan* (Tehran, 2536/1978), 500–2.
37. Al-Kashani, 'Sharh-i Sadr', 'al-Itidhar', in R. Jafariyan (ed.), *Da Resale-yi lil-Hakim . . . Muhammad Muhsin . . . al-Fayd al-Kashani* (Isfahan, 1371), 291, 450–2, 282–4, 68–70. Al-Kashani's reference herein to a group who, like he, opposed *ijtihad*, but also who opposed the prayer suggests the presence of some more 'extreme' than himself (see n. 43).
38. See al-Tihrani, *al-Dharia*, 5: 20; 15: 62–82, esp. 77, 80, 127. Over both centuries, nine are recorded by Jafariyan as opposing performance of the prayer during the occultation. In the sixteenth century, Ibrahim al-Qatifi advanced such an argument. See Newman, 'The Myth', 88–9. Another was a close associate of the court, Khalil Al-Qazwini (d. 1678–9), on whom, see Newman, 'Fayd', 49, n. 19.
39. See N. Calder, 'Legitimacy and Accommodation in Safawid Iran: The Juristic Theory of Muhammad Baqir al-Sabzewari (d. 1090/1679)', *Iran: Journal of the British Institute of Persian Studies*, 25 (1987), 91–105.
40. See his 'Risala fi' Salat al-Juma', in Jafariyan (ed.), *Da Resale-yi lil-Hakim*, 313 54.
41. Muhammad Tahir, 'Risala-yi Namaz-i Juma', in Jafariyan (ed.), *Davazda*, 637f, 656f.
42. Al-Kashani, *Mafatih*, 1: 209–10, 229.
43. Muhammad Tahir, 'Risala-yi Namaz-i Juma', 658. This confirms the classification of scholars such as al-Kashani, Khalil, Muhammad Tahir, al-Hurr and even Muhammad

Amin himself as *mujtahid-muhaddith* by Abdallah al-Samahiji (d. 1723) in his 1712–13 essay on the differences between Akhbaris and Usulis. The term referred to someone as well versed in the rationalist religious sciences as the *mujtahid*, but who both privileged the traditions – access to which was clearly increasing over the period – in arriving at legal decisions and also the need for the lay believer to seek recourse from senior clerics. The real 'radical', to whom al-Samahiji referred as the *muhaddith*, may have been among the critics of al-Kashani as Isfahan's Friday prayer leader. See n. 37 and Newman, 'The Nature', 55(2), 259–60, 260–1. On an instance of agreement on prayer between Ali al-Karaki and Muhammad Amin al-Astarabadi, see R. Gleave, 'Prayer and Prostration', in P. Khosronejad (ed.), *The Art and Material Culture of Iranian Shiism* (London, 2012), 247–8.

44.   See Newman, 'The Recovery of the Past'. Al-Majlisi failed to locate a copy of Ibn Babawayh's *Madinat al-Ilm* (112, 115, 115, nn. 23–4, 117, 125). Kohlberg ('Behar') notes the range of the materials comprised from before the occultation through to the early seventeenth century. See also n. 6.

45.   These are found in vol. 25 of the original, nineteenth-century lithograph of *Bihar* and vols 102–7 of the 1403/1983 Beirut edition.

46.   See Newman, 'The Recovery'; A. Newman (ed.), 'Baqir al-Majlisi and Islamicate Medicine: Safawid Medical Theory and Practice Re-examined', in *Society and Culture in the Early Modern Middle East. Studies on Iran in the Safawid Period* (Leiden, 2003), 371–96; A. Newman, 'Baqir al-Majlisi and Islamicate Medicine II: *al-Risala al-dhahabiyya* in *Bihar al-Anwar*', in Mohammad Ali Amir- Moezzi et al. (eds), *Le shi'ism imamite quarante ans après* (Turnout, 2009), 349–61.

47.   The most important of his Persian works are listed in R. Brunner, 'Majlesi, Mohammad-Baqir', *EIr*; Kohlberg, 'Behar', *EIr*. Al-Tihrani, *al-Dharia*, 21: 242f, 255, 258; 1: 76, 15; 13: 305, 1: 21f. By this period Persian was even being used for philosophical discourse, by Mulla Sadra's student and son-in-law Abd al-Razzaq Lahiji (d. 1662) and Mirza Rafia Naini (d. 1672). Abbas II had asked Sadra himself to undertake a Persian translation of portions of a work by al-Ghazali. On al-Kashani's other works in Persian, see al-Tihrani, *ibid.*, 15: 127, 10: 64. See also Newman, 'Fayd', 49, n. 17; S. Rizvi, 'Seeking the Face of God: The Safawid *hikmat* Tradition's Conceptualisation of *walaya takwiniya*', forthcoming.

48.   Afandi's *Riyad al-Ulama* has been cited. Al-Ardabili produced *Jami al-Ruwat*, 2 vols (Iran, n.d.). See Appendix III.

49.   J. Calmard, 'Shii Rituals and Power II. The Consolidation of Safawid Shiism: Folklore and Popular Religion', in C. Melville (ed.), *Safawid Persia* (London/New York, 1996), 139–90, esp. 158–9, 162–3, 165–6; Blake, *Half the World*, 170–1; Hunarfar, *Ganjinah-i Asar-I*, 531. Rahimi notes that even Iranian Sunnis took part in some of these rituals (Rahimi, 'Camel', 455–6, 460, 462). For a more detailed discussion of the period, see Newman, *Safavid Iran*.

50.   V. Minorsky (ed., trans.), *Tadhkirat al-Muluk. A Manual of Safawid Administration (c. 1137/1725)* (London, 1943), 13, n. 3; Abd al-Husayn al-Husayni Khatunabadi, *Waqai al-Sinin val-Avvam*, ed. M. Bihbudi (Tehran, 1352/1973), 549–50, 558.

51.   Blake, *Half the World*, 168, 152–3; Hunarfar, *Ganjinah-i Asar-I*, 649–50, 684, 652–66, 679–82, 660–2, 385, 476–7, 608, n. 1; N. Hamada, 'Chahar Waqfnama az Chahar Madrasah-yi Isfahan dar Dawra-yi Safawi', in R. Jafariyan (ed.), *Miras-i Islami-yi Iran* (Qum, 1375/1996), 3: 95–129, esp. 3: 99–100, 114f, 118, 128; R. Jafariyan, *Safawiyya dar Arsa-yi Din, Farhang, wa Siyasat*, (Qum, 1379/2000), 2: 903; M. Sifatgul, 'Safawid Administration of Avqaf: Structure, Changes and Functions, 1077–1135/1666–1722', in Newman (ed.), *Society and Culture*, 397–408, esp. 408.

52.   Nakash, *The Shiis of Iraq*, 19f.

53.   Blake, *Half the World*, 119; R. Jafariyan, 'Munasibat-i Isfahan wa Hijaz dar Dawra-yi

Safawi', paper presented at 'Isfahan and the Safawids', Isfahan, February 2002, 16–17; R. McChesney, 'Waqf and Public Policy: The Waqfs of Shah Abbas, 1011–1023/1602–1614', *Asian and African Studies*, 15 (1981), 173, 171; Nakash, *ibid.*, 19-22; Azzawi, *Tarikh al-Iraq*, 5: 35.

54. Azzawi, *ibid.*, 4: 35. See also S. Longrigg, *Four Centuries of Modern Iraq* (Oxford, 1925), 72–3.
55. S. Canby, *The Golden Age of Persian Art, 1501–1722* (London, 1999), 139–41; Blake, *Half the World*, 163–6.
56. Northridge, 'The Shrine in its Historical Context', 63.
57. Khatunabadi, *Waqai al-Sinin*, 506; al-Khwansari, *Raudat al-Jannat*, 4: 143f. See also Newman, 'Clerical Perceptions', 107, n. 35; Newman, 'Sufism', 149; D. Stewart, 'The Humor of the Scholars: The Autobiography of Nimat Allah al-Jazai'ri (d. 1112/1701)', *Iranian Studies*, 22(4) (1989), 72.
58. Winter, *The Shiites*, 58f, 109–10, 117f, 125
59. Al-Amin, *Ayan*, 10: 22–3; al-Hurr, *Kitab Amal al-Amil*, 1: 162; Afandi, *Riyad al-Ulama*, 5: 128; al-Amin, 2: 216, 7: 334.
60. Al-Amin, *Khitat*, 255f.
61. Mandaville, 'The Ottoman Province of al-Hasa', 498; Cole, 'Rival', 188f.
62. Note 53; Blake, *Half the World*, 168.
63. Jafariyan, 'Munasibat', 4–8, 16, 17, 19, 20f; Newman, 'Clerical Perceptions', 148f. See also R. Matthee, *The Politics of Trade in Safawid Iran. Silk for Silver 1600–1730* (Cambridge, 1999), 68; R. Matthee, 'Between Venice and Surat: The Trade in Gold in Late Safawid Iran', *Modern Asian Studies*, 34(1) (2000), 223–55, 243. R. McChesney, 'The Central Asian Hajj-Pilgrimage in the Time of the Early Modern Empires', in M. Mazzaoui (ed.), *Safawid Iran and Her Neighbors* (Salt Lake City, UT, 2003), 145f.
64. Khatunabadi, *Waqai al-Sinin*, 532; Jafariyan, *Safawiyya*, 2: 825–49; Matthee, 'Between Venice', 242–3.
65. M. Salati, 'A Shiite in Mecca', in R. Brunner and W. Ende (eds), *The Twelver Shia in Modern Times* (Leiden, 2001), 3–24.
66. Rizvi, *A Socio-intellectual History of the Isna Ashari Shiis in India*, 1: 292; Hollister, *The Shia of India*, 119, 116. The Safawid–Mughal contest over Qandahar – the Safawids took the city from the Mughals in 1557, lost it in 1594, retook it in 1622, lost it in 1638 and failed to retake it in 1649 – alone would seem to justify Mughal wariness of Safawid intentions in their missions to the Deccan. Newman, *Safawid Iran*, sv.
67. Rizvi, *ibid.*, 1: 325–37; Hollister, *ibid.*, 124–5.
68. Hollister, *ibid.*, 120f; Rizvi, *ibid.*, 1: 321f; T. Howarth, *The Twelver Shia as a Muslim Minority in India. Pulpit of Tears* (London, 2005), 11.
69. Al-Tihrani, *al-Dharia*, 8: 46; al-Amin, *Ayan*, 1: 192, 10: 10f, 10: 109, 2: 603, 9: 410, 432, 9: 251, 10: 58, 109, 3: 41; Rizvi, *ibid.*, 1: 303–19, 321f, 328f; Stewart, 'Humour', 63, 66; Hollister, *ibid.*, 123. On a doctor with the *nisba* Karaki, see n. 1. Mir Findiriski (d. 1640) a student of Mir Damad, also came to India, although when and where is not known, and returned to and died in Iran. Newman, 'Mir Damad' *EIr*; Blake, *Half the World*, 170. On Iranian merchants frequenting Hyderabad, see Subrahmanyam, 'Iranians Abroad', esp. 345f. The article also reviews the history of the Deccan Shii 'states'.
70. The Qadi having advised his oldest son not to return to Iran, his descendants settled in Najaf. Rizvi, *ibid.*, 1: 5f, 342–87; J. Calmard, 'Marashis', *EI2*; Rizvi, 2: 1–4; al-Tihrani, *ibid.*, 1: 290–1.
71. Rizvi, *ibid.*, 2: 37.
72. Rizvi, *ibid.*, 1: 313–14; n. 12.
73. An Amili also came to Kashmir in this period. See Rizvi, *ibid.*, 2: 15f, 36f, 93f, 105f; Cole,

Roots, 24–7. Haneda, 'Emigration of Iranian Elites', 135–6; Haneda, 'India xxviii. Iranian Immigrants in India', *EIr*; E. Lambourn, 'Of Jewels and Horses: the Career and Patronage of an Iranian Merchant under Shah Jahan', *Iranian Studies*, 36(2) (2003), esp. 221; A. Ahmad, 'Safawid Poets'; Subrahmanyam, 'Iranians Abroad, 345f, 353f; Newman, *Safavid Iran*, 68, n. 128, 88, n. 49.

74. M. Marcinkowski, 'Thailand–Iran Relations', *EIr*; M. Marcinkowski, 'Selected Historical Facets of the Presence of Shiism in Southeast Asia', *Muslim World*, 99 (2009), 391, 400, 402–5; M. Marcinkowski, 'The Iranian–Siamese Connection: An Iranian Community in the Thai Kingdom of Ayutthaya', *Iranian Studies*, 35 (2002), 23–46, 38, 42–3, 40. See also Subrahmanyam, *ibid.*, 348f.

75. Marcinkowski, 'The Iranian–Siamese', 27f; Marcinkowski, 'Selected', 391f, 394f; Marcinkowski, 'Thailand–Iran Relations'.

76. R. Ferrier, *A Journey to Persia, Jean Chardin's Portrait of a Seventeenth-century Empire* (London, 1996), 44–5. Blake (*Half the World*, 139–40) suggests that Chardin's figure of 162 mosques within the city and another twenty-eight outwith ignored many smaller neighbourhood mosques and those built by various notables in conjunction with the establishment of such other buildings as sarays, mansions and bathhouses. On Chardin and the dates of his sojourn in Iran over the 1660s and 1670s, see J. Emerson, 'Chardin', *EIr*.

Epilogue

In March 1722, Isfahan fell to invading Afghan forces. The Ottomans, in collusion with the Russians, invaded western Iran, capturing Hamadan in 1724. In 1726, the Afghans killed Sultan Husayn. In 1729, just three years later, the forces of Sultan Husayn's son Tahmasb II, led by Nader Quli Bik of the Afshar tribe, one of the original Qizilbash tribes, retook Isfahan. They were welcomed by the city's population when they did. Domestic and even foreign powers had hoped and expected the Afghan 'interlude' to be brief, and it was.[1] In 1732, Nadir deposed Tahmasb, in favour of the latter's infant son who, as Abbas III, 'ruled' for some four years. Nadir contracted marriages for himself and his son into the Safawid house, in the manner of the many earlier marriages between prominent Qizilbash tribal elements and members of the Safawid family, and in 1736 ascended the throne as Nadir Shah. He retook Qandahar from the Mughals in 1738–9, invaded India and, in 1740, executed both Tahmasb II and Abbas III.

Nadir's efforts to have the Ottomans recognise the Twelver faith as the 'Jafari *madhhab* (school)' alongside the four Sunni *madhhab*s – Hanafi, Shafii, Hanbali and Maliki – were more rooted in such practical goals as winning a peace with the Ottomans, which entailed their recognition of Iran's borders and their guarantee to safeguard Iranian pilgrims to the Hijaz more than they spoke to any fundamental disenchantment with the faith. Nadir was careful to devote considerable attention to, and designate as his new capital, Mashhad as well as the shrine cites in Iraq.[2]

In retrospect, the institutionalisation and popularisation of the faith in Iran that had taken place over the seventeenth century were not seriously challenged by the 'political' events of 1722 or by Nadir's efforts – the latest in a long line – to reach a *modus vivendi* with the Ottomans.

To be sure, complete copies of al-Majlisi's *Bihar*, when finally completed by his students, were hard to come by in subsequent years.[3] Too, in the years surrounding the Afghan invasion clerics were killed and many fled the country for Iraq and India.

By this time, however, as suggested by Appendix I, the number of clerics associated with the plateau had greatly expanded over any of the previous centuries. Many could not or did not emigrate. Of the al-Majlisi family, for example, some did depart for Iraq, but also for Mughal India, settling in Lucknow or Patna, and, further east, for Murshidbad, the capital of Bengal, under the control of the English East India Company from the 1760s. Some, however, stayed in and around Isfahan – in Khwansar, for example – while others moved further away, but remained on the plateau. Those family members who stayed in Iran both contracted alliances with middle- and lower-ranking commercial and artisanal elements and also staffed the many now well-established religious posts in larger and smaller communities throughout Iran.[4] Members of other scholarly families did the same.[5]

That Iraqi and Indian sites did witness an influx of Iran-based scholars in these years attest both to the reality, and the perception, of these precisely as such alternative sites in these years over the seventeenth century and into the eighteenth century as well. Indeed, that these other pockets of the faith remained so active over the seventeenth century owed itself not only, if not less, to Safawid efforts to influence/control them – as in the case of the Iraqi and Gulf sites – than to their access to their own, local resources. Comparatively, the numbers of scholars associated with these non-Iranian sites, let alone the scale of these sites' activities, were most likely less than those on the plateau. Nevertheless, at the time they remained on the 'map', more so than might be thought today. This was certainly the case with the Indian subcontinent, even well after the Deccan Shii city-states had been become incorporated by the Sunni Mughals, or in the Lebanon under the Ottomans.

A history of uncertainty, an uncertain history

This volume commenced by noting two salient facts about the Twelver Shii community today. First, and foremost, not all Shia are Iranians. Secondly, a range of sources composed in the ninth and tenth centuries suggest the existence of between fourteen and forty-five different Shii groups. The survival of the Twelvers as the largest, and perhaps the most scattered, of these today would seem to have been quite an accomplishment.

The myriad of scholarly studies on the faith and the faithful that have appeared in the last several decades attest that across the Shii world today each of the faith's pockets of believers has its own distinct historical and contemporary dynamic. These studies in whole or in part, intentionally or not, reveal the extent to which these local dynamics accentuate the differences between and among the faithful. Believers are both Lebanese, Hazara, Bahraini, Iraqi, Indian, Khoja,[6] Pakistani or Iranian and Twelvers. These studies also reveal a range of other, more 'personal', factors/axes – age, class, vocation, gender, wealth, education, for example – that further inform behaviour.

Those varied backgrounds mediate the manner in which believers even of one region not only understand, but also practice their faith, in private and in public. Differences in the latter are attested, especially in the many recent studies of Muharram commemorations, past and present.

The latter studies, in particular, reveal a diversity of attitudes and, indeed, schisms between and within lay and clerical elements across a variety of axes.

If studies of the faith in its variety of modern contexts reveal its diversity and vibrancy, studies of the past have not.

This volume has examined aspects of the appearance and development of Twelver Shiism, from its roots in the years following the death of the Prophet in 632, through to the political end of Iran's Safawid period in 1722.

Most accounts of the faith to the beginning of the modern period, or any portions thereof, approach their subject from a teleological perspective, assuming the survival of the faith from the first to some idealised 'norm' today. These accounts assume also that the trajectory of the evolution of the faith's doctrines and practices to those considered normative today are those articulated by, and discernible in the writings of, a handful of Twelver scholars most of whose careers and contributions have long been known both to scholars and the scholarly among believers.

To the contrary, this volume has suggested that at any, if not many, given moments across its history, the survival of the faith in any form whatsoever was not a given and could not have seemed so to the faithful at the time. Not until very late in seventeenth-century Iran can it be suggested that Twelver Shiism enjoyed any widespread elite and popular understanding and support across any large region of the Shii world.

The volume's first four chapters looked at the period from the Prophet's death to 1055, the date marking the end of the Buyid period of Abbasid history.

From the very earliest years of Islamic history following the 632 death of the Prophet, Shii discourse, and pro-Alid sentiments in particular, became a growing focal point for anti-establishment feeling and action on the part of elements of the *umma*. Alid-style risings did not end with the 750 Abbasid overthrow of the Umayyads, but none of these many movements were successful. The Husaynid Imams, the twelfth of whom went into occultation in 873–4, avoided identification with any of these failed, anti-establishment activities, but with the deaths of each Imam the numbers of their supporters became progressively smaller. The Imams did leave behind a legacy, however, both of followers scattered across the region and of statements and actions. The written record suggests that it was the literate faithful of ninth-century Qum who first collated the latter to meet the challenges from other Shii groups of the day, but also from the caliphate in Baghdad. In Baghdad at the same time, the community faced pressures from 'popular' Sunni traditionism and intolerant caliphs, together with extremist and also militant mass Shii-style movements such as the Zanj and the Qaramatians. Among the capital's rationalist elements, these pressures encouraged a rekindling of the early ninth-century Shii–Mutazili alliance.

In such an atmosphere, among the faithful across the various pockets of the community there was clearly a sense that the return of the Imam was imminent.

From west to east believers were thrown into confusion when the Imam did not appear. Chapter 3 notes that in an atmosphere of relative tolerance for Shii discourse during the early years of Zaydi Buyid rule (946–1055), during the Abbasid period a growing sense of self-confidence can be discerned among some, as they turned to traditions that offered solutions to the problem of the Imam's continued absence. Chapter 4 notes the extent to which the careers and, especially, the writings of the very few scholars of late Buyid Baghdad best known today shed light on both the external challenges and also, and more importantly, on the range of internal challenges facing the community over this period. In light of, and in response to, both sets of challenges – especially the internal challenges – these several scholars sought to assert their own authority over matters of both doctrine and practice based on their expertise in the rationalist religious sciences. But not all aspects of these scholars' visions were accepted by all segments within the community. Moreover, boundaries in doctrine and, especially, practice between different elements within the Twelver community and even between them, other Shii elements and even Sunni were not as finely and as firmly understood and accepted among the faithful of the period as these few scholars hoped. On balance, these scholars' own views on a range of issues of both doctrine and practice were most likely in the minority at the time.

The middle chapters note and address the impact of the three great invasions – those of Saljuks, the Mongols and the Timurids – that struck the Middle East over the following five centuries.

The Saljuks' capture of Baghdad in 1055 resulted in the destruction of key Twelver resources and the removal of the community and, especially, its elites from any favoured position enjoyed at court and in the region. The faithful commenced life as a unfavoured minority scattered across the region and generally without access to key works of the faith produced prior to 1055.

The Arab west remained home to many. Their fortunes were 'uneven' over these years. The written legacy suggests that initially elites were to some extent preoccupied with, and in disagreement over, al-Tusi's legacy, even if they did not necessarily challenge the rationalist methodology favoured by the scholarly elite of late Buyid Baghdad. In later years, however, evidence of both elite and popular traditionism is clearly discernible.

In Iran, the Shia were caught between the Saljuks' pro-Hanafi agenda and the plateau's existing Shafii tendencies. Traditionist-based discourse was influential among the 'popular' classes here as well, but, as in the Buyid period, sectarian distinctions could become blurred. Veneration of the Prophet's family in particular was widespread even among the Turkish newcomers to the area and was becoming mixed with Sufi messianic discourse. Iran-based elites were attuned to the region's complex discourse and, as earlier, being generally beholden to the faith's rationalist methodological tendencies, were also keen, and able, to identify with the anti-traditionist Sunnism of the political establishment. Some seem to have sought out points of common belief between Sunni and Shii, focusing, for example, on a common love for *ahl al-bayt*. There was support for the professionalisation of the clerical classes within the community and an effort to disavow the 'unorthodox' – which seemingly privileged the traditions.

Over the Mongol and Ilkhanid periods the community remained fragmented across the region. The already limited availability of the early sources only worsened with the destruction that befell Baghdad in 1258. At the same time, whether owing to the swathe that the Mongols are often said to have cut across the region – Iran in particular – or not, the thirteenth century commenced a long period in which scholarly activity, in Iran especially, was markedly less noticeable than in previous centuries. The written record suggests that al-Hilla emerged as centre of Twelver scholarly activity over these years. Its two most famous scholars enjoyed some measure of benefit from associations with the Khans. Their works document their efforts to encourage further the professionalisation of the clerical class and the expansion of authority of the senior clerics over doctrine and practice. Nevertheless, their works also attest to alternative views, if not outright challenges, both to their specific rulings, to the authority of the *faqih* generally and to themselves personally. As earlier in Twelver history, the views of those best known today were in a minority in their own time.

Across the region in the fourteenth and fifteenth centuries, the faith was under a challenge different, and arguably greater, that those presented by the arrival of the Saljuks and Mongols.

The faith's key written sources, both those completed prior to 1055 and even works by the Hillis, remained generally inaccessible over these years. Overall scholarly activity seems to have remained at low ebb over the period. Rationalist discourse would seem to have been confined mainly to the Arabic-speaking lands, although traditionist and Sufi-style discourse are also attested.

In these years, the east more than the west was affected by the political fragmentation of the post-Ilkhanid period, the Timurid invasion and subsequent further political disintegration. The events and trends in the political realm only further encouraged the Sufi–Shii messianic discourses and movements widespread across the region. Some of the latter took on the appearance of 'states'. Some in the Twelver scholarly tradition, as well as the region's post-Timurid polities, were associated with these. The politico-military 'base' of the latter polities included some of the very Turkmen tribal elements among which this Sufi–Shii messianism was most rife. By the end of the fifteenth century, traces of what might be considered normative Twelver doctrine and practice today, let alone in the latter years of the Buyid period, could only have been extremely hard to discern amidst the currents of messianic, and occasionally militant, heterodox movements sweeping the region.

One such movement was that of the Safawids. The originally quietist Sunni Sufi order experienced an influx of Turkmen tribal elements in the later 1400s. At the head of the Qizilbash coalition of such tribes, the first Safawid shah, Ismail I, captured Tabriz in 1501 and within a few more years had seized most of the territory associated with the borders of modern Iran.

Ismail also proclaimed Twelver Shiism to be the official faith of the realm. But, in fact, over the sixteenth century the doctrines and practices of the faith did not achieve widespread acceptance among elites or the 'popular' classes in Iran. Nor did large numbers of Shii clerics from across all the Arab lands suddenly or even gradually migrate to Iran over these years – given the manner of the Safawids' association with the faith, the continued strength of millenarian heterodoxy and the very dim future prospects of the Safawid realm itself.

Other Arab sites offered alternative, if not more promising, prospects over the century, as did sites in the Deccan. Even if the latter sites' prospects for survival and long-term association with the faith were at least as problematic as those of the Safawids, the absence of the extreme heterodoxy of Safawid spiritual discourse over the century may have been attractive to some.

Only in the next century did Iran become a Shii 'nation', but only in the midst of, and in response to, ongoing external political-military and internal economic, social and, especially, spiritual discord. By 1722, an established religious infrastructure enjoyed both elite and popular support and was producing ever greater numbers of teachers and students. Important pre-1501 and, especially, pre-1055 texts now became more accessible. These senior clerics both used and, in that use, encouraged the further productions of copies of these works, especially those of the Imams' traditions, in an effort to address the realm's spiritual turmoil, including especially the denouncing of certain problematic doctrines and practices, and the extension of clerics' authority over community life as a distinct professional body. To the same end, they made increasing use of Persian in religious discourse over the period. Late-Safawid Iran experienced popular unrest to be sure, but as compared with the middle years of the seventeenth century, over more specifically economic issues and much less over issues of 'popular' spiritual discourse.

Non-Iranian centres did continue to be active in these same years, despite the formal ending of the Deccan 'states' association with the faith and marked hostility in the Hijaz in the 1670s. The post-1722 flight of some Iran-based scholars to sites in Iraq and India bespeaks their perception of these as viable alternatives sites to Iran, as over the seventeenth century. Nevertheless, more stayed in Iran. There they allied with middle- and lowerranking elements and filled the many religious posts across the region's larger and smaller communities.

Four themes

Surveying this nearly 1,100 years of history, several themes emerge.

The first is that of challenges and pressures, both external, to be sure, but also internal more than is usually discussed in accounts of the faith over these years.

These years were fraught with such challenges, many of a very clearly existential nature. Some of the most prominent of these include, from the very first, the dwindling numbers of followers of each successive Husayni Imam in the face of Umayyad and Abbasid suspicion and hostility; external and internal pressures on Qum and Baghdadi believers in the ninth century; the disappearance of the twelfth Imam and the widespread 'confusion' that resulted across the community when the Imam did not return in the early tenth century; Sunni traditionist and caliphal hostility and challenges from non-Twelvers, and internal disagreement and discord in the later Buyid period; three sets of invasions from 1055 to the late fifteenth century that destroyed and scattered people and resources, and engendered a rising tide of Sufi–Shii millenarianism that threatened to engulf what was left; Ottoman and Uzbeg attacks, and ongoing heterodoxy and internal political feuding that threatened the nascent Safawid association with the faith.

Yet these challenges produced significant and similarly existential responses. The best known of these are reflected in the written legacy: the compilations of 'the four books' and the other volumes of traditions assembled across the years from the late ninth/early tenth centuries, the middle and later tenth century and the early eleventh century, each in very different atmospheres, but all proffering answers to the challenges of that time; al-Tusi's contributions to, and development of, a Twelver discourse across a range of the religious sciences unseen to his time. If the first Safawid century did not firmly establish the faith in the 'hearts and minds' of the elite and popular classes in Iran after nearly five centuries of what might be termed the faith's second period of 'confusion' and uncertainty, the legal arguments that were tabled in this century, which gave rise to the principle of *niyaba amma*, legitimised the further extension of the authority of the senior clerics within the community during the Imam's continued absence. The magnitude of the external and internal political and spiritual challenges that arose in Iran in the years following the death of Tahmasb in 1576, and continuing well into the later seventeenth century, produced a series of responses that, finally, 'mapped' the faith on both the elite and the popular conscience in a given territory for the first time its history.

Secondly, and just as clearly evident across all these centuries, is the presence of a diversity of views on a range of theological issues, on the processes of interpretation and on specific practices. Dependent as we are on the writings of the literate opponents of such views means we do not, and perhaps cannot, know as much about these other voices as we might like, especially in comparison, for example, with some of the studies of the faith and the faithful in the modern period that have appeared in the last few decades. But these voices are there in the past nevertheless. They seem to have in common a privileging of the traditions and a veneration for the persons of their sources – that is, the Imams themselves – rather than the scholarly elite. On the few occasions when these elements' 'voices' are heard, all indirectly to be sure, many of these seem partial to use of the vernacular, to memorisation, to choosing their own judges and to being critical of the authenticity of the Uthmanic Codex of the Quran. Overall, also, they are seen at times to be more confrontational, that is, less accommodating of non-Shii discourse than the faith's senior figures would have preferred and, too, less accommodating to these senior figures themselves – al-Mufid, al-Allama, Shaykh Bahai, Mulla Sadra and Fayd al-Kashani, all highly respected today, were all publicly hounded during their own lifetimes. At other times, in the Buyid, Saljuk, Timurid and Safawid periods, the lines of demarcation between Twelver, other Shii and non-Shii, and even Sufi discourse and practice, are seen to be rather more blurred than some of the scholarly elite would have liked.

In response, and thirdly, evident also across these centuries is a growing effort by the elite to postulate boundaries both between the lay believer and the religious professional and, in the process, between Twelver and non-Twelver doctrine and practice. The written record left by the literate minority reveals this effort clearly as on offer at least from the time of Ibn Babawayh, through the later Buyid period across the five hundred years to 1501, through the works of Ali al-Karaki and Shaykh Zayn al-Din, al-Kashani, Muhammad Tahir, Shaykh Ali al-Amili to Baqir al-Majlisi himself. Even those in the seventeenth century who privileged recourse to the Imams' traditions in the interpretation of doctrine and practice stood firm on the necessity for the layperson to refer to and heed the counsel of the *faqih* and otherwise involve the latter in his affairs.

Fourth, and finally, there is the theme of pockets or groups of believers scattered across the region. These are attested, for example, as early as the pre-Buyid collections of traditions through those of al-Numani and Ibn Babawayh to the works of the late Buyid period rationalists, some of the latter in response to questions from a range of sites outside Baghdad, but also in the *tabaqat* literature, for all periods.

Care needs to be exercised in the use of the latter. *Nisba* alone is hardly as reliable an indicator of place of birth, let alone residence, as might be hoped. Nor is inclusion in the *tabaqat* literature of today any guarantee of these past figures' credentials as a Shii, especially when these are, as already suggested, a matter of interpretation both at the time and later. Moreover, as also noted, there are periods, such as that from 1055 to 1501, wherein even the biographers cannot agree or make mistakes as to names, works and teachers/students of those in question. Compounding the problems in researching these years, even texts produced by authors living in these years, as in the case of works by al-Barqi, Ibn Babawayh and al-Allama, for example, became lost forever.

Nevertheless, pockets of believers across the region there were. Confirmed residence in, and movement to and from, these sites as well as manuscript copying identified with them underscores this.

Taken together such evidence suggests that no one site, not even seventeenth-century Iran, had a monopoly on scholarly activity, let alone authority across these centuries. To be sure, most believers were not members of the learned classes in these years, and most of the ulama did not travel. Nevertheless, these sites clearly possessed sufficient independent wherewithal to support such activity and/or, at least, afford to see students travel off to other sites. That these multiple sites existed was good for the community, contributing to its international reach and allowing for a measure of the independence of the dynamics of any one locale from others. If the fortunes of any one suffered, those of others did not necessarily suffer also, or as badly.

In unity, that is, in the sharing of an expectation of the return of the Hidden Imam, there was also diversity over the nearly 1,100 years from 632. In spite of, and also because of, this diversity, by the early eighteenth century the future of the faith was assured.

Post-1722, the history and experience of the faith has been and will continue to be marked by the very same diversity of experience.

Notes

1. W. Floor, *The Afghan Invasion of Safavid Persia, 1721–29* (Paris, 1998), 342–3, 336, 355, 358.
2. See E. Tucker, 'Nadir Shah and the Jafari Madhhab', *Iranian Studies*, 27 (1994), 163–79; E. Tucker, *Nadir Shah's Quest for Legitimacy in Post-Safavid Iran* (Gainesville, FL, 2006).
3. Kohlberg, 'Behar'.
4. J. Cole, 'Shii Clerics in Iraq and Iran, 1722–1780: The Akhbari–Usuli Conflict Reconsidered', *Iranian Studies*, 18(1) (1985), 6f. This article is available in slightly revised form in Cole, *Sacred Space and Holy War, The Politics, Culture and History of Shiite Islam* (London, 2002), 60f.
5. See A. Newman, 'Anti-Akhbari Sentiments among the Qajar Ulama: The Case of Muhammad Baqir al-Khwansari (d. 1313/1895)', in R. Gleave (ed.), *Religion and Society in Qajar Iran* (London, 2005), esp. 162, on the ancestors of the author of *Raudat al-Jannat* who remained in Iran following 1722.
6. On the Khoja community, see, most recently, I. Akhtar, 'The Oriental African: The Evolution of Postcolonial Islamic Identities Among the Globalised Khoja of Dar Es Salaam', unpublished PhD dissertation, University of Edinburgh, 2013.

Appendix I Scholars by region: fifth–twelfth Islamic centuries/eleventh–eighteenth centuries AD*

5th Islamic century 1009–1105	6th century 1106–1202	7th century 1203–1299	8th century 1300–1396	9th century 1397–1493	10th century 1494–1591	11th century 1592–1688	12th century 1689–1785
Iran 107	Iran 241	Iraq 65	Iran 71	Iran 59	Iran 190	Iran 530	Iran 975
(including) Tus/Nishabur 27 Rayy 13 Qazwin 11 Gurgan 9 Isfahan 9 Qum 9	(including) Rayy 43 Qum 32 Tus/Nishapur 29 Qazwin 21 Kashan 19 Hamadan 17 Varamin 10 Isfahan 8	(including) Hilla 22 Baghdad 19 Wasit 7 Kufa 4 Najaf 2	(including) Qum 8 Shiraz 7 Tabaristan 7 Kashan 6 Astarabad 5 Amol 4 Rayy 3 Yazd 3 Khurasan 3 Isfahan 2 Tus/Nishabur 2	(including) Astarabad 11 Gurgan 5 Yazd 5 Kashan 4 Isfahan 4 Amol 4 Sabzewar 3 Gilan 2 Khurasan 2 Qum 2 Shiraz 2	(including) Mazanderan 38 Khurasan 30 Shiraz 23 Kashan 17 Isfahan 15 Qazwin 9 Tabas 9 Tabriz 9 Qum 8 Yazd 7	(including) Isfahan 81 Mashhad 67 Astarabad 50 Shiraz 50 Kashan 19 Qazwin 15 Tabriz 11 Qum 9	(including) Shushtar 91 Mashhad 81 Qazwin 48 Shiraz 47 Kashan 44 Tabriz 37 Qum 29 Gilan 25 Astarbad 24 Sabzewar 21
Iraq 59	Iraq 61	Iran 50	Iraq 66	Jabal Amil 52	Jabal Amil 80	Iraq 166	Gulf 203
Baghdad 28 Basra 14 Kufa 10	Baghdad 15 Hilla 13 Najaf 13 Kufa 11	Qum 7 Yazd 4 Isfahan 4 Hamadan 4 Daylam 2 Rayy 2 Nishabur 2	Hilla 33 Karbala 5 Kufa 5 Wasit 5 Najaf 3 Baghdad 2		Amili 65 Juba 7 Mays 6	Najaf 79 Jazair 38 Hilla 12	Bahrain 102 Maqab 16 Qatif 15 Awal 14 Khatt 12 Diraz 9 Ahsa 8 Mahuz 5

Syria 15	Syria 25	Gulf 13	Syria 20	Iraq 43	Iraq 54	Lebanon 121	Iraq 191
Aleppo 11	Aleppo 20	Bahrain 11	Aleppo 16	Hilla 15	Najaf 17	Jabal Amil 118	Najaf 80
Damascus 3		Ahsa 2	Damascus 4	Najaf 8	Jazair 15		Jazair 47
				Baghdad 3	Hilla 9		Kazimayn 25
							Karbala 14
							Hilla 9
Lebanon 11	Gulf 4	Syria 12	Lebanon 18	Gulf 21	Gulf 27	Gulf 95	Lebanon 119
Tripoli 10	Bahrain 4	Aleppo 11	Jabal Amil 13	Bahrain 13	Bahrain 18	Bahrain 53	Jabal Amil 96
Jabal Amil 1		Hims 1	Karak 2	Ahsa 4	Ahsa 5	Ahsa 10	
				Qatif 4	Qatif 3	Qatif 2	
Egypt 7	Egypt 3	Lebanon 4	Gulf 6	Syria 4	Herat 7	India 34	India 42
		Jabal Amil 4	Bahrain 6	Herat 4		Hijaz 27	Kashmir 11
							Hyderabad 2
			Hijaz 4	Hijaz 4	India 6		Afghanistan 10
				India 1	Yemen 5		Herat 8
			Yemen 2				Hijaz 9
							Yemen 4
							Syria 3

* Based on Agha Buzurg Tihrani, Tabaqat Alam al-Shia, A. N. Munzavi ed., vols 2–6 (Qum, nd).

Appendix II Manuscript copies of key Twelver Shii written works, sixth–thirteenth Islamic centuries/twelfth–nineteenth centuries AD*

Author/Title	Centuries										
	6th 12th	7th 13th	8th 14th	9th 15th	900–50 1494–1543	951–1000 1544–91	1001–50 1591–1640	1051–1100 1641–88	1101–34 1689–1722	1135–1200 1722–85	1201–50 1786–1834

Al-Barqi (d. 887–994)

| Al-Mahasin | 0 | 0 | 0 | 1 | 0 | 0 | 0 | 9 | 1 | 0 | 1 |

post-1251/1835 = 0
undated copies of the text: 11
total number of mss = 23
total that can be dated: 12

Al-Saffar (d. 902–3)

| Basair | 1 | 0 | 0 | 0 | 0 | 1 | 1 | 14 | 1 | 2 | 0 |

post-1251/1835 = 3
undated copies of the text: 5
total number of mss = 28
total that can be dated: 23

Al-Kulayni (d. 941)

al-kāfī   0   10   17   158   24   28   0   1   2   0

post-1251/1835 = 4
   undated copies of the text: 93
      total number of mss = 338
      total that can be dated: 245

Ibn Qulawayh (d. 979–80)

Kāmil   0   0   0   3   0   2   0   0   0   0

post-1251/1835 = 3
   undated copies of the text: 5
      total number of mss = 13
      total that can be dated: 8

Ibn Babawayh (d. 991)

Al-Faqīh   0   2   9   52   9   4   0   0   0   1

post-1251/1835 = 6
   undated copies of the text: 15
      total number of mss = 98
      total that can be dated: 83

Author/Title	Centuries										
	6th 12th	7th 13th	8th 14th	9th 15th	900–50 1494–1543	951–1000 1544–91	1001–50 1591–1640	1051–1100 1641–88	1101–34 1689–1722	1135–1200 1722–85	1201–50 1786–1834
Ilal	0	0	0	0	0	2	2	18	2	4	0
al-Khisal	0	0	0	1	0	2	2	22	1	1	1
Maani	0	0	0	0	1	2	1	22	2	2	1
al-Tawhid	0	0	0	0	1	1	2	17	1	1	0

Ilal
post-1251/1835 = 2
undated copies of the text: 14
total number of mss = 44
total that can be dated: 30

al-Khisal
post-1251/1835 = 0
undated copies of the text: 16
total number of mss = 46
total that can be dated: 30

Maani
post-1251/1835 = 2
undated copies of the text: 14
total number of mss = 46
total that can be dated: 32

al-Tawhid
post-1251/1835 = 0
undated copies of the text: 6
total number of mss = 29
total that can be dated: 23

Ujun	0	0	1	1	0	2	2	53	11	10	0
post-1251/1835 = 1											
total number of mss = 115											
total that can be dated: 81											
Kamal/Ikmal	0	0	0	1	3	6	53	2	5	3	
post-1251/1835 = 0											
total number of mss = 89											
total that can be dated: 73											
Amali/Majalis	2	0	0	0	0	0	6	3	1	0	
post-1251/1835 = 0											
total number of mss = 22											
total that can be dated: 12											

Al-Mufid (d. 1022)

Al-Irshad	3	0	2	1	2	1	0	13	1	1	0
post-1251/1835 = 0											
total number of mss = 36											
total that can be dated: 24											

Author/Title	Centuries										
	6th 12th	7th 13th	8th 14th	9th 15th	900–50 1494–1543	951–1000 1544–91	1001–50 1591–1640	1051–1100 1641–88	1101–34 1689–1722	1135–1200 1722–85	1201–50 1786–1834
Al-Muqni'a	0	1	0	0	0	4	0	7	0	0	0
Awail	0	0	0	0	0	1	0	4	0	1	0
Al-Mazar	0	0	0	0	0	1	0	3	0	0	0
Amali	2	2	0	0	0	5	0	5	4	2	1

Al-Muqni'a

post-1251/1835 = 2
undated copies of the text: 9
    total number of mss = 23
    total that can be dated: 14

Awail

post-1251/1835 = 1
undated copies of the text: 4
    total number of mss = 11
    total that can be dated: 7

Al-Mazar

post-1251/1835 = 2
undated copies of the text: 3
    total number of mss = 9
    total that can be dated: 6

Al-Murtada (d. 1044)

Amali

post-1251/1835 = 2
undated copies of the text: 6

total number of mss = 29
total that can be dated: 23 (excl. 15th c copy)

	6th	7th	8th	9th	900–50	951–1000	1001–50	1051–1100	1101–34	1135–1200	1201–50
Al-Intisar	2	0	0	1	1	6	2	5	2	2	0

post-1251/1835 = 3
undated copies of the text: 17
total number of mss = 41
total that can be dated: 24

	6th	7th	8th	9th	900–50	951–1000	1001–50	1051–1100	1101–34	1135–1200	1201–50
Al-Shafi	0	0	0	0	0	1	1	4	8	1	0

post-1251/1835 = 1
undated copies of the text: 5
total number of mss = 21
total that can be dated: 16

	6th	7th	8th	9th	900–50	951–1000	1001–50	1051–1100	1101–34	1135–1200	1201–50
Al-Fusul	0	0	0	0	0	0	1	3	0	1	0

post-1251/1835 = 3
undated copies of the text: 3
total number of mss = 11
total that can be dated: 8

	6th	7th	8th	9th	900–50	951–1000	1001–50	1051–1100	1101–34	1135–1200	1201–50
Al-Dharia	0	0	0	1	1	0	2	0	2	0	3

post-1251/1835 = 4
undated copies of the text: 0
total number of mss = 12
total that can be dated: 12

Author/Title	Centuries										
	6th 12th	7th 13th	8th 14th	9th 15th	900–50 1494–1543	951–1000 1544–91	1001–50 1591–1640	1051–1100 1641–88	1101–34 1689–1722	1135–1200 1722–85	1201–50 1786–1834

Al-Tusi (d. 1067)

Tahdhib	0	0	2	2	6	28	42	221	34	17	3

post-1250/1835 = 11
undated copies of the text = 96
total number of all mss = 462
Total that can be dated = 366

Al-Istibsar	0	4	0	0	1	5	34	111	8	4	2

post-1251/1835 = 5
undated copies of the text: 29
total number of mss = 203
total that can be dated: 174

Al-Nihaya	6	2	0	0	1	1	0	3	0	1	

post-1251/1835 = 4
undated copies of the text = 3
total number of mss = 22
total that can be dated = 19

Al-Ghayba
None at all

Al-Mabsut	5	5	0	0	1	5	6	0	3	1
Al-Khilaf	3	1	1	0	1	2	2	0	1	0
Al-Tibyan	14	4	1	0	0	1	0	0	0	0
Udda	0	0	0	1	1	1	5	1	0	1

undated copies of the text = 1
  total number of mss = 1
  total that can be dated = 0

Al-Mabsut

post-1251 = 4
undated copies of the text: 8
  total number of mss = 38
  total that can be dated: 30

Al-Khilaf

post-1251 = 5
undated copies of the text: 7
  total number of mss = 23
  total that can be dated: 16

Al-Tibyan

post-1251/1835 =1
Undated copies of the text = 6
  total number of mss= 28
  total that can be dated = 22

Udda

post 1251/1835 = 2
Undated copies of the text = 3
  total number of mss= 14
  total that can be dated = 11

Author/Title	Centuries										
	6th 12th	7th 13th	8th 14th	9th 15th	900–50 1494–1543	951–1000 1544–91	1001–50 1591–1640	1051–1100 1641–88	1101–34 1689–1722	1135–1200 1722–85	1201–50 1786–1834
Rijal	1	0	0	0	0	0	0	0	0	0	1

post 1251/1835 = 0
Undated copies of the text = 2
    total number of mss = 4
    total that can be dated = 2

Fihrist	0	0	0	0	0	8	0	2	0	0	0

post 1251/1835 = 0
Undated copies of the text = 0
    total number of mss = 10
    total that can be dated = 10

Ikhtiyar	1	0	0	0	0	2	9	0	0	0	0

post 1251/1835 = 2
Undated copies of the text = 4
    total number of mss = 18
    total that can be dated = 14

Al-Najashi (d. 1058–9)

Rijal	0	0	0	0	1	5	1	2	0	2	1

post-1251/1835 = 2
undated copies of the text: 6

total number of mss = 20
total that can be dated: 14

Ibn al-Ghadairi (early 11th century)

Al-Duafa	0	0	0	0	0	0	0	0	0	0

post-1251/1835 = 0
undated copies of the text: 5
total number of mss = 5
total that can be dated: 0

Al-Tabrisi (d. 1154)

Majma	1	2	7	2	4	24	11	62	17	1	10

post-1251/1835 = 6
undated copies of the text: 52
total number of mss = 199
total that can be dated: 147

Al-Rawandi (d. 1178)

Al-Kharaij	0	0	0	0	0	0	0	4	0	1	2

post-1251/1835 = 1
undated copies of the text: 1
total number of mss = 9
total that can be dated: 8

Author/Title	Centuries										
	6th 12th	7th 13th	8th 14th	9th 15th	900–50 1494–1543	951–1000 1544–91	1001–50 1591–1640	1051–1100 1641–88	1101–34 1689–1722	1135–1200 1722–85	1201–50 1786–1834
Fiqh	0	0	3	3	0	0	0	1	0	0	0

post-1251/1835 = 0
  undated copies of the text: 2
    total number of mss = 9
    total that can be dated: 7

Ibn Idris (d. 1202)

Al-Sarair	0	0	0	1	0	2	6	4	0	0	3

post-1251/1835 = 8
  undated copies of the text: 5
    total number of mss = 29
    total that can be dated: 24

Al-Muhaqqiq (d. 1277)

Sharai	0	3	1	4	5	20	8	61	4	10	21

post-1251/1835 = 8
  undated copies of the text: 65
    total number of mss = 210
    total that can be dated: 145

Al-Mukhtasar	0	1	2	4	5	17	10	51	8	16	6
Muariǰ	0	0	0	0	0	1	3	0	1	1	6
Mutabar	0	0	0	0	0	5	1	4	0	1	4
Qawaid	0	0	13	18	17	24	18	49	9	8	5

Al-Mukhtasar

post-1251/1835 = 13
undated copies of the text: 59
total number of mss 192
total that can be dated: 133

Muariǰ

post-1251/1835 = 6
undated copies of the text: 10
total number of mss: 28
total that can be dated: 18

Mutabar

post-1251/1835 = 0
undated copies of the text: 3
total number of mss: 18
total that can be dated: 15

Al-Allama (d. 1325)

Qawaid

post-1251/1835 = 4
undated copies of the text: 76
total number of mss = 241
total that can be dated: 165

Author/Title	Centuries										
	6th 12th	7th 13th	8th 14th	9th 15th	900–50 1494–1543	951–1000 1544–91	1001–50 1591–1640	1051–1100 1641–88	1101–34 1689–1722	1135–1200 1722–85	1201–50 1786–1834
Tahrir	0	0	15	8	6	20	3	8	0	0	0
Irshad	0	0	9	6	19	33	33	73	10	12	3
Tadhkira	0	0	2	1	1	9	3	5	4	1	7
Mukhtalaf	0	0	7	2	1	13	6	20	4	4	3

Tahrir

post-1251/1835 = 1
undated copies of the text: 19
    total number of mss = 80
    total that can be dated: 61

Irshad

post-1251/1835 = 3
undated copies of the text = 89
    total number of mss = 290
    total that can be dated = 201

Tadhkira

post-1251/1835 = 10
undated copies of the text: 8
    total number of mss = 51
    total that can be dated: 43

Mukhtalaf

post-1251/1835 = 6
undated copies of the text: 16
    total number of mss = 82
    total that can be dated: 66

Tahdhib	0	0	2	0	1	13	7	6	2	1	14

post-1251/1835 = 11
undated copies of the text: 26
  total number of mss = 83
  total that can be dated: 57

Kashf al-Murad	0	1	2	4	0	3	0	4	1	0	0

post-1251/1835 = 3
undated copies of the text: 9
  total number of mss = 27
  total that can be dated: 18

Al-Bab	0	0	0	1	1	1	3	6	1	2	2

post-1251/1835 = 2
undated copies of the text: 37
  total number of mss = 56
  total that can be dated: 19

Nihaya	0	0	5	1	0	0	1	3	1	2	13

post-1251/1835 = 1
undated copies of the text: 8
  total number of mss = 35
  total that can be dated: 27

Khulasa	0	0	0	1	1	9	5	1	0	1	0

post-1251/1835 = 2
undated copies of the text: 34
  total number of mss = 54
  total that can be dated: 20

Author/Title	Centuries										
	6th 12th	7th 13th	8th 14th	9th 15th	900–50 1494–1543	951–1000 1544–91	1001–50 1591–1640	1051–1100 1641–88	1101–34 1689–1722	1135–1200 1722–85	1201–50 1786–1834

Ibn Makki (d. 1384)

Al-Lumaa	0	0	0	2	1	1	2	0	0	2	2

post-1251/1835 = 2
undated copies of the text: 4
    total number of mss = 16
    total that can be dated: 12

Dhikra	0	0	1	1	1	11	4	7	0	1	6

post-1251/1835 = 4
undated copies of the text: 10
    total number of mss = 46
    total that can be dated: 36

Al-Qawaid	0	0	0	0	1	3	2	4	6	0	1

post-1251/1835 = 3
undated copies of the text: 7
    total number of mss = 27
    total that can be dated: 20

Ali al-Karaki (d. 1534)

Jami al-Maqasid (*Sharh Qawaid*)	0	0	0	0	2	27	16	26	1	7	5

post-1251/1835 = 8
    undated copies of the text: 52
        total number of mss = 144
        total that can be dated: 92

Shaykh Zayn al-Din (d. 1558)

Text										
Al-Rauda (*Sharh al-Lumaa*)	0	0	0	0	4	14	49	11	28	26
Masalik (*Sharh al-Sharai*)	0	0	0	0	47	19	47	13	7	29
Raud al-Jinan (*Sharh al-Irshad*)	0	0	0	0	2	2	5	0	0	2

Al-Rauda
(*Sharh al-Lumaa*)
post-1251/1835 = 15
    undated copies of the text: 74
        total number of mss = 221
        total that can be dated: 147

Masalik
(*Sharh al-Sharai*)
post-1251/1835 = 47
    undated copies of the text = 49
        total number of mss = 258
        total that can be dated: 209

Raud al-Jinan
(*Sharh al-Irshad*)
post-1251/1835 = 1
    undated copies of the text: 7
        total number of mss = 19
        total that can be dated: 12

* These are organised in order of the known death dates of the authors. Note that the recorded dates of these manuscript copies are Hijri dates. The text discusses these with reference to the equivalent Christian centuries. Data gathered via www.aghabozorg.ir. Data for Ibn Babawayh's 'Itiqadat' could not be surveyed.

Appendix III Selected Safavid period *rijal* works*

Sixteenth century

Al-Amili, Yusuf n. Muhammad al-Husayni (d. 1574–5)
Jami al- aqval (al-Tihrani, 5: 42)
Tartib al-Kashshi (al-Tihrani, 4: 67)

Seventeenth century

Al-Quhpai, Inayat Allah b. Ali (d. 1607–8)
Majma al-Rijal, ed. Diya al-Din al-Allama (Esfahan, 1387)

Al-Shushtari, Nurallah (d. 1610–11)
Majalis al-mu'minin, 2 vols (Tehran, 1375/1955)

Al-Abraz, S. Husayn b Kamal al-Din (student of Shaykh Bahai)
Zubdat al-Aqval (al-Tihrani, 12: 19)

Al-Astarabadi, Mirza Muhammad (d. 1619)
'Sahib al-Rijal'. He authored three such works, of which one has
been published:
Manhaj al-maqal = Rijal al-Kabir, 7 vols (Qum, 2001)

Al-Tafrishi, Mir Mustafa b. Husayn (d. 1031/1621–2)
Naqd al-Rijal (Qum, 1998)

Mir Damad, Muhammad Baqir b. Muhammad (d. 1630–1).
*Ikhtiyar Marifat al-Rijal, al-Maruf bi Rijal al-Kashshi Tashih wa Taliq-e
Mir Damad*, ed. S. M. al-Rijai (Qum, 1404)

Al-Majlisi, Muhammad Taqi (d. 1659)
  Mashikhat kitab man la yahduruh al-faqih (al-Tihrani, 14: 68)

Al-Najafi, Fakhr al-Din b. Muhammad Ali b. Turayh (d. 1674)
  Jami al-Maqal (al-Tihrani, 5: 73f)

Al-Hurr al-Amili, Muhammad b. Hasan (d. 1693)
  Amal al-amil, ed. Ahmad al-Husayni, 2 vols (Najaf, 1965)

Al-Majlisi, Muhammad Baqir (d. 1699)
  Wajizah fi Ilm al-Rijal / Rijal al-Majlisi (Beirut, 1995)

Eighteenth century

Al-Ardabili, Muhammad b. Ali (d. 1101/1689–90 or later?)
  Jami al-Ruwat, 2 vols (Tehran, n.d.)

Sayyid Ali Khan Al-Madani (d. 1708–9)
  Sulafat al-Asr (Cairo, 1324)

Afandi, Abdallah Afandi (d. 1717)
  Riyad al-Ulama, 5 vols (Qum, 1401)

Al-Mahuzi, Sulayman (d. 1709–10)
  Fihrist Al Babawayh wa Ulama al-Bahrain (Qum, 1404)

* All references to al-Tihrani are from: Agha Buzurg al-Tihrani, *Al-Dharia ila Tasanif al-Shia*, 25 vols (Tehran and Najaf, 1353–98).

Appendix IV Shuruh/Hawashi of key Twelver works, sixth–twelfth Islamic centuries/twelfth–eighteenth centuries AD*

Author/Title	Centuries									
	6th 12th	7th 13th	8th 14th	9th 15th	900–50 1494–1543	951–1000 1544–91	1001–50 1591–1640	1051–1100 1641–88	1101–34 1689–1721	post-1134 post-1722
Shuruh										
Al-Kulayni (d. 941)										
al-Kafi	0	0	0	0	0	0	4	10	10	4
Ibn Babawayh (d. 991)										
al-Faqih	0	0	0	0	0	0	2	4	1	1
Tawhid	0	0	0	0	0	0	0	1	3	0
Uyun	0	0	0	0	0	0	0	0	1	2
Maani	0	0	0	0	0	0	0	0	0	1
Itiqadat	0	0	0	0	0	0	0	1	2	5
Al-Murtada (d. 1044)										
Al-Dharia	1	1	1	0	0	0	0	0	0	0
Al-Tusi (d. 1067)										
Tahdhib	0	0	0	0	0	0	4	4	4	2
Al-Istibsar	0	0	0	0	0	0	3	4	4	2

Al-Muhaqqiq (d. 1277)

Work									
Sharai	55	1	2	1	2	1	0	0	0
Al-Mukhtasar	0	0	0	1	1	0	0	0	0
Muarij	0	0	0	0	0	0	0	0	0

Al-Allama (d. 1325)

Work									
Qawaid	7	3	0	2	1	2	1	8	0
Tahrir	0	0	0	0	0	0	0	1	0
Irshad	8	0	7	5	4	2	3	2	0
Mukhtalaf	0	0	0	2	0	0	0	0	0
Tahdhib	6	0	0	2	1	4	0	5	0
Mabadi	1	0	1	0	1	0	1	2	0
Al-Bab	8	2	2	1	3	3	0	1	0

Hawashi

Al-Kulayni

Work									
Al-Kafi	3	6	6	3	0	0	0	0	0

Ibn Babawayh

Work									
Al-Faqih	0	5	4	5	1	0	0	0	0
Uyun	0	0	0	1	0	0	0	0	0
Amali	1	0	0	0	0	0	0	0	0

Al-Tusi

Work									
Tahdhib	4	4	2	8	2	0	0	0	0
Al-Istibsar	1	1	4	6	0	0	0	0	0

Author/Title	Centuries									
	6th 12th	7th 13th	8th 14th	9th 15th	900–50 1494–1543	951–1000 1544–91	1001–50 1591–1640	1051–1100 1641–88	1101–34 1689–1721	post-1134 post-1722
Al-Muhaqqiq										
Shara'i	0	0	0	0	2	1	2	1	2	3
Al-Mukhtasar	0	3	3	0	2	1	3	1	0	14
Al-Allama										
Qawa'id	0	0	4	0	1	0	1	0	2	3
Tahrir	0	0	2	1	2	0	1	0	0	5
Irshad	0	0	4	0	2	3	2	2	0	0
Mukhtalaf	0	0	0	0	1	0	6	3	0	2
Mabadi	0	0	0	0	0	0	0	0	0	3
Al-Bab	0	0	0	0	1	0	0	0	0	0
Tahdhib	0	0	1	1	0	0	2	0	0	2
Kashf	0	0	0	0	0	0	0	0	0	2
Khulasa	0	0	0	0	0	2	4	1	1	0

By author

Ali al-Karaki (d. 1534)

Sharh

Sharai
Qawaid
Mukhtalaf

Hawashi
  Sharai
  Qawaid
  Irshad
  Tahrir

Ibrahim al-Qatifi (d. after 1539)
Shuruh
  Al-Mukhtasar
  Irshad (al-Allama)

Hawashi
  Shara
  Irshad (al-Allama)

Son of al-Qatifi
Shuruh
  Al-Mukhtasar

Shayh Zayn al-Din al-Amili (d. 1558)
Shuruh
  Sharai
  Irshad (*Raud al-Jinan*)
  Qawaid
  Al-Luma'a (*al-Rauda*)

Hawashi
  Sharai
  Qawaid
  Irshad
  Khulasat al-Aqwal

Shaykh al-Husayn b. Abd al-Samad (d. 1576)

Sharah

  Qawaid

Hawashi

  Irshad

  Khulasat al-Aqwal

Ahmad b Muhammad al-Ardabili (d. 1585)

Sharah

  Irshad

S. al-Husayn b. al-Hasan al-Karaki (d. 1592–3)

Sharah

  Al-Kafi

Hawashi

  Uyun Akhbar al-Rida

Abd al-Ali b. Ali al-Karaki (d. 1593, son of Ali al-Karaki)

Sharah

  Irshad

Al-Hasan b. Shaykh Zayn al-Din (d. 1602)

Sharah

  Mukhtalaf

Hawashi

  Tahdhib al-Ahkam

Muhammad b. al-Hasan b. Shaykh Zayn al-Din (d. 1620)

Shuruh
  Al-Faqih
  Tahdhib al-Ahkam
  Mukhtalaf

Hawashi
  Al-Faqih
  Tahdhib al-Ahkam
  Tahdhib al-Wusul
  Khulasat al-Aqwal

Muhammad b. Ali al-Amili (d. 1600)

Shuruh
  Tahdhib
  Al-Mukhtasar

Hawashi
  Tahdhib
  Al-Istibsar
  Khulasat al-Aqwal

Nur Allah al-Shushtari (d. 1610–11)

Shuruh
  Tahdhib al-Ahkam
  Mukhtalaf

Hawashi
  Tahdhib al-Ahkam
  Qawaid
  Tahrir

Al-Astarabadi, Mirza Muhammad b. Ali (d. 1619)

Hawashi

Tahdhib al-Ahkam

Baha al-Din, Muhammad b. al-Husayn al-Amili (Shaykh Bahai) (d. 1621)

Shuruh

Al-Faqih

Mukhtalaf

Hawashi

Khulasat al-Aqwal

Muhammad Amin al-Astarabadi (d. 1626–7)

Shuruh

Al-Kafi

Tahdhib al-Ahkam

Al-Istibsar

Hawashi

Al-Kafi

Mir Damad, Muhammad Baqir al-Husayni (d. 1630–1)

Shuruh

Al-Kafi

Irshad

Mukhtalaf

Hawashi

Al-Kafi

Al-Faqih

Al-Istibsar

Ikhtiyar Marifat al-Rijal

Mulla Sadra (d. 1640)
  Shuruh
    Al-Kafi

Muhammad Taqi al-Majlisi (d. 1659)
  Shuruh
    Al-Faqih (Arabic, Persian)
    On the *shaykhs* of *al-Faqih*
    Tahdhib al-Ahkam

Muhammad Tahir (d. 1687)
  Shuruh
    Tahdhib al-Ahkam

Aziz Allah al-Majlisi (son of Taqi al-Majlisi)
  Hawashi
    Tahdhib al-Ahkam

Abd Allah al-Majlisi (son of Taqi al-Majlisi)
  Shuruh
    Tahdhib al-Ahkam

Muhammad Baqir al-Majlisi (son of Taqi al-Majlisi) (d. 1698–9)
  Shuruh
    Al-Kafi
    Tahdhib al-Ahkam

  Hawashi
    Tahdhib al-Ahkam

Muhammad Salih al-Mazandirani (son-in-law of Taqi al-Majlisi) (d. 1670)

   Shuruh

      Al-Kafi

Khalil al-Qazwini (d. 1678–9)

   Shuruh

      Al-Kafi (parts of it)

      Al-Kafi (Arabic and Persian)

      Uddat al-Usul

   Hawashi

      Uddat al-Usul

Muhammad Baqir al-Sabziwari (d. 1679)

   Shuruh

      Al-Tawhid

      Irshad

Muhammad b. al-Hasan al-Shirwani (son-in-law of Taqi al-Majlisi) (d. 1687)

   Shuruh

      Tahshib al-Ahkam

      Al-Mukhtasar

Nimatallah al-Jazairi (student of Baqir al-Majlisi) (d. 1701)

   Shuruh

      Al-Kafi

      Al-Istibsar

   Hawashi

      Al-Istibsar

Muhammad Salih al-Khatunabadi (son-in-law of Baqir al-Majlisi) (d. 1704)

Sharh
  Al-Faqih
  Al-Istibsar

Jamal al-Din al-Khwansari (d. 1713)

Hawashi
  Al-Faqih
  Tahdhib al-Ahkam

Abdallah Afandi (student of Baqir al-Majlisi) (d. 1717)

Sharh
  Al-Mukhtasar

Hawashi
  Tahdhib al-Ahkam

* Based on Al-Tihrani, Agha Buzurg, *Al-Dharia ila Tasanif al-Shia*, 25 vols (Tehran and Najaf, 1353–98).

Bibliography

EI2, refers to the *Encyclopaedia of Islam*, series 2. *EI3* to series 3.

EIr refers to the *Encyclopaedia Iranica*, available free online at: http://www.iranicaonline.org.

Primary sources

Afandi, A., *Riyad al-Ulama*, 5 vols, Qum, 1401.

Afshar, I. (ed.), *Tarikh-i Kashan*, Tehran, 2536/1978.

Ahmadi, N., 'Chahar Waqfnama az Chahar Madrasah-yi Isfahan dar Dawrah-yi Safavi', in R. Jafariyan (ed.), *Miras-i Islami-yi Iran*, Qum, 1375/1996, vol. 3, 95–129.

Alawi, A., 'Izhar al-Haqq' in R. Jafariyan (ed.), *Miras-i Islami-yi Iran*, Qum, 1374, vol. 2, 260–7.

Al-Amili, Husayn b. Abd al-Samad, *al-Iqd al-Husayni al-Tahmaspi*, ed. S. Jawad al-Mudarrisis al-Yazdi (Yazd, n.d.).

Al-Amili, Shaykh Zayn al-Din, 'Risala fi Salat al-Juma', in R. Jafariyan (ed.), *Davazda Risala-yi Fiqhi darbara-yi Namaz-i Juma*, Qum, 1423/1381/2003, 137–81.

Al-Amin, M., *Khitat Jabal Amil*, Beirut, 1961.

Al-Amin, M. *Ayan al-Shia*, 11 vols, Beirut, 1983.

Al-Ashari, Ali b. Ismail, *Maqalat al-Islamiyyin*, ed. H. Ritter, Wiesbaden, 1980.

Al-Astarabadi, M. A., *Al-Fawaid al-Madaniyya*, ed. R. al-Rahmati al-Araki, Qum 1424.

Al-Azzawi, A., *Tarikh al-Iraq bayn al-Ihtilalayn*, 8 vols, Baghdad, 1935–56.

Al-Bahrani, Y., *Luluat al-Bahrayn*, Najaf, 1969.

Al-Barqi, Ahmad b. Muhammad b. Khalid al-Qummi, *al-Rijal*, ed. J. M. Urmawi, Tehran, 1342.

Al-Barqi, Ahmad b. Muhammad b. Khalid al-Qummi, *al-Mahasin*, ed. J. M. Urmawi, Tehran, 1370/1950–1.

Danishpazhuh, M. T. (ed.), *Catalogue méthodique, descriptif et raisonné des manuscrits concernant la tradition, les principes de la jurisprudence et le droit musulman de la Bibliothèque de l'Universitè de Téhéran don de M. le professuer Meshkât*, 6 vols, Tehran, 1330–1335.

Al-Fadli, A., *Introduction to Hadith, including 'Dirayat al-hadith' by al-Shahid al-Thani*, trans. N. Virjee, London, 2002.

Al-Hamawi, Yaqut, *Mujam al-Buldan*, Beirut, 1397/1977.

Al-Hilli, al-Hasan b. Yusuf, al-Allama, *al-Bab al-hadi ashar*, trans. W. E. Miller, London, 1928.

Al-Hilli, al-Hasan b. Yusuf, al-Allama, *Irshad al-Adhan*, 2 vols, Qum, 1410.

Al-Hilli, al-Hasan b. Yusuf, al-Allama, *Mabadi al-Wusul*, n.pl., 1404.

Al-Hilli, al-Hasan b. Yusuf, al-Allama, *Khulasat al-Aqwal*, n.pl., 1417.

Al-Hilli, al-Hasan b. Yusuf, al-Allama, *Mukhtalaf al-Shia*, Tehran, n.d.

Al-Hilli, al-Hasan b. Yusuf, al-Allama, *Muntaha al-Matlab*, n.pl., 1412.

Al-Hilli, al-Hasan b. Yusuf, al-Allama, *Qawaid al-Ahkam*, 2 vols in 1, Qum, n.d.

Al-Hilli, al-Hasan b. Yusuf, al-Allama, *Tahdkira al-Fuqaha*, n.pl., n.d.

Al-Hilli, al-Hasan b. Yusuf, al-Allama, *Tahrir al-Ahkam*, 2 vols in 1, Mashhad, n.d.

Al-Hilli, Jafar b. al-Hasan, al-Muhaqqiq, *al-Mutabar*, 2 vols, n.pl., 1364.

Al-Hilli, Jafar b. al-Hasan, al-Muhaqqiq, *al-Mukhtasar al-Nafi*, Najaf, 1383/1964.

Al-Hilli, Jafar b. al-Hasan, al-Muhaqqiq, *Sharai al-Islam*, Najaf, 1389/1969.

Al-Hilli, H., *al-Hilla wa Atharuha al-Ilmi wal-Adabi*, Qum, 1432/1390/2011.

Hunarfar, L., *Ganjinah-i Asar-i Tarikhi-i Isfahan*, Isfahan, 1344.

Al-Hurr al-Amili, Muhammad b. al-Hasan, *Kitab Amal al-Amil*, 2 vols, Baghdad, 1385.

Ibn al-Barraj, A., *Sharh Jumal al-Ilm wal-Amal*, ed. K. M. Shanachi, Mashhad, 1974.

Ibn Daud, al-Hasan b. Ali, *Rijal Ibn Daud*, ed. S. Muhammad Sadiq, Al Bahr al-Ulum, n.pl., 1392/1972.

Ibn al-Ghadairi, Ahmad b. al-Husayn, *Rijal ibn al-Ghada'iri*, Qum, 1422/1380.

Ibn Idris, Muhammad b. Mansur, *al-Sarair al-Hawi li Tahrir al-Fatawi*, 3 vols, Qum, 1410.

Ibn Ishaq, *The Life of Muhammad*, trans. A. Guillaume, London, 1955.

Ibn al-Jawzi, Abd al-Rahman b. Ali, *al-Muntazam*, 5–6, Hyderabad, 1357.

Ibn Makki, Muhammad, *Dhikra al-Shia fi Ahkam al-Sharia*, 4 vols, Qum, 1419.

Ibn Makki, Muhammad, *Al-Lumaa al-Dimashqiyya*, 10 vols, Qum, 1387/1967.

Ibn Makki, Muhammad, *Kitab al-Mazar*, n.pl., 1410.

Ibn Qulawayh, Jafar b. Muhammad al-Qummi, *Kamil al-Ziyarat*, available at: http://www.rafed. net/books/doaa/kamil/index.html, accessed 12 January 2011.

Ibn Shahr Ashub, Muhammad b. Ali, *Maalim al-Din*, n.pl., n.d.

Ibn Shahr Ashub, Muhammad b. Ali, *Manaqib Al Abi Talib*, 3 vols, Najaf, 1376/1956.

Ibn Tawus, Ali B. Musa, *Al-Aman min Akhtar al-Asfar*, Qum, 1409.

Iqbal, A., *Khwandan-i Nawbakhti*, Tehran, 1345.

Jafariyan, R. (ed.), 'Mashaghal-i Idari-yi Ulama dar Dawlat-i Safawi', in *Din va Siyasat dar Dawrah-yi Safavi*, Qum, 1370/1991, 75–118.

Jafariyan, R., *Tarikh-i Tashayyu dar Iran*, 1, Qum, 1375.

Jafariyan, R., *Safawiyya dar Arsa-yi Din, Farhang, va Siyasat*, 2, Qum, 1379/2000.

Jafariyan, R., 'Munasibat-i Isfahan wa Hijaz dar Dawrah-yi Safavi', paper presented at 'Isfahan and the Safavids', Isfahan, February 2002.

Jafariyan, R. (ed.), *Davazda Risala-yi Fiqhi darbara-yi Namaz-i Juma*, Qum, 1423/1381/2003.

Al-Karaki, Ali, 'Risala fi Salat al-Juma', in R. Jafariyan (ed.), *Davazda Risala-yi Fiqhi darbara-yi Namaz-i Juma*, Qum, 1423/1381/2003, 103–30.

Al-Kashani, Fayd, *Da Resale-yi lil-Hakim … Muhammad Muhsin … al-Fayd al-Kashani*, ed. R. Jafariyan, Esfahan, 1371.

Al-Kashani, Fayd, *Mafatih al-Sharai*, 1, Beirut, 1388/1969.

Al-Kashani, Fayd, *al-Shihab al-Thaqib*, Beirut, 1980.

Al-Kashani, Fayd, *Kitab al-Wafi*, 3 vols, Qum, 1404.

Khatunabadi, A., *Waqai al-Sinin val-Avvam*, ed. M. Bihbudi, Tehran, 1352/1973.

Khomeini, Imam, *Clarification of Questions*, trans. J. Burujirdi, Boulder, CO, 1984.

Khomeini, Imam, *Islam and Revolution*, trans. H. Algar, London, 1985.

Al-Khwansari, M. B., *Raudat al-Jannat*, eds M. T. al-Kashfi and A. Ismaililiyan, 8 vols, Tehran and Qum, 1390–1392.

Al-Kulayni, Muhammad b. Yaqub, *al-Kafi*, ed. A. A. al-Ghaffari, 8 vols, Tehran, 1377–79/1957–60.

Lawhi, Mir, 'Salwat al-Shia', in R. Jafariyan (ed.), *Miras-i Islami-yi Iran*, 2, Qum, 1374, 343–59.

Al-Masudi, Ali b. al-Husayn, *Muruj al-Dhahab*, 4, Beirut, 1403/1982.

Membré, M., *Mission to the Lord Sophy of Persia (1539–1542)*, trans. with Introduction and Notes A. H. Morton, London, 1993.

Minorsky, V. (ed., trans.), *Tadhkirat al-Muluk. A Manual of Safavid Administration, (c. 1137/1725)*, London, 1943.

Miskawayh, Ahmad b. Muhammad, *The Eclipse of the Abbasid Caliphate, the Concluding Portion of the Experiences of Nations [Tajarib al-Umum]*, trans. D. S. Margoliouth, ed. H. F. Amedroz, 1, Oxford, 1921.

Al-Mufid, Muhammad b. Muhammad, *al-Ifsah*, in *Iddat Rasa'il*, 2nd edn, Qum, n.d., 1–163.

Al-Mufid, Muhammad b. Muhammad, *Awail al-Maqalat* including *Tashih al-Itiqadat*, ed. A. S. Wajdi, Tabriz, 1370–1.

Al-Mufid, Muhammad b. Muhammad, *Al-Fusul al-Mukhtara*, Qum, 1396.

Al-Mufid, Muhammad b. Muhammad, *Kitab al-Irshad*, trans. I. K. A. Howard, London, 1981.

Al-Mufid, Muhammad b. Muhammad, *Kitab al-Mazar*, Beirut, 1993/1414.

Al-Mufid, Muhammad b. Muhammad, *Al-Masail al-Ashara fil-Ghayba*, Qum, n.d.

Al-Mufid, Muhammad b. Muhammad, 'al-Masail al-Sarawiyya', in al-Mufid, *Iddat Rasa'il*, 2nd edn, Qum, n.d., 221–5.

Al-Mufid, Muhammad b. Muhammad, *Al-Muqnia fil-fiqh*, Qum, 1417.

Munshi, I., *History of Shah Abbas the Great*, trans. R. M. Savory, 3 vols, Boulder, CO, 1978–86.

Muntajab al-Din, Ali b. Ubayd, *Fihrist Muntajab al-Din*, ed. Jalal-Din Urmawi, Qum, 1366.

Al-Murtada, Ali b. al-Husayn, *Al-Intisar*, Qum, 1415.

Al-Murtada, Ali b. al-Husayn, *Jawabat al-Masail al-Miyyafariqin*, in *Rasa'il al-Sharif al-Murtada*, ed. S. M. Raja'i, 1, Qum, 1405, 271–306.

Al-Murtada, Ali b. al-Husayn, *Jawabat al-Masail al-Mosuliyyat al-Thalitha*, in *Rasa'il al-Sharif al-Murtada*, ed. S. M. Raja'i, 1, Qum, 1405, 201–13.

Al-Murtada, Ali b. al-Husayn, *Jumal al-Ilm wal-Amal*, in *Rasa'il al-Sharif al-Murtada*, ed. S. M. Raja'i, 3, Qum, 1405.

Al-Murtada, Ali b. al-Husayn, *al-Muqni'a*, Qum, 1416.

Al-Murtada, Ali b. al-Husayn, *al-Shafi fil-Imama*, ed. F. al-Milani, 4 vols, Qum, 1410.

Al-Najashi, Ahmad b. Ali al-Asadi, *Rijal al-Najashi*, ed. M. al-Zanjani, Qum, 1407.

Naraqi, H., *Asar-i Tarikhi-yi Shahristanha-yi Kashan wa Natanz*, Tehran, 1348/1969.

Al-Nawbakhti, Abu Muhammad al-Hasan b. Musa, *Firaq al-Shia*, Najaf, 1969.

Al-Numani, Muhammad b. Ibrahim, *Kitab al-Ghayba*, ed. and trans.M. J. al-Ghaffari, Tehran, 1363/1985.

Al-Nuri, al-Husayn b. Muhammad, *Mustadrak al-Wasail*, 3 vols, Tehran, 1382.

Al-Qummi, al-Hasan b. Muhammad b. al-Hasan al-Ashari, *Tarikh-i Qum*, trans. Hasan b. Ali al-Qummi, ed. Jalal al-Din al-Tehrani, Tehran, 1313/1934–5.

Al-Qummi, Muhammad b. Ali, Ibn Babawayh, *Kamal al-Din fi Timam al-Nima*, Qum, 1405/1363.

Al-Qummi, Ali b. Babawayh, *Kitab al-Imama wal-Tabsira min al-Hayra*, available at: http://www.aqaed.info/book/75/indexs.html, accessed 12 February 2010.

Al-Qummi, Sad b. Abdallah al-Ashari, *Kitab al-Maqalat wal-Firaq*, Tehran, 1963.

Al-Qummi, Muhammad b. Ali, Ibn Babawayh, *Maani al-Akhbar*, Qum, 1361.

Al-Qummi, Muhammad b. Ali, Ibn Babawayh, *Man la Yahdaruhu al-Faqih*, 2, ed. A. A. al-Ghaffari, Qum, n.d.

Al-Qummi, Muhammad b. Ali, Ibn Babawayh, *Man la Yahduruhu al-Faqih*, ed. H. M. al-Khurasan, 4 vols, Najaf, 1378; ed. A. A. al-Ghaffari, Qum, n.d.

Al-Qummi, Muhammad b. Ali, Ibn Babawayh, *A Shiiite Creed*, trans. A. A. A. Fyzee, Calcutta, 1942; revised version (Tehran, 1999), available at: http://www.wofis.com/Publications.aspx?bookID=4, accessed 19 May 2011.

Al-Qummi, Muhammad b. Ali, Ibn Babawayh, *Uyun Akhbar al-Rida*, Tehran, n.d.

Al-Rawandi, Qutb al-Din Said, *Fiqh al-Quran*, 2 vols, Qum, 1397–1399.

Al-Rawandi, Qutb al-Din Said, *al-Kharaij wal-Jaraih*, 3 vols, n.pl., 1409.

Al-Rizawi, Muhammad Zaman b. Muhammad Jafar, 'Sahifat al-Rishad', in R. Jafariyan (ed.), *Miras-i Islami-yi Iran*, 2 (Qum, 1374), 268–72.

Rumlu, Hasan Beg, *Ahsan al-Tawarikh*, Tehran, 1357.

Al-Sabziwari, Muhammad, 'Risala fi Salat al-Juma', in R. Jafariyan (ed.), *Davazda Risala-yi Fiqhi darbara-yi Namaz-i Juma*, Qum, 1423/1381/2003, 313–554.

Al-Saffar, Muhammad b. al-Hasan, *Basair al-Darajat fi Fadail Al Muhammad*, ed. M. Kuchabaghi, Qum, 1404.

Al-Tabari, Muhammad b. Jarir al-Tabari, *The History of al-Tabari*, ed. E. Yarshater, 40 vols, Albany, NY, 1989f.

Al-Tabatabai, S. A., *Maktabat al-Allama al-Hilli*, Qum, 1416.

Al-Tabrisi, Fadl b. Hasan, *Ilam al-Wara*, 2 vols, Qum, 1417.

Tahir, Muhammad, 'Risala-yi Namaz-i Juma', in R. Jafariyan (ed.), *Davazda Risala-yi Fiqhi darbara-yi Namaz-i Juma*, Qum, 1423/1381/2003, 611–78.

Taliqani, A., *Khulasat al-Fawaid*, in *Miras-i Islami-yi Iran*, ed. R. Jafariyan, 2, Qum, 1374, 273–300.

Al-Tihrani, Agha Buzurg, *Tabaqat Alam al-Shia*, 6 vols, ed. A. N. Munzavi, Qum, n.d.

Al-Tihrani, Agha Buzurg, *Al-Dharia ila Tasanif al-Shia*, 25 vols, Tehran and Najaf, 1353–98.

Al-Tusi, Muhammad b. al-Hasan, *Al-Istibsar*, ed. H. M. al-Khurasan, 4 vols, Najaf, 1375/1956–1376/1957.

Al-Tusi, Muhammad b. al-Hasan, *al-Fihrist*, ed. M. Bahr al-Ulum, Najaf, 1937.

Al-Tusi, Muhammad b. al-Hasan, *Kitab al-Ghayba*, eds A. al-Tehrani *et al.*, Qum, 1411.

Al-Tusi, Muhammad b. al-Hasan, *Al-Mabsut fil-Fiqh*, eds M. T. al-Kashfi and M. B. al-Bihbudi, 8 vols, Tehran, 1387–1393.

Al-Tusi, Muhammad b. al-Hasan, *al-Nihaya fi Mujjarad al-Fiqh wal-Fatawi*, Beirut, 1390/1970.

Al-Tusi, Muhammad b. al-Hasan, *Rijal al-Tusi*, ed. Bahr al-Ulum, Najaf, 1380/1961.

Al-Tusi, Muhammad b. al-Hasan, *Tahdhib al-Ahkam*, ed. H. M. al-Khurasan, 10 vols, Najaf, 1378/1959–1382/1962.

Al-Tusi, Muhammad b. al-Hasan, *Uddat al-Usul*, ed. M. R. Ansari Qummi, n.pl., 1376/1417.

Al-Tusi, Muhammad b. al-Hasan, *Tahdhib al-Ahkam*, ed. S. H. al-Musawi al-Khurasani, 6 vols, Tehran, 1365.

Al-Yaqubi, Ahmad b. Wadih, *Tarikh al-Yaqubi*, 3 vols, Najaf, 1384/1964.

Al Yasin, M. H., *Tarikh al-Mashhad al-Kazimi*, Baghdad, 1967/1387.

Secondary sources

Abd-Allah, U. F., 'Abu Hanifa', *EIr*.

Abisaab, R., *Converting Persia, Religion and Power in the Safavid Empire*, London, 2004.

Abisaab, R., 'Shiite Beginnnings and Scholastic Tradition in Jabal Amil in Lebanon', *Muslim World* (1999), 1–21.

Aghaie, K., 'The Karbala Narrative: Shii Political Discourse in Modern Iran in the 1960s and 1970s', *Journal of Islamic Studies*, 12 (2001), 151–76.

Aghaie, K., *The Martyrs of Karbala. Shii Symbols and Rituals in Modern Iran*, Seattle, WA, 2005.

Aghaie, K., *The Women of Karbala. Ritual Performance and Symbolic Discourses in Modern Shii Islam*, Austin, TX, 2005.

Ahmad, A., 'Safawid Poets and India', *IRAN: Journal of the British Institute of Persian Studies*, 14 (1976), 117–32.

Ahmed, M., 'The Shiis of Pakistan', in M. Kramer (ed.), *Shiism, Resistance and Revolution*, Boulder, CO, 1987, 275–88.

Akhavi, S., *Religion and Politics in Contemporary Iran. Clergy–State Relations in the Pahlavi Period*, Albany, NY, 1980.

Akhtar, I., 'The Oriental African: The Evolution of Postcolonial Islamic Identities Among the Globalised Khoja of Dar Es Salaam', unpublished PhD dissertation, University of Edinburgh, 2013.

Akhtar, S. W., *Early Shiite Imamiyyah Thinkers*, New Delhi, 1988.

Akhtar, W., 'An Introduction to Imamiyyah Scholars, Major Shii Thinkers of the Fifth/Eleventh Century', *Al-Tawhid*, 4(4) (1407), available at: http://www.al-islam.org/al-tawhid/scholars.htm, accessed 15 October 2011.

Algar, H., 'Bektash, Haji', *EIr.*

Algar, H., 'Iran IX. Religion in Iran (2), Islam in Iran (2.2) Mongol and Timurid Periods', *EIr.*

Algar, H., 'Kobrawiyya II. The Order', *EIr.*

Algar, H., 'The Oppositional Role of the Ulama in Twentieth Century Iran', in Keddie (ed.), *Scholars, Saints, and Sufis*, Berkeley, CA, 1969, 231–55.

Algar, H., *Religion and the State in Iran, 1785–1906*, Berkeley, CA, 1969.

Amanat, A., 'The Nuqtawi Movement of Mahmud Pisikhani and his Persian Cycle of Mystical-materialism', in F. Daftary (ed.), *Medieval Ismaili History and Thought*, Cambridge, 1996, 281–97.

Amir-Moezzi, M., 'Khattabiyya', *Eir.*

Amir-Moezzi, M. A., *The Divine Guide in Early Shiism. The Sources of Esotericism in Islam*, trans. David Streight, Albany, NY, 1994.

Amir-Moezzi, M. A., 'The Warrior of *Tawil*: A Poem about Ali by Mulla Sadra', in M. A. Amir-Moezzi, *The Spirituality of Shii Islam*, London, 2011, 307–37.

Anthony, S., *The Caliph and the Heretic. Ibn Saba and the Origins of Shiism*, Leiden, 2011.

Anthony, S., 'The Legend of Abdallah ibn Saba and the Date of Umm al-Kitab', *Journal of thr Royal Asiatic Society*, 21 (2011), 1–30.

Arjomand, S. A., *The Shadow of God and the Hidden Imam. Religion, Political Order, and Societal Change in Shiite Iran from the Beginning to 1890*, Chicago, 1984.

Arjomand, S. A. (ed.), 'Two Decrees of Shah Tahmasp Concerning Statecraft and the Authority of Shaykh Ali al-Karaki', in *Authority and Political Culture in Shiism*, Albany, NY, 1988, 250–62.

Asatryan, M., 'Bankers and Politics: The Network of Shii Moneychangers in 2nd/8th-century Kufa and their Role in the Shii Community', forthcoming.

Aubin, J., 'Notes sur quelques documents Aq Qoyunlu', *Mélanges Louis Massignon*, 1, Damas, 1956, 123–47.

Aubin, J., 'La fin de l'état sarbadar du Khorassan', *Journal Asiatique* (1974), 95–118.

Avery, P., *Modern Iran*, New York, 1965.

Ayoub, M., *Redemptive Suffering in Islam. A Study of the Devotional aspects Ashura in Twelver Shiism*, The Hague, 1978.

Babayan, K., 'The Waning of the Qizilbash: The Spiritual and the Temporal in Seventeenth Century Iran', unpublished PhD dissertation, Princeton University, 1993.

Baldick, J., *Mystical Islam*, London, 1989.

Bar-Asher, M., 'Variant Readings and Additions of the Imami Shia to the Quran', *Israel Oriental Studies*, 13 (1993), 39–74.

Bashir, S., 'The Imam's Return: Messianic Leadership in Later Medieval Shiism', in L. Walbridge (ed.), *The Most Learned of the Shia*, Oxford, 2001, 21–33.

Bausani, A., 'Religion in the Saljuq Period', in J. A. Boyle et al. (eds), *Cambridge History of Iran, vol. 5: The Saljuq and Mongol Periods*, Cambridge, 1968, 538–49.

Bill, J., *The Politics of Iran*, New York, 1972.

Birge, J., *The Bektashi Order of Dervishes*, London, 1937.

Blake, S., *Half the World. The Social Architecture of Safavid Isfahan, 1590–1722*, Costa Mesa, CA, 1999.

Bosworth, C. E., 'Saffarids', *EI2.*

Bosworth, C. E. *et al.*, 'Saldjukids', *EI2*.

Brown, J., *The Canonization of al-Bukhari and Muslim. The Formation and Function of the Sunni Hadith Canon*, Leiden, 2007.

Browne, E. G., *A Literary History of Persia*, 4, Cambridge, 1953.

Brunner, R., 'Majlesi, Mohammad-Baqir', *EIr*.

Buckley, R., 'The Early Shiite *Ghulah*', *Journal of Semitic Studies*, 42(2) (1997), 301–25.

Buhl, F., 'Muhammad b. Abd Allah … al-Nafs al-Zakiyya', *EI2*.

Buyukkara, A., 'The Schism in the Party of Musa al-Kazim and the Emergence of the Waqifa', *Arabica*, 47(1) (2000), 78–99.

Cahen, C., 'Baba Ishaq, Baba Ilyas, Hadjdji Bektash et quelques autres', *Turcica*, 1 (1969), 53–64.

Cahen, Cl. *et al.*, 'Ibn Abbad', *EI2*.

Calder, N., 'The Structure of Authority in Imami Shii Jurisprudence', unpublished PhD dissertation, School of Oriental and African Studies, 1980.

Calder, N., 'Zakat in Imami Shii Jurisprudence from the Tenth to the Sixteenth Century, AD', *Bulletin of the School of Oriental and African Studies*, 46(3) (1981), 468–80.

Calder, N., '*Khums* in Imami Shii Jurisprudence from the Tenth to the Sixteenth Century, AD', *Bulletin of the School of Oriental and African Studies*, 45(1) (1982), 39–47.

Calder, N., 'Legitimacy and Accommodation in Safavid Iran: The Juristic Theory of Muhammad Baqir al-Sabzewari (d. 1090/1679)', *IRAN: Journal of the British Institute of Persian Studies*, 25 (1987), 91–105.

Calmard, J., 'Imam Husayn in Popular Literature', *EIr*.

Calmard, J., 'Marashis', *EI2*.

Calmard, J., 'Le chiisme imamite en Iran à l'époque seljoukide d'après le *Kitab al-naqd*', *Le monde iranien et l'Islam*, 1 (1971), 43–67.

Calmard, J. (ed.), 'Les rituels shiites et le pouvoir. L'imposition du shiisme safavide: eulogies et malédictions canoniques', in *Études Safavides*, Paris/Tehran, 1993, 109–50.

Calmard, J., 'Shii Rituals and Power, II', in C. Melville (ed.), *Safavid Persia*, London/New York, 1996, 139–90.

Canard, M., 'Bagdad au IVe siècle de l'hégire (Xe siècle de l'ère chrétienne)', *Arabica*, 9 (1962), 267–87.

Canby, S., *The Golden Age of Persian Art, 1501–1722*, London, 1999.

Chelkowski, P., *Taziyeh. Ritual and Drama in Iran*, New York, 1979.

Cole, J., 'Conversion III. To Imami Shiism in India', *EIr*.

Cole, J., 'Shii Clerics in Iraq and Iran, 1722–1780: The Akhbari-Usuli Conflict reconsidered', *Iranian Studies*, 18(1) (1985), 3–34.

Cole, J., 'Rival Empires of Trade and Imami Shiism in Eastern Arabia, 1300–1800', *International Journal of Middle East Studies*, 19(2) (1987), 177–203.

Cole, J., *Roots of North Indian Shi'ism in Iran and Iraq. Religion and State in Awadh, 1722–1859*, Berkeley, CA, 1988.

Cole, J. and N. Keddie, *Shiism and Social Protest*, New Haven, CT, 1986.

Cottam, R., *Nationalism in Iran*, Pittsburgh, 1964.

Crone, P., 'Mawla', *EI2*.

Dabashi, H., *Shiism. A Religion of Protest*, Cambridge, MA, 2011.

Daftary, F., *The Ismailis. Their History and Doctrines*, London, 1992.

Daftary, F., *A Short History of the Ismailis*, Edinburgh, 1998.

Daiber, H., 'al-Tusi, Nasir al-Din', *EI2*.

Dale, S., 'A Safavid Poet in the Heart of Darkness: The Indian Poems of Ashraf Mazandarani', *Iranian Studies*, 36(2) (2003), 197–212.

Deeb, L., 'Living Ashura in Lebanon', *Comparative Studies of South Asia, Africa and the Middle East*, 25(1) (2005), 122–37.

Djebli, M., 'al-Sharif al-Radi', *EI2*.

Donahue, J., *The Buwayhid Dynasty in Iraq, 334 H./945 to 403 H./1012. Shaping Institutions for the Future*, Leiden, 2003.

Donaldson, D. M., *The Shiite Religion. A History of Islam in Persia and Irak*, London, 1933.

Durand-Guédy, D., *Iranian Elites and Turkish Rulers. A History of Isfahan in the Saljuq Period*, London, 2010.

Dutton, Y., *The Origins of Islamic Law. The Qur'an, the Muwatta' and Madinan Amal*, Richmond, 1999.

Ed., 'Hashwiyya', *EI2*.

Eisenstein, H., 'Sunnite Accounts of the Subdivisions of the Shia', in Frederick de Jong (ed.), *Shia Islam, Sects and Sufism. Historical Dimensions, Religious Practice and Methodological Considerations*, Utrecht, 1992, 1–9.

Emerson, J., 'Chardin', *EIr*.

Ende, W., 'The Flagellations of Muharram and the Shiite Ulama', *Islam*, 55 (1978), 19–36.

Fahd, T. (ed.), *Le Shi'isme imamite*, Paris, 1970.

Ferrier, R., *A Journey to Persia. Jean Chardin's Portrait of a Seventeenth-century Empire*, London, 1996.

Floor, W., *The Afghan Invasion of Safavid Persia*, 1721–29, Paris, 1998.

Floor, W., 'The *sadr* or Head of the Safavid Religious Administration, Judiciary and Endowments and other Members of the Religious Institution', *ZDMG*, 150 (2000), 461–500.

Fudge, B., *Quranic Hermeneutics. Al-Tabrisi and the Craft of Commentary*, London, 2011.

Gheisari, E. and J. Qasemi, 'Akhbariyya', *EI3*.

Gholsorkhi, S., 'Ismail II and Mirza Makhdum Sharifi: An Interlude in Safavid History', *International Journal of Middle Eastern Studies*, 26 (1994), 477–88.

Gimaret, D., 'Mutazila', *EI2*.

Gleave, R., 'Akhbariyya and Usuliyya', *EI3*.

Gleave, R., *Scripturalist Islam. The History and Doctrines of the Akhbari Shii School*, Leiden, 2007.

Gleave, R., 'Prayer and Prostration', in P. Khosronejad (ed.), *The Art and Material Culture of Iranian Shiism*, London, 2012, 247–8.

Gleave, R., 'Shii Jurisprudence during the Seljuq Period', in S. Mecit and C. Lange (eds), *The Seljuqs. Politics, Society and Culture*, Edinburgh, 2011, 205–27.

Goerke, A. *et al.*, 'First-century Sources for the Life of Muhammad? A Debate', *Der Islam*, 89 (2012), 2–59.

Gruber, C., 'When *Nubuvvat* Encounters *Valayat*', in P. Khosronejad (ed.), *The Art and Material Culture of Iranian Shiism*, London, 2012, 46–73.

Haidar, N., *The Origins of the Shia. Identity, Ritual, and Sacred Space in Eighth-century Kufa*, Cambridge, 2011.

Hallaq, W., *A History of Islamic Legal Theories*, Cambridge, 1997.

Halkin, A. S., 'The Hashwiyya', *Journal of the American Oriental Society*, 54 (1934), 1–28.

Halliday, F., *Iran: Dictatorship and Development*, London, 1979.

Halm, H., 'Golat', *EIr*.

Halm, H., *Shi'a Islam: from Religion to Revolution*, Princeton, 1997.

Halm, H., *Shiism*, 2nd edn, Edinburgh, 2004.

Halpern, M., *The Politics of Social Change in the Middle East and North Africa*, Princeton, 1963.

Hamza, F., *Anthology of Quranic Commentaries, vol. I: On the Nature of the Divine*, Oxford, 2008.

Hanaway, W. *et al.*, 'Ayyar', *EIr*.

Haneda, M., 'Emigration of Iranian Elites to India During the 16th–18th Centuries', in M.

Szuppe (ed.), *L'héritage timouride. Iran–Asie Centrale–Inde XVe–XVIIIe siècles*, Tashkent/Aix-en-Provence, 1997, 129–43.

Haneda, M., 'India XXVIII. Iranian Immigrants in India', *EIr.*

Hartmann, A., 'Al-Nasir Li-Din Allah', *EI2.*

Hawting, G. R., *The First Dynasty of Islam. The Umayyad Caliphate ad 661–750*, London, 2000.

Hegland, M., 'Mixed Blessing: The Majles – Shi'a Women's Rituals of Mourning in North-West Pakistan', in Judy Brink and Joan Mencher (eds.), *Mixed Blessings: Gender and Religious Fundamentalism Cross-Culturally*, New York, 1997, 179–96.

Hillenbrand, C., 'The Power Struggle Between the Saljuqs and the Ismailis of Alamut, 487–518/1094–1124: the Saljuq Perspective', in F. Daftary (ed.), *Medieval Ismaili's History and Thought*, Cambridge, 1996, 205–20.

Hillenbrand, R., 'Safavid Architecture', *The Cambridge History of Iran, vol. 6: The Timurid and Safavid Periods*, eds P. Jackson and L. Lockhart, Cambridge, 1986, 759–842.

Hollister, J. N., *The Shia of India*, London, 1953.

Howard, I., '*Muta* Marriage Reconsidered in the Context of the Formal Procedures for Islamic Marriage', *Journal of Semitic Studies*, 20 (1975), 82–92.

Howarth, T., *The Twelver Shia as a Muslim Minority in India: Pulpit of Tears*, London, 2005.

Hussain, J., *The Occultation of the Twelfth Imam. A Historical Background*, London, 1982.

Imber, C., 'The Persecution of the Ottoman Shiites According to the *muhimme defterleri*, 1565–85', *Der Islam*, 56 (1979), 245–73.

Irfanmunsh, J., *Jughrafiyi-yi Tarikihi-yi Hijrat Imam Rida Az Madina ta Marv*, Tehran, 1382.

Ishraqi, I., '"Noqtaviyya" à l'époque Safavides', in A. Newman (ed.), *Society and Culture in the Early Modern Middle East. Studies on Iran in the Safavid Period*, Leiden, 2003, 341–9.

Jafariyan, R., 'Four Centuries of Influence of Iraqi Shi'ism on Pre-Safavid Iran', available at: http://www.al-islam.org/mot/iraqishiism, chapter three, accessed 31 December 2012.

Jafri, S., *The Origins and Early Development of Shia Islam*, New York, 1979.

Johnson, R., 'Sunni Survival in Safavid Iran: Anti-Sunni Activities during the Reign of Tahmasp I', *Iranian Studies*, 27(1–4) (1994), 123–34.

Kabir, M., *The Buwayhid Dynasty of Baghdad, 334/946–447/1055*, Calcutta, 1964.

Keddie, N. (ed.), 'The Roots of the Ulama's Power in Modern Iran', in *Scholars, Saints, and Sufis*, Berkeley, CA, 1969, 211–29.

Kennedy, H., *The Early Abbasid Caliphate*, London, 1981.

Kennedy, H., *The Prophet and the Age of the Caliphates*, London, 1986.

Kohlberg, E., 'Akhbariyya', *EIr.*

Kohlberg, E., 'Amoli, Sayyed Baha' al-Din', *EIr.*

Kohlberg, E., 'Behar al-Anwar', *EIr.*

Kohlberg, E., 'Halabi, Abu al-Selah', *EIr.*

Kohlberg, E., 'al-Rafida', *EI2.*

Kohlberg, E., 'Some Notes on the Imamite Attitude to the Quran', in S. M. Stern *et al.* (eds), *Islamic Philosophy and the Classical Tradition*, Oxford, 1972, 209–24.

Kohlberg, E., 'The Development of the Imami Shii Doctrine of Jihad', *ZDMG*, 126(1) (1976), 64–86.

Kohlberg, E., 'From Imamiyya to Ithna' Ashariyya', *Bulletin of the School of Oriental and African Studies*, 39 (1976), 521–34.

Kohlberg, E., *A Medieval Muslim Scholar at Work. Ibn Tawus and His Library*, Leiden, 1992.

Kohlberg, E., 'The Term *Muhaddath* in Twelver Shiism', *Studia Orientalia Memoriae D. H. Baneth Dedicata*, Jerusalem, 1979, 39–47.

Kohlberg, E., 'al-Usul al-Arbaumia', *Jerusalem Studies in Arabic and Islam*, 10 (1987), 128–66.

Kohlberg, E. and M. A. Amir-Moezzi (eds), *Revelation and Falsification. The Kitab al-qira'at of Ahmad b. Muhammad al-Sayyari*, Leiden, 2009.

Kramer, J., *Humanism in the Renaissance of Islam. The Cultural Revival of the Buyid Age*, Leiden, 1986.

Kramer, M., *Shiism, Resistance and Revolution*, Boulder, CO, 1987.

Lalani, A., *Early Shii Thought. The Teachings of Imam Muhammad al-Baqir*, London, 2004.

Lambourn, E., 'Of Jewels and Horses: the Career and Patronage of an Iranian Merchant under Shah Jahan', *Iranian Studies*, 36(2) (2003), 213–58.

Lambton, A. K. S., 'Qum. The Evolution of a Medieval City', *Journal of the Royal Asiatic Society*, 2 (1990), 322–39.

Lawson, B. T., 'A 14th Century Shii Gnostic, Rajab Bursi and his Mashariq al-Anwar,' *Islamic Philosophy Yearbook*, 1, Moscow, 2009, 422–38.

Lerner, D., *The Passing of Traditional Society*, New York, 1958.

Litvak, M., 'Kazemayn', *EIr*.

Lockhart, L., *The Fall of the Safawi Dynasty and the Afghan Occupation of Persia*, Cambridge, 1958.

Longrigg, S., *Four Centuries of Modern Iraq*, Oxford, 1925.

Madelung, W., 'Abd al-Jalil Razi', *EIr*.

Madelung, W., 'Abd al-Jabbar b. Ahmad', *EIr*.

Madelung, W., 'Akhbariyya', *EI2*.

Madelung, W., 'Djabir al-Jufi', *EI2*.

Madelung, W., 'Khattabiyya', *EI2*.

Madelung, W., 'Shia', *EI2*.

Madelung, W., 'Imamism and Mutazilite Theology', in T. Fahd (ed.), *Le shi'isme imamite*, Paris, 1970, 13–29.

Madelung, W., 'The Shiite and Kharijite Contribution to Pre-Asharite *Kalam*', in Parviz Morewedge (ed.), *Islamic Philosophical Theology*, Albany, NY, 1979, 120–39.

Madelung, W., 'A Treatise of the Sharif al-Murtada on the Legality of Working for the Government (*Masala fil-Amal maal-sultan*)', *Bulletin of the School of Oriental and African Studies*, 43(1) (1980), 18–31.

Madelung, W., *Religious Trends in Early Islamic Iran*, Albany, NY, 1988.

Madelung, W., *The Succession to Muhammad. A Study of the Early Caliphate*, Cambridge, 1998.

Mahdjoub, M., 'The Evolution of Popular Eulogy of the Imams Among the Shia', in S. A. Ajomand (ed.), *Authority and Political Culture in Shi'ism*, Albany, NY, 1988, 54–79.

Makdisi, G., 'Notes on Hilla and the Mazyadids in Medieval Islam', *Journal of the American Oriental Society*, 74 (1954), 249–62.

Mandaville, J., 'The Ottoman Province of al-Hasa in the Sixteenth and Seventeenth Centuries', *Journal of the American Oriental Society*, 90(3) (1970), 486–513.

Marcinkowski, C., 'Thailand–Iran Relations', *EIr*.

Marcinkowski, C., 'Rapproachment and Fealty during the Buyids and Early Saljuks: The Life and Times of Muhammad ibn al-Hasan al-Tusi', *Islamic Studies*, 40(2) (2001), 273–96.

Marcinkowski, C., 'The Iranian–Siamese Connection: An Iranian Community in the Thai Kingdom of Ayutthaya', *Iranian Studies*, 35 (2002), 23–46.

Marcinkowski, C., 'Selected Historical Facets of the Presence of Shi'ism in Southeast Asia', *Muslim World*, 99 (2009), 381–416.

Marquet, Y., 'Le shi'isme au XIe siècle à travers l'histoire de Ya'qubi', *Arabica*, 19 (1972), 1–145.

Massignon, L. [L. Gardet], 'al-Hallaj', *EI2*.

Massignon, L., 'Recherches sur les shîites extrémistes à Bagdad à la fin du troisième siècle de l'Hégire', *Opera Minora*, ed. Y. Moubarac, Paris, 1969, 1: 523–26.

Matthee, R., *The Politics of Trade in Safavid Iran, Silk for Silver 1600–1730*, Cambridge, 1999.

Matthee, R., 'Between Venice and Surat: The Trade in Gold in Late Safavid Iran', *Modern Asian Studies*, 34(1) (2000), 223–55.

Mavani, H., *Religious Authority and Political Thought in Twelver Shiism*, forthcoming.

Mazzaoui, M., *The Origins of the Safawids. Shism, Sufism, and the Ghulat*, Wiesbaden, 1972.

Melville, C., 'Sarbadarids', *EI2*.

McChesney, R., 'Waqf and Public Policy: The Waqfs of Shah Abbas, 1011–1023/1602–1614', *Asian and African Studies*, 15 (1981), 165–90.

McChesney, R., 'The Central Asian Hajj Pilgrimmage in the Time of the Early Modern Empires', in M. Mazzaoui (ed.), *Safavid Iran and Her Neighbors*, Salt Lake City, UT, 2003, 129–56.

McDermott, M., 'Ebn Babawayh', *EIr*

McDermott, M., *The Theology of al-Shaikh al-Mufid*, Beirut, 1978.

Millward, W. G., 'Al-Yaqubi's Sources and the Question of Shia Partiality', *Abr Nahrain*, 12 (1971/2), 47–74.

Minorsky, V. [C. E. Bosworth], 'Uzun Hasan', *EI2*.

Minorsky, V., 'The Poetry of Shah Ismail I', *Bulletin of the School of Oriental and African Studies*, 10 (1942), 1006a–53a.

Minorsky, V., 'Jihan Shah Qaraquyunlu and his Poetry', *Bulletin of the School of Oriental and African Studies*, 16(2) (1954), 271–97.

Moazzen, M., 'Shiite Higher Learning and the Role of the *Madrasa-yi Sultani* in Late Safavid Iran', unpublished PhD dissertation, University of Toronto, 2011.

Modarressi, H., *Barqi az Tarikh-i Qazvin*, Qum, 1361.

Modarressi, H., *An Introduction to Shii Law*, London, 1984.

Modarressi, H., *Crisis and Consolidation in the Formative Period of Shiite Islam. Abu Jafar Ibn Qiba Al-Razi and His Contribution to Imamite Shiite Thought*, Princeton, 1993.

Momen, M., *An Introduction to Shii Islam*, New Haven, 1985.

Moosa, M., *Extremist Shiites*, Syracuse, NY, 1988.

Mortel, R. T., 'The Origins and Early History of the Husaynid Amirate of Madina to the End of the Ayyubid Period', *Studia Islamica*, 74 (1991), 63–78.

Mortel, R. T., 'Zaydi Shiism and the Hasanid Sharifs of Mecca', *International Journal of Middle Eastern Studies*, 19(4) (1987), 455–72.

Mousavi, S. A., *The Hazaras of Afghanistan. An Historical, Cultural, Economic and Political Study*, Richmond, 1998.

Nakash, Y., 'An attempt to Trace the Origin of the Rituals of Ashura', *Die Welt des Islams*, 33(2) (1993), 161–81.

Nakash, Y., *Reaching for Power. The Shia in the Modern Arab World*, Princeton, 2006.

Nakash, Y., *The Shiis of Iraq*, Princeton, 1995.

Nasr, S. H., 'The School of Ispahan', in M. M. Sharif (ed.), *A History of Muslim Philosophy*, 2, Wiesbaden, 1966, 904–32.

Nasr, S. H., H. Dabashi and S. V. Nasr, *Shiism, Doctrines, Thought and Spirituality*, Albany, NY, 1988.

Nasr, S. H., H. Dabashi and S. V. Nasr, *Expectation of the Millennium. Shiism in History*, Albany, NY, 1989.

Nasr, V., *The Shia Revival*, New York, 2006.

Newman, A., 'Anti-Akhbari Sentiments among the Qajar *Ulama*: The Case of Muhammad Baqir al-Khwansari (d. 1313/1895)', in R. Gleave (ed.), *Religion and Society in Qajar Iran*, London, 2005, 155–73.

Newman, A. (ed.), 'Baqir al-Majlisi and Islamicate Medicine: Safavid Medical Theory and Practice Re-examined', in *Society and Culture in the Early Modern Middle East. Studies on Iran in the Safavid Period*, Leiden, 2003, 371–96.

Newman, A., 'Baqir al-Majlisi and Islamicate Medicine II: *al-Risala al-dhahabiyya* in *Bihar al-anwar*' in Mohammad Ali Amir-Moezzi *et al.* (eds), *Le shi'isme imamite quarante ans après*, Turnhout, 2009, 349–61.

Newman, A., 'Between Qum and the West: The Occultation According to al-Kulayni and al-Katib al-Numani', in F. Daftary (ed.), *Culture and Memory in Medieval Islam: Essays in Honour of Wilferd Madelung* (London: I. B. Tauris, 2003), 94–108.

Newman, A., 'Clerical Perceptions of Sufi Practices in Late Seventeenth-Century Persia: Arguments Over the Permissibility of Singing (*Ghina*)', in L. Lewisohn and D. Morgan (eds), *The Heritage of Sufism, vol. III: Late Classical Persianate Sufism: the Safavid and Mughal Period (1501– 1750)*, Oxford, 1999, 135–64.

Newman, A., 'Clerical Perceptions of Sufi Practices in Late 17th Century Persia, II: al-Hurr al-Amili (d. 1693) and the Debate on the Permissibility of Ghina', in Y. Suleiman (ed.), *Living Islamic History. Studies in Honour of Professor Carole Hillenbrand*, Edinburgh, 2010, 192–207.

Newman, A., 'Fayd al-Kashani and the Rejection of the Clergy/State Alliance: Friday Prayer as Politics in the Safavid Period', in L. Walbridge (ed.), *The Most Learned of the Shi'a*, New York, 2001, 34–52.

Newman, A., *The Formative Period of Twelver Shiism*, Abingdon, 2000.

Newman, A., 'Minority Reports', in F. Daftary and G. Miskinzoda (eds), *The Study of Shi'i Islam. The State of the Field and Issues of Methodology* (London, 2013).

Newman, A., 'Mir Damad', *EIr.*

Newman, A., 'The Myth of the Clerical Migration to Safavid Iran: Arab Shiite Opposition to Ali al-Karaki and Safavid Shiism', *Die Welt des Islams*, 33 (1993), 66–112.

Newman, A., 'The Nature of the Akhbari/Usuli Dispute in Late-Safavid Iran. Part One: Abdallah al-Samahiji's "Munyat al-Mumarisin"', *Bulletin of the School of Oriental and African Studies*, 55(1) (1992), 22–51.

Newman, A., 'The Nature of the Akhbari/Usuli Dispute in Late-Safavid Iran. Part Two: The Conflict Reassessed', *Bulletin of the School of Oriental and African Studies*, 55(2) (1992), 250–61.

Newman, A., 'The Recovery of the Past: Ibn Babawayh, Baqir al-Majlisi and Safavid Medical Discourse', *IRAN: Journal of the British Institute of Persian Studies*, 50 (2012), 109–27.

Newman, A., *Safavid Iran. Rebirth of a Persian Empire*, London, 2006.

Newman, A., 'Sufism and Anti-Sufism in Safavid Iran: The Authorship of the "Hadiqat al-Shia" Revisited', *IRAN: Journal of the British Institute of Persian Studies*, 37 (1999), 95–108.

Newman, A., 'Towards a Reconsideration of the Isfahan School of Philosophy: Shaykh Bahai and the Role of the Safawid Ulama', *Studia Iranica*, 15(2) (1986), 165–99.

Northridge, A., 'The Shrine in Its Historical Context', in I. Panjwani (ed.), *The Shia of Samarra*, London, 2012, 49–66.

Al-Oraibi, A., 'Rationalism in the School of Bahrain: A Historical Perspective' in L. Clarke (ed.), *Shiite Heritage*, Binghamton, 2001, 331–44,

Pakatchi, A. and S. Umar, 'Halabi, Abu'l-Salah', *EI2*.

Peacock, A. *Early Seljuq History. A New Interpretation*, London, 2010.

Pellat, Ch., 'Muhammad b. Ali al-Shalmaghani', *EI2*.

Petrushevsky, I. P., *Islam in Iran*, trans. H. Evans, London, 1985.

Pierce, M., 'Remembering the Infallible Imams, Narrative and Memory in Medieval Twelver Shiism', unpublished PhD dissertation, Boston University, 2013.

Pinault, D., *The Shiites. Ritual and Popular Piety in a Muslim Community*, New York, 1992.

Pinault, D., *Horse of Karbala. Muslim Devotional Life in India*, New York, 2001.

Pinault, D., *Notes from a Fortune-telling Parrot. Islam and the Struggle for Religious Pluralism in Pakistan*, London, 2008.

Pomerantz, M., 'Ebn Abbad, Esmail', *EIr*.

Pomerantz, M., 'A Shii–Mutazili Poem of al-Sahib b. 'Abbad (d. 385/995)', in B. Craig (ed.), *Ismaili and Fatimid Studies in Honor of Paul E. Walker*, Chicago, 2010, 131–50.

Popovic, A., *The Revolt of the African Slaves in the Third/Ninth Century*, Princeton, 1999.

Pourjavady, R., *Philosophy in Early Safavid Iran, Najm al-Din Mahmud al-Nayrizi and His Writings*, Leiden, 2011.

Al-Qadi, W., 'The Development of the Term "Ghulat" in Muslim Literature with Special Reference to the Kaysaniyya', in E. Kohlberg (ed.), *Shiism*, Aldershot, 2003, 269–318.

Rahimi, B., 'The Rebound Theater State: The Politics of the Safavid Camel Sacrifice, 1598–1695 C E', *Iranian Studies*, 37(3) (2004), 451–78.

Rahimi, B., *Theater State and the Formation of Early Modern Public Sphere in Iran*, Leiden, 2011.

Richard, Y., *Shiite Islam. Polity, Ideology, and Creed*, Oxford, 1995.

Rizvi, S. A. A., *A Socio-intellectual History of the Isna Ashari Shiis in India*, 2 vols, Canberra, 1986.

Rizvi, S., *Mulla Sadra and the Later Islamic Philosophical Tradition*, Edinburgh, 2013.

Rizvi, S., 'Seeking the Face of God': The Safavid *hikmat* Tradition's Conceptualisation of *walaya takwiniya*', forthcoming.

Sabari, S., *Mouvements populaires à Bagdad à l'époque 'Abbasside, IXe–XIe siècles*, Paris, 1981.

Sachedina, A. A., *The Idea of the Mahdi in Twelver Shiism*, Albany, NY, 1981.

Sachedina, A. A., 'The Significance of Kashshi's *Rijal* in Understanding the Early Role of the Shiite *Fuqaha*', in R. Savory (ed.), *Logos Islamikos. Studia Islamica in honorem Georgii Michaelis Wickens*, Toronto, 1984, 183–206.

Sachedina, A. A., 'A Treatise on the Occultation of the Twelfth Imamite Imam', *Studia Islamica*, 48 (1978), 109–24.

Salati, M., 'A Shiite in Mecca', in R. Brunner and W. Ende (eds), *The Twelver Shia in Modern Times*, Leiden, 2001, 3–24.

Salati, M., 'Toleration, Persecution and Local Realities: Observations on the Shiism in the Holy Places and the Bilad al-Sham (16th–17th centuries)', *Convegno sul Tema La Shi'a Nell'Impero Ottomano*, Rome, 15 April 1991, Rome, 1993, 121–48.

Sarwar, G., *History of Shah Ismail*, Aligarh, 1939.

Sauvaget, J., 'Halab', *EI2*.

Savory, R., 'A Curious Episode of Safavid History', in C. E. Bosworth (ed.), *Iran and Islam*, Edinburgh, 1971, 461–73.

Savory, R., *Iran Under the Safavids*, Cambridge, 1980.

Savory, R., 'The Office of Khalifat al- Khulafa under the Safavids', *Journal of the American Oriental Society*, 85 (1965), 497–502.

Schmidtke, S., 'New Sources for the Life and Work of Ibn Abi Jumhur al-Ahsa'i', *Studia Iranica*, 38 (2009), 49–68.

Schimdtke, S., *The Theology of al-Allama al-Hilli (d. 725/1325)*, Berlin, 1991.

Schoeler, G., *The Biography of Muhammad. Nature and Authenticity*, Abingdon, 2010.

Schoeler, G., *The Genesis of Literature in Islam*, Edinburgh, 2009.

Sefatgol, M., 'Safavid Administration of Avqaf: Structure, Changes and Functions, 1077–1135/1666–1722', in A. J. Newman (ed.), *Society and Culture in the Early Modern Middle East. Studies on Iran in the Safavid Period*, Leiden, 2003, 397–408.

Shaban, M. A., *Islamic History. A New Interpretation*, 2, Cambridge, 1978.

Shams al-Din, M. M., *The Rising of al-Husayn*, trans. I. Howard, London, 1985.

Shomali, M. A., *Shii Islam*, London, 2003.

Shubbar, J. H., *Tarikh al-Mushashaiyin wa Tarajim Alaihim*, Najaf, 1385/1965.

Siddiqi, M. Z., *Hadith Literature, its Origin, Development and Special Features*, Cambridge, 1993.

Sindawi, K., 'Are there any Shi'ite Muslims in Israel?', *Holy Land Studies* 7(2) (2008), 183–99.

Sindawi, K., 'Visit to the Tomb of al-Husayn b. Ali in Shiite Poetry: First to Fifth Centuries AH (8th–11th Centuries CE)', *Journal of Arabic Literature*, 37(2) (2006), 230–58.

Smith, J. M., *The History of the Sarbadar Dynasty, 1336–1381 AD and its Sources*, The Hague, 1970.

Sobhani, J., *Doctrines of Shii Islam*, trans. R. Shah-Kazemi, London, 2001.

Stanfield, R., 'Mirza Makhdum Sharifi: A 16th Century Sunni *sadr* at the Safavid Court', unpublished PhD thesis, New York University, 1993.

Stetkevych, S., 'Al-Sharif al-Radi and the Poetics of Alid Legitimacy, Elegy for al-Husayn ibn Ali on Ashura', 391 AH', *Journal of Arabic Literature*, 38(3) (2007), 293–323.

Stewart, D., 'The First Shaykh al-Islam of the Safavid Capital of Qazvin', *Journal of the American Oriental Society*, 116(3) (1996), 387–405.

Stewart, D., 'Husayn b. Abd al-Samad al-Amili's Treatise for Sultan Suleiman and the Shii Shafii Legal Tradition', *Islamic Law and Society*, 4(2) (1997), 156–99.

Stewart, D., 'The Humor of the Scholars: The Autobiography of Nimat Allah al-Jaza'iri (d. 1112/1701)', *Iranian Studies*, 22(4) (1989), 47–81.

Stewart, D., 'The Genesis of the Akhbari Revival', in M. Mazzaoui (ed.), *Safavid Iran and Her Neighbors*, Salt Lake City, UT, 2003, 169–93.

Stewart, D., 'Notes on the Migration of Amili Scholars to Safavid Iran', *Journal of Near Eastern Studies*, 55(2) (1996), 81–103.

Stewart, D., 'The Ottoman Execution of Zayn al-Din al-Amili', *Die Welt des Islams*, 48 (2008), 289–347.

Sourdel, D., 'Ibn al-Furat', *EI2*.

Streck, M. and J. Lassner, 'al-Karkh', *EI2*.

Subrahmanyam, S., 'Iranians Abroad: Intra-Asian Elite Migration and Early Modern State Formation', *Journal of Asian Studies*, 51 (1992), 340–63.

Szuppe, M., 'La participation des femmes de la famille royale à l'exercice du pouvoir en Iran safavide au XVIe siècle (Première Partie)', *Studia Iranica*, 23(2) (1994), 211–58.

Szuppe, M., 'La participation des femmes de la famille royale à l'exercice du pouvoir en Iran safavide au XVIe siècle (Seconde Partie)', *Studia Iranica*, 24(1) (1995), 61–122.

Tabatabai, M. H., *Shiite Islam*, trans. S. H. Nasr, Albany, NY, 1975.

Taeschner, Fr., 'Ayyar', *EI2*

Thackston, W., 'The Diwan of Khata'i: Pictures for the Poetry of Shah Ismail', *Asian Art*, 1(4) (1988), 37–63.

Thomas, D., 'Two Muslim–Christian Debates from the Early Shi'ite Tradition', *Journal of Semitic Studies*, 33 (Spring 1988), 53–80.

Togan, Z. V., 'Sur l'origine des safavides', *Mélanges Louis Massignon* 3, Damas, 1957, 345–57.

Tor, D. G., 'Sovereign and Pious', in S. Mecit and C. Lange (eds), *The Seljuqs. Politics, Society and Culture*, Edinburgh, 2011, 39–62

Tucker, E., 'Nadir Shah and the Jafari *Madhhab*', *Iranian Studies*, 27 (1994), 163–79.

Tucker, E., *Nadir Shah's Quest for Legitimacy in Post-Safavid Iran*, Gainesville, FL, 2006.

Tucker, W. F., *Mahdis and Millenarians*, Cambridge, 2008.

van Ess, J., 'Ala-al-Dawlah Semnani', *EIr*.

van Ess, J., 'Haydar-i Amuli', *EI2*.

Varjavand, P. *et al.*, 'Emamzadeh', *EIr*.

Vilozny, R., 'A Shii Life Cycle according to al-Barqi's *Kitab al-Mahasin*', *Arabica*, 54(3) (2007), 362–96.

Waines, D., 'The Third Century Internal Crisis of the Abbasids', *Journal of the Economic and Social History of the Orient*, 20 (1977), 282–306.

Watt, W. M., 'Al-Ashari, Abu'l-Ḥasan', *EI2*.

Watt, W. M., *The Formative Period of Islamic Thought*, Edinburgh, 1973.

Watt, W. M., 'The Rafidites: a Preliminary Study, *Oriens*, 16 (1963), 110–21.

Watt, W. M., 'Shiism under the Umayyads', *Journal of the Royal Asiatic Society*, 3(4) (1960), 158–72.

Winter, S., 'Shams al-Din Muhammad ibn Makki 'al-Shahid al-Awwal' (d. 1384) and the Shiah of Syria', *Mamluk Studies Review*, 3 (1999), 149–82.

Winter, S., *The Shiites of Lebanon under Ottoman Rule, 1516–1788*, Cambridge, 2010.

Woods, J., *The Aqquyunlu. Clan, Confederation, Empire*, rev. edn, Salt Lake City, UT, 1999.

Yaghoubi, M. T. and A. Montazerolghaem, 'The Shia of Baghdad at the Time of the Abbassid Caliphate and the Seljuk Sultanate (447–575 AH), *Journal of Shia Islamic Studies*, 6(1) (2013), 53–74.

Zadeh, T., *The Vernacular Qur'an. Translation and the Rise of Persian Exegesis*, Oxford, 2012.

Zakeri, M., 'Javanmardi', *EIr*.

Zettersteen, K., 'al-Radi', *EI2*.

Zonis, M., *The Political Elite of Iran*, Princeton, 1971.

Index

Note: the index uses a transliteration system based on Arabic.